4th Workshop on Computational Approaches to Discourse (CODI 2023)

Toronto, Canada
13 - 14 July 2023

ISBN: 978-1-7138-8225-1

Printed from e-media with permission by:

Curran Associates, Inc.
57 Morehouse Lane
Red Hook, NY 12571

Some format issues inherent in the e-media version may also appear in this print version.

Printed with permission by Curran Associates, Inc. (2024)

Association for Computational Linguistics
209 N. Eighth Street
Stroudsburg, Pennsylvania 18360

Phone: 1-570-476-8006
Fax: 1-570-476-0860

acl@aclweb.org

Additional copies of this publication are available from:

Curran Associates, Inc.
57 Morehouse Lane
Red Hook, NY 12571 USA
Phone: 845-758-0400
Fax: 845-758-2633
Email: curran@proceedings.com
Web: www.proceedings.com

CODI 2023

4th Workshop on Computational Approaches to Discourse

Proceedings of the Workshop

July 13-14, 2023

Order copies of this and other ACL proceedings from:

Association for Computational Linguistics (ACL)
209 N. Eighth Street
Stroudsburg, PA 18360
USA
Tel: +1-570-476-8006
Fax: +1-570-476-0860
acl@aclweb.org

Preface

Welcome to the 4th Workshop on Computational Approaches to Discourse, CODI!

CODI provides a venue to bring together researchers working on all aspects of discourse in Computational Linguistics and NLP. Our aim is to provide a venue for the entire discourse processing community where we can present and exchange our theories, algorithms, software, datasets, and tools.

The workshop consists of invited talks, contributed papers, extended abstracts, and ACL Findings presentations. We received paper submissions that span a wide range of topics, addressing issues related to discourse representation and parsing, reference and coreference resolution, summarization, dialogue, pragmatics, applications, and more. As the workshop is hybrid this year, papers are presented live either in person or remotely and discussed during live Q&A sessions.

We are pleased that CODI 2023 features the third edition of the DISRPT (DIScourse Relation Parsing and Treebanking) shared task on Discourse Segmentation, Connective and Relation Identification across Formalisms. As we hope that the next CODI workshops will also feature shared tasks and other special events, the workshop also includes a discussion on future shared tasks, special sessions on discourse representation and parsing, coreference resolution, and multilingual discourse processing and machine translation.

We thank our invited speakers, **Yufang Hou**, IBM Research Ireland and adjunct senior lecturer and co-supervisor at UKP Lab-TU Darmstadt, who works on referential discourse modeling, argument mining, and scholarly document processing; and **Giuseppe Carenini**, University of British Columbia, known for his work on discourse parsing, summarization, and generation. We would also like to thank our reviewers for their thoughtful and instructive comments. They helped us to prepare an excellent and inclusive workshop program. Finally we would like to thank the ACL 2023 workshop chairs Eduardo Blanco, Yang Feng, and Annie Louis who organized the ACL workshops program.

The CODI Organizers,

Chloé Braud, Christian Hardmeier, Junyi Jessy Li, Sharid Loáiciga, Michael Strube, and Amir Zeldes

Program Committee

Chairs

Chloé Braud, IRIT - CNRS - ANITI
Christian Hardmeier, IT University of Copenhagen
Junyi Jessy Li, University of Texas at Austin
Sharid Loáiciga, University of Gothenburg
Michael Strube, Heidelberg Institute for Theoretical Studies
Amir Zeldes, Georgetown University

Program Committee

Katherine Atwell, University of Pittsburgh
Giuseppe Carenini, university of british columbia
Haixia Chai, Heidelberg Institute for Theoretical Studies gGmbH
Jackie Chi Kit Cheung, Mila / McGill University
Vera Demberg, Saarland University
Pascal Denis, INRIA
Elisa Ferracane, Abridge AI, Inc.
Zhengxian Gong, Computer Science and Technology School, Soochow University
Jie He, University of Edinburgh
Ryuichiro Higashinaka, Nagoya University/NTT
Sungho Jeon, Heidelberg Institute for Theoretical Studies
Prathyusha Jwalapuram, Rakuten
Murathan Kurfalı, Stockholm University
Ekaterina Lapshinova-Koltunski, Stiftung Universität Hildesheim
Ramesh Manuvinakurike, Intel labs
Philippe Muller, IRIT, University of Toulouse
Maciej Ogrodniczuk, Institute of Computer Science, Polish Academy of Sciences
Carolyn Rosé, Carnegie Mellon University
Manfred Stede, University of Potsdam
Francielle Vargas, University of São Paulo
Bonnie Webber, University of Edinburgh
Deniz Zeyrek, Middle East Technical University
Heike Zinsmeister, Universität Hamburg

Table of Contents

Program

Thursday, July 13, 2023

09:15 - 09:30 *Opening Remarks*

09:30 - 10:30 *Invited Talk - Yufang Hou: Bridging Resolution: A Journey Towards Modelling Referential Discourse Entities*

10:30 - 11:00 *Coffee Break*

11:00 - 12:20 *Session - Summarization/Generation*

Contrastive Hierarchical Discourse Graph for Scientific Document Summarization
Haopeng Zhang, Xiao Liu and Jiawei Zhang

Entity-based SpanCopy for Abstractive Summarization to Improve the Factual Consistency
Wen Xiao and Giuseppe Carenini

Two-step Text Summarization for Long-form Biographical Narrative Genre
Avi Bleiweiss

Improving Long Context Document-Level Machine Translation
Christian Herold and Hermann Ney

12:30 - 14:00 *Lunch*

14:00 - 14:50 *Session - Coreference*

Ensemble Transfer Learning for Multilingual Coreference Resolution
Tuan Lai and Heng Ji

Leveraging Structural Discourse Information for Event Coreference Resolution in Dutch
Loic De Langhe, Orphee De Clercq and Veronique Hoste

Entity Coreference and Co-occurrence Aware Argument Mining from Biomedical Literature
Boyang Liu, Viktor Schlegel, Riza Batista-navarro and Sophia Ananiadou

Thursday, July 13, 2023 (continued)

14:50 - 15:30 *Session - Discourse Relations/Other*

Unpacking Ambiguous Structure: A Dataset for Ambiguous Implicit Discourse Relations for English and Egyptian Arabic
Ahmed Ruby, Sara Stymne and Christian Hardmeier

Embedding Mental Health Discourse for Community Recommendation
Hy Dang, Bang Nguyen, Noah Ziems and Meng Jiang

15:30 - 16:00 *Coffee Break*

16:00 - 16:35 *Session - Rhetorical Structure Theory*

Encoding Discourse Structure: Comparison of RST and QUD
Sara Shahmohammadi, Hannah Seemann, Manfred Stede and Tatjana Scheffler

APA-RST: A Text Simplification Corpus with RST Annotations
Freya Hewett

16:35 - 17:25 *Session - Other*

Discourse Information for Document-Level Temporal Dependency Parsing
Jingcheng Niu, Victoria Ng, Erin Rees, Simon De Montigny and Gerald Penn

SAE-NTM: Sentence-Aware Encoder for Neural Topic Modeling
Hao Liu, Jingsheng Gao, Suncheng Xiang, Ting Liu and Yuzhuo Fu

Friday, July 14, 2023

09:30 - 10:30	*Invited Talk - Giuseppe Carenini: Discourse Processing in the era of Large Language Models*
10:30 - 11:00	*Coffee Break*
11:00 - 12:10	*Discourse Relation Parsing and Treebanking (DISRPT) Shared Task*
12:10 - 12:30	*Discussion of Future Shared Tasks*
12:30 - 14:00	*Lunch*
14:00 - 15:20	*Session - Discourse Relations/Other*
	MuLMS-AZ: An Argumentative Zoning Dataset for the Materials Science Domain Timo Schrader, Teresa Bürkle, Sophie Henning, Sherry Tan, Matteo Finco, Stefan Grünewald, Maira Indrikova, Felix Hildebrand and Annemarie Friedrich
	A Side-by-side Comparison of Transformers for Implicit Discourse Relation Classification Bruce W. Lee, Bongseok Yang and Jason Lee
	A Weakly-Supervised Learning Approach to the Identification of Alternative Lexicalizations in Shallow Discourse Parsing René Knaebel
	Exploiting Knowledge about Discourse Relations for Implicit Discourse Relation Classification Nobel Varghese, Frances Yung, Kaveri Anuranjana and Vera Demberg
	The distribution of discourse relations within and across turns in spontaneous conversation S. Magalí López Cortez and Cassandra L. Jacobs
15:20 - 17:00	*Coffee and Poster Session*
	Chinese-DiMLex: A Lexicon of Chinese Discourse Connectives Shujun Wan, Peter Bourgonje, Hongling Xiao, Clara Wan Ching Ho and Manfred Stede

Friday, July 14, 2023 (continued)

17:00 - 17:30 *Closing Remarks and Awards*

MuLMS-AZ: An Argumentative Zoning Dataset for the Materials Science Domain

Timo Pierre Schrader[1,6] **Teresa Bürkle**[2] **Sophie Henning**[1,3] **Sherry Tan**[4] **Matteo Finco**[2]
Stefan Grünewald[1,5] **Maira Indrikova**[2] **Felix Hildebrand**[2] **Annemarie Friedrich**[6]

[1]Bosch Center for Artificial Intelligence, Renningen, Germany
[2]Robert Bosch GmbH, Stuttgart, Germany [3]LMU Munich, Germany [4]TU Darmstadt, Germany
[5]University of Stuttgart, Germany [6]University of Augsburg, Germany

timo.schrader|teresa.buerkle|sophie.henning@de.bosch.com
annemarie.friedrich@informatik.uni-augsburg.de

Abstract

Scientific publications follow conventionalized rhetorical structures. Classifying the *Argumentative Zone* (AZ), e.g., identifying whether a sentence states a MOTIVATION, a RESULT or BACKGROUND information, has been proposed to improve processing of scholarly documents. In this work, we adapt and extend this idea to the domain of materials science research. We present and release a new dataset of 50 manually annotated research articles. The dataset spans seven sub-topics and is annotated with a materials-science focused multi-label annotation scheme for AZ. We detail corpus statistics and demonstrate high inter-annotator agreement. Our computational experiments show that using domain-specific pre-trained transformer-based text encoders is key to high classification performance. We also find that AZ categories from existing datasets in other domains are transferable to varying degrees.

1 Introduction

In academic writing, it is custom to adhere to a rhetorical argumentation structure to convince readers of the relevance of the work to the field (Swales, 1990). For example, authors typically first indicate a gap in prior work before stating the goal of their own research. *Argumentative Zoning* (AZ) is a natural language processing (NLP) task in which sentences are classified according to their argumentative roles with varying granularity (Teufel et al., 1999, 2009). AZ information can then be used for summarization (Teufel and Moens, 2002; El-Ebshihy et al., 2020), improved citation indexing (Teufel, 2006), or writing assistance (Feltrim et al., 2006).

Manually annotated AZ datasets (Teufel et al., 1999; Fisas et al., 2016; Soldatova and Liakata, 2007) only exist for few domains and employ differing annotation schemes. The resulting models are not directly applicable to our domain of interest, materials science research, which presents a challenging domain for current NLP methods (e.g., Mysore et al., 2019; Friedrich et al., 2020; O'Gorman et al., 2021). In this paper, we present MuLMS-AZ, the first dataset annotated for AZ in this domain. Working together with domain experts, we derive a hierarchical multi-label **annotation scheme** (see Table 1). Our scheme includes domain-specific labels such as descriptions of the materials' PREPARATION and CHARACTERIZATION, which are crucial distinctions also for NLP applications from the domain experts' view.

Label	Count	Label	Count
MOTIVATION	363	EXPLANATION	603
BACKGROUND	3155	RESULTS	2953
- PRIORWORK	1824	CONCLUSION	680
EXPERIMENT	2579	HEADING	702
- PREP.	962	CAPTION	485
- CHARACT.	1347	METADATA	210

Table 1: MuLMS-AZ label counts (multi-label).

This **resource paper** makes the following contributions:

- We present a **dataset** of 50 scientific articles (more than 10,000 sentences) in the domain of materials science manually annotated by domain experts with a hierarchical fine-grained **annotation scheme** for AZ with high agreement. The corpus will be publicly released.[1]
- We apply several neural models to our dataset that will serve as strong baselines for future work using our new benchmark. We find (a) that using domain-specific pre-trained transformers is key to a successful model, (b) that multi-task learning with existing AZ datasets leads to small benefits, and (c) that the effectiveness of transfer learning of materials science AZ labels from other corpora differs by label.

[1] https://github.com/boschresearch/mulms-az-codi2023

Proceedings of the 4th Workshop on Computational Approaches to Discourse (CODI 2023), pages 1–15
July 13-14, 2023

2 Related Work

In this section, we describe related work on AZ.

AZ Datasets. Table 2 shows the statistics of several related datasets. Three larger-scale datasets manually annotated with AZ information are the AZ-CL corpus (Teufel et al., 1999; Teufel and Moens, 1999), consisting of computational linguistics papers, the Dr. Inventor Multi-Layer Scientific Corpus (DRI, Fisas et al., 2016, 2015), featuring computer graphics papers, and, closest to our domain, the ART corpus (Soldatova and Liakata, 2007), covering topics in physical chemistry and biochemistry. Appendix E explains these datasets in more detail. Teufel et al. (2009) also apply and adapt the annotation scheme of the AZ-CL corpus to the chemistry domain. Accuosto et al. (2021) label sentences with argumentation-related categories (e.g., *proposal, means, observation*). Making use of sentence-wise author-provided keywords, a dataset of about 388k abstracts with silver standard rhetorical role annotations has been derived from PubMed/MEDLINE (de Moura and Feltrim, 2018).

Modeling. AZ has been modeled as a sentence classification task using maximum entropy models (Teufel and Kan, 2009), SVMs, and CRFs (Guo et al., 2011) leveraging a variety of word, grammatical, heuristic, and discourse features (Guo et al., 2013). Ensemble-based classifiers have also been shown to be effective (Badie et al., 2018; Asadi et al., 2019). LSTM-based models relying on word embeddings have been applied to AZ and to the fundamentally very similar task of assigning zones to sentences in job ads (Liu, 2017; de Moura and Feltrim, 2018; Gnehm and Clematide, 2020). BERT-style (Devlin et al., 2019) models work well for AZ (Mo et al., 2020; Brack et al., 2022). Multitask training has been found to be beneficial for these models both in-domain (Lauscher et al., 2018) as well as cross-domain (Brack et al., 2021).

Datasets in the Materials Science Domain. Several datasets targeting the domain of materials science research have recently been released. Mysore et al. (2019) annotate paragraphs describing synthesis procedures with graph structures capturing relations and typed arguments. Friedrich et al. (2020) mark similar graph structures corresponding to experiment information in 45 open-access publications. Several works and datasets address named entity recognition in the domain (Yamaguchi et al., 2020; O'Gorman et al., 2021).

	AZ-CL	ART	DRI	MuLMS-AZ
# docs	80	225	40	50
# sents	12818	34995	10784	10186
# labels	7	11	10	12

Table 2: Manually annotated AZ corpora.

3 Data Sources and Annotated Corpus

In this section, we present our new dataset.

Source of Texts and Preprocessing. We select 50 scientific articles licensed under CC-BY from seven sub-areas of materials science: electrolysis, graphene, polymer electrolyte fuel cell (PEMFC), solid oxide fuel cell (SOFC), polymers, semiconductors, and steel. The four SOFC papers were selected from the SOFC-Exp corpus (Friedrich et al., 2020). 11 papers were selected from the OA-STM corpus[2] and classified into the above subject areas by a domain expert. The majority of the papers were found via PubMed[3] and DOAJ[4] using queries prepared by a domain expert. For the OA-STM data, we use the sentence segmentation provided with the corpus, which has been created using GENIA tools (Tsuruoka and Tsujii, 2005). For the remaining texts, we rely on the sentence segmentation provided by INCEpTION v21.0 (Klie et al., 2018) with some manual fixes.

Annotation Scheme. AZs are functional sentence types, i.e., they capture the rhetorical function of a sentence. Together with several domain experts, we design a hierarchical scheme tailored to the materials science domain as shown in Table 3. In addition, we provide ABSTRACT, HEADING, METADATA, CAPTION, FIGURE/TABLE annotations for structural information. We assume a multi-label setting in which annotators may assign any number of labels to a sentence. Our detailed guidelines are available with our dataset.

Corpus Statistics. Documents are rather long (on average 203.7 sentences per document with a standard deviation of ± 73.2). There is a tendency towards long sentences (28.7 tokens per sentence on average), but with high variation of ± 17.9 due to, e.g., short headings. Table 1 shows how often each AZ label occurs. When ignoring tags for structural information 8133 sentences have exactly one AZ label (or the AZ label and its supertype), 1056 sentences have two labels, and 11 sentences have 3

[2] https://github.com/elsevierlabs/OA-STM-Corpus

[3] https://pubmed.ncbi.nlm.nih.gov/

[4] https://doaj.org/

Label	Description	Example
MOTIVATION	aims/motivation of the study	*In this study, we perform a systematic analysis of ...*
BACKGROUND	textbook-like technical background	*The method is based on the Kelvin equation.*
- PRIORWORK	specific prior work relevant to current study	*Irmawati et al. has concluded that ...*
EXPERIMENT	description of the experiment	*We evaluate PtCo nanoparticle catalyst ...*
- PREPARATION	steps describing the preparation of samples	*The mixture was subjected to stirring for 60 minutes.*
- CHARACT.	characterizations and characterization techniques of the involved materials	*Ni foam surface coverage of the WO3 thin film and its homogeneity were analyzed by energy–dispersive X-ray spectroscopy (EDS).*
EXPLANATION	statements (hypotheses or assumptions) relevant to results or experimental settings	*In our calculation, all Pt loadings were considered to be electrochemically active.*
RESULTS	details on experimental results	*The hydrogen adsorption/desorption peak is at about 0.2V.*
CONCLUSION	conclusions and take-aways	*This result indicated that ...*

Table 3: Content-based MuLMS-AZ Argumentative Zoning sentence labels.

labels. Labels are similarly distributed across data splits (see Appendix D).

Inter-Annotator Agreement. Our entire dataset has been annotated by a single annotator, a graduate student of materials science, who was also involved in the design of the annotation scheme. We compare the annotations of this main annotator to those of another annotator who holds a Master's degree in materials science and a PhD in engineering. The agreement study is performed on 5 documents (357 sentences). Due to the multi-label scenario, following Krippendorff (1980) we measure κ (Cohen, 1960) for each label separately, comparing whether each annotator used a particular label on an instance or not (see Table 4). Our annotators achieve "substantial" agreement (Landis and Koch, 1977) on most labels, "perfect" agreement on identifying HEADINGs (see also Appendix D). Lower, though still "moderate", agreement on MOTIVATION, EXPLANATION and CONCLUSION can in part be explained by their lower frequency which makes it generally harder to obtain high κ-values. Intuitively, they also have a more difficult nature compared to the other tags, e.g., we observe disagreements regarding what constitutes a MOTIVATION or an EXPLANATION versus what is purely reporting BACKGROUND. The full confusion matrix and a discussion of agreement on subtags are given in Appendix D; a discussion of multi-label examples can be found in Appendix F.

Our scores are in the same ballpark as those reported by Teufel et al. (1999) on a similar annotation task. For their 7-way task, they report κ scores around 0.71-0.75, with differences between categories in one-vs-all measurements ranging from about 0.49 to 0.78. In sum, we conclude that agreement on AZ is satisfactory in our dataset.

AZ Label	κ	AZ Label	κ
HEADING	0.89	METADATA	0.76
MOTIVATION	0.44	BACKGROUND	0.75
CONCLUSION	0.55	EXPERIMENT	0.78
EXPLANATION	0.39	RESULTS	0.70

Table 4: IAA for AZ on 357 sentences.

4 Modeling

We model AZ as a multi-label classification problem, using BERT (Devlin et al., 2019) as the underlying text encoder. We also test domain-specific pre-trained variants of BERT. SciBERT (Beltagy et al., 2019) has been pre-trained on articles in the scientific domain. MatSciBERT (Gupta et al., 2022) is a version of SciBERT further pre-trained on materials science articles. We use the CLS embedding as input to a linear layer, transform logits using a sigmoid function and choose labels if their respective score exceeds 0.5. For multi-task experiments with other datasets, we use a single shared language model and one linear output layer per dataset. For hyperparameters, see Appendix A.

As shown in Table 1, the dataset suffers from strong class imbalance. Classifiers tend to underperform on minority labels (Johnson and Khoshgoftaar, 2019). To address this problem, we apply the **multi-label random oversampling** (ML-ROS, Charte et al., 2015) algorithm during training. The main idea behind ML-ROS is to dynamically duplicate instances of minority classes while taking the multi-label nature of the problem into account. In a nutshell, the algorithm performs several oversampling iterations, keeping track of the imbalance ratios associated with each label and choosing instances that carry minority labels until a predefined number of additional samples have been chosen. Details are given in Appendix B.

Method	LM	mic.-F1	mac.-F1
No Oversampling	BERT	$72.6_{\pm 1.0}$	$65.5_{\pm 0.7}$
	MatSciBERT	$76.3_{\pm 0.7}$	$70.1_{\pm 0.7}$
	SciBERT	$76.2_{\pm 0.9}$	$70.2_{\pm 0.6}$
ML-ROS	SciBERT	$76.7_{\pm 0.7}$	$70.6_{\pm 0.9}$
+ MultiTask ART	SciBERT	$75.0_{\pm 0.9}$	$68.9_{\pm 1.1}$
+ MultiTask AZ-CL	SciBERT	$\mathbf{77.2}_{\pm 0.3}$	$\mathbf{71.1}_{\pm 0.5}$
*human agreement**		*78.7*	*74.9*

Table 5: AZ classification results on MuLMS-AZ test set. *Not directly comparable: computed on documents from agreement study (see Appendix D).

Training data	PM Label	P	R
PM, AZ-CL, ART, DRI	OBJECTIVE	36.1	28.3
PM, AZ-CL, ART, DRI	BACKGROUND	84.2	40.0
PM, ART, DRI	METHOD	58.1	74.7
PM, ART, DRI	RESULT	82.4	30.9
PM, ART, DRI	CONCLUSION	43.5	29.9
MuLMS-AZ	OBJECTIVE	56.8	54.3
MuLMS-AZ	BACKGROUND	82.1	78.8
MuLMS-AZ	METHOD	79.9	78.2
MuLMS-AZ	RESULT	82.1	83.2
MuLMS-AZ	CONCLUSION	43.5*	29.9*

Table 6: Results for transfer learning experiment. Precision and recall on MuLMS-AZ test set. *not a typo.

5 Experimental Results

We here detail our experimental results.

Settings. We split our corpus into train, dev, and test sets of 36, 7, and 7 documents. For all experiments and for hyperparameter tuning, we always train five models. The training data is split into five folds. Similar to cross-validation, we train on four folds and use the fifth fold for model selection (cf. van der Goot, 2021), repeating this process five times (also for hyperparameter tuning). The dev set is only used for tuning, and we report scores for the five models on test. In this setting, deviations are naturally higher than when reporting results for the same training data. For hyperparameters and implementation details, see Appendix A. To evaluate our experiments, we use hierarchical precision, recall, and F1 (Silla and Freitas, 2011). These scores operate on the sets of labels per instance, always including the respective supertypes of gold or predicted labels.

Results. Table 5 shows the performance of our neural models on MuLMS-AZ. Overall, the categories can be learned well, approaching our estimate of human agreement. SciBERT clearly outperforms BERT, i.e., using domain-specific embeddings is a clear advantage. However, MatSciBERT does not add upon SciBERT. We hence conduct the remaining experiments using SciBERT. Using ML-ROS results in minor increases for most labels (see also Appendix G). When multi-task learning with the AZ-CL dataset (using 40% of its samples), further increases are observed. It is worth noting that multi-task training with ART does not result in increases although the chemistry domain should be much closer to our domain. This might indicate that despite the domain discrepancy, AZ annotations in AZ-CL are more compatible with ours.

As a first step to explaining what part of rhetorical information can be induced based only on data from other corpora, we perform a transfer learning experiment. We carefully manually map the AZ labels of the various datasets (see Appendix E) to the coarse-grained categories used by PubMed (PM). Using these mapped labels, we train binary classifiers that aim to detect the presence of a particular PM label. As training data, we use ART, DRI, and a selection of documents from the PM dataset by de Moura and Feltrim (2018) that were published in materials science journals (see Appendix C). We add AZ-CL to the training data only if an unambiguous mapping of its categories to the PM label in question is possible. Here, we use the dev set of MuLMS-AZ for model selection and hyperparameter tuning. Results for running the resulting classifiers on MuLMS-AZ are reported in Table 6. For BACKGROUND and RESULTS, we observe a high precision, which indicates that similar rhetorical elements may be used. OBJECTIVE and METHOD seem to differ most across datasets as they are likely very domain- and problem-specific. When training with mapped labels on the entire MuLMS-AZ, we observe much higher recall scores across all label groups, again indicating the usefulness of our in-domain training data.

6 Conclusion and Outlook

We have presented a new AZ corpus in the field of materials science annotated by domain experts with high agreement. Our experimental results demonstrate that strong classifiers can be learned on the data and that AZ labels can be transferred from related datasets only to a limited extent.

Our new dataset opens up new research opportunities on cross-domain AZ, class imbalance scenarios, and integrating AZ information in information extraction tasks in materials science.

Limitations

This resource paper describes the dataset in detail, providing strong baselines and first initial cross-domain experiments. It does not aim to provide an extensive set of experiments on cross-domain argumentative zoning yet.

The entire dataset is only singly-annotated. The agreement study was performed on complete documents and hence has only limited data for several labels. Due to the limited funding of the project, we could double-annotate the entire dataset.

Finally, we only test one model class (BERT-based transformers). A potential next step is to test a bigger variety of models and embeddings. Because AZ labels are interdependent within a document, especially document-level models or CRF-based models are promising methods to try. We have also tested only one method (multi-label random oversampling) to deal with the strong class imbalance in the dataset. We have not yet tested further such methods (Henning et al., 2023) or data augmentation methods.

Ethical Considerations

We took care of potential license issue of the data underlying our dataset by exclusively selecting open-access articles published under CC BY.

The main annotator was paid above the minimum wage of our country in the context of a full-time internship. The annotator was aware of the goal of the study and consents to the public release of the data. The remaining domain experts participated on a voluntary basis due to their interest in the topic.

References

Pablo Accuosto, Mariana Neves, and Horacio Saggion. 2021. Argumentation mining in scientific literature: From computational linguistics to biomedicine. In *Frommholz I, Mayr P, Cabanac G, Verberne S, editors. BIR 2021: 11th International Workshop on Bibliometric-enhanced Information Retrieval; 2021 Apr 1; Lucca, Italy. Aachen: CEUR; 2021. p. 20-36.* CEUR Workshop Proceedings.

Nasrin Asadi, Kambiz Badie, and Maryam Tayefeh Mahmoudi. 2019. Automatic zone identification in scientific papers via fusion techniques. *Scientometrics*, 119(2):845–862.

Kambiz Badie, Nasrin Asadi, and Maryam Tayefeh Mahmoudi. 2018. Zone identification based on features with high semantic richness and combining results of separate classifiers. *Journal of Information and Telecommunication*, 2(4):411–427.

Iz Beltagy, Kyle Lo, and Arman Cohan. 2019. SciBERT: A pretrained language model for scientific text. In *Proceedings of the 2019 Conference on Empirical Methods in Natural Language Processing and the 9th International Joint Conference on Natural Language Processing (EMNLP-IJCNLP)*, pages 3615–3620, Hong Kong, China. Association for Computational Linguistics.

Arthur Brack, Anett Hoppe, Pascal Buschermöhle, and Ralph Ewerth. 2021. Sequential sentence classification in research papers using cross-domain multi-task learning. *CoRR*, abs/2102.06008.

Arthur Brack, Anett Hoppe, Pascal Buschermöhle, and Ralph Ewerth. 2022. Cross-domain multi-task learning for sequential sentence classification in research papers. In *Proceedings of the 22nd ACM/IEEE Joint Conference on Digital Libraries*, pages 1–13.

Francisco Charte, Antonio J. Rivera, María J. del Jesus, and Francisco Herrera. 2015. Addressing imbalance in multilabel classification: Measures and random resampling algorithms. *Neurocomputing*, 163:3–16. Recent Advancements in Hybrid Artificial Intelligence Systems and its Application to Real-World Problems Progress in Intelligent Systems Mining Humanistic Data.

Jacob Cohen. 1960. A coefficient of agreement for nominal scales. *Educational and Psychological Measurement*, 20(1):37–46.

G. Bennemann de Moura and V. Delisandra Feltrim. 2018. Using lstm encoder-decoder for rhetorical structure prediction. In *2018 7th Brazilian Conference on Intelligent Systems (BRACIS)*, pages 278–283, Los Alamitos, CA, USA. IEEE Computer Society.

Jacob Devlin, Ming-Wei Chang, Kenton Lee, and Kristina Toutanova. 2019. BERT: Pre-training of deep bidirectional transformers for language understanding. In *Proceedings of the 2019 Conference of the North American Chapter of the Association for Computational Linguistics: Human Language Technologies, Volume 1 (Long and Short Papers)*, pages 4171–4186, Minneapolis, Minnesota. Association for Computational Linguistics.

Alaa El-Ebshihy, Annisa Maulida Ningtyas, Linda Andersson, Florina Piroi, and Andreas Rauber. 2020. ARTU / TU Wien and artificial researcher@ LongSumm 20. In *Proceedings of the First Workshop on Scholarly Document Processing*, pages 310–317, Online. Association for Computational Linguistics.

Valéria D Feltrim, Simone Teufel, Maria Graças V das Nunes, and Sandra M Aluísio. 2006. Argumentative zoning applied to critiquing novices' scientific abstracts. In *Computing Attitude and Affect in Text: Theory and Applications*, pages 233–246. Springer.

Beatriz Fisas, Francesco Ronzano, and Horacio Saggion. 2016. A multi-layered annotated corpus of scientific papers. In *Proceedings of the Tenth International Conference on Language Resources and Evaluation (LREC'16)*, pages 3081–3088, Portorož, Slovenia. European Language Resources Association (ELRA).

Beatriz Fisas, Horacio Saggion, and Francesco Ronzano. 2015. On the discoursive structure of computer graphics research papers. In *Proceedings of The 9th Linguistic Annotation Workshop*, pages 42–51, Denver, Colorado, USA. Association for Computational Linguistics.

Annemarie Friedrich, Heike Adel, Federico Tomazic, Johannes Hingerl, Renou Benteau, Anika Marusczyk, and Lukas Lange. 2020. The SOFC-exp corpus and neural approaches to information extraction in the materials science domain. In *Proceedings of the 58th Annual Meeting of the Association for Computational Linguistics*, pages 1255–1268, Online. Association for Computational Linguistics.

Ann-Sophie Gnehm and Simon Clematide. 2020. Text zoning and classification for job advertisements in German, French and English. In *Proceedings of the Fourth Workshop on Natural Language Processing and Computational Social Science*, pages 83–93, Online. Association for Computational Linguistics.

Yufan Guo, Anna Korhonen, and Thierry Poibeau. 2011. A weakly-supervised approach to argumentative zoning of scientific documents. In *Proceedings of the 2011 Conference on Empirical Methods in Natural Language Processing*, pages 273–283, Edinburgh, Scotland, UK. Association for Computational Linguistics.

Yufan Guo, Roi Reichart, and Anna Korhonen. 2013. Improved information structure analysis of scientific documents through discourse and lexical constraints. In *Proceedings of the 2013 Conference of the North American Chapter of the Association for Computational Linguistics: Human Language Technologies*, pages 928–937, Atlanta, Georgia. Association for Computational Linguistics.

Tanishq Gupta, Mohd Zaki, N. M. Anoop Krishnan, and Mausam. 2022. MatSciBERT: A materials domain language model for text mining and information extraction. *npj Computational Materials*, 8(1):102.

Sophie Henning, William Beluch, Alexander Fraser, and Annemarie Friedrich. 2023. A survey of methods for addressing class imbalance in deep-learning based natural language processing. In *Proceedings of the 17th Conference of the European Chapter of the Association for Computational Linguistics*, pages 523–540, Dubrovnik, Croatia. Association for Computational Linguistics.

Justin M Johnson and Taghi M Khoshgoftaar. 2019. Survey on deep learning with class imbalance. *Journal of Big Data*, 6(1):1–54.

Jan-Christoph Klie, Michael Bugert, Beto Boullosa, Richard Eckart de Castilho, and Iryna Gurevych. 2018. The INCEpTION platform: Machine-assisted and knowledge-oriented interactive annotation. In *Proceedings of the 27th International Conference on Computational Linguistics: System Demonstrations*, pages 5–9, Santa Fe, New Mexico. Association for Computational Linguistics.

Klaus Krippendorff. 1980. *Krippendorff, Klaus, Content Analysis: An Introduction to its Methodology. Beverly Hills, CA: Sage, 1980.* Sage Publications, Inc.

J Richard Landis and Gary G Koch. 1977. An application of hierarchical kappa-type statistics in the assessment of majority agreement among multiple observers. *Biometrics*, pages 363–374.

Anne Lauscher, Goran Glavaš, Simone Paolo Ponzetto, and Kai Eckert. 2018. Investigating the role of argumentation in the rhetorical analysis of scientific publications with neural multi-task learning models. In *Proceedings of the 2018 Conference on Empirical Methods in Natural Language Processing*, pages 3326–3338, Brussels, Belgium. Association for Computational Linguistics.

Maria Liakata and Larisa Soldatova. 2008. Guidelines for the annotation of general scientific concepts. *Aberystwyth University, JISC Project Report http://ie-repository. jisc. ac. uk/88.*

Haixia Liu. 2017. Automatic argumentative-zoning using word2vec. *CoRR*, abs/1703.10152.

Ilya Loshchilov and Frank Hutter. 2019. Decoupled weight decay regularization.

Wang Mo, Cui Yunpeng, Chen Li, and Li Huan. 2020. A deep learning-based method of argumentative zoning for research articles. *Data Analysis and Knowledge Discovery*, 4(6):60–68.

Sheshera Mysore, Zachary Jensen, Edward Kim, Kevin Huang, Haw-Shiuan Chang, Emma Strubell, Jeffrey Flanigan, Andrew McCallum, and Elsa Olivetti. 2019. The materials science procedural text corpus: Annotating materials synthesis procedures with shallow semantic structures. In *Proceedings of the 13th Linguistic Annotation Workshop*, pages 56–64, Florence, Italy. Association for Computational Linguistics.

Tim O'Gorman, Zach Jensen, Sheshera Mysore, Kevin Huang, Rubayyat Mahbub, Elsa Olivetti, and Andrew McCallum. 2021. MS-mentions: Consistently annotating entity mentions in materials science procedural text. In *Proceedings of the 2021 Conference on Empirical Methods in Natural Language Processing*, pages 1337–1352, Online and Punta Cana, Dominican Republic. Association for Computational Linguistics.

Carlos N Silla and Alex A Freitas. 2011. A survey of hierarchical classification across different application domains. *Data Mining and Knowledge Discovery*, 22(1):31–72.

Larisa Soldatova and Maria Liakata. 2007. An ontology methodology and cisp-the proposed core information about scientific papers. *JISC Project Report*.

John M. Swales. 1990. Discourse analysis in professional contexts. *Annual Review of Applied Linguistics*, 11:103–114.

Simone Teufel. 2006. Argumentative zoning for improved citation indexing. In *Computing attitude and affect in text: Theory and Applications*, pages 159–169. Springer.

Simone Teufel, Jean Carletta, and Marc Moens. 1999. An annotation scheme for discourse-level argumentation in research articles. In *Ninth Conference of the European Chapter of the Association for Computational Linguistics*, pages 110–117, Bergen, Norway. Association for Computational Linguistics.

Simone Teufel and Min-Yen Kan. 2009. Robust argumentative zoning for sensemaking in scholarly documents. In *Advanced language technologies for digital libraries*, pages 154–170. Springer.

Simone Teufel and Marc Moens. 1999. Discourse-level argumentation in scientific articles: human and automatic annotation. In *Towards Standards and Tools for Discourse Tagging*.

Simone Teufel and Marc Moens. 2002. Articles summarizing scientific articles: Experiments with relevance and rhetorical status. *Computational Linguistics*, 28(4):409–445.

Simone Teufel, Advaith Siddharthan, and Colin Batchelor. 2009. Towards domain-independent argumentative zoning: Evidence from chemistry and computational linguistics. In *Proceedings of the 2009 Conference on Empirical Methods in Natural Language Processing*, pages 1493–1502, Singapore. Association for Computational Linguistics.

Yoshimasa Tsuruoka and Jun'ichi Tsujii. 2005. Bidirectional inference with the easiest-first strategy for tagging sequence data. In *Proceedings of Human Language Technology Conference and Conference on Empirical Methods in Natural Language Processing*, pages 467–474, Vancouver, British Columbia, Canada. Association for Computational Linguistics.

Rob van der Goot. 2021. We need to talk about train-dev-test splits. In *Proceedings of the 2021 Conference on Empirical Methods in Natural Language Processing*, pages 4485–4494, Online and Punta Cana, Dominican Republic. Association for Computational Linguistics.

Kyosuke Yamaguchi, Ryoji Asahi, and Yutaka Sasaki. 2020. SC-CoMIcs: A superconductivity corpus for materials informatics. In *Proceedings of the 12th Language Resources and Evaluation Conference*, pages 6753–6760, Marseille, France. European Language Resources Association.

Appendix

A Hyperparameters

We implement all our models using PyTorch. We use AdamW (Loshchilov and Hutter, 2019) as the optimizer for all our models and set the batch size to $16/32$ depending on what works best and GPU restrictions. The learning rate stays constant after a linear warmup phase. We set a dropout rate to 0.1 for the linear layer that takes the contextualized embeddings that are produced by BERT as input. Early stopping is applied if the micro-F1 score has not improved for more than 3 epochs. Binary cross entropy is the loss function for the MuLMS-AZ output layer, whereas cross entropy is the loss function used for optimizing the multi-task output heads corresponding to the other AZ datasets. Table 7 lists the various learning rates found during grid search. We tested different learning rates between 1e-4 and 1e-7. A refinement of the grid was done after an initial search, which almost always leads to a second search area within the range of 1e-6 to 9e-6. When using ML-ROS, we oversample by 20%. Training was performed on a single Nvidia A100 GPU or alternatively V100 GPU.

Method	LM	Learning Rate
No Oversampling	BERT	3e-6
	MatSciBERT	8e-6
	SciBERT	3e-6
ML-ROS	SciBERT	2e-6
+ MT (+PM)	SciBERT	7e-6
+ MT (+ART)	SciBERT	2e-6
+ MT (+AZ-CL)	SciBERT	2e-6
+ MT (+DRI)	SciBERT	1e-6
+ MT (+ART+AZ+DRI)	SciBERT	8e-6
Data Augm. (+PM)	SciBERT	8e-6

Table 7: Learning rates of the different model reported in Table 12

B Multi-Label Random Oversampling (ML-ROS) Algorithm

Figure 1 details our adaption of the multi-label random oversampling (ML-ROS) algorithm originally proposed by Charte et al. (2015). In the initialization (lines 3-7), for each label, all the instances that carry a particular label are collected in what Charte et al. call a *bag*. The main part of the algorithm (lines 10-24) does the following: For each label y, the *Imbalance Ratio per label* (IRLbl), which is the ratio between the count of the most frequent label and the count of y, is calculated:

$$\mathrm{IRLbl}(y) = \frac{\max_{y' \in L} \sum_{i=1}^{|D|} h(y', Y_i)}{\sum_{i=1}^{|D|} h(y, Y_i)}$$

D is the dataset, L is the label set, Y_i is the set of labels assigned to the i-th sample and h is an indicator function evaluating if $y \in Y_i$. Hence, the larger the value, the less frequently y occurs compared to the most frequent label.

The per-label values are then used to determine the *mean imbalance ratio* (MeanIR):

$$\mathrm{MeanIR} = \frac{1}{|L|} \sum_{y' \in L} \mathrm{IRLbl}(y')$$

For each of the labels with an imbalance ratio exceeding the current MeanIR, a random instance of this label is duplicated.

The main part is repeated until the pre-specified size of the oversampled dataset is reached. Our implementation differs from Charte et al. in that we update meanIR in each iteration step and also oversample labels originally not being a minority label when their IRLbl exceeds MeanIR at the beginning of an iteration step.

C List of Materials Science Journals

We used the list of materials-science related journals collected on Wikipedia to filter for abstracts in the PubMed Medline corpus published in journals.[5]

D Further Corpus Statistics for MuLMS-AZ

Table 8 gives the counts of sentences carrying a particular AZ label. Distributions are similar across data splits. Table 8 also lists counts for ABSTRACT, which we decide to exclude from our modeling experiments because including it resulted in performance decreases due to confusion with other labels. Locating the abstract in a document can usually be solved in rule-based ways as abstracts of publications are commonly available in a machine-readable format.

During annotation, we introduced two subtypes of EXPLANATION, HYPOTHESIS and ASSUMPTION, distinguishing between scientific hypotheses and assumptions made by the author in cases where often choices are possible. As the overall counts

[5]https://en.wikipedia.org/w/index.php?title=List_of_materials_science_journals&oldid=1078212543

```
Inputs: <Dataset> D, <Percentage> P
Outputs: Oversampled dataset
samplesToDuplicate <-- |D|/100 * P # P % size increment
L <-- labelsInDataset(D) # Obtain the full set of labels
for each label in L do # Bags of samples for each label
    Bag_label <-- getSamplesPerLabel(label)
end for

while samplesToDuplicate > 0 do # Loop duplicating instances
    MeanIR <-- calculateMeanIR(D, L)
    # Gather minority bags (bag: all instances of a given label)
    minBags = []
    for each label in L do
        IRLbl_label <-- calculateIRperLabel(D, label)
        if IRLbl_label > MeanIR then
            minBags += Bag_label
        end if
    end for
    # Duplicate a random sample from each minority bag
    for each minBag_i in minBags do
        x <-- random(1, |minBag_i|)
        duplicateSample(minBag_i, x)
        --samplesToDuplicate
    end for
end while
```

Figure 1: Pseudocode for adapted (dynamic) ML-ROS algorithm.

and agreement were low, we decided to only use the supertype EXPLANATION in all experiments.

Figure 2a shows the label coincidence matrix between the two annotators in the inter-annotator agreement study, i.e., how often each pair of labels co-occurred on an instance. For all labels except MOTIVATION, the majority of coincidences occur on the diagonal. RESULTS is the label most mixed up with others, possibly because these sentences often are long and also contain interpretative information of the other rhetorical types.

Figure 2a breaks this information down the level including subtypes. CHARACTERIZATION and PREPARATION are rarely confused by the domain experts. Similarly, BACKGROUND and PRIORWORK are reliably distinguished.

Agreement on sub-labels. Our agreement study contained only 12 CAPTION instances. Data inspection showed that the additional (not the main) annotator neglected to use this tag where appropriate, using only content-related tags on these instances. There were also not enough instances of the subtypes PREPARATION and EXPERIMENT_CHARACTERIZATION to measure agreement. On identifying the subtype BACKGROUND_PRIORWORK, annotators achieve a κ of 0.8, with (minor) disagreements mainly with regard to using BACKGROUND or its subtype.

Label	total	train	dev	test
MOTIVATION	363	273	44	46
BACKGROUND	3155	2423	440	292
-PRIORWORK	1824	1387	265	172
EXPERIMENT	2579	1896	394	289
-CHARACTERIZATION	1347	982	200	165
-PREPARATION	962	705	146	111
EXPLANATION	603	430	91	82
RESULTS	2953	2146	440	367
CONCLUSION	680	507	106	67
ABSTRACT	269	190	28	51
CAPTION	485	309	91	85
HEADING	702	536	96	70
METADATA	210	142	40	28

Table 8: **Label counts** on the complete dataset and on data split subsets. **Multi-label counts:** Number of sentences in which the label is present. Due to multi-labeling, the sum of these columns exceeds the total amount of sentences. For hierarchical labels, the super-label count includes all sub-label counts.

Agreement on HEADING. As it should be straightforward to identify headings, we looked at the 6 cases that one annotator labeled as HEADING but not the other. We found 4 cases to result from broken formatting. One METADATA sentence was wrongly labeled HEADING, and the remaining HEADING sentence was missed by the other annotator.

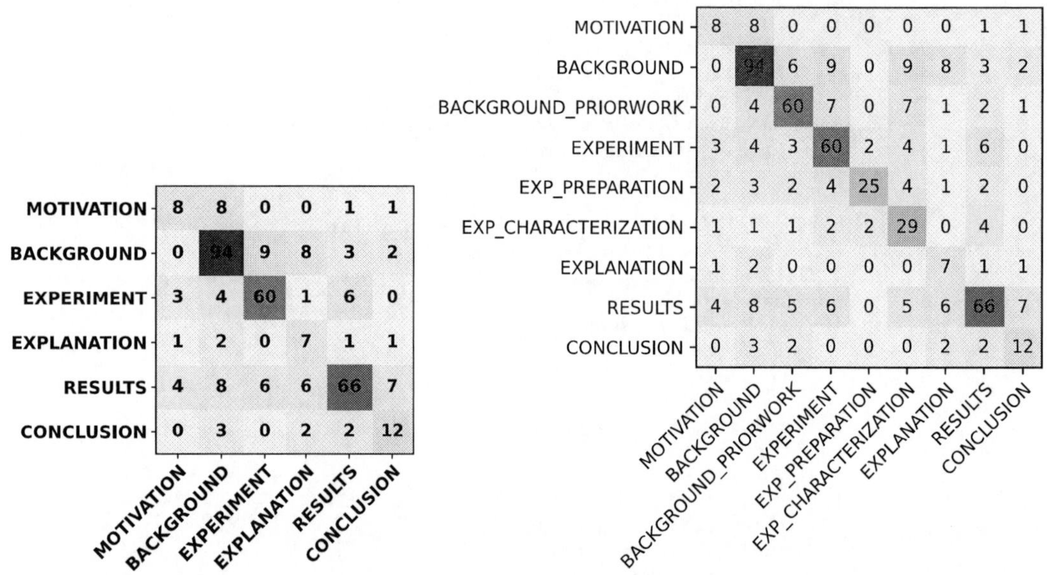

(a) Coincidence matrix for coarse AZ labels.

(b) Coincidence matrix for AZ labels with subtypes.

Figure 2: Coincidence matrices of inter-annotator agreement study for AZ labels on 357 sentences.

	Precision	Recall	F1	support
micro avg.	77.3	80.0	78.7	
macro avg.	75.0	76.1	74.9	
HEADING	100.0	81.2	89.7	32
METADATA	75.0	81.8	78.3	11
MOTIVATION	50.0	44.4	47.1	18
BACKGROUND	77.0	89.5	82.8	105
-PRIORWORK	77.9	90.9	83.9	66
EXPERIMENT	80.0	84.5	82.2	71
-PREPARATION	92.6	73.5	82.0	34
CHARACTERIZATION	61.7	78.4	69.0	37
RESULTS	85.7	70.2	77.2	94
CONCLUSION	50.0	66.7	57.1	18

Table 9: Human agreement computed in terms of hierarchical precision, recall, and F1.

Human "upper bound". In order to provide a *rough* estimate of how humans would perform on the classification task, we use the data from the agreement study to compute hierarchical precision, recall, and F1 scores. Due to insufficient data for the remaining labels, we only compute the scores over the following labels: HEADING, METADATA, MOTIVATION, BACKGROUND, PRIORWORK, EXPERIMENT, PREPARATION, CHARACTERIZATION, RESULTS, and CONCLUSION. Table 9 reports detailed scores per label. Scores have been computed using scikit-learn[6].

[6]https://scikit-learn.org/stable

E Description and Comparison of AZ Datasets.

In this section, we provide a detailed description and comparison of existing AZ datasets. The various corpora try to capture very similar information. However, each corpus defines its set of labels in a slightly different way. Table 10 lists the various labels used in the datasets and groups labels used for the same or very similar purpose. Table 11 shows the label distributions of the corpora.

AZ-CL corpus. The Argumentative Zoning (AZ, Teufel et al., 1999; Teufel and Moens, 1999) corpus[7] consists of 80 manually annotated open-access **computational linguistics** research articles. Sentences are marked according to their argumentative zone or rhetorical function as one of the following classes: AIM, BACKGROUND, BASIS, CONTRAST, OTHER, OWN or TEXT. Inter-annotator agreement is reported as substantial ($\kappa = 0.71$). The distribution of classes is quite skewed towards OTHER and OWN.

ART corpus. The ART corpus[8] (Soldatova and Liakata, 2007) covers topics in **physical chemistry** and **biochemistry**. Articles are annotated according to the CISP/CoreSC annotation scheme (Liakata and Soldatova, 2008). Sentences are

[7]https://github.com/WING-NUS/RAZ

[8]https://www.aber.ac.uk/en/cs/research/cb/projects/art/art-corpus/

PubMed	AZ-CL	ART	DRI	MuLMS-AZ	Description
OBJECTIVE	AIM	HYPOTHESIS MOTIVATION GOAL	CHALLENGE	MOTIVATION	A sentence describing the research target, goal, aim or the motivation for the research.
BACKGROUND	BACKGROUND CONTRAST BASIS	BACKGROUND	BACKGROUND	BACKGROUND PRIORWORK	A statement concerning the knowledge domain or previous related work.
METHOD	OWN	OBJECT, METHOD MODEL EXPERIMENT OBSERVATION	APPROACH	EXPERIMENT PREPARATION CHARACTERIZ. EXPLANATION	A sentence describing the research procedure, models used, or observations made during the research.
RESULT	OWN	RESULT	OUTCOME	RESULTS EXPLANATION	A sentence describing the study findings, effects, consequences, and/or analysis of the results.
CONCLUSION	OWN	CONCLUSION	OUTCOME FUTUREWORK	CONCLUSION	A statement concerning the support or rejection of the hypothesis or suggestions of future research.
–	TEXT OTHER	–	SENTENCE UNSPECIFIED	–	Example sentences, broken sentences, etc.

Table 10: AZ Corpus Zones Mapping and Descriptions. Compare to Table 3.

labeled with one of the categories HYPOTHESIS, MOTIVATION, GOAL OF INVESTIGATION, BACKGROUND, OBJECT OF INVESTIGATION, RESEARCH METHOD, MODEL, EXPERIMENT, OBSERVATION, RESULT or CONCLUSION. The annotation scheme also defines subcategories for some of these. The corpus has been annotated by domain experts. In a preliminary study, κ was measured as 0.55, however, for the final corpus, only the annotators that had the highest average agreement were selected. Hence, the agreement in the final corpus is expected to be higher.

DRI corpus. The Dr. Inventor Multi-Layer Scientific Corpus[9] (DRI, Fisas et al., 2016, 2015), contains 40 scientific articles taken from the domain of **computer graphics**. Each of the 10,784 sentences was annotated with one of the rhetorical categories: CHALLENGE, BACKGROUND, APPROACH, OUTCOME or FUTUREWORK. They have also included two other categories SENTENCE for sentences that are characterized by segmentation or character encoding errors and UNSPECIFIED for sentences where identification is not possible. Also to note was the possibility to annotate a combination of two different categories as seen in the example of: OUTCOME_CONTRIBUTION, CHALLENGE_GOAL and CHALLENGE_HYPOTHESIS. Manual annotation reaches a κ value of 0.66.

[9] http://sempub.taln.upf.edu/dricorpus

PubMed corpus. The PubMed corpus[10] (de Moura and Feltrim, 2018) contains abstracts of papers in the **biomedical** domain extracted from PUBMED/MEDLINE. The collected abstracts were written in English and annotated with predefined section names by their authors; based on the mapping provided by the U.S. National Library of Medicine (NLM), the section names were collapsed into five rhetorical roles: BACKGROUND, OBJECTIVE, METHODS, RESULTS, and CONCLUSIONS. The abstracts that did not contain the five mentioned rhetorical roles were removed from the dataset with the resulting corpus containing close to 5 million sentences. The dataset is not particularly challenging: a simple CRF model achieves an F-score of 93.75, an LSTM-based model achieves 94.77 according to de Moura and Feltrim (2018).

F Examples

In this section, we present and discuss several examples from our dataset.

F.1 Example Sentences

- MOTIVATION: *Therefore, it is highly desirable to develop an innovative technology to raise the mass activity of Ir-based OER catalysts to the targeted level.*

[10] https://github.com/dead/rhetorical-structure-pubmed-abstracts

Dataset	Label	Count
AZ-CL	Own	8624
	Other	2019
	Background	789
	Contrast	600
	Aim	313
	Basis	246
	Text	227
ART	Result	7373
	Background	6657
	Observation	4659
	Method	3751
	Model	3456
	Conclusion	3083
	Experiment	2841
	Object	1190
	Hypothesis	656
	Goal	548
	Motivation	466
DRI	Approach	5038
	Background	1760
	Sentence	1247
	Outcome	1175
	Unspecified	759
	Challenge	351
	Outcome_Contribution	219
	FutureWork	136
	Challenge_Hypothesis	7
MatSci PubMed	Results	1282
	Objective	1264
	Methods	1198
	Conclusion	380
	Background	60

Table 11: Label counts for the different AZ corpora.

- Background: *For photocatalytic water splitting using photoelectrochemical cells (PECs), the charge carriers are created from the photovoltaic effect close to the catalytic site.*

- PriorWork: *Proton exchange membrane (PEM) electrolysis, which occurs in acidic electrolytes (pH 0–7), has better efficiency and enhanced ramping capability over other types of electrolysis [7].*

- Experiment: *In order to find an optimum efficiency of the PV–electrolysis, different combinations of the electrolyzer with A-CIGS-based thin film solar cell modules with different band gaps of the cell were examined.*

- Preparation: *Pre-sputtering was performed for 5 min in argon plasma in order to remove surface impurities.*

- Characterization: *The current density-potential (j–V) characteristics of the A-CIGS cells were recorded under simulated AM 1.5G sunlight in a set-up with a halogen lamp (ELH).*

- Explanation: *A possible explanation for the superior ECSA-specific activity in the 3D WP-structured catalysts is efficient removal of oxygen bubbles from the catalyst layer.*

- Results: *The load curves were similar for the electrolyzers with different WO3 thin films and the lowest potential needed for 10 mA cm-2 in the overall reaction was 1.77 V.*

- Conclusion: *The Cu-N- rGO demonstrated superior catalytic activity to the counterpart N-rGO, and enhanced durability compared to commercial Pt/C.*

Structural tags are used, for example, in the following cases.

- Heading: *4. Discussion and concluding remarks*

- Metadata: *This research was funded by Hubei Superior and Distinctive Discipline Group of "Mechatronics and Automobiles" (No.XKQ2019009).*

- Caption: *Figure 8. Enlarged view of the shaded portion of Figure 7.*

F.2 Multi-Label Examples

In contrast to earlier works on AZ, our approach to labeling AZ in materials science publications uses a multi-label approach. In this section, we discuss some multi-label examples.

- Background, PriorWork, Results: *This indicates that the HER follows a rate-determining Volmer or Heyrovsky step for different sputtering conditions without any order [40,41].* In this example, a result obtained in the current paper confirms a result known from prior work.

- Experiment, Characterization, Results, Explanation: *Attributing this enthalpy release exclusively to the removal of grain boundaries in stage B, a specific grain boundary energy(2)γ=Hρ3dini-1-dfin-1=0.85±0.08Jm-2is estimated using the initial and final crystallite diameters of stage B, as given above (dini=222nm, dfin=764nm),* *as well as the Cu bulk value of 8.92gcm-3 for the mass density ρ.* The first subordinate clause of this sentence (*Attributing ... stage B*) is an EXPLANATION. The remainder of the sentence states a CHARACTERIZATION.

- BACKGROUND, PRIORWORK, RESULTS, CONCLUSION: *Furthermore, the fatigue life decreased approximately by more than 12% when the pre-corroded time was doubled, and the fatigue life decreased approximately by more than 11% when the applied stress level was doubled, indicating that both pre-corroded time and applied stress level can significantly affect the fatigue life of specimens, which shows a good agreement with the previous works [37,38].* This example illustrates a case where our simplification of labeling entire sentences comes to its limits: The first part of the sentence (*Furthermore ... was doubled*) reports RESULTS while the second part draws a CONCLUSION drawing connections to specific PRIORWORK.

G Detailed Results

In this section, we provide detailed results for the experiments presented in the main part of the paper.

Table 13 (no oversampling and ML-ROS) and Table 14 (multi-task AZ-CL) show the results in terms of precision, recall and (hierarchical) F1 for each label individually. We report the results on both dev and test of the specific model that performed best on dev compared to all other models.

First, we compare the difference between no oversampling at all and when using ML-ROS. As shown in Table 1, MOTIVATION, METADATA, and CAPTION are the least frequent labels in our dataset. Except for METADATA on the test set, there is always an increase in terms of F1-score when applying ML-ROS on minority labels during training. The biggest increase of 5.8 happened for MOTIVATION on the test set. Furthermore, there is also an improvement of 1.2 points on dev and 2.5 points on test in terms of F1-score for EXPLANATION, which is fourth in the list of rarest AZ labels.

During our experimentation, we observed that ML-ROS tends to be especially helpful for models that show strong performance on majority labels, but not on minority labels. Other models with different hyperparameters achieve even better scores on minority labels without oversampling; however, they tend to have worse overall performance.

Method	LM	mic.-F1	mac.-F1
No Oversampling	BERT	$72.6_{\pm 1.0}$	$65.5_{\pm 0.7}$
	MatSciBERT	$76.3_{\pm 0.7}$	$70.1_{\pm 0.7}$
	SciBERT	$76.2_{\pm 0.9}$	$70.2_{\pm 0.6}$
ML-ROS	SciBERT	$76.7_{\pm 0.7}$	$70.6_{\pm 0.9}$
+ MT (+PM)	SciBERT	$76.5_{\pm 0.4}$	$69.5_{\pm 0.5}$
+ MT (+ART)	SciBERT	$75.0_{\pm 0.9}$	$68.9_{\pm 1.1}$
+ MT (+AZ-CL)	SciBERT	**77.2**$_{\pm 0.3}$	**71.1**$_{\pm 0.5}$
+ MT (+DRI)	SciBERT	$76.6_{\pm 0.3}$	$70.5_{\pm 0.4}$
+ MT (+ART+AZ+DRI)	SciBERT	$76.4_{\pm 0.6}$	$70.2_{\pm 0.5}$
Data Augm. (+PM)	SciBERT	$77.1_{\pm 0.8}$	$70.8_{\pm 1.3}$
*human agreement**		*78.7*	*74.9*

Table 12: Results on MuLMS-AZ test set, hierarchical micro/macro F1: MT=Multi-Task models, *not directly comparable.

Next, we describe the effects of **multi-task training** with the AZ-CL dataset. We also apply ML-ROS to MuLMS-AZ in our multi-task experiments. Both micro-F1 and macro-F1 increase by 0.5 points in terms of micro- and macro-F1 when using multi-tasking instead of ML-ROS only. Most of the per-label F1-scores increased when using multi-tasking, interestingly with notable differences for CHARACTERIZATION (4.8) and METADATA (5.6). We conclude that multi-tasking with AZ-CL helps supporting common majority labels even though the domain of this dataset is clearly different from ours.

In contrast, multi-task learning with the other datasets consistently resulted in *decreases* of performance. The chemistry domain is intuitively closest to that of materials science, hence, we would have expected ART to be a good additional dataset in multi-task learning. Brack et al. (2022) provide some insights into cross-domain learning of AZ categories using datasets from biomedicine, chemistry, and computer graphics. Our MuLMS-AZ, alongside AZ-CL, opens up new research opportunities.

In addition, we perform a **data augmentation** experiment using AZ data from scientific abstracts of the PubMed Medline corpus[11], filtering for abstracts that were published in journals related to the materials science domain (see Appendix C). We map the four PubMed AZ labels BACKGROUND, OBJECTIVE, RESULTS, and CONCLUSIONS to our four AZ labels BACKGROUND, MOTIVATION, RESULTS and CONCLUSION. Augmenting with data from the PubMed Medline dataset also helps to

[11] https://www.nlm.nih.gov/databases/download/pubmed_medline.html

achieve better performance. However, the micro-F1 score is 0.1 lower and the macro-F1 score is 0.3 lower compared to the MT (+AZ-CL) model. On the other hand, training is much more time-efficient since a low augmentation percentage of 10% is sufficient to get good results.

Label	dev			test			
	P	R	H. F1	P	R	H. F1	Count
SciBERT, no oversampling							
MOTIVATION	65.5	46.8	54.4	68.5	36.5	47.6	363
BACKGROUND	89.2	80.0	**84.3**	85.0	76.6	80.6	3155
-PRIORWORK	97.0	84.5	**90.3**	92.9	67.9	78.4	1824
EXPERIMENT	82.1	85.8	83.9	80.6	82.6	**81.6**	2579
-CHARACTERIZATION	72.0	68.9	**70.3**	75.8	67.3	**71.1**	962
-PREPARATION	65.2	65.1	65.0	78.6	69.7	**73.7**	1347
EXPLANATION	46.3	33.0	38.4	55.0	35.9	43.4	603
RESULTS	75.0	84.6	79.5	79.9	85.9	82.8	2953
CONCLUSION	56.7	55.3	**56.0**	42.4	43.0	**42.6**	680
CAPTION	92.4	75.2	82.9	80.9	68.9	74.4	485
HEADING	84.8	97.9	90.9	87.4	96.6	91.7	702
METADATA	93.1	68.0	78.6	78.6	72.9	**75.2**	210
Average	**76.6**	70.4	72.9	**75.5**	67.0	70.2	
SciBERT, ML-ROS							
MOTIVATION	56.3	55.9	**55.9**	72.9	43.0	**53.4**	363
BACKGROUND	82.2	84.8	83.5	79.7	84.2	**81.9**	3155
-PRIORWORK	96.0	84.5	89.9	90.5	71.3	**79.7**	1824
EXPERIMENT	85.1	83.2	**84.1**	81.1	81.7	81.4	2579
-CHARACTERIZATION	73.3	67.3	70.1	73.2	67.5	70.2	962
-PREPARATION	69.4	63.4	**66.3**	73.8	69.5	71.5	1347
EXPLANATION	45.7	35.2	**39.6**	53.4	40.2	**45.9**	603
RESULTS	77.6	83.4	**80.4**	83.6	83.8	**83.7**	2953
CONCLUSION	60.6	44.5	51.3	46.8	35.2	40.1	680
CAPTION	91.7	79.6	**85.2**	77.9	73.6	**75.7**	485
HEADING	85.4	97.5	**91.1**	90.6	96.3	**93.4**	702
METADATA	89.3	70.5	**78.8**	61.9	80.0	69.8	210
Average	76.1	**70.8**	**73.0**	73.8	**68.9**	**70.6**	

Table 13: Per label scores on dev and test of MuLMS-AZ in terms of precision, recall, and hierarchical F1. **Bold**: best result for label. P, R, and F1 scores are averages over the P, R, F1 scores of 5 folds each.

Label	dev			test		
	P	R	H. F1	P	R	H. F1
MOTIVATION	62.7	54.1	58.0	71.2	43.9	54.3
BACKGROUND	85.6	82.1	83.8	80.9	81.6	81.2
-PRIORWORK	95.4	84.2	89.4	93.7	68.8	79.3
EXPERIMENT	83.6	82.8	83.2	83.1	83.0	83.0
-CHARACTERIZATION	73.7	65.9	69.3	77.4	73.0	75.0
-PREPARATION	69.4	55.6	61.7	79.4	67.2	72.8
EXPLANATION	42.6	35.8	38.8	51.2	35.9	41.7
RESULTS	76.6	84.4	80.3	81.5	85.1	83.2
CONCLUSION	61.8	49.6	55.0	41.0	32.8	36.4
CAPTION	90.5	77.6	83.5	79.2	76.2	77.7
HEADING	84.7	97.7	90.7	88.9	97.4	92.9
METADATA	84.3	72.0	77.6	70.6	81.4	75.4

Table 14: Per label scores on dev and test in terms of precision, recall, and hierarchical F1 using multi-task learning with the AZ-CL dataset, SciBERT, ML-ROS.

A Side-by-side Comparision of Transformers for English Implicit Discourse Relation Classification

Bruce W. Lee[1,2], **BongSeok Yang**[2], **Jason Hyeong-Jong Lee**[2]
[1]University of Pennsylvania - PA, USA
[2]LXPER AI Research - Seoul, South Korea
brucelws@seas.upenn.edu
bongseok@lxper.com
jasonlee@lxper.com

Abstract

Though discourse parsing can help multiple NLP fields, there has been no wide language model search done on implicit discourse relation classification. This hinders researchers from fully utilizing public-available models in discourse analysis. This work is a straightforward, fine-tuned discourse performance comparison of seven pre-trained language models. We use PDTB-3, a popular discourse relation annotated dataset. Through our model search, we raise SOTA to 0.671 ACC and obtain novel observations. Some are contrary to what has been reported before (Shi and Demberg, 2019b), that sentence-level pre-training objectives (NSP, SBO, SOP) generally fail to produce the best performing model for implicit discourse relation classification. Counterintuitively, similar-sized PLMs with MLM and full attention led to better performance.

1 Introduction

An utterance has multiple dimensions of meaning. Discourse relation classification identifies one such dimension: the coherence relation between clauses or sentences arising from low-level textual cues (Zhao and Webber, 2022; Webber et al., 2019). This makes the task important to several NLP fields, including multi-party dialogue analysis (Li et al., 2022), social media postings analysis (Siskou et al., 2022), and student literary writing analysis (Fiacco et al., 2022). A discourse relation is often marked with explicit connectives such as *but, because, and.* Consider the following example:

> Although Philip Morris typically tries to defend the rights of smokers, [*"this has nothing to do with cigarettes, nor will it ever," the spokesman says*]$_{Arg1}$. [<u>But</u>]$_{Conn}$ [**some anti-smoking activists disagree**]$_{Arg2}$, expressing anger... → `Comparison.Contrast`

The explicit connective, <u>Conn</u> (But), is informative. Hence, it is fairly easy to know that the two arguments, *Arg1* and **Arg2**, are compared, likely in a contrasting relationship rather than similarity. This task is often referred to as explicit discourse relation classification. Pitler and Nenkova (2009) achieves a 94.15% accuracy (4-way) with Naive Bayes.

Implicit discourse relation classification, on the other hand, aims to classify discourse relationships in cases without an explicit connective. It has received constant attention (Li et al., 2022) since the release of Penn Discourse Tree Bank 2.0 (PDTB-2) (Prasad et al., 2008). Consider the following:

> ["*Last year we probably bought one out of every three new deals,*]$_{Arg1}$," he says. "[**This year, at best, it's in one in every five or six.**]$_{Arg2}$" → `Comparison.Contrast`

Without an explicit connective, <u>Conn</u>, discourse relation classification only relies on low-level semantic cues from the arguments, *Arg1* and **Arg2**. Such "implicit" discourse relation classification is very challenging as it requires a language model to conceptualize the unstated goal the speaker is trying to achieve, not only the literal content (Shi and Demberg, 2019b; Sileo et al., 2019).

With XLNet$_{large}$ (Yang et al., 2019) achieving ~60% accuracy (Kim et al., 2020), pre-trained language models showed promising improvements from the past studies: Maximum-Entropy Learning (~40% F1) (Lin et al., 2014), Adversarial Network (~46% ACC) (Qin et al., 2017), Seq2Seq + Memory Network (~48% ACC) (Shi and Demberg, 2019a). Implicit discourse relation classification gives relatively small textual information for a language model to infer from. Thus, pre-training large text helps establish typical relations within/across clauses and sentences (Shi and Demberg, 2019b).

Proceedings of the 4th Workshop on Computational Approaches to Discourse (CODI 2023), pages 16–23
July 13-14, 2023 ©2023 Association for Computational Linguistics

Configurations	ALBERT$_{large}$	BART$_{large}$	BigBird-R.	DeBERTa$_{large}$	Longformer$_{large}$	RoBERTa$_{large}$	SpanBERT$_{large}$
Release	2019	2020	2020	2020	2020	2019	2020
Parameters	17M	406M	-	350M	435M	340M	340M
Hidden	1024	1024	-	1024	1024	1024	1024
Layers	24 (Enc)	24 (Enc+Dec)*	-	24 (Enc)	24 (Enc)	24 (Enc)	24 (Enc)
Attention Heads	16	16	-	16	16	16	16
Self-Attention	Full	Full	Block-Sparse	Full**	Global+Window	Full	Full
Max Seq. Length	512	512	4096	512	4096	512	512
Pre-train Obj.	MLM & SOP	TI & SS	-	MLM	MLM	MLM	MLM & SBO

Table 1: Tested language models and their varying configurations. *: BART follows the original encoder-decoder architecture, 12 layers allocated for each. **: DeBERTa uses disentangled attention. MLM: masked language modelling. SOP: sentence order prediction. SBO: span boundary objective. TI: text infilling. SS: sentence shuffling.

Pre-trained language models, like BERT (Devlin et al., 2018), follow transformer-type (Vaswani et al., 2017) architecture and have only been recently introduced into implicit discourse relation classification (Kishimoto et al., 2020). To the best of our knowledge, BERT and XLNet are the only pre-trained language models (fine-tuned and) evaluated for implicit discourse relation classification on PDTB-3 (Kim et al., 2020). However, language models vary in architecture, training objective, data, etc.

Instead of performing a focused study on a single model, we fine-tune seven state-of-the-art (SOTA) language models **(§2)**. Our wider approach brings weaknesses **(§5)** (as we ignore some model-specific characteristics), but it allows the bird's-eye view of several downstream performances in PDTB-3 **(§3)** (Webber et al., 2019) and raises SOTA (~67% ACC) on Kim et al. (2020)'s evaluation protocol. By contrasting performances, we show that certain language model characteristics can benefit implicit discourse relation classification.

Additionally, we take the best-performing language model and check if the "full-sentence(s)" setup gives better performance **(§3.4)**. As we elaborate further in the following sections, our sanity checks on PDTB-3 hint that some argument annotations are questionable in terms of consistency and coverage. Hence, implicit discourse relation classification accuracy might improve by simply training the language model with a full sentence(s) instead of human-annotated argument spans (*Arg1* and **Arg2**). We evaluate this idea toward the end.

2 Background

The pre-train and fine-tune paradigm have been led by the remarkable downstream task performances of pre-trained language models (Kalyan et al., 2021; Devlin et al., 2018). For several NLP tasks, a pre-trained language model could have likely done a fine job at learning syntax, semantics, and world knowledge – given enough data and model size (Wang et al., 2019).

A pre-trained language model's competence in discourse was questionable until Shi and Demberg (2019b) proposed that BERT's pre-training objective can benefit implicit discourse relation classification. However, Iter et al. (2020) hints that BERT is not the language model best suited to the task.

Implicit discourse relation classification is an active area of research (Kurfalı, 2022; Zhao and Webber, 2022; Kurfalı and Östling, 2021b; Knaebel, 2021; Munir et al., 2021; Kurfalı and Östling, 2021a; Kishimoto et al., 2020; Bourgonje and Stede, 2019; Shi and Demberg, 2019b; Bai and Zhao, 2018; Dai and Huang, 2018; Rutherford et al., 2017). However, there has been no wide-range model study on implicit discourse relation classification, limiting a researcher's scope of model choice. This issue is further complicated by the fact that discourse task performances do not always correlate with popular semantics-based natural language understanding (NLU) scores, such as GLUE (Sileo et al., 2019). Thus, it is difficult to predict which language model can perform well without a dedicated empirical exploration.

With the a version update to Penn Discourse Tree Bank (PDTB-3) (Webber et al., 2019) and the correspondingly updated evaluation method (Kim et al., 2020), we fine-tune seven language models to implicit discourse relation classification.

The chosen language models are: RoBERTa$_{large}$ (Liu et al., 2019), ALBERT$_{large}$ (Lan et al., 2019), BigBird-RoBERTa$_{large}$ (Zaheer et al., 2020), BART$_{large}$ (Lewis et al., 2020), Longformer$_{large}$ (Beltagy et al., 2020), SpanBERT$_{large}$ (Joshi et al., 2020), DeBERTa$_{large}$ (He et al., 2020a). These models are selected with diversity in mind, especially in terms of input sequence length, attention type, and pre-train objectives. These models fol-

	ALBERT$_{large}$	BART$_{large}$	BigBird-R.	DeBERTa$_{large}$	Longformer$_{large}$	RoBERTa$_{large}$	SpanBERT$_{large}$
Hyperparameters							
Learning Rate	5e-6	5e-6	5e-6	2e-6	5e-6	2e-6	5e-6
a: Argument Spans							
Accuracy	0.565	0.657	0.649	0.671	0.668	0.670	0.627
Variance	2.53e-4	2.15e-4	4.02e-4	2.70e-4	2.15e-4	3.32e-4	1.78e-4
b: Full Sentence(s)							
Accuracy	0.534	0.629	0.620	0.634	0.627	0.617	0.598
Variance	2.27e-4	4.28e-4	2.79e-4	3.75e-4	4.18e-4	3.62e-4	2.84e-4

Table 2: Language model performances (test set) on Level-2 14-way implicit discourse relation classification.

low the popular transformer architecture (Vaswani et al., 2017), and we will not review each model in detail. A brief comparison is shown in Table 1.

3 Experiments

3.1 Data Preparation

We obtained the official PDTB-3 data from the Linguistic Data Consortium[1]. PDTB-3 is a large-scale resource of annotated discourse relations and their arguments over the 1 million words Wall Street Journal Corpus (Marcus et al., 1993). From a public repository[2], we retrieved the corresponding evaluation script (Kim et al., 2020). We describe some characteristics of the evaluation protocol below.

Cross-validation is used on the section level to preserve paragraph and document structures. Cross-validation likely solves label sparsity issue (Shi and Demberg, 2017). The 25 sections of PDTB-3 are divided into 12 folds with 2 development, 2 test, and 21 training sections in each fold. The sliding window of two sections is used, creating 12 folds.

Label set is composed of 14 senses on L2 discourse relations (see Appendix B). Only the senses with $\geq$100 instances are used. This is to produce results that are in align with Kim et al. (2020). This alignment is crucial as we directly compared our results against fine-tuend BERT from Kim et al. (2020), which is trained with next sentence prediction (NSP) objective. Multiply-annotated labels become separate training instances.

3.2 Fine-Tuning

To ensure reproducibility, we only take pre-trained language models from the now ubiquitous Huggingface (Wolf et al., 2019) `transformers` library. Fine-tuning was done with PyTorch (Paszke et al., 2019) and our scripts are publicly available.

[1]www.ldc.upenn.edu

[2]github.com/najoungkim/pdtb3

During fine-tuning, each training instance is a concatenation of two arguments (= sequence of tokens in *Arg1* and **Arg2**). BERT-type models carry special tokens ([CLS], [SEP], [EOS]) for segmentation: [CLS], $Arg1_1$ ... $Arg1_N$, [SEP], $\mathbf{Arg2}_1$ ... $\mathbf{Arg2}_M$, [EOS]. Depending on the model, these special tokens are modified or completely removed.

As for hyperparameter searches, we mostly focus on the learning rate. We use the popular AdamW optimizer with a linear scheduler (no warm-up steps). As for the learning rate, we start from 2e-5, a value commonly used for text classification since Sun et al. (2019). We test lower learning rates of 2e-6 and 5e-6; we find that 5e-6 (which is slightly lower than what is usually used in sequence classification) performs best for almost all models. The batch size is 8 and the max input length is set at 256.

Lastly, for each experiment step (i.e. BART on fold 1), we train for 10 epochs with an early stop. The training stops if the current epoch's validation loss (see development set **§3.1**) did not decrease from the previous epoch. Model training time, GPU, language model repository address, and other details on hyperparameters are in Appendix C.

3.3 Evaluation and Observations

In Table 2-a, we report the mean test set accuracy of 12 folds along with variance. This is in alignment with what was recommended by Kim et al. (2020). Development set performances are given in Table 3 to facilitate reproducibility. For multiply-annotated labels (also discussed in **§3.1**), the model only has to get one label correct. We reach some surprising observations, which we share below.

1) Sentence-level pre-train objectives are not necessary to create best-performing models. This is contrary to Shi and Demberg (2019b), which proposed that NSP helps implicit discourse

	ALBERT$_{large}$	BART$_{large}$	BigBird-R.	DeBERTa$_{large}$	Longformer$_{large}$	RoBERTa$_{large}$	SpanBERT$_{large}$
a: Argument Spans							
Accuracy	0.566	0.663	0.653	0.673	0.669	0.670	0.629
Variance	2.94e-4	1.33e-4	1.62e-4	2.47e-4	1.68e-4	1.01e-4	2.03e-4
b: Full Sentence(s)							
Accuracy	0.567	0.660	0.645	0.656	0.661	0.652	0.639
Variance	3.92e-4	4.59e-4	3.50e-4	1.85e-4	2.56e-4	4.10e-4	3.45e-4

Table 3: Language model performances (**dev set**) on Level-2 14-way implicit discourse relation classification.

relation classification after conducting an ablation study on BERT. Their finding was intuitive as well because implicit discourse relation classification aims to find the relationship between two argument spans.

But in a more general scope, the necessity of NSP has been questioned multiple times (Yang et al., 2019; Lample and Conneau, 2019). In other words, NSP – or any other sentence-level pre-train objective for that matter – could have been only helpful in some specific ablation study of BERT-type models but not in other cases (Liu et al., 2019). We obtain supporting results in Table 2-a, where language models with sentence-level objectives performed worse than MLM-only models given similar model sizes (ALBERT is an exception).

2) Long-document modifications (mostly done by altering attention schemes of an existing model) decrease the original model performance. At first, we postulated that long-document models could lead to performance increases because they can learn long-span discourse relations during pre-training. But using sparse or block attention mechanisms eventually led to a performance decrease.

The decrease is clearly demonstrated by BigBird-RoBERTa$_{large}$ and Longformer$_{large}$. Both models start from the existing RoBERTa$_{large}$ checkpoint and modify it to process longer sequences. Such modifications achieved performance increases in other NLP tasks like question-answering, coreference resolution, and some cases of sequence classification. But implicit discourse relation classification, which requires the model's understanding of dense discourse relations hidden within a few tokens, long-document modification is a drawback.

3) The simplest combination of MLM and full attention is best suited for implicit discourse relation classification. We are making this argument within the scope of what we have tested. We believe that MLM and full attention (e.g., RoBERTa, DeBERTa) work best because the model has to make inferences based on a relatively small number of tokens. Hence, trivial textual cues should not be risked being overlooked. MLM, with full attention, forces every token to attend to every other and learn the token-specific relations, likely to lose the least textual cues and nuances.

3.4 Train Full Sentence or Argument Span?

Following the aforementioned observations, we postulated that fine-tuning language models using full sentence(s) could further improve classification accuracy. By full sentence(s), we refer to the sentence(s) (usually up to two) that the annotated argument spans appeared. We had two reasons for our postulation: 1. textual cues that hint at underlying discourse relation could be spread throughout the sentence(s), 2. argument span annotation is sometimes inconsistent, especially at punctuation marks, unnecessarily confusing the language model. Implicit discourse relation classification has rarely been tested using the full sentence.

We built an argument matcher to find the source sentence of each annotated argument span. For inter-sentential relations, we only considered argument spans that came from two adjacent source sentences. We share the test set results in Table 2-b. The results bring us to our fourth observation.

4) As input, concatenating argument spans generally perform better than full sentence(s). Opposed to our postulation, using full sentence(s) as input decreased performance on the test set. Though we see mixed results on the development set in Table 3, training full sentences as input generally decrease performance. But when it comes to implicit discourse sense classification from the raw text (that means in practical, end-to-end applications), the benefits of using argument spans must be weighed against the low accuracies (50% $\sim$ 60%) of the available argument extractors.

4 Conclusion

Researchers often build or modify a neural network to improve task performance. While such effort is essential, this paper shows that SOTA can also be raised through extensive search and application of existing resources. Through a side-by-side comparison of seven PLMs, we also make handy observations on pre-training objectives, long-document modifications, and full-sentence setups. Though some might consider these phenomena rather expected, nothing is scientifically conclusive until an analysis is performed at an adequate scale. We hope that our report helps researchers working towards discourse understanding, and we continue to discuss the missing details in the appendices.

5 Acknowledgement

We thank the anonymous reviewers for their crisp and realistic advices on cleaning the language of the paper and experiments. Most of the review opinions were accepted and were reflected in the paper as they were valid.

References

Hongxiao Bai and Hai Zhao. 2018. Deep enhanced representation for implicit discourse relation recognition. In *Proceedings of the 27th International Conference on Computational Linguistics*, pages 571–583.

Iz Beltagy, Matthew E Peters, and Arman Cohan. 2020. Longformer: The long-document transformer. *arXiv preprint arXiv:2004.05150*.

Peter Bourgonje and Manfred Stede. 2019. Explicit discourse argument extraction for german. In *International Conference on Text, Speech, and Dialogue*, pages 32–44. Springer.

Zeyu Dai and Ruihong Huang. 2018. Improving implicit discourse relation classification by modeling inter-dependencies of discourse units in a paragraph. *arXiv preprint arXiv:1804.05918*.

Jacob Devlin, Ming-Wei Chang, Kenton Lee, and Kristina Toutanova. 2018. Bert: Pre-training of deep bidirectional transformers for language understanding. *arXiv preprint arXiv:1810.04805*.

James Fiacco, Shiyan Jiang, David Adamson, and Carolyn Rosé. 2022. Toward automatic discourse parsing of student writing motivated by neural interpretation. In *Proceedings of the 17th Workshop on Innovative Use of NLP for Building Educational Applications (BEA 2022)*, pages 204–215, Seattle, Washington. Association for Computational Linguistics.

Pengcheng He, Xiaodong Liu, Jianfeng Gao, and Weizhu Chen. 2020a. Deberta: Decoding-enhanced bert with disentangled attention. In *International Conference on Learning Representations*.

Ruifang He, Jian Wang, Fengyu Guo, and Yugui Han. 2020b. TransS-driven joint learning architecture for implicit discourse relation recognition. In *Proceedings of the 58th Annual Meeting of the Association for Computational Linguistics*, pages 139–148, Online. Association for Computational Linguistics.

Dan Iter, Kelvin Guu, Larry Lansing, and Dan Jurafsky. 2020. Pretraining with contrastive sentence objectives improves discourse performance of language models. *arXiv preprint arXiv:2005.10389*.

Mandar Joshi, Danqi Chen, Yinhan Liu, Daniel S Weld, Luke Zettlemoyer, and Omer Levy. 2020. Spanbert: Improving pre-training by representing and predicting spans. *Transactions of the Association for Computational Linguistics*, 8:64–77.

Katikapalli Subramanyam Kalyan, Ajit Rajasekharan, and Sivanesan Sangeetha. 2021. Ammus: A survey of transformer-based pretrained models in natural language processing. *arXiv preprint arXiv:2108.05542*.

Najoung Kim, Song Feng, Chulaka Gunasekara, and Luis Lastras. 2020. Implicit discourse relation classification: We need to talk about evaluation. In *Proceedings of the 58th Annual Meeting of the Association for Computational Linguistics*, pages 5404–5414, Online. Association for Computational Linguistics.

Yudai Kishimoto, Yugo Murawaki, and Sadao Kurohashi. 2020. Adapting bert to implicit discourse relation classification with a focus on discourse connectives. In *Proceedings of The 12th Language Resources and Evaluation Conference*, pages 1152–1158.

René Knaebel. 2021. discopy: A neural system for shallow discourse parsing. In *Proceedings of the 2nd Workshop on Computational Approaches to Discourse*, pages 128–133, Punta Cana, Dominican Republic and Online. Association for Computational Linguistics.

Murathan Kurfalı. 2022. *Contributions to Shallow Discourse Parsing: To English and beyond*. Ph.D. thesis, Department of Linguistics, Stockholm University.

Murathan Kurfalı and Robert Östling. 2021a. Let's be explicit about that: Distant supervision for implicit discourse relation classification via connective prediction. *arXiv preprint arXiv:2106.03192*.

Murathan Kurfalı and Robert Östling. 2021b. Probing multilingual language models for discourse. In *Proceedings of the 6th Workshop on Representation Learning for NLP (RepL4NLP-2021)*, pages 8–19.

Guillaume Lample and Alexis Conneau. 2019. Crosslingual language model pretraining. *arXiv preprint arXiv:1901.07291*.

Zhenzhong Lan, Mingda Chen, Sebastian Goodman, Kevin Gimpel, Piyush Sharma, and Radu Soricut. 2019. Albert: A lite bert for self-supervised learning of language representations. *arXiv preprint arXiv:1909.11942*.

Mike Lewis, Yinhan Liu, Naman Goyal, Marjan Ghazvininejad, Abdelrahman Mohamed, Omer Levy, Veselin Stoyanov, and Luke Zettlemoyer. 2020. Bart: Denoising sequence-to-sequence pre-training for natural language generation, translation, and comprehension. In *Proceedings of the 58th Annual Meeting of the Association for Computational Linguistics*, pages 7871–7880.

Jiaqi Li, Ming Liu, Bing Qin, and Ting Liu. 2022. A survey of discourse parsing. *Frontiers of Computer Science*, 16(5):1–12.

Ziheng Lin, Hwee Tou Ng, and Min-Yen Kan. 2014. A pdtb-styled end-to-end discourse parser. *Natural Language Engineering*, 20(2):151–184.

Yinhan Liu, Myle Ott, Naman Goyal, Jingfei Du, Mandar Joshi, Danqi Chen, Omer Levy, Mike Lewis, Luke Zettlemoyer, and Veselin Stoyanov. 2019. Roberta: A robustly optimized bert pretraining approach. *arXiv preprint arXiv:1907.11692*.

Mitchell P. Marcus, Beatrice Santorini, and Mary Ann Marcinkiewicz. 1993. Building a large annotated corpus of English: The Penn Treebank. *Computational Linguistics*, 19(2):313–330.

Kashif Munir, Hongxiao Bai, Hai Zhao, and Junhan Zhao. 2021. Memorizing all for implicit discourse relation recognition. *Transactions on Asian and Low-Resource Language Information Processing*, 21(3):1–20.

Adam Paszke, Sam Gross, Francisco Massa, Adam Lerer, James Bradbury, Gregory Chanan, Trevor Killeen, Zeming Lin, Natalia Gimelshein, Luca Antiga, Alban Desmaison, Andreas Kopf, Edward Yang, Zachary DeVito, Martin Raison, Alykhan Tejani, Sasank Chilamkurthy, Benoit Steiner, Lu Fang, Junjie Bai, and Soumith Chintala. 2019. Pytorch: An imperative style, high-performance deep learning library. In H. Wallach, H. Larochelle, A. Beygelzimer, F. d'Alché-Buc, E. Fox, and R. Garnett, editors, *Advances in Neural Information Processing Systems 32*, pages 8024–8035. Curran Associates, Inc.

Emily Pitler and Ani Nenkova. 2009. Using syntax to disambiguate explicit discourse connectives in text. In *Proceedings of the ACL-IJCNLP 2009 Conference Short Papers*, pages 13–16, Suntec, Singapore. Association for Computational Linguistics.

Rashmi Prasad, Nikhil Dinesh, Alan Lee, Eleni Miltsakaki, Livio Robaldo, Aravind Joshi, and Bonnie Webber. 2008. The penn discourse treebank 2.0. In *Proceedings of the Sixth International Conference on Language Resources and Evaluation (LREC'08)*.

Lianhui Qin, Zhisong Zhang, Hai Zhao, Zhiting Hu, and Eric Xing. 2017. Adversarial connective-exploiting networks for implicit discourse relation classification. In *Proceedings of the 55th Annual Meeting of the Association for Computational Linguistics (Volume 1: Long Papers)*, pages 1006–1017, Vancouver, Canada. Association for Computational Linguistics.

Attapol Rutherford, Vera Demberg, and Nianwen Xue. 2017. A systematic study of neural discourse models for implicit discourse relation. In *Proceedings of the 15th Conference of the European Chapter of the Association for Computational Linguistics: Volume 1, Long Papers*, pages 281–291.

Wei Shi and Vera Demberg. 2017. On the need of cross validation for discourse relation classification. In *Proceedings of the 15th Conference of the European Chapter of the Association for Computational Linguistics: Volume 2, Short Papers*, pages 150–156, Valencia, Spain. Association for Computational Linguistics.

Wei Shi and Vera Demberg. 2019a. Learning to explicitate connectives with Seq2Seq network for implicit discourse relation classification. In *Proceedings of the 13th International Conference on Computational Semantics - Long Papers*, pages 188–199, Gothenburg, Sweden. Association for Computational Linguistics.

Wei Shi and Vera Demberg. 2019b. Next sentence prediction helps implicit discourse relation classification within and across domains. In *Proceedings of the 2019 conference on empirical methods in natural language processing and the 9th international joint conference on natural language processing (EMNLP-IJCNLP)*, pages 5790–5796.

Damien Sileo, Tim Van-de Cruys, Camille Pradel, and Philippe Muller. 2019. Discourse-based evaluation of language understanding. *arXiv preprint arXiv:1907.08672*.

Wassiliki Siskou, Clara Giralt Mirón, Sarah Molina-Raith, and Miriam Butt. 2022. Automatized detection and annotation for calls to action in Latin-American social media postings. In *Proceedings of the 6th Joint SIGHUM Workshop on Computational Linguistics for Cultural Heritage, Social Sciences, Humanities and Literature*, pages 65–69, Gyeongju, Republic of Korea. International Conference on Computational Linguistics.

Chi Sun, Xipeng Qiu, Yige Xu, and Xuanjing Huang. 2019. How to fine-tune bert for text classification? In *China national conference on Chinese computational linguistics*, pages 194–206. Springer.

Ashish Vaswani, Noam Shazeer, Niki Parmar, Jakob Uszkoreit, Llion Jones, Aidan N Gomez, Łukasz Kaiser, and Illia Polosukhin. 2017. Attention is all you need. *Advances in neural information processing systems*, 30.

Alex Wang, Jan Hula, Patrick Xia, Raghavendra Pappagari, R. Thomas McCoy, Roma Patel, Najoung Kim, Ian Tenney, Yinghui Huang, Katherin Yu, Shuning Jin, Berlin Chen, Benjamin Van Durme, Edouard Grave, Ellie Pavlick, and Samuel R. Bowman. 2019. Can you tell me how to get past sesame street? sentence-level pretraining beyond language modeling. In *Proceedings of the 57th Annual Meeting of the Association for Computational Linguistics*, pages 4465–4476, Florence, Italy. Association for Computational Linguistics.

Bonnie Webber, Rashmi Prasad, Alan Lee, and Aravind Joshi. 2019. The penn discourse treebank 3.0 annotation manual. *Philadelphia, University of Pennsylvania.*

Thomas Wolf, Lysandre Debut, Victor Sanh, Julien Chaumond, Clement Delangue, Anthony Moi, Pierric Cistac, Tim Rault, Rémi Louf, Morgan Funtowicz, et al. 2019. Huggingface's transformers: State-of-the-art natural language processing. *arXiv preprint arXiv:1910.03771.*

Nianwen Xue, Hwee Tou Ng, Sameer Pradhan, Rashmi Prasad, Christopher Bryant, and Attapol Rutherford. 2015. The conll-2015 shared task on shallow discourse parsing. In *Proceedings of the Nineteenth Conference on Computational Natural Language Learning-Shared Task*, pages 1–16.

Nianwen Xue, Hwee Tou Ng, Sameer Pradhan, Attapol Rutherford, Bonnie Webber, Chuan Wang, and Hongmin Wang. 2016. Conll 2016 shared task on multilingual shallow discourse parsing. In *Proceedings of the CoNLL-16 shared task*, pages 1–19.

Zhilin Yang, Zihang Dai, Yiming Yang, Jaime Carbonell, Russ R Salakhutdinov, and Quoc V Le. 2019. Xlnet: Generalized autoregressive pretraining for language understanding. *Advances in neural information processing systems*, 32.

Manzil Zaheer, Guru Guruganesh, Kumar Avinava Dubey, Joshua Ainslie, Chris Alberti, Santiago Ontanon, Philip Pham, Anirudh Ravula, Qifan Wang, Li Yang, et al. 2020. Big bird: Transformers for longer sequences. *Advances in Neural Information Processing Systems*, 33:17283–17297.

Zheng Zhao and Bonnie Webber. 2022. Revisiting shallow discourse parsing in the pdtb-3: Handling intra-sentential implicits. *arXiv preprint arXiv:2204.00350.*

A "Full sentence(s)" Experiment

A.1 What Makes the Experiment Important?

This section is a continuation of §3.4. Here, we discuss implicit discourse relation classification from raw sentence(s), which we believe is the best practical example of real-world applications of the related fields. Such an *end-to-end* concept has been popularized through CoNLL-2016 (Xue et al., 2016) and CoNLL-2015 (Xue et al., 2015), and most systems develop a separate argument span identification model. Then, the identified argument spans would be fed to the discourse relation classification model for sense prediction (refer to examples given in **§1**) (He et al., 2020b).

Such a double-step process makes sense. Indeed, feeding the exact argument spans (that only contain the tokens that imply a certain discourse sense) will increase sense prediction performance.

But the problem arises because identifying argument spans from raw sentence(s) is a low accuracy operation (Knaebel, 2021). A wrong span identification eventually leads to error propagation, providing a discourse relation classification model that lacks textual information. We give a theoretical error propagation example and conduct a simple experiment to prove our point.

A.2 Theoretical Example of Error Propagation

—

1. A set of two raw sentences is given.

> "Last year we probably bought one out of every three new deals," he says. "This year, at best, it's in one in every five or six."

—

2. Where correct argument spans are as below.

> ["*Last year we probably bought one out of every three new deals,*]$_{Arg1}$" he says. "[**This year, at best, it's in one in every five or six.**]$_{Arg2}$"

—

3. But an argument span identification model often makes wrong predictions (best system (**?**) at CoNLL-2016 scores 52.02 F1, for exact span match).

> ["*Last year we probably bought one*]$_{Arg1}$ out of every three new deals," he says. "This year, at best, [**it's in one in every five or six.**]$_{Arg2}$"

—

4. Now, compare the amount of textual information passed over to the implicit discourse relation classification model, under three setups. Note that setup 1 cannot be used in real-world settings because it requires PDTB-3's gold annotations.

Setup 1) PDTB-3 (with gold annotations)

> Last year we probably bought one out of every three new deals This year, at best, it's in one in every five or six.

Setup 2) A low accuracy argument span model

> Last year we probably bought one it's in one in every five or six.

Fine-tuned PLM	Argument Span	
	ACC	F1
BERT$_{large}$	0.912	0.742

Table 4: BERT's performance (12-folds test set) on PDTB-3's argument spans.

Setup 3) Full sentence(s)

> "Last year we probably bought one out of every three new deals," he says. "This year, at best, it's in one in every five or six."

A.3 Experiment on Error Propagation

Though not all tokens are valuable under a full sentence(s) setup, we can notice that it is a foolproof way to input all meaningful tokens. Table 4 reports the classification performance of BERT$_{large}$, which was trained to identify argument spans using PDTB-3. Our argument span scoring scheme approximately matches CoNLL-16's partial scoring scheme, essentially a relaxed version of conlleval. That means we consider a prediction correct if more than 70% of argument span tokens are identified. For implicit discourse relation classification, a sense prediction is correct if it matches any of the multiply-annotated senses.

BERT's 0.912 ACC score implies that the model could correctly identify at least 70% of the gold argument span tokens more than 9 out of 10 times. Nonetheless, error propagation detrimentally affected implicit discourse relation classification performance in Table 5. This empirically proves our ideas in Appendix A.1.

Fine-tuned PLM	Implicit Sense	
	ACC	F1
DeBERTa$_{large}$	0.670	0.671
with error propagation	0.476	0.491
full sentence(s)	0.634	0.637

Table 5: DeBERTa performances (12-fold test set) on PDTB-3's Level-2 14-way implicit discourse relation classification, but under three different pipeline setups.

B 14-way Label Set

Label	Counts
Comparison.Concession	1494
Comparison.Contrast	983
Contingency.Cause	5785
Contingency.Cause+Belief	202
Contingency.Condition	199
Contingency.Purpose	1373
Expansion.Conjunction	4386
Expansion.Equivalence	336
Expansion.Instantiation	1533
Expansion.Level-of-detail	3361
Expansion.Manner	739
Expansion.Substitution	450
Temporal.Asynchronous	1289
Temporal.Synchronous	539

Table 6: Counts of 14-way implicit discourse senses.

C More on Fine-tuning Set Up

We ran all our experiments on a single NVIDIA Tesla V100 GPU. Model train time and repositories are listed below. Training times below suppose no early stop. The performances reported in Table 2 are obtained **with** early stop.

ALBERT$_{large}$
- huggingface.co/albert-large-v1
- $\sim$2.4 days, for 12 folds $\times$ 10 epochs

BART$_{large}$
- huggingface.co/facebook/bart-large
- $\sim$3.6 days, for 12 folds $\times$ 10 epochs

BigBird-RoBERTa$_{large}$
- huggingface.co/google/bigbird-roberta-large
- $\sim$3.2 days, for 12 folds $\times$ 10 epochs

DeBERTa$_{large}$
- huggingface.co/microsoft/deberta-large
- $\sim$4.6 days, for 12 folds $\times$ 10 epochs

Longformer$_{large}$
- huggingface.co/allenai/longformer-large-4096
- $\sim$11 days, for 12 folds $\times$ 10 epochs

RoBERTa$_{large}$
- huggingface.co/roberta-large
- $\sim$2.9 days, for 12 folds $\times$ 10 epochs

SpanBERT$_{large}$
- .../SpanBERT/spanbert-large-cased
- $\sim$2.9 days, for 12 folds $\times$ 10 epochs

Ensemble Transfer Learning for Multilingual Coreference Resolution

Tuan Lai, Heng Ji
Department of Computer Science
University of Illinois Urbana-Champaign
{tuanml2, hengji}@illinois.edu

Abstract

Entity coreference resolution is an important research problem with many applications, including information extraction and question answering. Coreference resolution for English has been studied extensively. However, there is relatively little work for other languages. A problem that frequently occurs when working with a non-English language is the scarcity of annotated training data. To overcome this challenge, we design a simple but effective ensemble-based framework that combines various transfer learning (TL) techniques. We first train several models using different TL methods. Then, during inference, we compute the unweighted average scores of the models' predictions to extract the final set of predicted clusters. Furthermore, we also propose a low-cost TL method that bootstraps coreference resolution models by utilizing Wikipedia anchor texts. Leveraging the idea that the coreferential links naturally exist between anchor texts pointing to the same article, our method builds a sizeable distantly-supervised dataset for the target language that consists of tens of thousands of documents. We can pre-train a model on the pseudo-labeled dataset before finetuning it on the final target dataset. Experimental results on two benchmark datasets, OntoNotes and SemEval, confirm the effectiveness of our methods. Our best ensembles consistently outperform the baseline approach of simple training by up to 7.68% in the F1 score. These ensembles also achieve new state-of-the-art results for three languages: Arabic, Dutch, and Spanish[1].

1 Introduction

Within-document entity coreference resolution is the process of clustering entity mentions in a document that refer to the same entities (Ji et al., 2005; Luo and Zitouni, 2005; Ng, 2010, 2017). It is an important research problem, with applications in various downstream tasks such as entity linking (Ling et al., 2015; Kundu et al., 2018), question answering (Dhingra et al., 2018), and dialog systems (Gao et al., 2019). Researchers have recently proposed many neural methods for coreference resolution, ranging from span-based end-to-end models (Lee et al., 2017, 2018) to formulating the task as a question answering problem (Wu et al., 2020b). Given enough annotated training data, deep neural networks can learn to extract useful features automatically. As a result, on English benchmarks with abundant labeled training documents, the mentioned neural methods consistently outperform previous handcrafted feature-based techniques (Raghunathan et al., 2010; Lee et al., 2013), achieving new state-of-the-art (SOTA) results.

Compared to the amount of research on English coreference resolution, there is relatively little work for other languages. A problem that frequently occurs when working with a non-English language is the scarcity of annotated training data. For example, the benchmark OntoNotes dataset contains about eight times more documents in English than in Arabic (Pradhan et al., 2012). Some recent studies aim to overcome this challenge by applying standard cross-lingual transfer learning (TL) methods such as continued training or joint training (Kundu et al., 2018; Pražák et al., 2021). In continued training, a model pretrained on a source dataset is further finetuned on a (typically smaller) target dataset (Xia and Van Durme, 2021). In joint training, a model is trained on the concatenation of the source and target datasets (Min, 2021). The mentioned studies only use one transfer method at a time, and they do not explore how to combine multiple TL techniques effectively. This can be sub-optimal since different learning methods can be complementary (Liu et al., 2019; Li et al., 2021). For example, our experimental results to be discussed later show that continued training and joint training are highly complementary. Furthermore, a disadvantage of using a cross-lingual transfer method is the require-

[1]Data and code will be made available upon publication.

Proceedings of the 4th Workshop on Computational Approaches to Discourse (CODI 2023), pages 24–36
July 13-14, 2023 ©2023 Association for Computational Linguistics

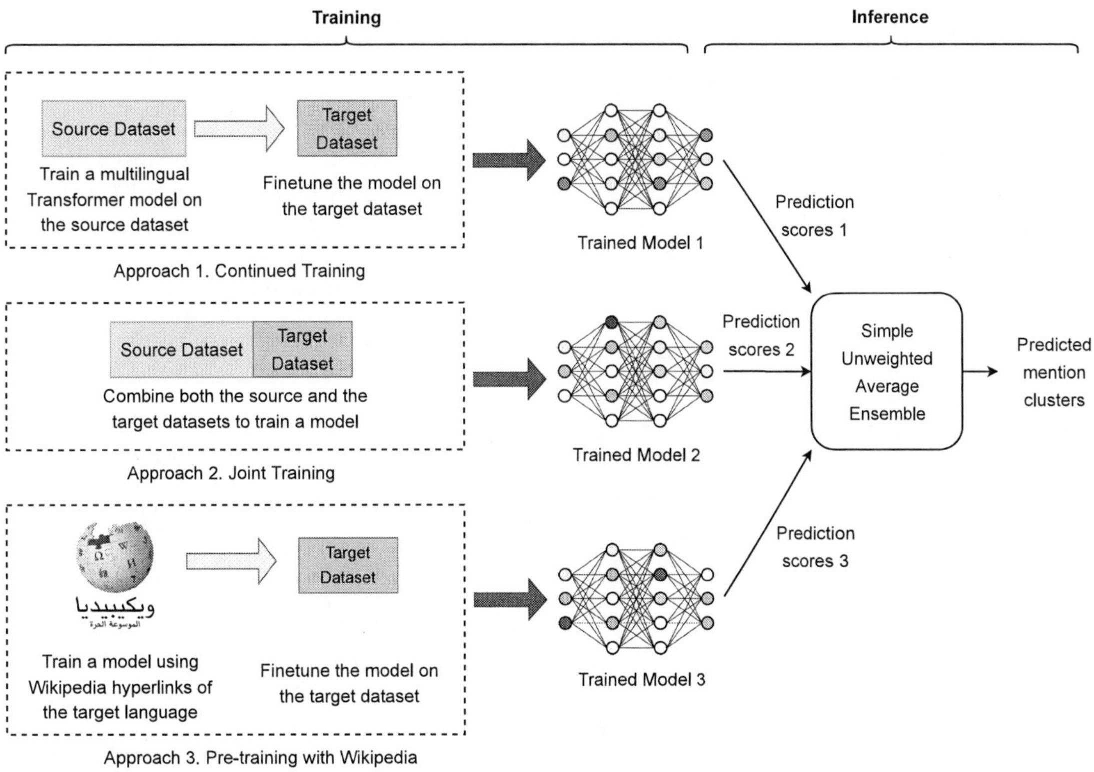

Figure 1: An overview of our framework. We first train several coreference resolution models using different TL approaches. During inference, we use a simple unweighted averaging method to combine the models' predictions.

ment of a labeled coreference resolution dataset in some source language (usually English).

In this work, we propose an effective ensemble-based framework for combining various TL techniques. We first train several coreference models using different TL methods. During inference, we compute the unweighted average scores of the models' predictions to extract the final set of mention clusters. We also propose a low-cost TL method that bootstraps coreference models without using a labeled dataset in some source language. The basic idea is that the coreference relation often holds between anchor texts pointing to the same Wikipedia article. Based on this observation, our TL method builds a sizable distantly-supervised dataset for the target language from Wikipedia. We can then pretrain a model on the pseudo-labeled dataset before finetuning it on the final target dataset. Experimental results on two datasets, OntoNotes and SemEval (Recasens et al., 2010), confirm the effectiveness of our proposed methods. Our best ensembles outperform the baseline approach of simple training by up to 7.68% absolute gain in the F1 score. These ensembles also achieve new SOTA results for three languages: Arabic, Dutch, and Spanish.

In summary, our main contributions include:

- We introduce an ensemble-based framework that combines various TL methods effectively.
- We design a new TL method that leverages Wikipedia to bootstrap coreference models.
- Extensive experimental results show that our proposed methods are highly effective and provide useful insights into entity coreference resolution for non-English languages.

2 Methods

Figure 1 shows an overview of our framework. During the training stage, we train several coreference resolution models using various TL approaches. For simplicity, we use the same span-based architecture (Section 2.1) for every model to be trained. However, starting from the same architecture, using different learning methods typically results in models with different parameters. In this work, our framework uses two types of TL methods: (a) cross-lingual TL approaches (Section 2.2) and (b) our newly proposed Wikipedia-based approach (Section 2.3). The cross-lingual TL methods require a labeled coreference resolution dataset in some source language, but our Wikipedia-based method does not have that limitation. Our framework is general as it can work with other learning methods (e.g., self-distillation). During inference, we use a simple unweighted averaging method to combine the trained models' predictions (Section 2.4).

2.1 Span-based End-to-End Coreference Resolution

In this work, the architecture of every model is based on the popular span-based *e2e-coref* model (Lee et al., 2017). Given an input document consisting of n tokens, our model first forms a contextualized representation for each input token using a multilingual Transformer encoder such as XLM-R (Conneau et al., 2020). Let $\mathbf{X} = (\mathbf{x}_1, ..., \mathbf{x}_n)$ be the output of the encoder. For each candidate span i, we define its representation $\mathbf{g}_i$ as:

$$\mathbf{g}_i = [\mathbf{x}_{\text{START(i)}}, \mathbf{x}_{\text{END(i)}}, \hat{\mathbf{x}}_i, \phi(s_i)] \quad (1)$$

where START(i) and END(i) denote the start and end indices of span i respectively. $\hat{\mathbf{x}}_i$ is an attention-weighted sum of the token representations in the span (Lee et al., 2017). $\phi(s_i)$ is a feature vector encoding the size of the span.

To maintain tractability, we only consider spans with up to L tokens. The value of L is selected empirically and set to be 30. All the span representations are fed into a mention scorer $s_m(.)$:

$$s_m(i) = \text{FFNN}_m(\mathbf{g}_i) \quad (2)$$

where FFNN_m is a feedforward neural network with ReLU activations. Intuitively, $s_m(i)$ indicates whether span i is indeed an entity mention.

After scoring the spans using FFNN_m, we only keep spans with high mention scores[2]. We denote the set of the unpruned spans as S. Then, for each remaining span $i \in S$, the model predicts a distribution $\hat{P}(j)$ over its antecedents[3] $j \in Y(i)$:

$$\hat{P}(j) = \frac{\exp{(s(i,j))}}{\sum_{k \in Y(i)} \exp{(s(i,k))}} \quad (3)$$

$$s(i,j) = \text{FFNN}_s([\mathbf{g}_i, \mathbf{g}_j, \mathbf{g}_i \circ \mathbf{g}_j, \phi(i,j)])$$

where $Y(i) = \{\epsilon, 1, ..., i-1\}$ is a set consisting of a dummy antecedent ϵ and all spans that precede i. The dummy antecedent ϵ represents two possible cases: (1) the span i is not an entity mention, or (2) the span i is an entity mention, but it is not coreferential with any remaining preceding span. FFNN_s is a feedforward network, and $\circ$ is element-wise multiplication. $\phi(i,j)$ encodes the distance between the two spans i and j. Finally, note that $s(i,\epsilon)$ is fixed to be 0.

Given a labeled document D and a model with parameters θ, we define the mention detection loss:

$$\mathcal{L}_{detect}(\theta, D) = -\frac{1}{|S|}\sum_{i \in S} \mathcal{L}_{detect}(\theta, i)$$

$$\mathcal{L}_{detect}(\theta, i) = y_i \log \hat{y}_i + (1-y_i)\log{(1-\hat{y}_i)}$$

where $\hat{y}_i = \text{sigmoid}(s_m(i))$, and $y_i = 1$ if and only if span i is in one of the gold-standard mention clusters. In addition, we also want to maximize the marginal log-likelihood of all correct antecedents implied by the gold-standard clustering:

$$\mathcal{L}_{cluster}(\theta, D) = -\log \prod_{i \in S} \sum_{\hat{y} \in Y(i) \cap \text{GOLD}(i)} \hat{P}(\hat{y})$$

where GOLD(i) are gold antecedents for span i. $\hat{P}(\hat{y})$ is calculated using Equation 3. Our final loss combines mention detection and clustering:

$$\mathcal{L}(\theta, D) = \mathcal{L}_{detect}(\theta, D) + \mathcal{L}_{cluster}(\theta, D) \quad (4)$$

2.2 Cross-Lingual Transfer Learning

Inspired by previous studies (Xia and Van Durme, 2021; Min, 2021; Pražák et al., 2021), we investigate two different cross-lingual transfer learning methods: *continued training* and *joint training*. Both methods assume the existence of a labeled dataset in some source language. In this work, we use the English OntoNotes dataset (Pradhan et al., 2012) as the source dataset, as it contains nearly 3,500 annotated documents (Table 1).

Continued Training. We first train a coreference resolution model on the source dataset until convergence. After that, we further finetune the pre-trained model on a target dataset. More formally, let $M(f, \theta_0)$ denote an optimization procedure for f with initial guess θ_0. This optimization procedure can, for example, be the application of some stochastic gradient descent algorithm. Also, let $\mathbb{S}$ be the set of all training documents in the source dataset, and let $\mathbb{T}$ denote the set of all training documents in the target dataset. Then, the first stage of continued training can be described as:

$$\hat{\theta}_1 = M\left(\sum_{D \in \mathbb{S}} \mathcal{L}(\theta, D), \hat{\theta}_0\right) \quad (5)$$

[2] We describe the exact filtering criteria in Section 3.1.

[3] All spans are ordered based on their start indices. Spans with the same start index are ordered by their end indices.

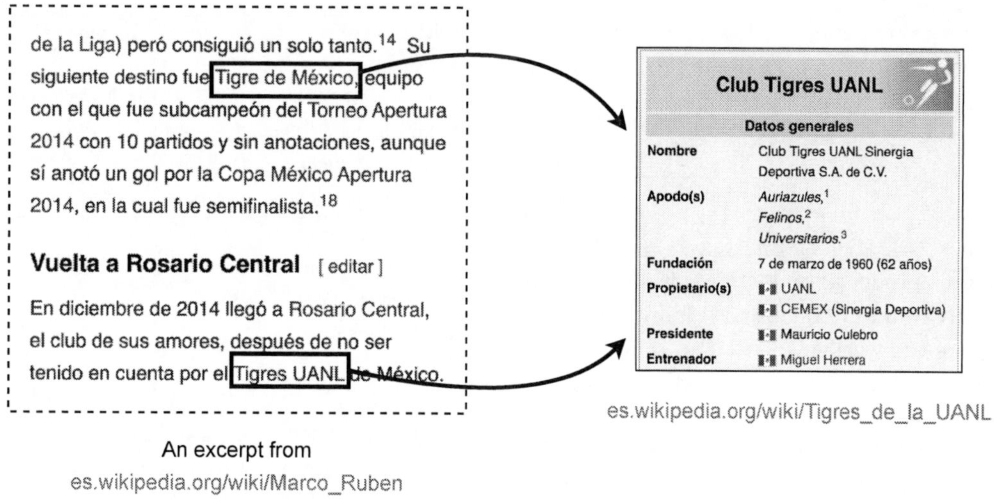

Figure 2: Since the hyperlinks of *Tigre de México* and *Tigres UANL* point to the same Wikipedia page, a person who does not know Spanish can still guess that the two mentions are likely to be coreferential. In fact, the two mentions both refer to Tigres UANL, a Mexican professional football club.

where $\hat{\theta}_0$ is randomly initialized. Then, the second stage can be described using Equation 6:

$$\hat{\theta}_2 = M\Bigg(\sum_{D \in \mathbb{T}} \mathcal{L}(\theta, D), \hat{\theta}_1 \Bigg) \tag{6}$$

Here, $\hat{\theta}_2$ is the parameter set of the final model.

Joint Training. We combine both the source and target datasets to train a model. More specifically, using the same notations as above, we can describe joint training by the following equation:

$$\hat{\theta}_1 = M\Bigg(\sum_{D \in \mathbb{T} \cup \mathbb{S}} \mathcal{L}(\theta, D), \hat{\theta}_0 \Bigg) \tag{7}$$

where $\hat{\theta}_0$ is randomly initialized, and $\hat{\theta}_1$ is the parameter set of the final model.

2.3 Bootstrapping using Wikipedia Hyperlinks

While cross-lingual methods such as continued training and joint training are conceptually simple and typically effective (Huang et al., 2020), they require the existence of a labeled dataset in some source language. To overcome this limitation, we propose an inexpensive TL method that bootstraps coreference models by utilizing Wikipedia anchor texts. The basic idea is that two anchor texts pointing to the same Wikipedia page are likely coreferential (See Figure 2 for an example). Our method builds a large distantly-supervised dataset $\mathbb{W}$ for the target language by leveraging this observation:

$$\mathbb{W} = \{D_1, D_2, ..., D_m\} \tag{8}$$

where D_i is a text document constructed from some Wikipedia page written in the target language. The number of mentions in D_i is the same as the number of anchor texts in the text portion of the original Wikipedia article. We consider two mentions in D_i to be coreferential if and only if their corresponding anchor texts point to the same article.

After constructing $\mathbb{W}$, we follow a two-step process similar to the continued training approach. We first train a conference resolution model on $\mathbb{W}$ until convergence. Then, we finetune the pre-trained model on the final target dataset.

Compared to a manually-labeled dataset, $\mathbb{W}$ has several disadvantages. Not all entity mentions are exhaustively marked in Wikipedia documents. For example, in Spanish Wikipedia, pronouns are typically not annotated. Nevertheless, since Wikipedia is one of the largest multilingual repositories for information, $\mathbb{W}$ is generally large (see Table 1 for some statistics), and it contains documents on various topics. As such, $\mathbb{W}$ can still provide some useful distant supervision signals, and so it can serve as a source dataset in the TL process.

2.4 Ensemble-Based Coreference Resolution

During the training stage, we train three different coreference resolution models using the TL approaches described above. At test time, we use a simple unweighted averaging method to combine the models' predictions. More specifically, for a candidate span i with no more than L tokens, we compute its mention score as follows:

$$s_{m,\text{ensemble}}(i) = \frac{(s_{m,1}(i) + s_{m,2}(i) + s_{m,3}(i))}{3} \quad (9)$$

where $s_{m,1}(i)$, $s_{m,2}(i)$, and $s_{m,3}(i)$ are the mention scores produced by the three trained models separately (refer to Equation 2). Intuitively, these scores indicate whether span i is an entity mention.

Similar to the process described in Section 2.1, after scoring every span whose length is no more than L using Equation 9, we only keep spans with high mention scores[4]. Then, for each remaining span i, we predict a distribution over its antecedents $j \in Y(i)$ as follows:

$$\hat{P}_{\text{ensemble}}(j) = \frac{\exp(s_{\text{ensemble}}(i,j))}{\sum_{k \in Y(i)} \exp(s_{\text{ensemble}}(i,k))}$$

$$s_{\text{ensemble}}(i,j) = \frac{s_1(i,j) + s_2(i,j) + s_3(i,j)}{3} \quad (10)$$

where $s_1(i,j)$, $s_2(i,j)$, and $s_3(i,j)$ are the pairwise scores produced by the trained models separately (Eq. 3). We fix $s_{\text{ensemble}}(i,\epsilon)$ to be 0.

After computing the antecedent distribution for each remaining span, we can extract the final set of mention clusters. Note that while we consider only three individual TL methods in this work, Equation 9 and Equation 10 can easily be extended for the case when we use more TL methods.

3 Experiments

3.1 Data and Experiments Setup

Evaluation metrics Following prior work (Pradhan et al., 2012), we evaluate coreference using the average F_1 between B^3 (Bagga and Baldwin, 1998), MUC (Vilain et al., 1995), and $CEAF_{\phi_4}$ (Luo, 2005). We refer to this metric as AVG.

Datasets Table 1 shows the basic statistics of all the datasets we used in this work. When using a cross-lingual TL method, we use the English portion of OntoNotes (Pradhan et al., 2012) as the source dataset. We explore three target datasets: OntoNotes Arabic (Pradhan et al., 2012), SemEval Dutch (Recasens et al., 2010), and SemEval Spanish(Recasens et al., 2010). These datasets contain data in three different languages.

[4]We describe the exact filtering criteria in Section 3.1.

Dataset	Training	Dev	Test
Source Datasets			
OntoNotes English	2,802	343	348
Wikipedia-based Arabic Dataset	64,850	250	250
Wikipedia-based Dutch Dataset	46,715	250	250
Wikipedia-based Spanish Dataset	104,520	250	250
Target Datasets			
OntoNotes Arabic	359	44	44
SemEval Dutch	145	23	72
SemEval Spanish	875	140	168

Table 1: Number of documents for each of the datasets.

OntoNotes does not annotate singleton mentions (i.e., noun phrases not involved in any coreference chain). It only has annotations for non-singleton mentions. SemEval has annotations for singletons.

Wikipedia-based Dataset Construction To construct a distantly-supervised dataset, we first download a complete Wikipedia dump in the target language. We then extract clean text and hyperlinks from the dump using WikiExtractor[5]. For each preprocessed article, we cluster its anchor texts based on the destinations of their hyperlinks. We also filter out articles with too few coreference links (e.g., articles that only have singleton mentions).

General Hyperparameters We use two different learning rates, one for the lower pretrained Transformer encoder and one for the upper layers. For every setting, the lower learning rate is 1e-5, the upper learning rate is 1e-4, and the span length limit L is 30. The number of training/pre-training epochs is set to be 25 in most cases. When pretraining a model on a Wikipedia-based dataset, the number of epochs is 5. When fine-tuning a model already pre-trained on Dutch Wikipedia or Spanish Wikipedia, the number of epochs is 50. During each training/pre-training process, we pick the checkpoint which achieves the best AVG score on the appropriate dev set as the final checkpoint.

Transformer Encoders When the target dataset is OntoNotes Arabic, we use GigaBERT (Lan et al., 2020) as the Transformer encoder. GigaBERT is an English-Arabic bilingual language model pretrained from the English and Arabic Gigaword corpora. When the target dataset is SemEval Dutch or SemEval Spanish, we use the multilingual XLM-RoBERTa (XLM-R) Transformer model (Conneau et al., 2020). More specifically, we use the base version of XLM-R (i.e., `xlm-roberta-base`).

[5]`https://tinyurl.com/wikiextractor`

	Arabic	Dutch	Spanish
Baselines			
◆ Previous SOTA (Table 3)	64.55	55.40	51.30
◆ Baseline Approach (trained using the target dataset)	63.70	52.81	72.18
Individual Transfer/Pretraining Methods (Sections 2.2 and 2.3)			
■ Continued Training	64.96	58.90	74.05
■ Joint Training	65.50	58.76	73.53
■ Wikipedia Pre-Training	63.78	53.15	73.35
Ensembles (Section 2.4)			
♦ Three models, each trained using the baseline approach	64.70	54.44	73.35
♦ Baseline Approach ⊕ Wikipedia Pre-Training	65.75	55.25	74.19
♦ Joint Training ⊕ Wikipedia Pre-Training	66.63	58.18	74.82
♦ Continued Training ⊕ Wikipedia Pre-Training	66.24	57.88	75.43
♦ Continued Training ⊕ Joint Training	65.79	**60.49**	74.93
♦ Continued Training ⊕ Joint Training ⊕ Wikipedia Pre-Training	**66.72**	59.66	**75.62**
Oracle-Guided Ensembles (Section 3.3.1)			
◇ Continued Training ⊕ Joint Training ⊕ Wikipedia Pre-Training	77.53	75.19	83.12

Table 2: Overall F_1 (in %) on OntoNotes Arabic, SemEval Dutch, and SemEval Spanish.

Dataset	Prior Work	Approach	Prev. Score	Our Best
OntoNotes Arabic	(Min, 2021)	GigaBERT + C2F + Joint Training	64.55	**66.72**
SemEval Dutch	(Xia and Van Durme, 2021)	XLM-R + ICoref + Continued Training	55.40	**60.49**
SemEval Spanish	(Xia and Van Durme, 2021)	XLM-R + ICoref + Continued Training	51.30	**75.62**

Table 3: Test F_1 (in %) on the target datasets and the previous SOTA on each dataset (to the best of our knowledge).

Span Pruning As described in Section 2.1, after computing a mention score for each span whose length is not more than L, we only keep spans with high scores. More specifically, when working with a dataset from OntoNotes (e.g., OntoNotes Arabic), we only keep up to λn spans with the highest mention scores (Lee et al., 2017). The value of λ is selected empirically and set to be 0.18. When working with any other dataset, we keep every span that has a positive mention score.

3.2 Overall Results

Table 2 shows the overall performance of different approaches. Our baseline approach is to simply train a model with the architecture described in Section 2.1 using only the target dataset of interest. Overall, the performance of a model trained using the baseline approach is positively correlated with the size of the corresponding target dataset, which is expected. A surprising finding is that our baseline approach already outperforms the previous SOTA method for SemEval Spanish (Xia and Van Durme, 2021) by 20.98% in the F1 score. We speculate that the previous SOTA model for SemEval Spanish is severely undertrained.

Table 2 also shows the results of using different TL methods individually. Each of the TL methods can help improve the coreference resolution performance. While continued training seems to be the most effective approach, it requires the existence of a source dataset (OntoNotes English in this case). On the other hand, our newly proposed Wikipedia-based method can help improve the performance without relying on any labeled source dataset.

Finally, Table 2 also shows the results of using different combinations of learning approaches. Our simple unweighted averaging method is effective across almost all model combinations. In particular, by combining all of the three TL methods discussed previously, we can outperform the previous SOTA methods by large margins. In addition, even without using any labeled source dataset, the combination [Baseline Approach ⊕ Wikipedia Pre-Training] can still outperform the previous SOTA

Approaches	AVG
Baseline Approach	40.10
Wikipedia Pre-Training	42.67
Baseline Approach ⊕ Wikipedia Pre-Training	**45.28**

Table 4: Test F-score (in %) of various approaches on OntoNotes Arabic when we restrict the size of the gold Arabic training dataset to only 10 documents.

methods for Arabic and Spanish. This further confirms the usefulness of our Wikipedia-based TL method. Lastly, combining three models trained using the same baseline approach leads to smaller gains than combining the three TL methods. This is expected as ensemble methods typically work best when the individual learners are diverse (Krogh and Vedelsby, 1994; Melville and Mooney, 2003).

3.3 Analysis

3.3.1 How optimal is our simple unweighted averaging method?

Our averaging approach is equivalent to linear interpolation with equal weights. To analyze the optimality of our method, we compare it to the "best possible" interpolation method.

More specifically, we assume that there is an oracle that can tell us which model in an ensemble gives the most accurate prediction for a particular latent variable. Then, for example, suppose we want to score a span i using an ensemble of three models. If i is an entity mention, the oracle will tell us that the model that returns the highest mention score for i is the most accurate. Thus, we can set the score for i to be $\max(s_{m,1}(i), s_{m,2}(i), s_{m,3}(i))$. Following the same logic, if i is not an entity mention, we will set its score to be $\min(s_{m,1}(i), s_{m,2}(i), s_{m,3}(i))$. The same idea can be applied to compute the linking score $s_{\text{ensemble}}(i,j)$ between i and j.

In Table 2, we see a considerable gap between the performance of our simple averaging method and the oracle-guided interpolation method. Therefore, a promising future direction is to experiment with a more context-dependent ensemble method. Nevertheless, our averaging method is simple, and it does not require any further parameter tuning to combine a set of existing models. Finally, the performance of each oracle-guided ensemble is far from perfect, implying that improving the underlying architecture of each model can also be a worthwhile effort.

... el director del centro, Anna Mas, asegurar que el acto pretender "rechazar el agresión y concienciar a el alumno del incremento de este ataque". el director recordar otro dos agresión "por llevar hierro dental o el pelo largo". en mucho ocasión se producir asalto a niño, y el alumno, añadir Mas, "ver como algo normal que les parir por el calle y les quitar el poco dinero que llevar encima" ...
... Het vakblad Hormones and Behavior beschrijven hoe het voldoend zijn dat mannelijk muis een vleug vrouw roken om hen weinig bang te maken van kat en wezel ...

Table 5: Examples of mention clusters that were correctly predicted by our ensembles. Blue spans represent coreferential mentions. The first example is in Spanish. The second example is in Dutch.

3.3.2 How effective is our framework in extremely low-resource settings?

We conduct experiments on OntoNotes Arabic where we assume that the training dataset for Arabic only has 10 documents and that we do not have any source dataset (Table 4). In this setting, our ensemble substantially outperforms the baseline approach by up to 5.18% in the F1 score.

3.3.3 Qualitative Analysis

We provide some qualitative analyses to demonstrate the strengths of our ensembles in Table 5.

In the first example, the three highlighted mentions refer to Anna Mas, the director of a center. Our model trained using joint training merged this cluster with a different cluster that refers to a different entity (not shown in the example because of space constraints). In contrast, our models trained using other TL methods did not make that error. As a result, our best ensemble for Spanish predicted the correct cluster for Anna Mas.

The second example is in Dutch. Here, *mannelijk muis* can be translated as *male mouses*, while *hen* can be translated as *them*. Our model trained using continued training failed to extract the mention *mannelijk muis*. Nevertheless, in the end, our ensemble for Dutch was able to extract the mention and correctly link it to the pronoun *hen*.

4 Related Work

4.1 Entity Coreference Resolution

Recently, neural models for entity coreference resolution have shown superior performance over approaches using hand-crafted features. Lee et al. (2017) proposed the first end-to-end neural coreference resolution model named *e2e-coref*. The model uses a bi-directional LSTM and a head-finding attention mechanism to learn mention representations and calculate mention and antecedent scores. Lee et al. (2018) extended the *e2e-coref* model by introducing a coarse-to-fine pruning mechanism and a higher-order inference mechanism. The model uses ELMo representations (Peters et al., 2018) instead of traditional word embeddings. The model is typically referred to as the *c2f-coref* model.

Almost all recent studies on entity coreference resolution are influenced by the design of *c2f-coref.* Joshi et al. (2019) built the *c2f-coref* system on top of BERT representations (Devlin et al., 2019). Fei et al. (2019) transformed *c2f-coref* into a policy gradient model that can optimize coreference evaluation metrics directly. Xu and Choi (2020) studied in depth the higher-order inference (HOI) mechanism of *c2f-coref.* The authors concluded that given a high-performing encoder such as SpanBERT (Joshi et al., 2020), the impact of HOI is negative to marginal. Another line of work aims to simplify and/or reduce the computational complexity of *c2f-coref* (Xia et al., 2020; Kirstain et al., 2021; Lai et al., 2021; Dobrovolskii, 2021).

The studies mentioned above only trained and evaluated models using English datasets such as OntoNotes English (Pradhan et al., 2012) and the GAP dataset (Webster et al., 2018). On the other hand, there is significantly less work on coreference resolution for other languages. For example, while *e2e-coref* was introduced in 2017, the first neural coreference resolver for Arabic was only recently proposed in 2020 (Aloraini et al., 2020). For Dutch, many existing systems are still using rule-based (van Cranenburgh, 2019) or traditional learning-based approaches (Hendrickx et al., 2008; De Clercq et al., 2011). Recently, Poot and van Cranenburgh (2020) evaluated the performance of *c2f-coref* on Dutch datasets of two different domains: literary novels and news/Wikipedia text.

While our models' architecture is based on *e2e-coref* (Section 2.1), we go beyond just applying the models to a non-English language in this work. We propose new TL approaches that can take advantage of existing source datasets and Wikipedia to improve the final performance.

4.2 Transfer Learning for Coreference Resolution

Compared to English datasets, the size of a coreference resolution dataset for a non-English language is typically smaller. Several recent studies aim to overcome this challenge by applying standard cross-lingual TL methods such as continued training or joint training (Kundu et al., 2018; Xia and Van Durme, 2021; Pražák et al., 2021; Min, 2021). These studies only use one transfer method at a time, and they do not explore how to combine multiple TL techniques effectively. Our experimental results (Section 3.2) show that combining various TL techniques can substantially improve the final coreference resolution performance.

A closely related work by Yang et al. (2012) proposed an adaptive ensemble method to adapt coreference resolution across domains. Their study did not explicitly focus on improving coreference resolution for non-English languages. In addition, they experimented with the settings where gold standard mentions are assumed to be provided. We do not make that assumption. Each of our models does both mention extraction and linking.

4.3 Leveraging Wikipedia for Coreference Resolution

There have been studies on leveraging Wikipedia for coreference resolution. Eirew et al. (2021) recently created a large-scale cross-document event coreference dataset from English Wikipedia. For cross-document entity coreference, Singh et al. (2012) created Wikilinks by finding hyperlinks to English Wikipedia from a web crawl and using anchor text as mentions. Different from these studies, we focus on within-document entity coreference resolution. In addition, we explore coreference resolution for languages beyond English in this work.

Many previous studies leveraged Wikipedia for related tasks such as name tagging (Alotaibi and Lee, 2012; Nothman et al., 2013; Althobaiti et al., 2014) and entity linking (Pan et al., 2017; Wu et al., 2020a; Cao et al., 2021). We leave the extension of our methods to these tasks for future research.

5 Conclusions and Future Work

In this work, we propose an ensemble-based framework that combines various TL techniques. We also introduce a low-cost Wikipedia-based TL approach that does not require any labeled source dataset. Our approaches are highly effective, as our best ensembles achieve new SOTA results for three different languages. An interesting future direction is to explore the use of model compression techniques (Hinton et al., 2015; Han et al., 2016; Lai et al., 2020) to reduce the computational complexity of our ensembles.

6 Limitations

Multilingual language models such as XLM-R (Conneau et al., 2020) and GigaBERT (Lan et al., 2020) are typically pre-trained on large amounts of unlabeled text crawled from the Web. Since these models are optimized to capture the statistical properties of the training data, they tend to pick up on and amplify social stereotypes present in the data (Kurita et al., 2019). Since our coreference resolution models use such pre-trained language models, they may also exhibit social biases present on the Web. Identifying and mitigating social biases in neural models is an active area of research (Zhao et al., 2018; Sheng et al., 2021; Gupta et al., 2022). In the future, we plan to work on removing social biases from coreference resolution models.

Furthermore, while our proposed methods are highly effective, the performance of our best ensembles is still far from perfect. On OntoNotes Arabic, our best system only achieves an F1 score of 66.72%. Such performance may not be acceptable for some downstream tasks (e.g., information extraction from critical clinical notes).

Finally, even though Wikipedia is available in more than 300 languages, there are still very few Wikipedia pages for some very rare languages. Our proposed methods are likely to be less effective for such rare languages.

References

Abdulrahman Aloraini, Juntao Yu, and Massimo Poesio. 2020. Neural coreference resolution for Arabic. In *Proceedings of the Third Workshop on Computational Models of Reference, Anaphora and Coreference*, pages 99–110, Barcelona, Spain (online). Association for Computational Linguistics.

Fahd Alotaibi and Mark Lee. 2012. Mapping Arabic Wikipedia into the named entities taxonomy. In *Proceedings of COLING 2012: Posters*, pages 43–52, Mumbai, India. The COLING 2012 Organizing Committee.

Maha Althobaiti, Udo Kruschwitz, and Massimo Poesio. 2014. Automatic creation of Arabic named entity annotated corpus using Wikipedia. In *Proceedings of the Student Research Workshop at the 14th Conference of the European Chapter of the Association for Computational Linguistics*, pages 106–115, Gothenburg, Sweden. Association for Computational Linguistics.

Amit Bagga and Breck Baldwin. 1998. Algorithms for scoring coreference chains. In *The first international conference on language resources and evaluation workshop on linguistics coreference*, volume 1, pages 563–566. Citeseer.

Nicola De Cao, Gautier Izacard, Sebastian Riedel, and Fabio Petroni. 2021. Autoregressive entity retrieval. In *International Conference on Learning Representations*.

Alexis Conneau, Kartikay Khandelwal, Naman Goyal, Vishrav Chaudhary, Guillaume Wenzek, Francisco Guzmán, Edouard Grave, Myle Ott, Luke Zettlemoyer, and Veselin Stoyanov. 2020. Unsupervised cross-lingual representation learning at scale. In *ACL*.

Orphée De Clercq, Véronique Hoste, and Iris Hendrickx. 2011. Cross-domain Dutch coreference resolution. In *Proceedings of the International Conference Recent Advances in Natural Language Processing 2011*, pages 186–193, Hissar, Bulgaria. Association for Computational Linguistics.

Jacob Devlin, Ming-Wei Chang, Kenton Lee, and Kristina Toutanova. 2019. BERT: Pre-training of deep bidirectional transformers for language understanding. In *Proceedings of the 2019 Conference of the North American Chapter of the Association for Computational Linguistics: Human Language Technologies, Volume 1 (Long and Short Papers)*, pages 4171–4186, Minneapolis, Minnesota. Association for Computational Linguistics.

Bhuwan Dhingra, Qiao Jin, Zhilin Yang, William Cohen, and Ruslan Salakhutdinov. 2018. Neural models for reasoning over multiple mentions using coreference. In *Proceedings of the 2018 Conference of the North American Chapter of the Association for Computational Linguistics: Human Language Technologies, Volume 2 (Short Papers)*, pages 42–48, New Orleans, Louisiana. Association for Computational Linguistics.

Vladimir Dobrovolskii. 2021. Word-level coreference resolution. In *Proceedings of the 2021 Conference on Empirical Methods in Natural Language Processing*, pages 7670–7675, Online and Punta Cana, Dominican Republic. Association for Computational Linguistics.

Alon Eirew, Arie Cattan, and Ido Dagan. 2021. WEC: Deriving a large-scale cross-document event coreference dataset from Wikipedia. In *Proceedings of the 2021 Conference of the North American Chapter of the Association for Computational Linguistics: Human Language Technologies*, pages 2498–2510, Online. Association for Computational Linguistics.

Hongliang Fei, Xu Li, Dingcheng Li, and Ping Li. 2019. End-to-end deep reinforcement learning based coreference resolution. In *Proceedings of the 57th Annual Meeting of the Association for Computational Linguistics*, pages 660–665, Florence, Italy. Association for Computational Linguistics.

Yifan Gao, Piji Li, Irwin King, and Michael R. Lyu. 2019. Interconnected question generation with coreference alignment and conversation flow modeling. In *Proceedings of the 57th Annual Meeting of the Association for Computational Linguistics*, pages 4853–4862, Florence, Italy. Association for Computational Linguistics.

Umang Gupta, Jwala Dhamala, Varun Kumar, Apurv Verma, Yada Pruksachatkun, Satyapriya Krishna, Rahul Gupta, Kai-Wei Chang, Greg Ver Steeg, and Aram Galstyan. 2022. Mitigating gender bias in distilled language models via counterfactual role reversal. In *ACL Finding*.

Song Han, Huizi Mao, and William J. Dally. 2016. Deep compression: Compressing deep neural network with pruning, trained quantization and huffman coding. *arXiv: Computer Vision and Pattern Recognition*.

Iris Hendrickx, Gosse Bouma, Frederik Coppens, Walter Daelemans, Veronique Hoste, Geert Kloosterman, Anne-Marie Mineur, Joeri Van Der Vloet, and Jean-Luc Verschelde. 2008. A coreference corpus and resolution system for Dutch. In *Proceedings of the Sixth International Conference on Language Resources and Evaluation (LREC'08)*, Marrakech, Morocco. European Language Resources Association (ELRA).

Geoffrey E. Hinton, Oriol Vinyals, and Jeffrey Dean. 2015. Distilling the knowledge in a neural network. *ArXiv*, abs/1503.02531.

Jocelyn Huang, Oleksii Kuchaiev, Patrick O'Neill, Vitaly Lavrukhin, Jason Li, Adriana Flores, Georg Kucsko, and Boris Ginsburg. 2020. Cross-language transfer learning, continuous learning, and domain adaptation for end-to-end automatic speech recognition. *arXiv preprint arXiv:2005.04290*.

Heng Ji, David Westbrook, and Ralph Grishman. 2005. Using semantic relations to refine coreference decisions. In *Proceedings of Human Language Technology Conference and Conference on Empirical Methods in Natural Language Processing*, pages 17–24, Vancouver, British Columbia, Canada. Association for Computational Linguistics.

Mandar Joshi, Danqi Chen, Yinhan Liu, Daniel S. Weld, Luke Zettlemoyer, and Omer Levy. 2020. Spanbert: Improving pre-training by representing and predicting spans. *Transactions of the Association for Computational Linguistics*, 8:64–77.

Mandar Joshi, Omer Levy, Luke Zettlemoyer, and Daniel Weld. 2019. BERT for coreference resolution: Baselines and analysis. In *Proceedings of the 2019 Conference on Empirical Methods in Natural Language Processing and the 9th International Joint Conference on Natural Language Processing (EMNLP-IJCNLP)*, pages 5803–5808, Hong Kong, China. Association for Computational Linguistics.

Yuval Kirstain, Ori Ram, and Omer Levy. 2021. Coreference resolution without span representations. In *Proceedings of the 59th Annual Meeting of the Association for Computational Linguistics and the 11th International Joint Conference on Natural Language Processing (Volume 2: Short Papers)*, pages 14–19, Online. Association for Computational Linguistics.

Anders Krogh and Jesper Vedelsby. 1994. Neural network ensembles, cross validation, and active learning. *Advances in neural information processing systems*, 7.

Taku Kudo and John Richardson. 2018. Sentencepiece: A simple and language independent subword tokenizer and detokenizer for neural text processing. *arXiv preprint arXiv:1808.06226*.

Gourab Kundu, Avi Sil, Radu Florian, and Wael Hamza. 2018. Neural cross-lingual coreference resolution and its application to entity linking. In *Proceedings of the 56th Annual Meeting of the Association for Computational Linguistics (Volume 2: Short Papers)*, pages 395–400, Melbourne, Australia. Association for Computational Linguistics.

Keita Kurita, Nidhi Vyas, Ayush Pareek, Alan W Black, and Yulia Tsvetkov. 2019. Measuring bias in contextualized word representations. In *Proceedings of the First Workshop on Gender Bias in Natural Language Processing*, pages 166–172, Florence, Italy. Association for Computational Linguistics.

Tuan Manh Lai, Trung Bui, and Doo Soon Kim. 2021. End-to-end neural coreference resolution revisited: A simple yet effective baseline. *arXiv preprint arXiv:2107.01700*.

Tuan Manh Lai, Quan Hung Tran, Trung Bui, and Daisuke Kihara. 2020. A simple but effective bert model for dialog state tracking on resource-limited systems. In *ICASSP 2020-2020 IEEE International Conference on Acoustics, Speech and Signal Processing (ICASSP)*, pages 8034–8038. IEEE.

Wuwei Lan, Yang Chen, Wei Xu, and Alan Ritter. 2020. An empirical study of pre-trained transformers for Arabic information extraction. In *Proceedings of the 2020 Conference on Empirical Methods in Natural Language Processing (EMNLP)*, pages 4727–4734, Online. Association for Computational Linguistics.

Heeyoung Lee, Angel Chang, Yves Peirsman, Nathanael Chambers, Mihai Surdeanu, and Dan Jurafsky. 2013. Deterministic Coreference Resolution Based on Entity-Centric, Precision-Ranked Rules. *Computational Linguistics*, 39(4):885–916.

Kenton Lee, Luheng He, Mike Lewis, and Luke Zettlemoyer. 2017. End-to-end neural coreference resolution. In *Proceedings of the 2017 Conference on Empirical Methods in Natural Language Processing*, pages 188–197, Copenhagen, Denmark. Association for Computational Linguistics.

Kenton Lee, Luheng He, and Luke Zettlemoyer. 2018. Higher-order coreference resolution with coarse-to-fine inference. In *Proceedings of the 2018 Conference of the North American Chapter of the Association for Computational Linguistics: Human Language Technologies, Volume 2 (Short Papers)*, pages 687–692, New Orleans, Louisiana. Association for Computational Linguistics.

Shiyang Li, Semih Yavuz, Wenhu Chen, and Xifeng Yan. 2021. Task-adaptive pre-training and self-training are complementary for natural language understanding. In *Findings of the Association for Computational Linguistics: EMNLP 2021*, pages 1006–1015, Punta Cana, Dominican Republic. Association for Computational Linguistics.

Xiao Ling, Sameer Singh, and Daniel S. Weld. 2015. Design challenges for entity linking. *Transactions of the Association for Computational Linguistics*, 3:315–328.

Xiaodong Liu, Pengcheng He, Weizhu Chen, and Jianfeng Gao. 2019. Multi-task deep neural networks for natural language understanding. In *ACL*.

Xiaoqiang Luo. 2005. On coreference resolution performance metrics. In *HLT*.

Xiaoqiang Luo and Imed Zitouni. 2005. Multi-lingual coreference resolution with syntactic features. In *Proceedings of Human Language Technology Conference and Conference on Empirical Methods in Natural Language Processing*, pages 660–667, Vancouver, British Columbia, Canada. Association for Computational Linguistics.

Prem Melville and Raymond J. Mooney. 2003. Constructing diverse classifier ensembles using artificial training examples. In *IJCAI*.

Bonan Min. 2021. Exploring pre-trained transformers and bilingual transfer learning for Arabic coreference resolution. In *Proceedings of the Fourth Workshop on Computational Models of Reference, Anaphora and Coreference*, pages 94–99, Punta Cana, Dominican Republic. Association for Computational Linguistics.

Kevin Musgrave, Serge Belongie, and Ser-Nam Lim. 2020. Pytorch metric learning.

Vincent Ng. 2010. Supervised noun phrase coreference research: The first fifteen years. In *Proceedings of the 48th Annual Meeting of the Association for Computational Linguistics*, pages 1396–1411, Uppsala, Sweden. Association for Computational Linguistics.

Vincent Ng. 2017. Machine learning for entity coreference resolution: A retrospective look at two decades of research. In *Proceedings of the 31st AAAI Conference on Artificial Intelligence*, pages 4877–4884.

Joel Nothman, Nicky Ringland, Will Radford, Tara Murphy, and James R. Curran. 2013. Learning multilingual named entity recognition from wikipedia. *Artif. Intell.*, 194:151–175.

Xiaoman Pan, Boliang Zhang, Jonathan May, Joel Nothman, Kevin Knight, and Heng Ji. 2017. Cross-lingual name tagging and linking for 282 languages. In *Proceedings of the 55th Annual Meeting of the Association for Computational Linguistics (Volume 1: Long Papers)*, pages 1946–1958, Vancouver, Canada. Association for Computational Linguistics.

Adam Paszke, S. Gross, Francisco Massa, A. Lerer, J. Bradbury, G. Chanan, T. Killeen, Z. Lin, N. Gimelshein, L. Antiga, Alban Desmaison, Andreas Köpf, E. Yang, Zach DeVito, Martin Raison, Alykhan Tejani, Sasank Chilamkurthy, B. Steiner, Lu Fang, Junjie Bai, and Soumith Chintala. 2019. Pytorch: An imperative style, high-performance deep learning library. In *NeurIPS*.

Matthew E. Peters, Mark Neumann, Mohit Iyyer, Matt Gardner, Christopher Clark, Kenton Lee, and Luke Zettlemoyer. 2018. Deep contextualized word representations. In *Proceedings of the 2018 Conference of the North American Chapter of the Association for Computational Linguistics: Human Language Technologies, Volume 1 (Long Papers)*, pages 2227–2237, New Orleans, Louisiana. Association for Computational Linguistics.

Corbèn Poot and Andreas van Cranenburgh. 2020. A benchmark of rule-based and neural coreference resolution in Dutch novels and news. In *Proceedings of the Third Workshop on Computational Models of Reference, Anaphora and Coreference*, pages 79–90, Barcelona, Spain (online). Association for Computational Linguistics.

Sameer Pradhan, Alessandro Moschitti, Nianwen Xue, Olga Uryupina, and Yuchen Zhang. 2012. CoNLL-2012 shared task: Modeling multilingual unrestricted coreference in OntoNotes. In *Joint Conference on EMNLP and CoNLL - Shared Task*, pages 1–40, Jeju Island, Korea. Association for Computational Linguistics.

Ondřej Pražák, Miloslav Konopík, and Jakub Sido. 2021. Multilingual coreference resolution with harmonized annotations. In *Proceedings of the International Conference on Recent Advances in Natural Language Processing (RANLP 2021)*, pages 1119–1123, Held Online. INCOMA Ltd.

Karthik Raghunathan, Heeyoung Lee, Sudarshan Rangarajan, Nathanael Chambers, Mihai Surdeanu, Dan Jurafsky, and Christopher Manning. 2010. A multi-pass sieve for coreference resolution. In *Proceedings of the 2010 Conference on Empirical Methods in Natural Language Processing*, pages 492–501, Cambridge, MA. Association for Computational Linguistics.

Marta Recasens, Lluís Màrquez, Emili Sapena, M. Antònia Martí, Mariona Taulé, Véronique Hoste, Massimo Poesio, and Yannick Versley. 2010. SemEval-2010 task 1: Coreference resolution in multiple languages. In *Proceedings of the 5th International Workshop on Semantic Evaluation*, pages 1–8, Uppsala, Sweden. Association for Computational Linguistics.

Emily Sheng, Kai-Wei Chang, Prem Natarajan, and Nanyun Peng. 2021. Societal biases in language generation: Progress and challenges. In *ACL*.

Sameer Singh, Amarnag Subramanya, Fernando Pereira, and Andrew McCallum. 2012. Wikilinks: A large-scale cross-document coreference corpus labeled via links to wikipedia. *University of Massachusetts, Amherst, Tech. Rep. UM-CS-2012*, 15.

Andreas van Cranenburgh. 2019. A dutch coreference resolution system with an evaluation on literary fiction. *Computational Linguistics in the Netherlands Journal*, 9:27–54.

Marc B. Vilain, John D. Burger, John S. Aberdeen, Dennis Connolly, and Lynette Hirschman. 1995. A model-theoretic coreference scoring scheme. In *MUC*.

Kellie Webster, Marta Recasens, Vera Axelrod, and Jason Baldridge. 2018. Mind the GAP: A Balanced Corpus of Gendered Ambiguous Pronouns. *Transactions of the Association for Computational Linguistics*, 6:605–617.

Thomas Wolf, Lysandre Debut, Victor Sanh, Julien Chaumond, Clement Delangue, Anthony Moi, Pierric Cistac, Tim Rault, Remi Louf, Morgan Funtowicz, Joe Davison, Sam Shleifer, Patrick von Platen, Clara Ma, Yacine Jernite, Julien Plu, Canwen Xu, Teven Le Scao, Sylvain Gugger, Mariama Drame, Quentin Lhoest, and Alexander Rush. 2020. Transformers: State-of-the-art natural language processing. In *Proceedings of the 2020 Conference on Empirical Methods in Natural Language Processing: System Demonstrations*, pages 38–45, Online. Association for Computational Linguistics.

Ledell Wu, Fabio Petroni, Martin Josifoski, Sebastian Riedel, and Luke Zettlemoyer. 2020a. Scalable zero-shot entity linking with dense entity retrieval. In *Proceedings of the 2020 Conference on Empirical Methods in Natural Language Processing (EMNLP)*, pages 6397–6407, Online. Association for Computational Linguistics.

Wei Wu, Fei Wang, Arianna Yuan, Fei Wu, and Jiwei Li. 2020b. CorefQA: Coreference resolution as query-based span prediction. In *Proceedings of the 58th Annual Meeting of the Association for Computational Linguistics*, pages 6953–6963, Online. Association for Computational Linguistics.

Patrick Xia, João Sedoc, and Benjamin Van Durme. 2020. Incremental neural coreference resolution in constant memory. In *Proceedings of the 2020 Conference on Empirical Methods in Natural Language Processing (EMNLP)*, pages 8617–8624, Online. Association for Computational Linguistics.

Patrick Xia and Benjamin Van Durme. 2021. Moving on from OntoNotes: Coreference resolution model transfer. In *Proceedings of the 2021 Conference on Empirical Methods in Natural Language Processing*, pages 5241–5256, Online and Punta Cana, Dominican Republic. Association for Computational Linguistics.

Liyan Xu and Jinho D. Choi. 2020. Revealing the myth of higher-order inference in coreference resolution. In *Proceedings of the 2020 Conference on Empirical Methods in Natural Language Processing (EMNLP)*, pages 8527–8533, Online. Association for Computational Linguistics.

Jian Bo Yang, Qi Mao, Qiao Liang Xiang, Ivor Wai-Hung Tsang, Kian Ming Adam Chai, and Hai Leong Chieu. 2012. Domain adaptation for coreference resolution: An adaptive ensemble approach. In *Proceedings of the 2012 Joint Conference on Empirical Methods in Natural Language Processing and Computational Natural Language Learning*, pages 744–753, Jeju Island, Korea. Association for Computational Linguistics.

Jieyu Zhao, Tianlu Wang, Mark Yatskar, Vicente Ordonez, and Kai-Wei Chang. 2018. Gender bias in coreference resolution: Evaluation and debiasing methods. In *Proceedings of the 2018 Conference of the North American Chapter of the Association for Computational Linguistics: Human Language Technologies, Volume 2 (Short Papers)*, pages 15–20, New Orleans, Louisiana. Association for Computational Linguistics.

A Reproducibility Information

In this section, we present the reproducibility information of our paper.

Implementation Dependencies Libraries Pytorch 1.11.0 (Paszke et al., 2019), Transformers 4.17.0 (Wolf et al., 2020), SentencePiece 0.1.96 (Kudo and Richardson, 2018), PyTorch Metric Learning (Musgrave et al., 2020).

Computing Infrastructure The experiments were conducted on a server with Intel(R) Xeon(R) Gold 5120 CPU @ 2.20GHz and NVIDIA Tesla V100 GPUs. GPU memory is 16G.

Number of Model Parameters When the target dataset is OntoNotes Arabic, we use GigaBERT (Lan et al., 2020) as the Transformer encoder. GigaBERT has about 125M parameters.

When the target dataset is SemEval Dutch or SemEval Spanish, we use the base version of XLM-R (i.e., `xlm-roberta-base`) (Conneau et al., 2020). `xlm-roberta-base` has about 278M parameters.

Hyperparameters The information about the hyperparameters is available in the main paper.

Expected Validation Performance We report the validation performance of the ensemble *[Continued Training ⊕ Joint Training ⊕ Wikipedia Pre-Training]*.

The validation F1 score of the ensemble for Arabic coreference resolution is 66.60%. The total time needed for the evaluation is about 1 minute and 19 seconds.

The validation F1 score of the ensemble for Dutch coreference resolution is 57.81%. The total time needed for the evaluation is about 20 seconds.

The validation F1 score of the ensemble for Spanish coreference resolution is 75.73%. The total time needed for the evaluation is about 1 minute and 42 seconds.

Contrastive Hierarchical Discourse Graph for Scientific Document Summarization

Haopeng Zhang, Xiao Liu, Jiawei Zhang
IFM Lab, Department of Computer Science, University of California, Davis, CA, USA
haopeng,xiao,jiawei@ifmlab.org

Abstract

The extended structural context has made scientific paper summarization a challenging task. This paper proposes CHANGES, a contrastive hierarchical graph neural network for extractive scientific paper summarization. CHANGES represents a scientific paper with a hierarchical discourse graph and learns effective sentence representations with dedicated designed hierarchical graph information aggregation. We also propose a graph contrastive learning module to learn global theme-aware sentence representations. Extensive experiments on the PubMed and arXiv benchmark datasets prove the effectiveness of CHANGES and the importance of capturing hierarchical structure information in modeling scientific papers.

1 Introduction

Extractive document summarization aims to extract the most salient sentences from the original document and form the summary as an aggregate of these sentences. Compared to abstractive summarization approaches that suffer from hallucination generation problems (Kryściński et al., 2019; Zhang et al., 2022b), summaries generated in an extractive manner are more fluent, faithful, and grammatically accurate, but may lack coherence across sentences. Recent advances in deep neural networks and pre-trained language models (Devlin et al., 2018; Lewis et al., 2019) have led to significant progress in single document summarization (Nallapati et al., 2016a; Narayan et al., 2018; Liu and Lapata, 2019; Zhong et al., 2020). However, these methods mainly focus on short documents like news articles in CNN/DailyMail (Hermann et al., 2015) and New York Times (Sandhaus, 2008), and struggle when dealing with relatively long documents such as scientific papers.

The challenges of lengthy scientific paper summarization lie in several aspects. First, the extended input context hinders cross-sentence relation modeling, the critical step of extractive summarization (Wang et al., 2020). Thus, sequential models like RNN are incapable of capturing the long-distance dependency between sentences, and hard to differentiate salient sentences from others. Furthermore, scientific papers tend to cover diverse topics and contain rich hierarchical discourse structure information. The internal hierarchy structure, like sections, paragraphs, sentences, and words, is too complex for sequential models to capture. Scientific papers generally follow a standard discourse structure of problem definition, methodology, experiments and analysis, and conclusions (Xiao and Carenini, 2019). Moreover, the lengthy input context also makes the widely adopted self-attention Transformer-based models (Vaswani et al., 2017) inapplicable. The input length of a scientific paper can range from 2000 to $7,000$ words, which exceeds the input limit of the Transformer due to the quadratic computation complexity of self-attention. Thus, sparse Transformer models like BigBird (Zaheer et al., 2020) and Longformer (Beltagy et al., 2020) are proposed.

Recently, researchers have also turned to graph neural networks (GNN) as an alternative approach. Graph neural networks have been demonstrated to be effective at tasks with rich relational structure and can preserve global structure information (Yao et al., 2019; Xu et al., 2019; Zhang and Zhang, 2020). By representing a document as a graph, GNNs update and learn sentence representations by message passing, and turn extractive summarization into a node classification problem. Among all attempts, one popular way is to construct cross-sentence similarity graphs (Erkan and Radev, 2004; Zheng and Lapata, 2019), which uses sentence representation cosine similarity as edge weights to model cross-sentence semantic relations. Xu et al. (2019) proposed using Rhetorical Structure Theory (RST) trees and coreference mentions to capture cross-sentence discourse relations. Wang et al. (2020) proposed constructing a word-document het-

Proceedings of the 4th Workshop on Computational Approaches to Discourse (CODI 2023), pages 37–47
July 13-14, 2023

erogeneous graph by using words as the intermediary between sentences. Despite their success, how to construct an effective graph to capture the hierarchical structure for academic papers remains an open question.

To address the above challenges, we propose CHANGES (**C**ontrastive **H**ier**A**rchical **G**raph neural network for **E**xtractive **S**ummarization), a hierarchical graph neural network model to fully exploit the section structure of scientific papers. CHANGES first constructs a sentence-section hierarchical graph for a scientific paper, and then learns *hierarchical* sentence representations by dedicated designed information aggregation with iterative intra-section and inter-section message passing. Inspired by recent advances in contrastive learning (Liu and Liu, 2021; Chen et al., 2020), we also propose a graph contrastive learning module to learn global theme-aware sentence representations and provide fine-grained discriminative information. The local sentence and global section representations are then fused for salient sentence prediction. We validate CHANGES with extensive experiments and analyses on two scientific paper summarization datasets. Experimental results demonstrate the effectiveness of our proposed method. Our main contributions are as follows:

- We propose a hierarchical graph-based model for long scientific paper extractive summarization. Our method utilizes the hierarchical discourse of scientific documents and learns effective sentence representations with iterative intra-section and inter-section sentence message passing.

- We propose a plug-and-play graph contrastive module to provide fine-grained discriminative information. The graph contrastive module learns global theme-aware sentence representations by pulling semantically salient neighbors together and pushing apart unimportant sentences. Note that the module could be added to any extractive summarization system.

- We validate our proposed model on two benchmark datasets (arXiv and PubMed), and the experimental results demonstrate its effectiveness over strong baselines.

2 Related Work

2.1 Extractive Summarization on Scientific Papers

Despite the superior performance on news summarization by recent neural network models (Zhou et al., 2018; Zhang et al., 2023a,b; Fonseca et al., 2022) and pre-trained language models (Liu and Lapata, 2019; Lewis et al., 2019), progress in long document summarization such as scientific papers is still limited.

Traditional approaches to summarize scientific articles rely on supervised machine learning algorithms such as LSTM (Collins et al., 2017) with surface features such as sentence position, and section categories. Recently, Xiao and Carenini (2019) proposed a neural-based method by incorporating both the global context of the whole document and the local context within the current topic with an encoder-decoder model. Ju et al. (2021) designed an unsupervised extractive approach to summarize long scientific documents based on the Information Bottleneck principle. Dong et al. (2020) proposed an unsupervised ranking model by incorporating two-level hierarchical graph representation and asymmetrical positional cues to determine sentence importance. Recent works also apply pretrained sparse language models like Longformer for modeling long documents (Beltagy et al., 2020; Ruan et al., 2022; Cho et al., 2022).

2.2 Graph-based Summarization

Graph models have been widely applied to extractive summarization due to the capability of modeling cross-sentence relations within a document. The sparsity nature of graph structure also brings scalability and flexibility, making it a good fit for long documents. Graph neural networks' memory costs are generally linear with regard to the input size compared to the quadratic self-attention mechanism.

Researchers have explored supervised graph neural network methods for summarization (Cui and Hu, 2021; Jia et al., 2020; Huang and Kurohashi, 2021; Xie et al., 2022; Phan et al., 2022). Yasunaga et al. (2017) first proposed to use Graph Convolutional Network (GCN) on the approximate discourse graph. Xu et al. (2019) then applied GCN on structural discourse graphs based on RST trees and coreference mentions. Recently, Wang et al. (2020) proposed constructing a word-document heterogeneous graph by using words as the intermediary

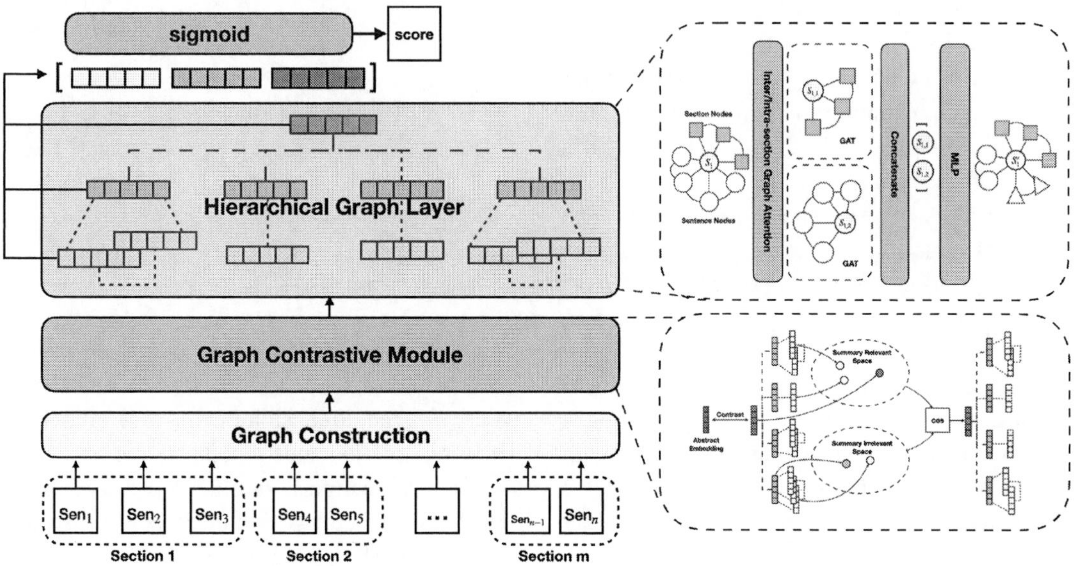

Figure 1: The overall model architecture of CHANGES. We first construct a hierarchical graph for an input document, and then learn representations with a graph contrastive module and hierarchical graph layers. The concatenation representations of sentence node and its section node will be fused for summary sentence selection.

between sentences. Zhang et al. (2022a) proposed to use hypergraph to capture the high-order sentence relations within the document. Our paper follows the series of work but incorporates hierarchical graphs for scientific paper discourse structure modeling and graph contrastive learning for theme-aware sentence representation learning.

3 Method

Given a document $D = \{s_1, s_2, ..., s_n\}$ with n sentences and m sections, we first represent it as a hierarchical graph and formulate extractive summarization as a node labeling task. The objective is to predict labels $y_i \in (0, 1)$ for all sentences, where $y_i = 1$ and $y_i = 0$ represent whether the i-th sentence should be included in the summary or not, respectively.

The overall model architecture of CHANGES is shown in Figure 1. CHANGES consists of two modules: a graph contrastive learning module to learn global theme-aware sentence representations and a hierarchical graph layer module to learn hierarchical graph node representations with iterative message passing. The learned sentence node and section node representations will be used as indicators for salient sentence selection.

3.1 Graph Construction

Given an academic paper D, we first construct a hierarchical graph $\mathcal{G} = (\mathcal{V}, \mathcal{E})$, where $\mathcal{V}$ stands for the node set and $\mathcal{E}$ represents edges between nodes. In order to utilize the sentence-section hierarchical structure of academic papers, the undirected hierarchical graph $\mathcal{G}$ contains both sentence nodes and section nodes, defined by $\mathcal{V} = \mathcal{V}_{sen} \cup \mathcal{V}_{sec}$, where each sentence node $v_{sen_i} \in \mathcal{V}_{sen}$ represents a sentence s_i in the document D and $v_{sec_j} \in \mathcal{V}_{sec}$ represents one section in the document. The edge connection of $\mathcal{G}$ is defined as $\mathcal{E} = \mathcal{E}_{sen} \cup \mathcal{E}_{sec} \cup \mathcal{E}_{cross}$, where $\mathcal{E}_{sen}$ denotes the connection between sentence nodes within the same section, $\mathcal{E}_{sec}$ denotes the connection between section nodes, and $\mathcal{E}_{cross}$ denotes the cross-connection between a sentence node and its corresponding section node. Note that we also add a special section supernode v_D that represents the whole document D. An illustration of the hierarchical graph is shown in Figure 2.

Edge Connection Unlike prior work (Zheng and Lapata, 2019; Dong et al., 2020) that uses cosine similarity of sentence semantic representations as edge weights, we construct unweighted hierarchical graphs to disentangle structural information (adjacency matrix $\mathbf{A}$) from semantic information (node representation $\mathbf{H}$). In other words, connected nodes have weight 1, and disconnected nodes have weight 0 in the adjacency matrix $\mathbf{A}$.

Formally, sentence-level edge $e_{sen_{i,j}}$ connects sentence nodes v_{sen_i} and v_{sen_j} if they are within the same section, aiming to aggregate local intra-section information. All section nodes are fully connected by section-level edges $e_{sec_{p,q}}$, aiming to aggregate global inter-section information. The cross-level edge $e_{cross_{i,p}}$ connects the sentence node v_{sen_i} to its corresponding section node v_{sec_p}, which allow message passing between sentence-level and section-level nodes.

In a hierarchical graph, a sentence node could only directly interact with local neighbor nodes within the same section, and indirectly interact with sentence nodes of other sections via section-level node connections.

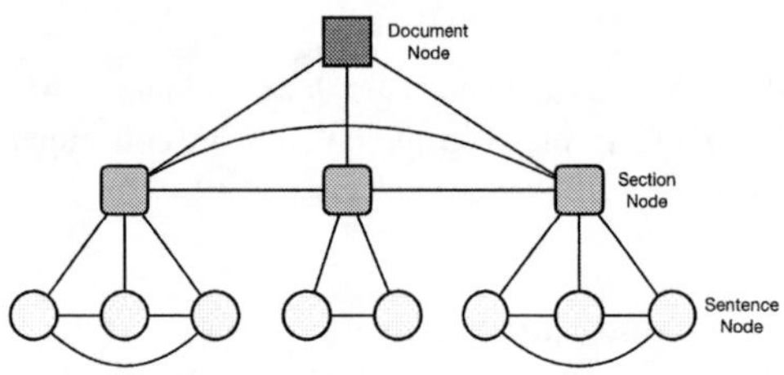

Figure 2: An illustration of a hierarchical graph for a long input document with rich discourse structures.

Node Representation We adopt BERT (Bidirectional Encoder Representations from Transformers) (Devlin et al., 2018) as sentence encoder to embed the semantic meanings of sentences $\{s_1, s_2, ..., s_n\}$ as initial node representations $\mathbf{X} = \{\mathbf{x}_1, \mathbf{x}_2, ..., \mathbf{x}_n\}$. Note that BERT here is only used for initial sentence embedding, but is not updated during the training process to reduce model computing cost and increase efficiency.

In addition to the semantic representation of sentences, we also inject positional encoding following Transformer (Vaswani et al., 2017) to preserve the sequential order information. We apply the hierarchical position embedding by (Ruan et al., 2022) to model sentence positions accompanying our hierarchical graph. Specifically, the position of each sentence s_i can be represented as two parts: its corresponding section index p_i^{sec}, and its sentence index within section p_i^{sen}. Formally, the hierarchical position embedding (HPE) of sentence s_i can be calculated as:

$$\mathrm{HPE}(s_i) = \mathrm{PE}(p_i^{sec}) + \mathrm{PE}(p_i^{sen}), \tag{1}$$

where $\mathrm{PE}(\cdot)$ refers to the position encoding function in (Vaswani et al., 2017):

$$\mathrm{PE}(pos, 2i) = \sin(pos/10000^{2i/d}), \tag{2}$$

$$\mathrm{PE}(pos, 2i+1) = \cos(pos/10000^{2i/d}). \tag{3}$$

Overall, we can get the initial sentence node representations $\mathbf{H}_{sen}^0 = \{\mathbf{h}_{sen_1}^0, \mathbf{h}_{sen_2}^0, ..., \mathbf{h}_{sen_n}^0\}$, with vector $\mathbf{h}_i^0 \in \mathbb{R}^d$ defined as:

$$\mathbf{h}_i^0 = \mathbf{x}_i + \mathrm{HPE}(s_i), \tag{4}$$

where d is the dimension of the node embedding. The initial section node representation $\mathbf{h}_{sec_j}^0 \in \mathbb{R}^d$ for the j-th section is the mean of its connected sentences embeddings, and the document node representation $\mathbf{h}_{doc}^0 \in \mathbb{R}^d$ is the mean of all section node embeddings.

3.2 Graph Contrastive Module

After constructing the hierarchical graph with adjacency matrix $\mathbf{A}$ and node representation $\mathbf{H}_{sen}^0 \in \mathbb{R}^{n\times d}$, we apply a graph contrastive learning (GCL) module to capture global context information. Motivated by the principal idea that a good summary sentence should be more semantically similar to the source document than the unqualified sentences (Radev et al., 2004; Zhong et al., 2020), our GCL module updates sentence representations using Graph Attention Network (Veličković et al., 2017) with a contrastive objective to learn the global theme-aware sentence representations. Note that the module could be added to any extractive summarization system.

Graph Attention Network Given a constructed graph $\mathcal{G} = (\mathcal{V}, \mathcal{E})$ with node representations $\mathbf{H}$ and adjacent matrix $\mathbf{A}$, a GAT layer updates a node v_i with representation $\mathbf{h}_i$ by:

$$\begin{aligned} e_{ij} &= \mathrm{LeakyReLU}\left(\mathbf{W}_a\left[\mathbf{W}_{in}\mathbf{h}_i \| \mathbf{W}_{in}\mathbf{h}_j\right]\right), \\ \alpha_{ij} &= \frac{\exp\left(e_{ij}\right)}{\sum_{l\in\mathcal{N}_i}\exp\left(e_{il}\right)}, \\ \mathbf{h}_i' &= \sigma\left(\sum_{j\in\mathcal{N}_i}\alpha_{ij}\mathbf{W}_v\mathbf{h}_j\right), \end{aligned} \tag{5}$$

where $\mathcal{N}_i$ denotes the 1-hop neighbors of node v_i, α_{ij} denotes the attention weight between nodes $\mathbf{h}_i$ and $\mathbf{h}_j$, $\mathbf{W}_{in}, \mathbf{W}_a, \mathbf{W}_v$ are trainable weight matrices, and $\|$ denotes concatenation operation.

The above single-head graph attention is further extended to multi-head attention, where T independent attention mechanisms are conducted and their outputs are concatenated as:

$$\mathbf{h}_i' = \|_{t=1}^{T} \sigma \left(\sum_{j \in \mathcal{N}_i} \alpha_{ij}^t \mathbf{W}_h^k \mathbf{h}_j \right) \quad (6)$$

Contrastive Loss Contrastive learning aims to learn effective representation by pulling semantically close neighbors together and pushing apart non-neighbors (Marelli et al., 2014). Recent works have demonstrated contrastive learning to be effective in high-order representation learning (Chen et al., 2020; Gao et al., 2021). Thus, we optimize our GCL module in a contrastive manner with the following contrastive loss. The goal of contrastive learning is to learn theme-aware sentence embedding by pulling semantically salient neighbors together and pushing apart less salient sentences. The contrastive loss is formally defined as:

$$\mathcal{L}_c = -\log \frac{\exp(sim((\mathbf{h}_D', \mathbf{h}_i')/\tau)}{\sum_{j=1}^{n} \exp(sim(\mathbf{h}_D', \mathbf{h}_j')/\tau)}, \quad (7)$$

where $\mathbf{h}_D'$ is the document node embedding, $\mathbf{h}_i'$ is the updated representaion of sentence s_i , and τ is the temperature factor.

After passing through the GCL module, the learned global theme-aware sentence embeddings $\mathbf{H}_{sen}^c = \{\mathbf{h}_{sen_1}^c, \mathbf{h}_{sen_2}^c, ..., \mathbf{h}_{sen_n}^c\} \in \mathbb{R}^{n \times d}$ are then passed to the hierarchical graph layer module.

3.3 Hierarchical Graph Layer

To exploit the sentence structure of academic papers, CHANGES then updates sentence and section node representations with hierarchical graph layers in an iterative manner.

The hierarchical graph layer first updates sentence embeddings with the local neighbor sentences within the same section with GAT for intra-section message passing, then update section nodes with sentence nodes for cross-level information aggregation to exploit the hierarchical structure of academic papers. Next, inter-section message passing allow *global* context information interaction. Finally, the sentence nodes are updated based on their corresponding section node, fusing both local and global context information.

Formally, each iteration contains four update processes: one intra-section message passing, one sentence-to-section aggregation, one inter-section message passing, and finally one section-to-sentence aggregation. For the l-th iteration, the process can be represented as:

$$\begin{aligned} \mathbf{H}_{sen}' &= \text{GAT}(\mathbf{H}_{sen}^l) \\ \mathbf{H}_{sec}' &= \text{GAT}(\mathbf{H}_{sen}') \\ \mathbf{H}_{sec}^{l+1} &= \text{GAT}(\mathbf{H}_{sec}') \\ \mathbf{H}_{sen}^{l+1} &= \sigma(\mathbf{W}_b[\mathbf{H}_{sen}' \| \mathbf{H}_{sec}^{l+1}]) \end{aligned} \quad (8)$$

where $\mathbf{H}_{sen}', \mathbf{H}_{sec}'$ denotes the intermediate representations of sentence and section nodes, $\mathbf{H}_{sen}^{l+1}, \mathbf{H}_{sec}^{l+1}$ denotes the updated sentence and section node representations, and $[\mathbf{H}_{sen}' \| \mathbf{H}_{sec}^{l+1}]$ denotes the concatenation of intermediate sentence node representation and its corresponding updated section node representation.

In this way, CHANGES updates and learns hierarchy-aware sentence embeddings through the hierarchical graph layers.

	Arxiv	PubMed
# train	201,427	112,291
# validation	6,431	6,402
# test	6,436	6,449
avg. word/doc	4,938	3,016
avg. word/summary	203	220
avg. sent./doc	205	140
avg. sent./summary	5	6

Table 1: Statistics of PubMed and Arxiv datasets.

3.4 Optimization

After passing L hierarchical graph layers, we obtain the final sentence node representations $\mathbf{H}_{sen}^L = \{\mathbf{h}_{sen_1}^L, \mathbf{h}_{sen_2}^L, ..., \mathbf{h}_{sen_n}^L\} \in \mathbb{R}^{n \times d}$. We then add a multi-layer perceptron (MLP) followed by a sigmoid activation function to indicate the confidence scores for extracting each sentence in the summary.

Formally, the predicted confidence score $\hat{y}_i$ to extract a sentence s_i in section sec_j as a summary sentence is:

$$\mathbf{z}_i = \text{LeakyReLU}(\mathbf{W}_{o1}[\mathbf{h}_{sen_i}^L \| \mathbf{h}_{sec_j}^L]), \quad (9)$$

$$\hat{y}_i = \text{sigmoid}(\mathbf{W}_{o2}\mathbf{z}_i), \quad (10)$$

where $\mathbf{W}_{o1}, \mathbf{W}_{o2}$ are both trainable parameters, and $[\mathbf{h}_{sen_i}^L \| \mathbf{h}_{sec_j}^L]$ denote the concatenation of sentence embedding and its corresponding section embedding. During the inference phase, we will select the k sentences with the highest predicted confidence scores as the extractive summary for the input long document.

Since the extractive ground truth labels for long documents are highly imbalanced, we optimize hierarchical graph layers using weighted cross entropy loss following (Xiao and Carenini, 2019) as:

$$\mathcal{L}_s = -\frac{1}{NN_d}\sum_{d=1}^{N}\sum_{i=1}^{N_d}(\eta \cdot y_i \log \hat{y}_i + (1-y_i)\log(1-\hat{y}_i)), \tag{11}$$

where N denotes the number of training instances in the training set, N_d denotes the number of sentences in the document, $\eta = \frac{\#negative}{\#positive}$ denote the ratio of the number of negative and positive sentences in the document, and y_i represent the ground-truth of sentence i.

Training Loss Overall, we optimize CHANGES in an end-to-end manner, by optimizing the graph contrastive module and hierarchical graph layers simultaneously.

The overall training loss of CHANGES is:

$$\mathcal{L} = \mathcal{L}_s + \lambda\mathcal{L}_c, \tag{12}$$

where λ is a re-scale hyperparameter and $\mathcal{L}_c$ denotes the contrastive loss in Equation 7.

4 Experiment

4.1 Experiment Setup

Dataset To validate the effectiveness of CHANGES, we conduct extensive experiments on two benchmark datasets: arXiv and PubMed (Cohan et al., 2018). The arXiv dataset contains papers in scientific domains, while the PubMed dataset contains scientific papers from the biomedical domain. These two benchmark datasets are widely adopted in long document summarization research and we use the original train, validation, and testing splits as in (Cohan et al., 2018). The detailed statistics of datasets are shown in Table 1.

Evaluation Following the common setting, we use ROUGE F-scores (Lin, 2004) as the automatic evaluation metrics. Specifically, we report the ROUGE-1/2 scores to measure summary informativeness and ROUGE-L scores to measure summary fluency. Following prior work (Liu and Lapata, 2019; Nallapati et al., 2016b), we also construct extractive ground truth labels (ORACLE) for training by greedily optimizing the ROUGE score on gold-reference abstracts.

4.2 Implementation Details

We use the publicly released BERT-base [1] (Devlin et al., 2018) as the sentence encoder. The BERT encoder is only used to generate initial sentence embeddings, but is not updated during training to improve model efficiency. We adopt the Graph Attention Network [2] (Veličković et al., 2017) implementation with 8 attention heads and 2 stack layers for graph message passing. The hidden size of our model is set to 2048.

Our model is trained with the Adam optimizer (Loshchilov and Hutter, 2017) with a learning rate of 0.0001 and a dropout rate of 0.1. We train our model on a single RTX A6000 GPU for 10 epochs and validate after each epoch using ROUGE-1 F-score. We employ early stopping to select the best model for a patient duration of 3 epochs. We searched the training loss re-scale factor λ in the range of 0 to 1 with 0.1 step size and got the best value of 0.5.

4.3 Baseline Methods

We perform a systematic comparison with recent approaches in both extractive and abstractive summarization for completeness. We keep the same train/validation/test splitting in all the experiments and report ROUGE scores from the original papers if available, or scores from (Xiao and Carenini, 2019) otherwise. Specifically, we compare with the following strong baseline approaches:

Unsupervised methods: LEAD method that selects the first few sentences as a summary, SumBasic (Vanderwende et al., 2007), graph-based unsupervised models LexRank (Erkan and Radev, 2004), PACSUM (Zheng and Lapata, 2019) and HIPORANK (Dong et al., 2020).

Neural extractive models: encoder-decoder based model Cheng&Lapata (Cheng and Lapata, 2016) and SummaRuNNer (Nallapati et al., 2016a); local and global context model ExtSum-LG (Xiao and Carenini, 2019) and its variants ExtSum-LG+RdLoss/MMR (Xiao and Carenini, 2020); language model-based methods SentCLF and SentPTR (Subramanian et al., 2019).

Neural abstractive models: pointer network generation model PGN (See et al., 2017), hierarchical attention generation model DiscourseAware (Cohan et al., 2018), and transformer-based generation model TLM-I+E (Subramanian et al., 2019).

[1] https://github.com/google-research/bert
[2] https://github.com/PetarV-/GAT

	PubMed			ArXiv		
Model	ROUGE-1	ROUGE-2	ROUGE-L	ROUGE-1	ROUGE-2	ROUGE-L
Oracle(15k tok.)	53.04	29.08	48.31	53.58	26.19	47.76
Lead-10	38.59	13.05	34.81	37.37	10.85	33.17
LexRank (2004)	39.19	13.89	34.59	33.85	10.73	28.99
SumBasic (2007)	37.15	11.36	33.43	29.47	6.95	26.30
PACSUM (2019)	39.79	14.00	36.09	38.57	10.93	34.33
HIPORANK (2021)	43.58	17.00	39.31	39.34	12.56	34.89
Cheng&Lapata (2016)	43.89	18.53	30.17	42.24	15.97	27.88
SummaRuNNer (2016)	43.89	18.78	30.36	42.81	16.52	28.23
ExtSum-LG (2019)	44.85	19.70	31.43	43.62	17.36	29.14
SentCLF (2020)	45.01	19.91	41.16	34.01	8.71	30.41
SentPTR (2020)	43.30	17.92	39.47	42.32	15.63	38.06
ExtSum-LG + RdLoss (2021)	45.30	20.42	40.95	44.01	17.79	39.09
ExtSum-LG + MMR (2021)	45.39	20.37	40.99	43.87	17.50	38.97
PGN (2017)	35.86	10.22	29.69	32.06	9.04	25.16
DiscourseAware (2018)	38.93	15.37	35.21	35.80	11.05	31.80
TLM-I+E (2020)	42.13	16.27	39.21	41.62	14.69	38.03
CHANGES (ours)	**46.43**	**21.17**	**41.58**	**45.61**	**18.02**	**40.06**

Table 2: ROUGE F1 results on PubMed and Arxiv datasets. We keep the same train/validation/test splitting in all the experiments and report ROUGE scores from the original papers if available, or scores from (Xiao and Carenini, 2019) otherwise.

4.4 Experiment Results

Table 2 shows the performance comparison of CHANGES and all baseline methods on both PubMed and arXiv datasets. The first blocks include the extractive ground truth ORACLE, position-based sentence selection method LEAD, and other unsupervised baseline approaches. The second block covers state-of-the-art supervised extractive neural baselines, and the third block covers the supervised abstractive baselines.

According to the results, HIPORANK (Dong et al., 2020) achieves state-of-the-art performance for graph-based unsupervised methods. Compared to PACSUM (Zheng and Lapata, 2019), the only difference is that HIPORANK incorporates section structural information for degree centrality calculation. The performance gain demonstrates the significance of capturing the hierarchical structure of academic papers when modeling cross-sentence relations.

Interestingly, the LEAD approach performs far better when summarizing short news like CNN/DailyMail (Hermann et al., 2015) and New York Times (Sandhaus, 2008) than summarizing academic papers, as shown in Table 2. The results show that the distribution of ground truth sentences in academic papers is more even. In other words, academic papers have less positional bias than news articles.

We also notice that the neural extractive models tend to outperform the neural abstractive methods in general, possibly because the extended context is more challenging for generative models during decoding. ExtSum-LG (Xiao and Carenini, 2019) is a benchmarked extractive method with section information by incorporating both the global context of the whole document and the local context within the current topic. We argue that CHANGES could better model the complex sentence structural information with the hierarchical graph than the LSTM-minus in ExtSum-LG.

According to the experimental results, our model CHANGES outperforms all baseline approaches significantly in terms of ROUGE F1 scores on both PubMed and arXiv datasets. The performance improvements demonstrate the usefulness of the global theme-aware representations from the graph contrastive learning module and the hierarchical graph structure for identifying the salient sentences.

5 Analysis

5.1 Ablation Study

We first analyze the influence of different components of CHANGES in Table 3. Here the second row 'w/o Contra' means we remove the GCL module and do not update the theme-aware sentence embeddings. The third row 'w/o Hierarchical' denotes that we only use the theme-aware sentence embedding for prediction without hierarchical graph layers. As shown in the table, removing either

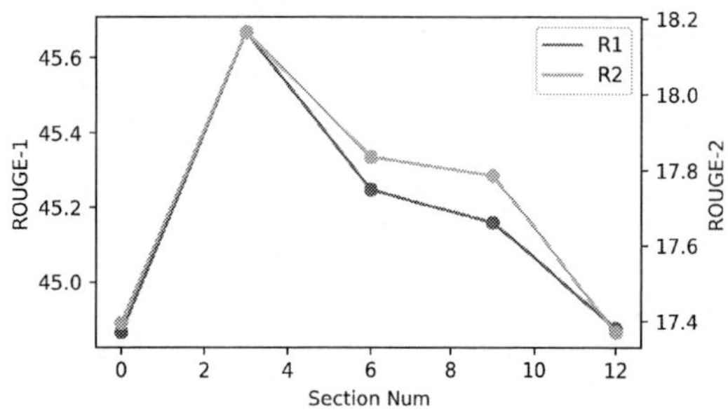

(a) ArXiv

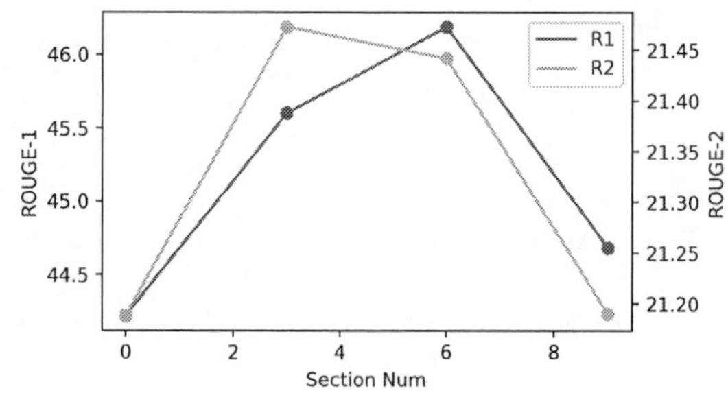

(b) PubMed

Figure 3: ROUGE-1,2 performance of CHANGES for test papers with different section numbers.

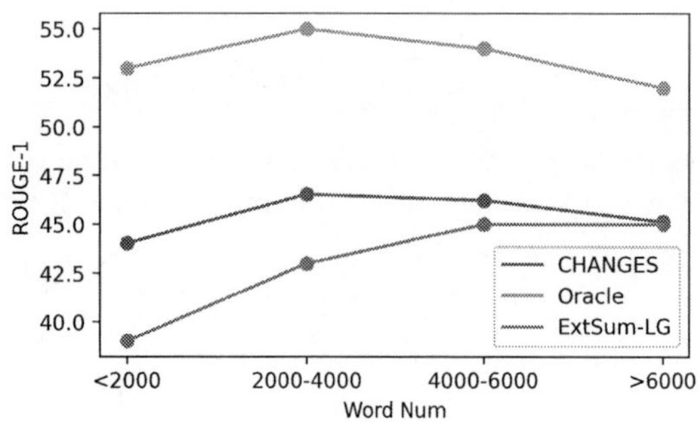

(a) ArXiv

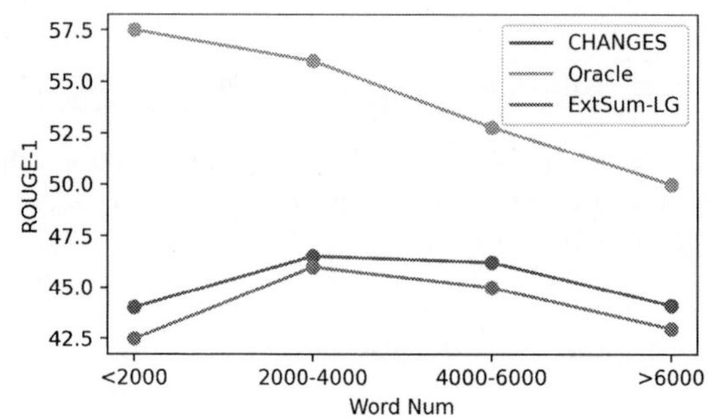

(b) PubMed

Figure 4: ROUGE-1 performance of ExtSum-LG, CHANGES, ORACLE for test papers with different lengths.

Model	ROUGE-1	ROUGE-2	ROUGE-L
PubMed			
CHANGES	**46.43**	**21.17**	**41.58**
w/o GCL	43.91	18.57	40.01
w/o Hierarchical	43.76	18.30	39.88
arXiv			
CHANGES	**45.61**	**18.02**	**40.06**
w/o GCL	44.47	16.58	38.87
w/o Hierarchical	44.72	16.79	39.10

Table 3: Ablation study results of removing components of CHANGES on PubMed and arXiv datasets.

component causes a significant model performance drop, which indicates that modeling sequential order information, semantic information, and hierarchical structural information are all necessary for academic paper summarization.

Interestingly, the theme-aware sentence embeddings and the hierarchy structure-aware sentence embeddings are almost equally critical to sentence salience modeling. The finding indicates the importance of modeling cross-sentence relations from both semantic and discourse structural perspectives.

5.2 Performance Analysis

We also analyze the sensitivity of CHANGES to section structure and length of academic papers. As shown in Figure 3, we see a performance drop trending when the number of sections increases. This is likely because the complex section structure hinders the inter-section sentence interactions. The model performance on the arXiv dataset is more stable compared to the PubMed dataset although documents in the arXiv dataset are relatively longer. We notice the same trend in Figure 4, model performance is also more stable on arXiv datasets across different document lengths. We argue this may imply that our model is more fit for longer documents that have richer discourse structures.

Regarding the document length, we see a steady performance gain when comparing to benchmark baseline methods ExtSum-LG on both datasets as shown in Figure 4. We also see as the document length increases, the performance gap between CHANGES and extractive summary performance ceiling ORACLE becomes smaller. The finding also verifies that CHANGES is especially effective and fit for long academic papers modeling.

6 Conclusion

In this paper, we propose CHANGES, a contrastive hierarchical graph-based model for scientific paper extractive summarization. CHANGES first leans global theme-aware sentence representations by graph contrastive learning module. Moreover, CHANGES incorporates the sentence-section hierarchical structure by separating intra-section and inter-section message passing and aggregating both global and local information for effective sentence embedding. Automatic evaluation on the PubMed and arXiv benchmark datasets proves the effectiveness of CHANGES and the importance of capturing both semantic and discourse structure information in modeling scientific papers.

In spite of the strong zero-shot performance of large language models like ChatGPT on various downstream tasks, long document modeling is still a challenging problem in the LLM era. Transformer-based GPT-like systems still suffer from the attention computing complexity problem and will benefit from effective and efficient modeling of long documents.

Limitations

In spite of the strong performance of CHANGES, its design still has the following limitations. First, CHANGES only extracts the sentence-section-document hierarchical structure of academic papers. We believe the model performance could be further improved by incorporating document hierarchy of different granularity like dependency parsing trees and Rhetorical structure theory trees. We leave this for future work. In addition, we only focus on single academic paper summarization in this work. Academic papers generally contain a large amount of domain knowledge, thus introducing domain knowledge from peer papers or citation networks should further boost model performance.

Acknowledgment

This work is supported by NSF through grants IIS-1763365 and IIS-2106972. We also thank the anonymous reviewers for their helpful feedback.

References

Iz Beltagy, Matthew E Peters, and Arman Cohan. 2020. Longformer: The long-document transformer. *arXiv preprint arXiv:2004.05150*.

Ting Chen, Simon Kornblith, Mohammad Norouzi, and Geoffrey Hinton. 2020. A simple framework for contrastive learning of visual representations. In *International conference on machine learning*, pages 1597–1607. PMLR.

Jianpeng Cheng and Mirella Lapata. 2016. Neural summarization by extracting sentences and words. *arXiv preprint arXiv:1603.07252*.

Sangwoo Cho, Kaiqiang Song, Xiaoyang Wang, Fei Liu, and Dong Yu. 2022. Toward unifying text segmentation and long document summarization. *arXiv preprint arXiv:2210.16422*.

Arman Cohan, Franck Dernoncourt, Doo Soon Kim, Trung Bui, Seokhwan Kim, Walter Chang, and Nazli Goharian. 2018. A discourse-aware attention model for abstractive summarization of long documents. *arXiv preprint arXiv:1804.05685*.

Ed Collins, Isabelle Augenstein, and Sebastian Riedel. 2017. A supervised approach to extractive summarisation of scientific papers. *arXiv preprint arXiv:1706.03946*.

Peng Cui and Le Hu. 2021. Topic-guided abstractive multi-document summarization. *arXiv preprint arXiv:2110.11207*.

Jacob Devlin, Ming-Wei Chang, Kenton Lee, and Kristina Toutanova. 2018. Bert: Pre-training of deep bidirectional transformers for language understanding. *arXiv preprint arXiv:1810.04805*.

Yue Dong, Andrei Mircea, and Jackie CK Cheung. 2020. Discourse-aware unsupervised summarization of long scientific documents. *arXiv preprint arXiv:2005.00513*.

Günes Erkan and Dragomir R Radev. 2004. Lexrank: Graph-based lexical centrality as salience in text summarization. *Journal of artificial intelligence research*, 22:457–479.

Marcio Fonseca, Yftah Ziser, and Shay B Cohen. 2022. Factorizing content and budget decisions in abstractive summarization of long documents by sampling summary views. *arXiv preprint arXiv:2205.12486*.

Tianyu Gao, Xingcheng Yao, and Danqi Chen. 2021. Simcse: Simple contrastive learning of sentence embeddings. *arXiv preprint arXiv:2104.08821*.

Karl Moritz Hermann, Tomas Kocisky, Edward Grefenstette, Lasse Espeholt, Will Kay, Mustafa Suleyman, and Phil Blunsom. 2015. Teaching machines to read and comprehend. In *Advances in neural information processing systems*, pages 1693–1701.

Yin Jou Huang and Sadao Kurohashi. 2021. Extractive summarization considering discourse and coreference relations based on heterogeneous graph. In *Proceedings of the 16th Conference of the European Chapter of the Association for Computational Linguistics: Main Volume*, pages 3046–3052.

Ruipeng Jia, Yanan Cao, Hengzhu Tang, Fang Fang, Cong Cao, and Shi Wang. 2020. Neural extractive summarization with hierarchical attentive heterogeneous graph network. In *Proceedings of the 2020 Conference on Empirical Methods in Natural Language Processing (EMNLP)*, pages 3622–3631.

Jiaxin Ju, Ming Liu, Huan Yee Koh, Yuan Jin, Lan Du, and Shirui Pan. 2021. Leveraging information bottleneck for scientific document summarization. *arXiv preprint arXiv:2110.01280*.

Wojciech Kryściński, Bryan McCann, Caiming Xiong, and Richard Socher. 2019. Evaluating the factual consistency of abstractive text summarization.

Mike Lewis, Yinhan Liu, Naman Goyal, Marjan Ghazvininejad, Abdelrahman Mohamed, Omer Levy, Ves Stoyanov, and Luke Zettlemoyer. 2019. Bart: Denoising sequence-to-sequence pre-training for natural language generation, translation, and comprehension. *arXiv preprint arXiv:1910.13461*.

Chin-Yew Lin. 2004. Rouge: A package for automatic evaluation of summaries. In *Text summarization branches out*, pages 74–81.

Yang Liu and Mirella Lapata. 2019. Text summarization with pretrained encoders. *arXiv preprint arXiv:1908.08345*.

Yixin Liu and Pengfei Liu. 2021. Simcls: A simple framework for contrastive learning of abstractive summarization. *arXiv preprint arXiv:2106.01890*.

Ilya Loshchilov and Frank Hutter. 2017. Decoupled weight decay regularization. *arXiv preprint arXiv:1711.05101*.

Marco Marelli, Stefano Menini, Marco Baroni, Luisa Bentivogli, Raffaella Bernardi, and Roberto Zamparelli. 2014. A sick cure for the evaluation of compositional distributional semantic models. In *Proceedings of the Ninth International Conference on Language Resources and Evaluation (LREC'14)*, pages 216–223.

Ramesh Nallapati, Feifei Zhai, and Bowen Zhou. 2016a. Summarunner: A recurrent neural network based sequence model for extractive summarization of documents. *arXiv preprint arXiv:1611.04230*.

Ramesh Nallapati, Bowen Zhou, Caglar Gulcehre, Bing Xiang, et al. 2016b. Abstractive text summarization using sequence-to-sequence rnns and beyond. *arXiv preprint arXiv:1602.06023*.

Shashi Narayan, Shay B Cohen, and Mirella Lapata. 2018. Ranking sentences for extractive summarization with reinforcement learning. *arXiv preprint arXiv:1802.08636*.

Tuan-Anh Phan, Ngoc-Dung Ngoc Nguyen, and Khac-Hoai Nam Bui. 2022. Hetergraphlongsum: Heterogeneous graph neural network with passage aggregation for extractive long document summarization. In *Proceedings of the 29th International Conference on Computational Linguistics*, pages 6248–6258.

Dragomir R Radev, Hongyan Jing, Małgorzata Styś, and Daniel Tam. 2004. Centroid-based summarization of multiple documents. *Information Processing & Management*, 40(6):919–938.

Qian Ruan, Malte Ostendorff, and Georg Rehm. 2022. Histruct+: Improving extractive text summarization with hierarchical structure information. *arXiv preprint arXiv:2203.09629*.

Evan Sandhaus. 2008. The new york times annotated corpus. *Linguistic Data Consortium, Philadelphia*, 6(12):e26752.

Abigail See, Peter J Liu, and Christopher D Manning. 2017. Get to the point: Summarization with pointer-generator networks. *arXiv preprint arXiv:1704.04368*.

Sandeep Subramanian, Raymond Li, Jonathan Pilault, and Christopher Pal. 2019. On extractive and abstractive neural document summarization with transformer language models. *arXiv preprint arXiv:1909.03186*.

Lucy Vanderwende, Hisami Suzuki, Chris Brockett, and Ani Nenkova. 2007. Beyond sumbasic: Task-focused summarization with sentence simplification and lexical expansion. *Information Processing & Management*, 43(6):1606–1618.

Ashish Vaswani, Noam Shazeer, Niki Parmar, Jakob Uszkoreit, Llion Jones, Aidan N Gomez, Łukasz Kaiser, and Illia Polosukhin. 2017. Attention is all you need. In *Advances in neural information processing systems*, pages 5998–6008.

Petar Veličković, Guillem Cucurull, Arantxa Casanova, Adriana Romero, Pietro Lio, and Yoshua Bengio. 2017. Graph attention networks. *arXiv preprint arXiv:1710.10903*.

Danqing Wang, Pengfei Liu, Yining Zheng, Xipeng Qiu, and Xuanjing Huang. 2020. Heterogeneous graph neural networks for extractive document summarization. *arXiv preprint arXiv:2004.12393*.

Wen Xiao and Giuseppe Carenini. 2019. Extractive summarization of long documents by combining global and local context. *arXiv preprint arXiv:1909.08089*.

Wen Xiao and Giuseppe Carenini. 2020. Systematically exploring redundancy reduction in summarizing long documents. *arXiv preprint arXiv:2012.00052*.

Qianqian Xie, Jimin Huang, Tulika Saha, and Sophia Ananiadou. 2022. Gretel: Graph contrastive topic enhanced language model for long document extractive summarization. *arXiv preprint arXiv:2208.09982*.

Jiacheng Xu, Zhe Gan, Yu Cheng, and Jingjing Liu. 2019. Discourse-aware neural extractive model for text summarization. *arXiv preprint arXiv:1910.14142*.

Liang Yao, Chengsheng Mao, and Yuan Luo. 2019. Graph convolutional networks for text classification. In *Proceedings of the AAAI conference on artificial intelligence*, volume 33, pages 7370–7377.

Michihiro Yasunaga, Rui Zhang, Kshitijh Meelu, Ayush Pareek, Krishnan Srinivasan, and Dragomir Radev. 2017. Graph-based neural multi-document summarization. *arXiv preprint arXiv:1706.06681*.

Manzil Zaheer, Guru Guruganesh, Kumar Avinava Dubey, Joshua Ainslie, Chris Alberti, Santiago Ontanon, Philip Pham, Anirudh Ravula, Qifan Wang, Li Yang, et al. 2020. Big bird: Transformers for longer sequences. *Advances in neural information processing systems*, 33:17283–17297.

Haopeng Zhang, Xiao Liu, and Jiawei Zhang. 2022a. Hegel: Hypergraph transformer for long document summarization. *arXiv preprint arXiv:2210.04126*.

Haopeng Zhang, Xiao Liu, and Jiawei Zhang. 2023a. Diffusum: Generation enhanced extractive summarization with diffusion. *arXiv preprint arXiv:2305.01735*.

Haopeng Zhang, Xiao Liu, and Jiawei Zhang. 2023b. Extractive summarization via chatgpt for faithful summary generation. *arXiv preprint arXiv:2304.04193*.

Haopeng Zhang, Semih Yavuz, Wojciech Kryscinski, Kazuma Hashimoto, and Yingbo Zhou. 2022b. Improving the faithfulness of abstractive summarization via entity coverage control. *arXiv preprint arXiv:2207.02263*.

Haopeng Zhang and Jiawei Zhang. 2020. Text graph transformer for document classification. In *Conference on Empirical Methods in Natural Language Processing (EMNLP)*.

Hao Zheng and Mirella Lapata. 2019. Sentence centrality revisited for unsupervised summarization. *arXiv preprint arXiv:1906.03508*.

Ming Zhong, Pengfei Liu, Yiran Chen, Danqing Wang, Xipeng Qiu, and Xuanjing Huang. 2020. Extractive summarization as text matching. *arXiv preprint arXiv:2004.08795*.

Qingyu Zhou, Nan Yang, Furu Wei, Shaohan Huang, Ming Zhou, and Tiejun Zhao. 2018. Neural document summarization by jointly learning to score and select sentences. *arXiv preprint arXiv:1807.02305*.

Leveraging Structural Discourse Information for Event Coreference Resolution in Dutch

Loic De Langhe, Orphée De Clercq, Veronique Hoste
LT3, Language and Translation Technology Team, Ghent University, Belgium
Groot-Brittanniëlaan 45, 9000 Ghent, Belgium
firstname.lastname@ugent.be

Abstract

Structural information is known to be important in resolving coreferential relations. We directly embed discourse structure information (subsection, paragraph and text location) in a transformer-based Dutch event coreference resolution model in order to more explicitly provide it with structural information. Results reveal that integrating this type of knowledge leads to a significant improvement in CONLL F1 for within-document settings (+ 8.6%) and a minor improvement for cross-document settings (+ 1.1%).

1 Introduction

Large Language models (LLMs) and transformer-based architectures have significantly changed the domain of Natural Language Processing (NLP) in recent years. Through pre-training and fine-tuning masked language models (MLMs) such as BERT (Devlin et al., 2018), state-of-the-art results can be obtained for tasks requiring deep semantic or syntactic knowledge such as readability assessment (Imperial, 2021), syntactic parsing (He and Choi, 2019) and conversational question-answering (Staliūnaitė and Iacobacci, 2020). However, despite their apparent dominance over other methods, transformer-based language models are still not the 'one-size-fits-all' solution for a subset of NLP tasks. In particular, discourse-based tasks such as Event Coreference Resolution (ECR) still pose a major challenge. Within ECR, the goal is to determine whether or not two textual events refer to the same real-life or fictional event, as is the case in Examples 1 and 2

1. Frankrijk Verslaat België in de halve finales van de FIFA wereldbeker voetbal *EN: France beats Belgium in the semi-final of the FIFA world cup.*

2. België verliest halve finale *EN: Belgium loses semi-final.*

Understanding that these two Examples, which have been sourced from a Dutch newspaper article, refer in fact to the same real-world occurrence is straightforward for human readers. Tasks like these typically require understanding of long-distance semantic relationships and dependencies within a given text, or even across multiple texts. While human readers can take advantage of both their extensive extra-linguistic knowledge and structural awareness of the text, AI algorithms typically do not possess such skills. For transformer-based language models in particular long-distance semantic dependencies throughout texts might pose a particular problem. Because MLM pre-training is typically limited to the immediate (sentence) context, the model is unable to learn these dependencies. Additionally, while models such as ALBERT (Lan et al., 2019) have tried to explicitly integrate textual and discourse structure in transformer-based architectures, these models still tend to focus on immediate local context and not on the discourse as a whole.

These limitations pose significant problems for ECR. Recent work has indicated that the correct classification of coreferential links between events in BERT-based models is primarily dependent on the outward lexical similarity of those events (De Langhe et al., 2023b). While logical in principle, this is highly problematic in cases such as Example 3 and Example 4, as there exist many instances in which two events are lexically similar, but that do not corefer.

3. De Franse president Macron ontmoette de Amerikaanse president voor de eerste keer vandaag *EN: The French president Macron met with the American president for the first time today*

4. Frans President Sarkozy ontmoette de Amerikaanse president *EN: French President Sarkozy met de American president*

Proceedings of the 4th Workshop on Computational Approaches to Discourse (CODI 2023), pages 48–53
July 13-14, 2023 ©2023 Association for Computational Linguistics

Vice versa, non-similar event mentions are not necessarily not in a coreferential relation. Although the latter cases are more exceptional, the overall sparseness of ECR results makes that the bulk of training data often consists of similar, but not-coreferring event mentions. Overall, transformer-based approaches have made significant strides within the field of ECR (Joshi et al., 2020). Nonetheless, the over-reliance on lexical similarity between event mentions might impede further improvement. Interestingly, earlier feature-based studies have shown that integrating certain structural features, such as the proximity of two events in a given text can have a positive effect (Lu and Ng, 2018). We aim to improve an existing Dutch transformer-based ECR model (De Langhe et al., 2022b) by enriching it with structural discourse-level information. The goal of this paper is two-fold. First, it is our ambition to illustrate that concepts rooted in general linguistic theory and fundamental to our own understanding of coreferential relations can also improve the performance of LLMs on this task. Second, we wish to address the gap between ECR studies in the English language domain and those in lower-resourced languages. Currently, there exists very little data or available research for languages other than English. In our experiments we show that including discourse-level information leads to a significant and consistent improvement for within-document ECR models. We also note minor improvements in cross-document contexts.

2 Related Work

There exist two important model paradigms within the domain of ECR. First, mention-ranking approaches focus on finding all possible antecedents for a given event and on generating a ranking of those antecedents based on the likelihood of coreference with the event in question. In Lu and Ng (2017a) a feature-based probabilistic model was used for within-document ECR. The authors show that lexical features such as full or partial overlap of events and cosine similarity between event mentions are among the most important information sources of the model. In addition, they revealed that distance-based features such as the number of sentences between two events also have a noticeable positive effect on the classifier's performance. A second and more important series of models are mention-pair approaches. This method generates all possible event pairs and reduces the classification to a binary decision (coreferring or not-coreferring) between each event pair. Earlier models within this paradigm were entirely feature-based and relied on a series of lexical, structural and logical constraining features. A large variety of classical machine learning algorithms has been tested using the mention-pair paradigm such as decision trees (Cybulska and Vossen, 2015), support vector machines (Chen et al., 2015) and standard deep neural networks (Nguyen et al., 2016). More recent work has focused on the use of LLMs and transformer encoders (Cattan et al., 2021a,b), with span-based architectures attaining the best overall results (Joshi et al., 2020; Lu and Ng, 2021). It has to be noted that mention-pair approaches relying on LLMs suffer most from the limitations discussed in Section 1. Therefore, recent studies have attempted, with some success, to integrate insights regarding discourse coherence (Held et al., 2021) and domain-specific document discourse information (Choubey et al., 2020) into existing pipelines. Research for comparatively lower-resourced languages has generally followed the paradigms and methods described above and has focused on languages such as Chinese (Mitamura et al., 2015), Arabic (NIST, 2005) and Dutch (Minard et al., 2016).

3 Experimental setup

3.1 Data

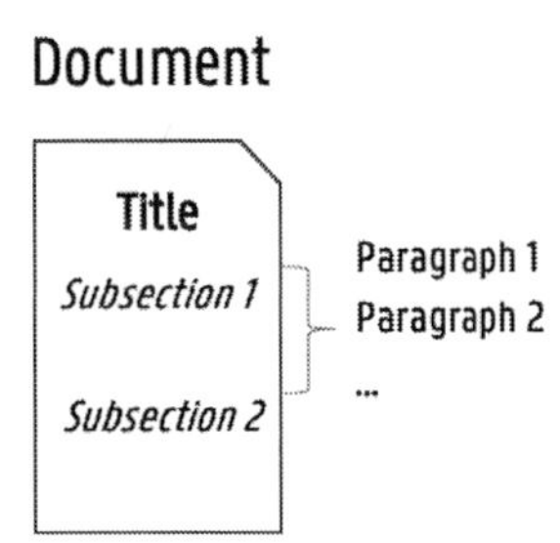

Figure 1: News article structure in the ENCORE dataset

Our data consists of a subset of the Dutch ENCORE corpus (De Langhe et al., 2022a), which in its totality consists of 15,407 annotated events spread over 1,015 documents that were sourced from a collection of Dutch (Flemish) newspaper articles. Coreferential relations between events were annotated at both the within- and cross-document level. For the research presented in this paper a

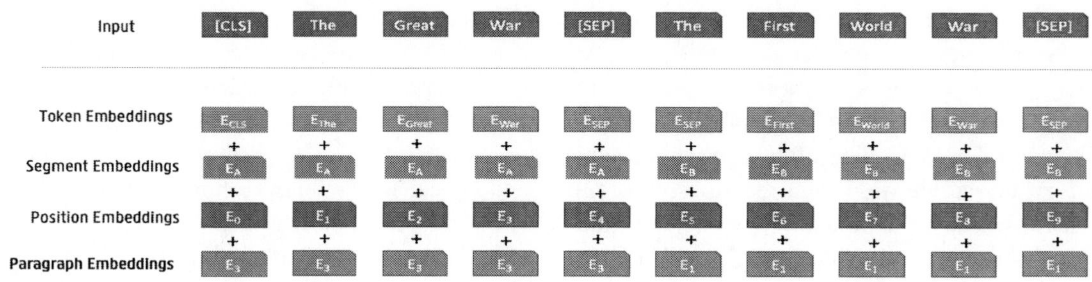

Figure 2: Visualisation of BERT's input embeddings with added discourse-level paragraph embeddings. Event 1 (*The Great War*) is found in paragraph 3 of the document, while potential antecedent Event 2 (*The First World War*) is found in the first paragraph of the document

subset of 8,794 events was selected which all come from documents for which a detailed discourse structure was available. Each of these documents can be broken down into subsections, which in turn consist of a number of paragraphs. Subsections are preceded by a subtitle in bold and typically group together a piece of related information. Figure 1 visualizes the general structure of a document in the ENCORE corpus.

For each event in our dataset we thus know at which subsection and paragraph level it is located within a given article. Additionally, for each event we can derive its *Text Location*, depending on where in the article the event is located. There are 5 possible locations, being the *Article Header*, *Article Subheader*, *Article Introduction*, *Subsection Title* and *Paragraph*.

3.2 Experiments

In our experiments we draw inspiration from earlier work on feature-based models (Lu and Ng, 2018) and integrate specific event proximity and structural information into a state-of-the-art Dutch transformer-based ECR model (De Langhe et al., 2023b). We focus on the usage of the readily available discourse and document-level information which was described in Section 3.1.

3.2.1 Baseline coreference algorithm

The ECR model consists of the fine-tuned Dutch BERT model BERTje (de Vries et al., 2019). For this model, the mention-pair approach has demonstratively better results compared to other existing methods (Lu and Ng, 2018, 2021). Concretely, pairwise scores for each pair of event mentions in the dataset are obtained. First, each possible event pair in the data is encoded by concatenating and tokenizing the two events and by subsequently feeding these to the BERTje encoder. A special *[SEP]* token is inserted between the two event mentions to indicate where one event ends and the other begins. We use the token representation of the classification token *[CLS]* as the aggregate embedding of each event pair, which is subsequently passed to a softmax-activated classification function. Finally, the results of the binary text pair classification are passed through a clustering algorithm in order to obtain output in the form of coreference chains.

3.2.2 Discourse Embeddings Model

In our proposed algorithm discourse-level positional information (paragraph, subsection and text location) is passed to BERT's first encoder layer for each individual event during the fine-tuning process. This is done in a similar way as how the positional, segment and token embeddings are used in the original BERT implementation. We believe that this structural information corresponds well with established general theories on discourse structure where related concepts are usually found within close proximity of each other, be it at the sentence, paragraph or section level (Hoeken and Van Vliet, 2000; Glasbey, 1994). By directly integrating this knowledge into the model it would ideally learn that, overall, coreferring mentions are grouped closer together compared to non-coreferring mentions at the document level. As mentioned before in Section 2, it has already been shown that knowledge regarding the proximity of two events can have a positive impact on the classification decision in feature-based models (Lu and Ng, 2017b, 2018). Earlier research has also shown that currently this knowledge is not encoded by BERT-like models (De Langhe et al., 2023a). These findings led us to believe that this specific knowledge can be leveraged by the model to learn about a fundamental aspect of coreferential relations, as well as

Model	CONLL
BERTje$_{Baseline}$	0.432
BERTje$_{Paragraph}$	0.466 ± 0.012
BERTje$_{Subsection}$	0.517 ± 0.008
BERTje$_{Text\ Location}$	0.424 ± 0.032
BERTje$_{Paragraph\ +\ Subsection}$	**0.518** ± 0.009
BERTje$_{Paragraph\ +\ TextLocation}$	0.434 ± 0.028
BERTje$_{Subsection\ +\ TextLocation}$	0.437 ± 0.019
BERTje$_{Paragraph\ +\ Subsection\ +\ Text\ Location}$	0.516 ± 0.022

(a) Results for the Within-document setting

Model	CONLL
BERTje$_{Baseline}$	0.519
BERTje$_{Paragraph}$	**0.530** ± 0.014
BERTje$_{Subsection}$	0.517 ± 0.011
BERTje$_{Text\ Location}$	0.460 ± 0.009
BERTje$_{Paragraph\ +\ Subsection}$	0.481 ± 0.032
BERTje$_{Paragraph\ +\ TextLocation}$	0.476 ± 0.048
BERTje$_{Subsection\ +\ TextLocation}$	0.468 ± 0.064
BERTje$_{Paragraph\ +\ Subsection+\ Text\ Location}$	0.472 ± 0.026

(b) Results for the Cross-document setting

Table 1: Subtables report average CONLL results and standard deviation over 3 trials using different random seeds for the discourse-level embeddings in a within-document and cross-document setting respectively. All results in the cross-document table, except the baseline model, automatically include document-level embeddings

break away from its aforementioned dependency on outward lexical similarity of events.

In our implementation, all possible subsection, paragraph and text location levels are encoded using a tokenizer-like mechanism where each level of the respective subsection, paragraph or text location is assigned a unique ID, much like individual tokens are encoded using BERT's own tokenizer. Then, an input embedding matrix of size *A x 768* is randomly initiated for each type of segment information (subsection, paragraph and text location), where *A* is the maximum depth level of a given segment across the dataset and 768 is the standard embedding length for a BERT$_{Base}$ model. Concretely, the maximum depth at the paragraph level is 10 if the longest document across the dataset (in number of paragraphs) has 10 paragraphs. The resulting input embedding matrix will then be of dimension *10x768* and a total of 7680 trainable parameters (*A x 768*) will be added to the model. The first paragraph in each document is encoded by the same unique ID (i.e., 1) and the paragraph-level embedding for each individual token is obtained by embedding the unique ID through the generated input embedding matrix. The same process is followed for the subsection and text location embeddings. Finally, the resulting discourse-level embeddings are summed with the token, segment and positional embeddings to obtain the input for the first encoder layer. As is the case in the original BERT implementation, the weights of our custom discourse input embedding matrices are also optimized during the fine-tuning process. A high-level visualization of the integration of a paragraph embedding can be found in Figure 2. Subsection and text location embeddings are implemented in an analogous manner.

While, intuitively, our proposed structural embeddings would most likely be most useful in a within-document setting, we also include results for a cross-document setting in order to gauge the effectiveness of discourse-level features in those contexts specifically. Our setup for cross-document ECR is identical to the one described above with the notable exception that we add a fourth type of discourse-level embedding, namely a document embedding. When events are found within the same document this embedding is identical.

4 Results and discussion

Tables 1a and 1b show the results of testing various discourse-level embeddings in a within-document and cross-document context, respectively. We evaluate our results using the established CONLL metric, which is an average of 3 commonly used metrics for coreference evaluation: MUC (Vilain et al., 1995), B^3 (Bagga and Baldwin, 1998) and CEAF (Luo, 2005). We report the average and standard deviations of 3 runs of experiments with different random seeds for the discourse-level input embedding matrices. For the within-document experiments, we see a significant impact on overall performance when including paragraph- and subsection-level information in the fine-tuning process. A combination of paragraph embeddings and subsection embeddings provides the best results. Conversely, we find that the inclusion of Text Location embeddings does not have any noticeable impact on the classification of within-document event coreference.

In the cross-document setting, we find that including structural discourse information does not have a significant impact on classifier performance. While including document and paragraph-level embeddings results in a minor improvement over the baseline coreference model, we find that in general including discourse-specific embeddings does not help with cross-document event coreference.

5 Conclusion and Future Work

In this paper we explored the potential of using discourse-level embeddings in transformer-based models for event coreference resolution. Motivated by general linguistic theory on the overall structure of language we integrate paragraph, subsection and text location information in a Dutch BERT-based mention-pair event coreference algorithm. We find that in within-document contexts the inclusion of discourse-level information has a significant positive effect on overall classifier performance. In particular, the inclusion of paragraph and subsection information consistently leads to better results. Results for the cross-document setting show only minimal improvement over the baseline model. In future work, we aim to further develop structurally informed models for event coreference resolution as well as look into improving the existing cross-document setup.

Acknowledgements

This work was supported by Ghent University under grant BOFGOA2018000601 and by the Research Foundation–Flanders under project grant number FWO.OPR.2020.0014.01.

References

Amit Bagga and Breck Baldwin. 1998. Algorithms for scoring coreference chains. In *The first international conference on language resources and evaluation workshop on linguistics coreference*, volume 1, pages 563–566. Citeseer.

Arie Cattan, Alon Eirew, Gabriel Stanovsky, Mandar Joshi, and Ido Dagan. 2021a. Cross-document coreference resolution over predicted mentions. *arXiv preprint arXiv:2106.01210*.

Arie Cattan, Alon Eirew, Gabriel Stanovsky, Mandar Joshi, and Ido Dagan. 2021b. Realistic evaluation principles for cross-document coreference resolution. *arXiv preprint arXiv:2106.04192*.

Yubo Chen, Liheng Xu, Kang Liu, Daojian Zeng, and Jun Zhao. 2015. Event Extraction via Dynamic Multi-Pooling Convolutional Neural Networks. *Proceedings of the 53rd Annual Meeting of the Association for Computational Linguistics and the 7th International Joint Conference on Natural Language Processing*, pages 167–176.

Prafulla Kumar Choubey, Aaron Lee, Ruihong Huang, and Lu Wang. 2020. Discourse as a function of event: Profiling discourse structure in news articles around the main event. In *Proceedings of the 58th Annual Meeting of the Association for Computational Linguistics*, pages 5374–5386, Online. Association for Computational Linguistics.

Agata Cybulska and Piek Vossen. 2015. Translating Granularity of Event Slots into Features for Event Coreference Resolution. In *Proceedings of the The 3rd Workshop on EVENTS: Definition, Detection, Coreference, and Representation*, pages 1–10, Denver, Colorado. Association for Computational Linguistics.

Loic De Langhe, Orphée De Clercq, and Veronique Hoste. 2022a. Constructing a cross-document event coreference corpus for dutch. *Language Resources and Evaluation*, pages 1–30.

Loic De Langhe, Orphee De Clercq, and Veronique Hoste. 2023a. What does bert actually learn about event coreference? probing structural information in a fine-tuned dutch language model. *Accepted.*

Loic De Langhe, Orphée De Clercq, and Veronique Hoste. 2022b. Investigating cross-document event coreference for dutch.

Loic De Langhe, Thierry Desot, Orphée De Clercq, and Veronique Hoste. 2023b. A benchmark for dutch end-to-end cross-document event coreference resolution. *Electronics*, 12(4).

Wietse de Vries, Andreas van Cranenburgh, Arianna Bisazza, Tommaso Caselli, Gertjan van Noord, and Malvina Nissim. 2019. Bertje: A dutch bert model. *arXiv preprint arXiv:1912.09582*.

Jacob Devlin, Ming-Wei Chang, Kenton Lee, and Kristina Toutanova. 2018. Bert: Pre-training of deep bidirectional transformers for language understanding. *arXiv preprint arXiv:1810.04805*.

Sheila R Glasbey. 1994. *Event structure in natural language discourse*. Ph.D. thesis, University of Edinburgh.

Han He and Jinho D Choi. 2019. Establishing strong baselines for the new decade: Sequence tagging, syntactic and semantic parsing with bert. *arXiv preprint arXiv:1908.04943*.

William Held, Dan Iter, and Dan Jurafsky. 2021. Focus on what matters: Applying discourse coherence theory to cross document coreference. *arXiv preprint arXiv:2110.05362*.

Hans Hoeken and Mario Van Vliet. 2000. Suspense, curiosity, and surprise: How discourse structure influences the affective and cognitive processing of a story. *Poetics*, 27(4):277–286.

Joseph Marvin Imperial. 2021. BERT embeddings for automatic readability assessment. In *Proceedings of the International Conference on Recent Advances in Natural Language Processing (RANLP 2021)*, pages 611–618, Held Online. INCOMA Ltd.

Mandar Joshi, Danqi Chen, Yinhan Liu, Daniel S Weld, Luke Zettlemoyer, and Omer Levy. 2020. Spanbert: Improving pre-training by representing and predicting spans. *Transactions of the Association for Computational Linguistics*, 8:64–77.

Zhenzhong Lan, Mingda Chen, Sebastian Goodman, Kevin Gimpel, Piyush Sharma, and Radu Soricut. 2019. Albert: A lite bert for self-supervised learning of language representations. *arXiv preprint arXiv:1909.11942*.

Jing Lu and Vincent Ng. 2017a. Learning antecedent structures for event coreference resolution. In *2017 16th IEEE International Conference on Machine Learning and Applications (ICMLA)*, pages 113–118. IEEE.

Jing Lu and Vincent Ng. 2017b. Learning Antecedent Structures for Event Coreference Resolution. In *Machine Learning and Applications (ICMLA), 2017 16th IEEE International Conference on*, pages 113–118. IEEE.

Jing Lu and Vincent Ng. 2018. Event Coreference Resolution: A Survey of Two Decades of Research. In *Proceedings of the Twenty-Seventh International Joint Conference on Artificial Intelligence*, pages 5479–5486, Stockholm, Sweden. International Joint Conferences on Artificial Intelligence Organization.

Jing Lu and Vincent Ng. 2021. Conundrums in event coreference resolution: Making sense of the state of the art. In *Proceedings of the 2021 Conference on Empirical Methods in Natural Language Processing*, pages 1368–1380.

Xiaoqiang Luo. 2005. On coreference resolution performance metrics. In *Proceedings of Human Language Technology Conference and Conference on Empirical Methods in Natural Language Processing*, pages 25–32.

Anne-Lyse Minard, Manuela Speranza, Ruben Urizar, Marieke van Erp, Anneleen Schoen, and Chantal van Son. 2016. MEANTIME, the NewsReader Multilingual Event and Time Corpus. In *Proceedings of the 10th language resources and evaluation conference (LREC 2016)*, page 6, Portorož, Slovenia. European Language Resources Association (ELRA).

Teruko Mitamura, Yukari Yamakawa, Susan Holm, Zhiyi Song, Ann Bies, Seth Kulick, and Stephanie Strassel. 2015. Event Nugget Annotation: Processes and Issues. In *Proceedings of the The 3rd Workshop on EVENTS: Definition, Detection, Coreference, and Representation*, pages 66–76, Denver, Colorado. Association for Computational Linguistics.

Thien Huu Nguyen, Adam Meyers, and Ralph Grishman. 2016. New york university 2016 system for kbp event nugget: A deep learning approach. In *TAC*.

NIST. 2005. The ACE 2005 (ACE 05) Evaluation Plan.

Ieva Staliūnaitė and Ignacio Iacobacci. 2020. Compositional and lexical semantics in roberta, bert and distilbert: a case study on coqa. *arXiv preprint arXiv:2009.08257*.

Marc Vilain, John D Burger, John Aberdeen, Dennis Connolly, and Lynette Hirschman. 1995. A model-theoretic coreference scoring scheme. In *Sixth Message Understanding Conference (MUC-6): Proceedings of a Conference Held in Columbia, Maryland, November 6-8, 1995*.

Entity Coreference and Co-occurrence Aware Argument Mining from Biomedical Literature

Boyang Liu[1], **Viktor Schlegel**[1,2], **Riza Batista-Navarro**[1], **Sophia Ananiadou**[1]
[1] Department of Computer Science, The University of Manchester, UK
[2] ASUS Intelligent Cloud Services (AICS), Singapore
{boyang.liu-2@postgrad., riza.batista@, sophia.ananiadou@}manchester.ac.uk
viktor_schlegel@asus.com

Abstract

Biomedical argument mining (BAM) aims at automatically identifying the argumentative structure in biomedical texts. However, identifying and classifying argumentative relations (AR) between argumentative components (AC) is challenging since it not only needs to understand the semantics of ACs but also need to capture the interactions between them. We argue that entities can serve as bridges that connect different ACs since entities and their mentions convey significant semantic information in biomedical argumentation. For example, it is common that related AC pairs share a common entity. Capturing such entity information can be beneficial for the Relation Identification (RI) task. In order to incorporate this entity information into BAM, we propose an Entity Coreference and Co-occurrence aware Argument Mining (ECCAM) framework based on an edge-oriented graph model for BAM. We evaluate our model on a benchmark dataset and from the experimental results we find that our method improves upon state-of-the-art methods.

1 Introduction

There is a growing interest in evidence-based decision making in the biomedical field, as it can assist medical practitioners in selecting the best treatment for a given medical case. However, extracting relevant evidence from vast amounts of biomedical publications is time-consuming for practitioners. Thus, biomedical Argument Mining (BAM), which is the application of Argument Mining (AM) to biomedical texts, is proposed to automatically extract argumentative structures in biomedical texts by identifying Argument Components (AC) and Argument Relations (AR) between ACs (Mayer et al., 2020). BAM includes three primary tasks (Si et al., 2022): (1) argument component identification (ACI)—i.e., distinguishing argumentative components from non-argumentative content; (2) argument component classification (ACC)—categorizing ACs into different types (e.g., claim, and evidence); and (3) relation identification (RI)—recognizing ARs (e.g., support, attack, or none) between a pair of ACs.

Among these tasks, the RI task is the hardest one and existing models tend to underperform on this task, compared to the ACI and ACC tasks (Mayer et al., 2020; Galassi et al., 2021; Si et al., 2022). One possible reason is that these models do not incorporate the information about the co-occurrence of common entities between different ACs. This is a valuable source of semantic information and can be particularly important in BAM. As shown in Fig 1, the AC pairs connected by an AR share entities with coreference relations. Furthermore, entity co-occurrence suggests the direction of the ARs (i.e. ACs with several entities are usually the tail of ARs, like in Figure 1).

Based on this intuition, we propose an Entity Coreference and Co-occurrence aware Argument Mining (ECCAM) framework that effectively captures ARs through entity coreference and co-occurrence. ECCAM is a graph-based model. We build a heterogeneous graph that consists of nodes that represent ACs and entities, and edges between nodes. The entity nodes can serve as bridges that connect different ACs. Considering that the entity coreference and co-occurrence relations exist between nodes and thus are represented by edge embeddings, we employ an edge-oriented graph model (Christopoulou et al., 2019) that learns edge representations of any two connected nodes by combing all paths between the two nodes. This enables information flow between different relations and iteratively updates the edge representations, which is finally used as the representations of ARs. Here, the edges between AC nodes and entity nodes are used to pass the entity coreference information while the edges between entity nodes aim to leverage entity co-occurrence information.

Proceedings of the 4th Workshop on Computational Approaches to Discourse (CODI 2023), pages 54–60
July 13-14, 2023

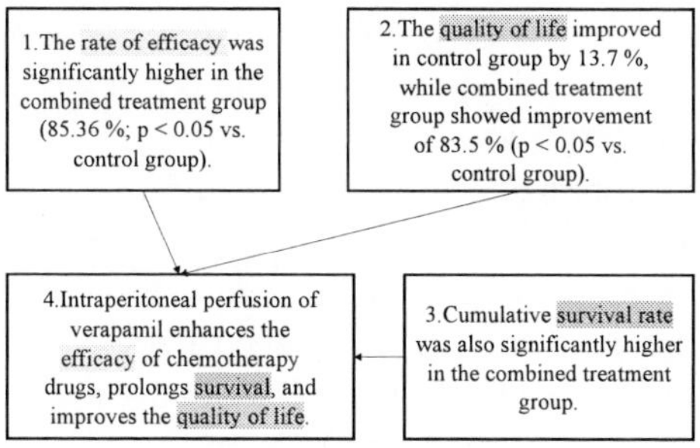

Figure 1: Part of the argument structure of the abstracts from PubMed 23589316. Each text in the rectangle represents an AC. Two ACs connected with an arrow means that there is an AR between them. Entities with the same colour are in the same coreference clusters.

Our contributions are shown below:

- To our best knowledge, this paper is the first to incorporate entity coreference and co-occurrence information into an argument mining model.
- We propose the ECCAM framework based on an edge-oriented model to leverage the entity coreference and co-occurrence information.
- Experimental results show that the entity coreference and co-occurrence information can improve the performance of the RI task significantly.

2 Related Work

Recently, the research community has shown growing interest in the task of BAM. Mayer et al. (2018) created a dataset by annotating ACs within randomized controlled trial abstracts and employ the SubSet Tree Kernel to classify the types of ACs with Bag-Of-Words of biomedical text as input. Further, a dataset with both ACs and ARs are created by Mayer et al. (2020) to deal with three tasks of BAM: ACI, ACC and RI. Various contextualized word embeddings, such as BERT (Devlin et al., 2019), BioBERT (Lee et al., 2020), SciBERT (Beltagy et al., 2019a), and RoBERTa (Liu et al., 2019) are explored to address these tasks. Liu et al. (2022) incorporate zoning information (such as background, result and conclusion) to tackle the ACI and ACC tasks at the same time. Galassi et al. (2021) employed a multi-task framework with an attentive residual network to address the ACC task, RI task, and link prediction task of BAM, based on the assumption that ACs had been detected. SeqMT (Si et al., 2022) also assumes the ACI task is solved and pays attention to the ACC and RI tasks. It utilises a multi-task learning approach to benefit from the sequential dependency between the ACC and RI tasks by transferring the representation of the input and output of the ACC task to the RI task.

However, none of the previous models leverages the entity coreference and co-occurence information for the RI task, which is the focus of this paper.

3 Model Architecture

Following previous models (Galassi et al., 2018; Si et al., 2022; Galassi et al., 2021), we assume that the outputs of the ACI task are provided, i.e., all ACs have been detected without AC types. Inspired by Christopoulou et al. (2019) who employ an edge-oriented graph model (Christopoulou et al., 2018) to leverage interactions among sentences that share the same entities for document-level relation extraction, we propose a framework for the RI task based on a similar edge-oriented model. Our framework contains three parts: the entity cluster extraction module, the document encoder module and the entity co-occurrence and coreference-aware argument mining module.

3.1 Entity Cluster Extraction Module

Since we cannot assume golden annotation of entities and their mentions, the first step of our framework is to identify all named entities in the AM dataset. One simple way is to train a model on biomedical coreference resolution datasets and use such model to predict entity clusters. However, most biomedical coreference resolution datasets concern diseases (Doğan et al., 2014; Li et al., 2015), species (Gerner et al., 2010; Pafilis et al., 2013) or proteins and genes (Wei et al., 2015; Collier and Kim, 2004). Most noteably, datasets with entity annotations related to cancer experiments, such as "quality of life" and "survival rate", are absent from the literature, while the biomedical argument mining dataset (Mayer et al., 2020) is about the cancer research. Thus, we choose another method that first predicts the entities in the AM datasets, and then disambiguates them by mapping to the Unified Medical Language System (UMLS) (Bodenreider, 2004) to obtain a unique identifier of a medical concept to obtain entity clusters.

Specifically, we use the Transformed NER model (Stylianou and Vlahavas, 2021) to obtain entities in the abstracts. This model is trained on the EMB-NLP (Nye et al., 2018) dataset and thus extracts four types of entities, namely Patient, Intervention, Comparison and Outcome (PICO). Since ACs mainly exist in sentences that describe experimental results and conclusions (Liu et al., 2022), we only use outcome entities, to avoid noise. Then, we use all the extracted entities as input of the QuickUMLS tool (Soldaini and Goharian, 2016) to obtain the corresponding UMLS identifiers (IDs). It is worth mentioning that given one mention, the QuickUMLS usually returns multiple IDs. We handle this situation as follows: when there is an exact match between the predicted entities and the given mention, we will use the ID of the exactly matched entity as the ID for the mention. If there is no exact match entity, we will reserve all the entities whose Jaccard similarity score with the given mention is higher than a specific threshold.

All entities in a document that share the same UMLS ID in a document form an entity cluster. The extracted entity clusters are denoted as $C = \{C_1, C_2, ..., C_{l_c}\}$, where $C_i = \{m_1, m_2, ..., m_l\}$, and l is total number of mentions in the i-th cluster.

3.2 Document Encoder Module

Given a document $D = \{t_1, t_2, ..., t_n\}$ consisting of n tokens as the input of our framework, a SciBERT model is employed as the encoder to generate the embeddings of tokens $X = \{x_1, x_2, ..., x_n\}$ in D.

$$X = SciBERT(D) \tag{1}$$

To leverage the entity coreference and co-occurrence information, a two-step method is proposed to generate the embeddings of all entities occurring in the document D. First, our model generates the embeddings of each mention m_i by averaging all token embeddings $\{x_{i1}, x_{i2}, ..., x_{iM}\}$ in m_i. Similarly, the embeddings of each AC n_a and each entity n_e are also an average of the tokens in the AC and entity, respectively.

3.3 Graph Construction

We initially construct a heterogeneous graph that consists of two different types of nodes (AC nodes and entity nodes) and three types of edges between the nodes. The rules for edge generation are outlined below.

AC-AC edge. If two ACs are adjacent, an edge will connect the two AC nodes. There are two situations where two ACs are adjacent. The first one is that the sequences of this two ACs are adjacent in the document. Another situation is that the words between the two ACs in the document are all non-argumentative. This type of edge is used to learn the context.

AC-Entity edge. If an AC mentions an entity at least once, there will be an edge between the entity and the related AC. This type of edge is used to learn the coreference information.

Entity-Entity edge. We connect all entity pairs so that the model can learn which co-occurrence of entity pairs is helpful for the RI task.

We use a concatenation operation to get the representation of an edge $e_{ij} = [n_i, n_j]$ given the representations of the source node n_i and the destination node n_j of the edge, where $n_i, n_j \in n_e \cup n_a$.

3.4 Entity Co-occurrence and Coreference aware Argument Mining model Module

Given the constructed graph, we employ an edge-oriented graph model (Christopoulou et al., 2018) to leverage the entity coreference and co-occurrence information. The model uses a two step method to iteratively update the edge embeddings of two nodes based on the paths between the two nodes.

First, a path between two nodes i and j is generated using intermediate nodes k. Then, the representations of two consecutive edges e_{ik} and e_{kj} are combined by a modified bilinear transformation. Through this action, an edge representation of double the length is generated. All existing paths between i and j through k are combined. The i, j, and k nodes can be either entity nodes or AC nodes. Intermediate nodes without adjacent edges to the target nodes are ignored. Formally, this is written as:

$$f(e_{ik}^{(l)}, e_{kj}^{(l)}) = \sigma(e_{ik}^{(l)} \otimes W e_{kj}^{(l)}) \tag{2}$$

where σ is the sigmoid non-linear function, W is a learned parameter matrix, $\otimes$ represents element-wise multiplication, l denotes the length of the edge and e_{ik} refers to the representation of the edge between nodes i and k.

At the second step, the original (short) edge representation and the new (longer) edge representation resulting from Equation 2 is aggregated as follows:

$$e_{ij}^{(2l)} = \beta e_{ij}^{(l)} + (1-\beta) \sum_{k \neq i,j} (e_{ik}^{(l)}, e_{kj}^{(l)}) \tag{3}$$

where $\beta \in [0, 1]$ is a scalar used to assign the weight of the shorter edge representation.

A finite number N of iterations is conducted for the two steps. The final length of path is directly proportional to the number of iterations. After N iterations, the number of edges of the longest path will be up to 2^N.

3.5 Classification Module

Finally, to classify relations between AC pairs, we incorporate a softmax classifier which takes the AC-to-AC edges e_{aa} as input:

$$y = softmax(We_{aa} + b) \tag{4}$$

where W and b are learned parameters of the classification layer. The whole model is trained end-to-end by minimising the cross-entropy loss between predicted and gold ACs.

4 Experiment

4.1 Datasets

Following Si et al. (2022), we use the AbstRCT (Mayer et al., 2020) benchmark to evaluate our model and compare it with previous approaches. The AbstRCT dataset is composed of three categories of ACs (major claim, claim, and evidence) and two kinds of ARs (support and attack). It consists of three parts, with the largest being the neoplasm corpus, which is divided into training, development, and testing sets. Moreover, there are two additional test sets. The first one solely consists of abstracts related to glaucoma, while the second one is a mixed set containing 20 abstracts for each disease in the dataset (neoplasm, glaucoma, hypertension, hepatitis, and diabetes).

	Documents	All ARs	Avg. AR
Neo_train	350	1427	4.1
Neo_dev	50	210	4.2
Neo_test	100	424	4.2
Gla_test	100	367	3.7
Mix_test	100	329	3.3

Table 1: Statistics of the AbstRCT dataset. The data statistics of the three test sets are reported separately. Here, *Neo*, *Gla* and *Mix* represent neoplasm, glaucoma and mixed, respectively.

4.2 Implementation

We use the same train-development-test split for the AbstRCT dataset as was used in Si et al. (2022). We fine-tune cased SciBERT (Beltagy et al., 2019b) and set the maximum sequence length to 256. A learning rate of $2 \cdot 10^{-5}$ is used. We train for 50 epochs with early stopping to avoid overfitting. Our model is implemented in PyTorch (Paszke et al., 2019). We employ an AdamW optimizer (Loshchilov and Hutter, 2019) for parameter optimization and report the macro-averaged F1 scores of models trained with three different random seeds.

4.3 Baselines

In order to evaluate our proposed method, we compare it with the following baselines:

ResArg (Galassi et al., 2018) is a hybrid of residual networks and long short-term memory network. This model is designed to tackle both the ACC and RI tasks simultaneously.

ResAttArg (Galassi et al., 2021) is an upgraded version of ResArg model featuring an attention module. ResArg and ResAttArg have two versions: an average version that calculates the final scores as an average of scores from 10 distinct networks trained with 10 different seeds, and an ensemble version that assigns the class based on the majority vote of the same 10 networks.

SeqMT (Si et al., 2022) utilises a multi-task learning approach to benefit from the sequential dependency between the ACC and RI tasks. It transfers the representation of the input and output of the ACC task to the RI task.

4.4 Main Results

We report the main results in Table 2. It can be observed that our model improves upon the state-of-the-art on two of three test sets even though our model is a single task model while all other baselines are multi-task/ensemble models. To be specific, our model outperforms the current best model on the neoplasm test set by 1.68% F1 score and the mixed test set by 1.11% F1 score. However, there is a gap between the performance of our model and SeqMT on the glaucoma test set. This might be due to the lack of multi-task training: compared with the results of SeqMT, the performance of the single task version model of SeqMT(SeqMT(-$\mathcal{L}_{acc}$)) similarly experiences a large drop of performance of 8.44% F1 score. Without the additional signal

models	NEO	GLA	MIX
RA(avg)	59.15	57.23	60.31
RA(Ensemble)	63.16	61.86	68.35
RAA(avg)	66.49	62.68	63.47
RAA(Ensemble)	70.92	68.40	67.66
SeqMT(-$\mathcal{L}_{acc}$)	68.58	64.83	70.30
SeqMT	71.24	**73.27**	72.71
ECCAM	**72.92**	68.96	**73.82**

Table 2: Main results of different models. The best scores are marked in bold. All the results of baselines are copied from the related papers. Here, *NEO*, *GLA* and *MIX* represent neoplasm, glaucoma and mixed.

from the ACC task, SeqMT(-$\mathcal{L}_{acc}$) performs significantly worse than our model on the glaucoma test set by 4.13% F1 score.

4.5 Ablation Study

To validate the effects of the entity coreference and entity co-occurrence information, we conduct two ablation experiments. **ECCAM(-EE)** is a model where the edges between the entities are excluded to test whether the entity co-occurrence information can improve the performance of RI. **ECCAM(-EA)** aims to reveal the impact of entity coreference information by removing both edges between entities and between entities and ACs. The results in Table 3 show the effectiveness of the entity coreference and entity co-occurrence information. Without the entity co-occurrence information, the performance of our model drops by 0.84%, 2.52% and 1.43% F1 score on the neoplasm, glaucoma and mixed test sets, respectively. The performance of **ECCAM(-EA)** decreases even more significantly—2.3%, 5.12% and 4.09% F1 score on the neoplasm, glaucoma and mixed test sets—showing the positive impact of entity coreference information.

models	NEO	GLA	MIX
ECCAM	**72.92**	**68.96**	**73.82**
ECCAM(-EE)	72.08	66.44	72.39
ECCAM(-AE)	70.62	63.84	69.73

Table 3: Ablation study of our model. **ECCAM(-EE)** is a model where the edges between the entities are excluded. **ECCAM(-EA)** removes both edges between entities and between entities and ACs. The best scores are marked in bold.

iterations	DEV	NEO	GLA	MIX
$N = 1$	60.20	65.32	53.49	66.90
$N = 2$	62.75	67.34	58.67	71.14
$N = 3$	66.04	71.84	63.37	71.80
$N = 4$	67.31	72.92	**68.96**	**73.82**
$N = 5$	**69.64**	**73.85**	66.30	68.83

Table 4: Results of hyper-parameter analysis. Here, *NEO*, *GLA* and *MIX* represent the results of on the neoplasm, glaucoma and mixed test sets, respectively. *DEV* denotes the results on the development set.

4.6 Hyper-parameter Analysis

We further test, whether number of iterations N affects the model performance on the three different test sets. We conduct experiments with $N = 1, 2, 3, 4, 5$. The results are shown in Table 4. From the results on the development set we can see that as the number of iterations increases, the performance of the model on the development set also increases. However, though our model obtains the best score on the neoplasm test set when $N = 5$, considering all three test sets, the best overall performance is achieved with four iterations. It is worth noting that the abstracts in the development set are all about neoplasm. Taking all these results into consideration, we can conclude that the more iterations the edges representations are updated, the more information is utilised from more distant nodes, with too many iterations causing overfitting.

5 Conclusion

In this paper, we propose the ECCAM model that is based on an edge-oriented graph model (Christopoulou et al., 2019) to incorporate entity coreference and co-occurrence information into BAM. We introduce edges between entity nodes and AC nodes in a heterogeneous graph to help our model capture entity coreference and co-occurrence information respectively. Experiments on the AbstRCT dataset show the effectiveness of these two types of information for the RI task. In the future, we will apply our method to other argument mining domains, such as student essays (Eger et al., 2017).

Limitations

Although our model improves upon state-of-the-art methods of BAM by incorporating entity coreference and co-occurrence information, there are still some limitations to our model. First, it is not easy to apply our model to other domains where no coreference resolution tool is available. Second, the number of nodes and edges of the generated heterogeneous graph will become enormous if the documents are long and many entities are extracted, which requires more GPU resources.

References

Iz Beltagy, Kyle Lo, and Arman Cohan. 2019a. SciBERT: A pretrained language model for scientific text. In *Proceedings of the 2019 Conference on Empirical Methods in Natural Language Processing and the 9th International Joint Conference on Natural Language Processing (EMNLP-IJCNLP)*, pages 3615–3620, Hong Kong, China. Association for Computational Linguistics.

Iz Beltagy, Kyle Lo, and Arman Cohan. 2019b. Scibert: A pretrained language model for scientific text. *arXiv preprint arXiv:1903.10676*.

Olivier Bodenreider. 2004. The unified medical language system (umls): integrating biomedical terminology. *Nucleic acids research*, 32(suppl_1):D267–D270.

Fenia Christopoulou, Makoto Miwa, and Sophia Ananiadou. 2018. A walk-based model on entity graphs for relation extraction. In *Proceedings of the 56th Annual Meeting of the Association for Computational Linguistics (Volume 2: Short Papers)*, pages 81–88, Melbourne, Australia. Association for Computational Linguistics.

Fenia Christopoulou, Makoto Miwa, and Sophia Ananiadou. 2019. Connecting the dots: Document-level neural relation extraction with edge-oriented graphs. In *Proceedings of the 2019 Conference on Empirical Methods in Natural Language Processing and the 9th International Joint Conference on Natural Language Processing (EMNLP-IJCNLP)*, pages 4925–4936, Hong Kong, China. Association for Computational Linguistics.

Nigel Collier and Jin-Dong Kim. 2004. Introduction to the bio-entity recognition task at jnlpba. In *Proceedings of the International Joint Workshop on Natural Language Processing in Biomedicine and its Applications (NLPBA/BioNLP)*, pages 73–78.

Jacob Devlin, Ming-Wei Chang, Kenton Lee, and Kristina Toutanova. 2019. BERT: Pre-training of deep bidirectional transformers for language understanding. In *Proceedings of the 2019 Conference of the North American Chapter of the Association for Computational Linguistics: Human Language Technologies, Volume 1 (Long and Short Papers)*, pages 4171–4186, Minneapolis, Minnesota. Association for Computational Linguistics.

Rezarta Islamaj Doğan, Robert Leaman, and Zhiyong Lu. 2014. Ncbi disease corpus: a resource for disease name recognition and concept normalization. *Journal of biomedical informatics*, 47:1–10.

Steffen Eger, Johannes Daxenberger, and Iryna Gurevych. 2017. Neural end-to-end learning for computational argumentation mining. In *Proceedings of the 55th Annual Meeting of the Association for Computational Linguistics (Volume 1: Long Papers)*, pages 11–22, Vancouver, Canada. Association for Computational Linguistics.

Andrea Galassi, Marco Lippi, and Paolo Torroni. 2018. Argumentative link prediction using residual networks and multi-objective learning. In *Proceedings of the 5th Workshop on Argument Mining*, pages 1–10, Brussels, Belgium. Association for Computational Linguistics.

Andrea Galassi, Marco Lippi, and Paolo Torroni. 2021. Multi-task attentive residual networks for argument mining. *arXiv preprint arXiv:2102.12227*.

Martin Gerner, Goran Nenadic, and Casey M Bergman. 2010. Linnaeus: a species name identification system for biomedical literature. *BMC bioinformatics*, 11(1):1–17.

Jinhyuk Lee, Wonjin Yoon, Sungdong Kim, Donghyeon Kim, Sunkyu Kim, Chan Ho So, and Jaewoo Kang. 2020. Biobert: a pre-trained biomedical language representation model for biomedical text mining. *Bioinformatics*, 36(4):1234–1240.

Jiao Li, Yueping Sun, R Johnson, Daniela Sciaky, Chih-Hsuan Wei, Robert Leaman, Allan Peter Davis, Carolyn J Mattingly, Thomas C Wiegers, and Zhiyong Lu. 2015. Annotating chemicals, diseases, and their interactions in biomedical literature. In *Proceedings of the fifth BioCreative challenge evaluation workshop*, pages 173–182. The Fifth BioCreative Organizing Committee.

Boyang Liu, Viktor Schlegel, Riza Batista-Navarro, and Sophia Ananiadou. 2022. Incorporating zoning information into argument mining from biomedical literature. In *Proceedings of the Thirteenth Language Resources and Evaluation Conference*, pages 6162–6169, Marseille, France. European Language Resources Association.

Yinhan Liu, Myle Ott, Naman Goyal, Jingfei Du, Mandar Joshi, Danqi Chen, Omer Levy, Mike Lewis, Luke Zettlemoyer, and Veselin Stoyanov. 2019. Roberta: A robustly optimized bert pretraining approach. *arXiv preprint arXiv:1907.11692*.

Ilya Loshchilov and Frank Hutter. 2019. Decoupled weight decay regularization. In *International Conference on Learning Representations*.

Tobias Mayer, Elena Cabrio, Marco Lippi, Paolo Torroni, Serena Villata, et al. 2018. Argument mining on clinical trials. In *COMMA*, pages 137–148.

Tobias Mayer, Elena Cabrio, and Serena Villata. 2020. Transformer-based argument mining for healthcare applications. In *ECAI 2020*, pages 2108–2115. IOS Press.

Benjamin Nye, Junyi Jessy Li, Roma Patel, Yinfei Yang, Iain Marshall, Ani Nenkova, and Byron Wallace. 2018. A corpus with multi-level annotations of patients, interventions and outcomes to support language processing for medical literature. In *Proceedings of the 56th Annual Meeting of the Association for Computational Linguistics (Volume 1: Long Papers)*, pages 197–207, Melbourne, Australia. Association for Computational Linguistics.

Evangelos Pafilis, Sune P Frankild, Lucia Fanini, Sarah Faulwetter, Christina Pavloudi, Aikaterini Vasileiadou, Christos Arvanitidis, and Lars Juhl Jensen. 2013. The species and organisms resources for fast and accurate identification of taxonomic names in text. *PloS one*, 8(6):e65390.

Adam Paszke, Sam Gross, Francisco Massa, Adam Lerer, James Bradbury, Gregory Chanan, Trevor Killeen, Zeming Lin, Natalia Gimelshein, Luca Antiga, et al. 2019. Pytorch: An imperative style, high-performance deep learning library. *Advances in neural information processing systems*, 32.

Jiasheng Si, Liu Sun, Deyu Zhou, Jie Ren, and Lin Li. 2022. Biomedical argument mining based on sequential multi-task learning. *IEEE/ACM Transactions on Computational Biology and Bioinformatics*, pages 1–1.

Luca Soldaini and Nazli Goharian. 2016. Quickumls: a fast, unsupervised approach for medical concept extraction. In *MedIR workshop, sigir*, pages 1–4.

Nikolaos Stylianou and Ioannis Vlahavas. 2021. Transformed: End-to-end transformers for evidence-based medicine and argument mining in medical literature. *Journal of Biomedical Informatics*, 117:103767.

Chih-Hsuan Wei, Hung-Yu Kao, and Zhiyong Lu. 2015. Gnormplus: an integrative approach for tagging genes, gene families, and protein domains. *BioMed research international*, 2015.

A Weakly-Supervised Learning Approach to the Identification of "Alternative Lexicalizations" in Shallow Discourse Parsing

René Knaebel
Applied Computational Linguistics
Department of Linguistics
University of Potsdam
Germany
rene.knaebel@uni-potsdam.de

Abstract

Recently, the identification of free connective phrases as signals for discourse relations has received new attention with the introduction of statistical models for their automatic extraction. The limited amount of annotations makes it still challenging to develop well-performing models. In our work, we want to overcome this limitation with semi-supervised learning from unlabeled news texts. We implement a self-supervised sequence labeling approach and filter its predictions by a second model trained to disambiguate signal candidates. With our novel model design, we report state-of-the-art results and in addition, achieve an average improvement of about 5% for both exactly and partially matched alternatively–lexicalized discourse signals due to weak supervision.

1 Introduction

Understanding the underlying structure of a text is a fundamental problem in computational linguistics. In discourse analysis, shallow discourse parsing in particular, we aim to identify individual discourse relations within a text. Thus we can gain information that helps in downstream tasks such as automatic summarization, machine translation, and document classification. The study of *connecting phrases* not only helps in understanding the way people connect their thoughts but also in the identification of discourse relations anchored by them. For our work, we use the third version of the **Penn Discourse Treebank** (PDTB) (Prasad et al., 2018) that distinguishes between **explicit** relations (signaled by a closed set of discourse connectives, e.g *because*, *and*, *if-then*, and *before*) and **alternative lexicalizations** (signaled by connecting phrases other than discourse connectives, e.g. *this means*, *for that reason*, and *it all adds up to*). In total, the PDTB contains 25878 signaled relations, most of which belong to the group of explicit relations (94%). Only 1638 connecting phrases build the group of free connective phrases, in the corpus referred to as alternative lexicalizations. While explicit relations are more commonly used to verbalize expansions and comparisons between text spans, alternative lexicalizations often point to lexically grounded causal relations. Also, they potentially contain information, e.g. the phrase *the most crucial reason for that* gives also evidence about the reason's importance, which is useful for understanding the full discourse.

In our work, we aim to overcome the problem of very limited training data available for free connective phrases and examine a weakly-supervised scenario for continuously improving a model through its own predictions. We regularize these predictions by re-ranking the extracted signals through a separate model trained to discriminate possible signal candidates into signals with or without discourse usage. Summarized, our contributions are: We (i) present a novel architecture and provide state-of-the-art results for recognizing alternative lexicalizations in the recent version of the PDTB. Further, we (ii) improve its performance of recognizing phrases by integrating unlabeled data into the training process using weak supervision.

2 Related Work

Self-supervised learning (Yarowsky, 1995), the most simple semi-supervised learning algorithm, extends its training data by adding new samples with confident predictions on different data. Self-training has been successfully applied on constituent parsing (McClosky et al., 2006) by incorporating a re-ranking strategy (Charniak and Johnson, 2005; Collins and Koo, 2005) to improve parsing results and reduce the bias of the trained model. Also, Suzuki and Isozaki (2008) improved performance on part-of-speech tagging via sequence labeling. In recent work, Nishida and Matsumoto (2022) study the empirical effectiveness of bootstrapping annotations from out-of-domain data and

Proceedings of the 4th Workshop on Computational Approaches to Discourse (CODI 2023), pages 61–69
July 13-14, 2023 ©2023 Association for Computational Linguistics

show its positive impact for BERT-based discourse dependency parsers. For candidates selection, they study criteria inspired by Steedman et al. (2003).

Chou et al. (2014) approach semi-supervised learning for named entity recognition, a similar training problem (sequence labeling) as ours. They propose an additional model for estimating confidence (self-testing) and removing samples with low scores. Braud et al. (2016) first apply semi-supervised learning to RST discourse parsing using multiple views on the data by incorporating various auxiliary tasks, such as PDTB discourse parsing. Knaebel and Stede (2020b) improved their argument extraction by jointly training three separate models so-called tri-training on additional news documents. Recently, Kobayashi et al. (2021) successfully bootstrapped RST sub-trees using a combination of simpler feature-based teachers to train a more complex neural student.

The group of alternative lexicalized relations has been rarely studied. Prasad et al. (2010) did initial work on the identification and analysis of alternative lexicalized relations in an older PDTB version. Synková et al. (2017); Rysová and Rysová (2015) distinguished two classes of alternative lexicalizations and developed a dictionary approach for more regular alternative lexicalized phrases. Most recently, Knaebel and Stede (2022) implemented the first automatic neural-based model for recognizing alternative lexicalizations on a sentence level using a binary sequence labeling approach. In this work, we build on their approach and adapt this model to the paragraph level, similar to the explicit connective model of Kurfalı (2020).

3 Method

3.1 Recognizing alternative lexicalizations

The recognition of alternative-lexicalized discourse signals (AltLex) in the PDTB corpus is challenging due to the higher complexity of the phrases when compared to explicit signals for example, and the limited number of training samples. While Knaebel and Stede (2022) predict binary labels (*is-part-of* the signal) on the sentence level, we follow Kurfalı (2020) and integrate more context into the model by training the whole model on the paragraph level. Accessing more context seems unavoidable for improving performance as discourse signals naturally link to phrases outside their sentence. We make use of pre-trained large language models and fine-tune the base model combined with an additional token classification layer on top of it.

Shifting from sentences to paragraphs results in potentially having an arbitrary number of signals. For this purpose, we use a three-class encoding similar to Kurfalı (2020): single signals, e.g. *following*, *resulting*, *not*, and *soon*, multi-word signals, e.g. *for this reason* and *in addition to*, and no signal otherwise. We limited our experiments to continuous signals, e.g. we removed phrases like *the more [...], the more*, which removes a minor number of samples but allows for decoding the labeled sequence without redundancy. We did not choose a more complex signal encoding, such as BIOS and BIOES, due to the lack of available training data and the resulting class imbalance.[1]

3.2 Learning from unlabeled data

In this work, we study self-training, which is a very basic but effective semi-supervised learning technique that uses a model's self-estimation to integrate confident predictions from unlabeled data. However, this technique has a high bias due to reinforcing its own false predictions. We overcome this problem by, first, improving the base performance of our signal extractor by building an ensemble of three separately trained models. Second, we follow the idea of McClosky et al. (2006) and introduce a separate model for confidence estimation that not only reduces the bias of a singly self-trained model but also simplifies the determination of a confidence score.

To estimate the model's confidence in its predicted alternatively–lexicalized phrases, referred to as candidates, we design an auxiliary task to disambiguate signal candidates produced by the labeling model. We want to learn to discriminate candidate phrases into those related to an AltLex or not. We adapt previous work on explicit sense classification (Knaebel and Stede, 2020a) to alternative lexicalizations and simultaneously predict whether a possible candidate phrase is used as a discourse signal and if so, we learn to predict its sense. Instead of learning only a single sense level, we jointly learn sense versus no-sense prediction on coarse and fine senses as Long and Webber (2022) suggest in their work. In a short ablation study (see Appendix A), we show that our chosen disambiguation architecture works with similar performance as a simple binary classifier.

[1]We did some initial studies with BIOS and BIOES encodings, but the performance was not satisfying.

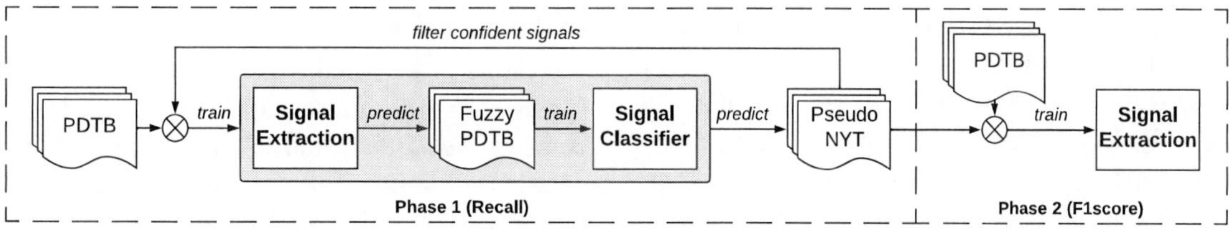

Figure 1: Overview of the learning process: Phase 1 refers to the cyclic self-supervised learning procedure (alternates between labeling and candidate discrimination). Phase 2 concludes the final training on combined data.

Our self-learning approach consists of two phases (compare Figure 1). In **Phase 1 (Recall)**, we optimize our signal labeling model (**Signal Extraction**) with respect to high recall. Therefore, we lower the weight for the **None** class, which is the dominating class label, and thus implicitly reinforce a higher focus on the other class labels. The resulting increase in the recall value simultaneously leads to a reduction in the precision value of the model. We first extract signal candidates from the PDTB which results in a fuzzy version, in order to train a second model for signal disambiguation (**Signal Classifier**). In the final step of a single iteration, we extract signals from a different corpus (here NYT see Section 4.1) and filter these signals, based on the confidence score, before we use the confident paragraph samples together with the original training data. Confident paragraphs are defined based on the individual signal confidence, such that signals are removed if the confidence is below a *relation threshold* τ_{rel} and the remaining signals' minimum is higher than a *paragraph threshold* τ_{par}. In **Phase 2 (F1Score)**, we use the finally extracted confident paragraphs and train a new model on signal extraction, but this time all class labels are equally weighted and the model is optimized for F1 score.

4 Experiments

4.1 Experimental Settings

The Unlabeled Corpus Most, but not all (Webber, 2009), documents of the PDTB are news articles. To learn about alternative lexicalizations from a different corpus, as there is relatively little annotated data currently available, we choose another news wire corpus, under the assumption of an easier adaption of a similar domain compared to other genres. *The New York Times Annotated Corpus* [2], referred to as NYT, contains about 1.8 million documents published by the New York Times between 1987 and 2007. For our work, we use a random subset of documents, 200 per month from the years 2000–2002, sampled only once before the experiments. The reduced corpus is due to computational feasibility, the years were selected randomly. We selected NYT to complement the PDTB training data because much more data is available and it has similar quality and structure of articles as in the Wallstreet Journal corpus, which is used for the PDTB. For example, we decided against the CNN/DM corpus used in a different study (Kobayashi et al., 2021) because of the largely absent paragraph structure.

Hyper-Parameter Settings For data preparation, we split 10% of documents from the PDTB corpus for testing purposes. While we use varying test splits for the general evaluation of the architecture, also to compare to previous work, we use the same test split for the evaluation of the self-supervised setting. After creating a separate test set, in each run, we split another 10% of the remaining training documents for validation. To increase the reproducibility of our experiments, we use the same validation splits for each model run, e.g. we have the same 3 and 5 splits for model ensembles and evaluations, respectively. For both types of models, signal labeling and sense classification, the batch size is 32. We train for at most 10 epochs and stop after 3 epochs without any improvement. For optimization, we chose Adam with decoupled weight decay (Loshchilov and Hutter, 2019) and an initial learning rate of 1e−4 that is reduced linearly over the maximum training epochs. As we observed overfitting with a too-small dropout rate, we set it to 0.4 for both models. For embedding paragraphs, we chose the base architecture of RoBERTa (Liu et al., 2019) that has shown good performance on several other tasks related to discourse processing (Long and Webber, 2022; Koto et al., 2021; Guz et al., 2020). We fix all but the last two layers

[2] https://doi.org/10.35111/77ba-9x74

for signal labeling. For the disambiguation model, we extract all hidden units from the model and propagate them to our classifier. As the input size of RoBERTa is limited, we truncate the tokenized paragraph. Only less than 1% of the paragraphs are affected by this truncation. For signal classification, we remove training examples where a signal occurs after the limit.

During the adaption phase, we focus on the recognition of alternative lexicalizations rather than whether predictions are correct or not, as we later train an additional model that filters wrong predictions. We identify two crucial hyper-parameters: First, we examine changing the **majority class weight** (None class) for the cross-entropy loss. Second, we study the influence of **negative samples** on the training progress. In agreement with our experiments (for details see Appendix B), we chose 0.01 for the majority class weight as the next step's small increase in recall did not justify the higher decrease in precision. Further, our results indicate that there is no advantage in reducing the number of negative samples.

For both phases, we set the relation threshold τ_{rel} to 0.33 as we measured a good balance of true and false predictions on the PDTB data. For the paragraph threshold τ_{par} we use a value of 0.7 during training, as we focus on optimizing the recognition rate (recall) of the extraction model in this phase. In the second phase, we study varying thresholds ranging from 0.4 to 0.9 for minimal paragraph relation confidence.

4.2 Experimental Results

First, we evaluate our novel architecture and compare its base performance with the initial work by Knaebel and Stede (2022). In their work, they measure the overlap within sentences containing an alternative lexicalization. We, therefore, re-run their neural labeling model and use the same evaluation metrics (exact–match) as for this paper. Results are averaged over 10 random splits and presented as mean (M) and standard deviation (SD). In our evaluation under similar conditions, the baseline (M=34.07% F1, SD=6.09) is clearly outperformed by our introduced model (M=45.48% F1, SD=5.08). We also study the performance of ensembles as used in our self-learning setting and simply combine the output probabilities of three random models. The performance further improves (M=51.68% F1, SD=3.28) and we observe a decreasing standard deviation.

Results of our final experiments are shown in Figure 2 and in more detail in Appendix D. We compare the baseline trained on the original PDTB dataset with models of varying paragraph thresholds τ_{par} (0.4 to 0.9) that incorporate data from the NYT corpus into their training data. We utilize partial matching as introduced by Xue et al. (2016), and define the matching overlap based on the F1 score of two connecting phrases. *Partial-Match* and *Exact-Match* refer to 70% and 90% F1 matching thresholds, respectively. For example, our model recognizes two of three words of the signal *greatly expanding collaboration* correctly, resulting in 0.66 recall, 1.0 precision, and thus 0.83 F1, this signal would count as partially matched but not exactly. All Experiments run on the same test set, with varying training and validation splits, 5 repetitions each. Interestingly, all models perform best at a τ_{par} of 0.6, which is in accordance with the threshold suggested by Nishida and Matsumoto (2022). Our model (M=47.38% F1, SD=1.22) with all unlabeled data and $\tau = 0.6$ improves the baseline (M=42.95% F1, SD=2.52) by more than 4% F1 score on exact match.

4.3 Analysis of Selected Cases

In this section, we would like to show some selected signal examples that we noticed while reviewing the results. First, we look at the predictions of our recall-optimized signal extraction model (without filtering predictions by our second classifier) within the PDTB training data. This model has repeatedly recognized phrases (*after*, *and*, *on the other hand*, *at the same time*, *further*, *if*, *because [of]*, among others) as alternative lexicalizations although, in terms of their surface form, they should rather belong to the group of explicit connectors. We assume some of these phrases are only partially recognized alternative phrases e.g. signals in which the referential expression is missing *after this situation* and *because of that event*. We also identify cases where individual parts of the signal belong to explicit connectives, while their conjunction is rather considered as an alternative lexicalization, e.g. *since* and *then*. Despite a large number of possible explicit signals, most of the confused signals are filtered in the second step and are therefore not considered signals at all. Interestingly, we noticed that the model identifies a few signals at the beginning of a paragraph, similar as discussed by Prasad

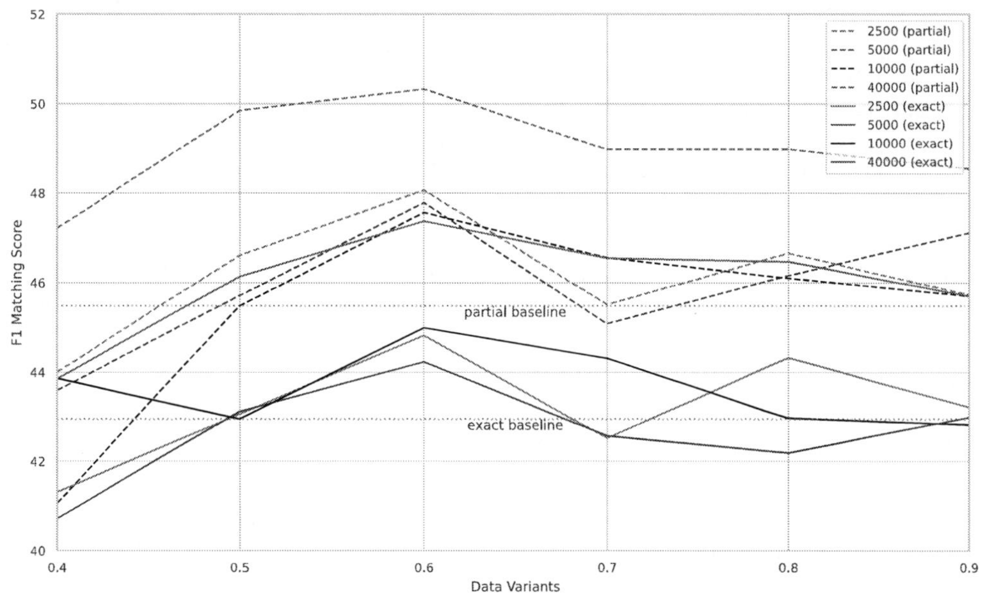

Figure 2: Final model evaluation: Comparison of baseline trained on the original dataset (horizontal dotted) and final models trained on data including NYT corpus with varying paragraph threshold τ_{par} (0.4 to 0.9) during prediction phase. All experiments run on the same test set, with varying training and validation splits, 5 repetitions. Evaluation is done using partial (dashed lines) and exact (straight lines) matching as explained in Section 4.2.

et al. (2017), that are per definition not included in the PDTB annotations, e.g. *That explains why*, *To illustrate*, *All this illustrates that*, and *What's more*. Besides different variations of gerunds, we found phrases such as *at the most*, *that may mean*, and *even that* that are likely being used as discourse signals without checking their context. The integration of the model's output in future annotation processes may be beneficial in identifying more discourse signals.

Next, we examine the predicted alternative lexicalizations in the NYT data. Here, we found quite a few change verbs, e.g. *dimishing*, *bolstering*, *stimulating*, *absorbing*, *contributing* and *negating*, that never occurred in the training data. There is about the same number (20 each) of variants of alternative lexicalizations containing the word *reason* in both data sets which have no overlap with the respective other data set, e.g. *the reason is probably that*, *the reasons for that finding*, and *that alone is reason for* where identified in NYT but not in PDTB. We further found, that our model tends to predict shorter signals (average length of 9) compared with the PDTB training dataset (average length of 13). The longest extracted signals with respect to token counts are *one reason for the cooperative ads is that*, *the overhaul was spurred in part by*, and *and that might partly explain why*.

5 Discussion and Conclusions

We developed a new paragraph-based architecture to extract alternatively–lexicalized discourse signals and presented state-of-the-art performance. Initial experiments on incorporating non-annotated data showed a further increase in performance.

Size seems to matter for this learning too, as this principle often holds for deep learning models. Although the gaps are rather small for up to 10,000 sampled documents, we think the distance for the largest set of documents is very clear. Due to time and computation constraints, we could not identify an upper performance bound yet.

We notice throughout our signal extraction experiments a confusion between alternative lexicalizations and explicit connectives. We assume the model to have problems clearly understanding their difference, as both kinds of phrases signal discourse relations. Filtering the connecting phrases as we have done seems unavoidable. Contrary to this, however, it seems worthwhile to soften the boundaries between these two categories and develop models that combine both types. This is not trivial due to the differences between both signal types (explicit signals are usually shorter recurring phrases with higher frequencies; AltLex signals tend to be longer phrases with more variance).

Limitations

Although the new architecture works well on PDTB-like structured data, we are often challenged with texts without clear paragraph structure. This would make it either necessary to pre-process texts and split sentences into semantically closed paragraphs such that our proposed model takes advantage of the surrounding context, or develop a new sentence-based model which was not successful in previous work.

Limiting the model to predict only continuous alternative lexicalizations does not highly affect results on the PDTB, but might have a more considerable impact on other text genres, e.g. speeches and debates. This would require the use of a more complex signal encoding as mentioned in Section 3.1.

Acknowledgements

This research has been supported by the German Research Foundation (DFG) with grant number 455911521, project "LARGA" in SPP "RATIO". I would like to thank Manfred Stede and Freya Hewett as well as the anonymous reviewers for their valuable feedback.

References

Chloé Braud, Barbara Plank, and Anders Søgaard. 2016. Multi-view and multi-task training of RST discourse parsers. In *Proceedings of COLING 2016, the 26th International Conference on Computational Linguistics: Technical Papers*, pages 1903–1913, Osaka, Japan. The COLING 2016 Organizing Committee.

Eugene Charniak and Mark Johnson. 2005. Coarse-to-fine n-best parsing and MaxEnt discriminative reranking. In *Proceedings of the 43rd Annual Meeting of the Association for Computational Linguistics (ACL'05)*, pages 173–180, Ann Arbor, Michigan. Association for Computational Linguistics.

Chien-Lung Chou, Chia-Hui Chang, and Shin-Yi Wu. 2014. Semi-supervised sequence labeling for named entity extraction based on tri-training: Case study on Chinese person name extraction. In *Proceedings of the Third Workshop on Semantic Web and Information Extraction*, pages 33–40, Dublin, Ireland. Association for Computational Linguistics and Dublin City University.

Michael Collins and Terry Koo. 2005. Discriminative reranking for natural language parsing. *Computational Linguistics*, 31(1):25–70.

Grigorii Guz, Patrick Huber, and Giuseppe Carenini. 2020. Unleashing the power of neural discourse parsers - a context and structure aware approach using large scale pretraining. In *Proceedings of the 28th International Conference on Computational Linguistics*, pages 3794–3805, Barcelona, Spain (Online). International Committee on Computational Linguistics.

René Knaebel and Manfred Stede. 2020a. Contextualized embeddings for connective disambiguation in shallow discourse parsing. In *Proceedings of the First Workshop on Computational Approaches to Discourse*, pages 65–75, Online. Association for Computational Linguistics.

René Knaebel and Manfred Stede. 2020b. Semi-supervised tri-training for explicit discourse argument expansion. In *Proceedings of the Twelfth Language Resources and Evaluation Conference*, pages 1103–1109, Marseille, France. European Language Resources Association.

René Knaebel and Manfred Stede. 2022. Towards identifying alternative-lexicalization signals of discourse relations. In *Proceedings of the 29th International Conference on Computational Linguistics*, pages 837–850, Gyeongju, Republic of Korea. International Committee on Computational Linguistics.

Naoki Kobayashi, Tsutomu Hirao, Hidetaka Kamigaito, Manabu Okumura, and Masaaki Nagata. 2021. Improving neural RST parsing model with silver agreement subtrees. In *Proceedings of the 2021 Conference of the North American Chapter of the Association for Computational Linguistics: Human Language Technologies*, pages 1600–1612, Online. Association for Computational Linguistics.

Fajri Koto, Jey Han Lau, and Timothy Baldwin. 2021. Discourse probing of pretrained language models. In *Proceedings of the 2021 Conference of the North American Chapter of the Association for Computational Linguistics: Human Language Technologies*, pages 3849–3864, Online. Association for Computational Linguistics.

Murathan Kurfalı. 2020. Labeling explicit discourse relations using pre-trained language models. In *Text, Speech, and Dialogue*, pages 79–86, Cham. Springer International Publishing.

Yinhan Liu, Myle Ott, Naman Goyal, Jingfei Du, Mandar Joshi, Danqi Chen, Omer Levy, Mike Lewis, Luke Zettlemoyer, and Veselin Stoyanov. 2019. Roberta: A robustly optimized BERT pretraining approach. *CoRR*, abs/1907.11692.

Wanqiu Long and Bonnie Webber. 2022. Facilitating contrastive learning of discourse relational senses by exploiting the hierarchy of sense relations. In *Proceedings of the 2022 Conference on Empirical Methods in Natural Language Processing*, pages 10704–10716, Abu Dhabi, United Arab Emirates. Association for Computational Linguistics.

Ilya Loshchilov and Frank Hutter. 2019. Decoupled weight decay regularization. In *7th International Conference on Learning Representations, ICLR 2019, New Orleans, LA, USA, May 6-9, 2019*. OpenReview.net.

David McClosky, Eugene Charniak, and Mark Johnson. 2006. Reranking and self-training for parser adaptation. In *Proceedings of the 21st International Conference on Computational Linguistics and 44th Annual Meeting of the Association for Computational Linguistics*, pages 337–344, Sydney, Australia. Association for Computational Linguistics.

Noriki Nishida and Yuji Matsumoto. 2022. Out-of-domain discourse dependency parsing via bootstrapping: An empirical analysis on its effectiveness and limitation. *Transactions of the Association for Computational Linguistics*, 10:127–144.

Rashmi Prasad, Katherine Forbes Riley, and Alan Lee. 2017. Towards full text shallow discourse relation annotation: Experiments with cross-paragraph implicit relations in the PDTB. In *Proceedings of the 18th Annual SIGdial Meeting on Discourse and Dialogue*, pages 7–16, Saarbrücken, Germany. Association for Computational Linguistics.

Rashmi Prasad, Aravind Joshi, and Bonnie Webber. 2010. Realization of discourse relations by other means: Alternative lexicalizations. In *Coling 2010: Posters*, pages 1023–1031, Beijing, China. Coling 2010 Organizing Committee.

Rashmi Prasad, Bonnie Webber, and Alan Lee. 2018. Discourse annotation in the PDTB: The next generation. In *Proceedings 14th Joint ACL - ISO Workshop on Interoperable Semantic Annotation*, pages 87–97, Santa Fe, New Mexico, USA. Association for Computational Linguistics.

Magdaléna Rysová and Kateřina Rysová. 2015. Secondary connectives in the Prague dependency treebank. In *Proceedings of the Third International Conference on Dependency Linguistics (Depling 2015)*, pages 291–299, Uppsala, Sweden. Uppsala University, Uppsala, Sweden.

Mark Steedman, Rebecca Hwa, Stephen Clark, Miles Osborne, Anoop Sarkar, Julia Hockenmaier, Paul Ruhlen, Steven Baker, and Jeremiah Crim. 2003. Example selection for bootstrapping statistical parsers. In *Proceedings of the 2003 Human Language Technology Conference of the North American Chapter of the Association for Computational Linguistics*, pages 236–243.

Jun Suzuki and Hideki Isozaki. 2008. Semi-supervised sequential labeling and segmentation using giga-word scale unlabeled data. In *Proceedings of ACL-08: HLT*, pages 665–673, Columbus, Ohio. Association for Computational Linguistics.

Pavlína Synková, Magdaléna Rysová, Lucie Poláková, and Jiří Mírovský. 2017. Extracting a lexicon of discourse connectives in Czech from an annotated corpus. In *Proceedings of the 31st Pacific Asia Conference on Language, Information and Computation*, pages 232–240. The National University (Phillippines).

Bonnie Webber. 2009. Genre distinctions for discourse in the Penn TreeBank. In *Proceedings of the Joint Conference of the 47th Annual Meeting of the ACL and the 4th International Joint Conference on Natural Language Processing of the AFNLP*, pages 674–682, Suntec, Singapore. Association for Computational Linguistics.

Nianwen Xue, Hwee Tou Ng, Sameer Pradhan, Attapol Rutherford, Bonnie Webber, Chuan Wang, and Hongmin Wang. 2016. CoNLL 2016 shared task on multilingual shallow discourse parsing. In *Proceedings of the CoNLL-16 shared task*, pages 1–19, Berlin, Germany. Association for Computational Linguistics.

David Yarowsky. 1995. Unsupervised word sense disambiguation rivaling supervised methods. In *33rd Annual Meeting of the Association for Computational Linguistics*, pages 189–196, Cambridge, Massachusetts, USA. Association for Computational Linguistics.

Model	Precision	Recall	F1
Baseline	83.54 (5.99)	59.45 (12.34)	68.84 (9.68)
Coarse	86.32 (4.83)	51.78 (9.22)	64.36 (7.82)
Binary	85.18 (4.81)	56.81 (8.80)	67.80 (6.87)

Table 1: Ablation Study for the AltLex Candidate Classifier. Results show mean and standard deviation for 10 runs each.

A Candidate Disambiguation: Ablation Study

Discourse signal disambiguation is a fundamental step in our weakly-supervised learning cycle for improving the prediction quality of our signal extraction model. We intuitively followed previous work on signal-based sense classification (Knaebel and Stede, 2020a) with the assumption of better results learning multiple sense levels at once. (Long and Webber, 2022) Our ablation study in Table 1 shows, that contrary to our assumption the baseline and a binary classifier that is limited to predicting the discourse usage of a free connective phrase have similar performances. Removing the model's fine-sense classification drastically reduces the recall of identified signals but increases precision. This holds for the binary case, too. Further investigations are necessary to identify specific differences in these classifiers.

B Hyperparameters: Loss Weight and Negative Sampling

During the adaption phase, we focus on the recognition of alternative lexicalizations rather than whether predictions are correct or not, as we later train an additional model that filters wrong predictions. Therefore, we adjust the majority class weights (None class) of the cross-entropy loss. In Table 2a, we report macro averaged results for weights ranging from 1.0 (normal weight) to 0.001 (inverse occurrence weight). As expected, the results indicate an increase in average recall with a decrease in average precision at the same time. We chose 0.01 for the majority class weight as the next step's small increase in recall did not justify the higher decrease in precision.

We also study the influence of negative samples on the training progress. The results in Table 2b indicate no advantage of reducing negative samples for training data, as already mentioned so in the paper. However, in contrast, a broader study with varying test partitions showed an increase in recall while reducing the number of negative samples.

Weight	Precision	Recall	F1
1.0	41.63 (1.81)	32.75 (2.22)	36.63 (1.88)
0.5	33.93 (1.06)	39.49 (2.46)	36.43 (0.53)
0.1	21.41 (3.35)	51.52 (1.54)	30.03 (3.23)
0.01	8.13 (0.40)	61.39 (0.37)	14.35 (0.61)
0.001	3.59 (0.77)	63.34 (1.20)	6.78 (1.38)

(a) Weighting the majority class: None. '1.0' refers to normal training while '0.001' is close to the inverse of the class occurrences. By Reducing the None class weight, errors on remaining classes are stronger penalized, and thus the model parameters are optimized for recall.

ratio	Precision	Recall	F1
0.0	39.37 (1.29)	35.68 (1.83)	37.42 (1.44)
0.2	40.96 (2.54)	33.14 (0.24)	36.60 (0.95)
0.4	35.78 (1.15)	33.63 (1.59)	34.63 (0.74)
0.6	33.20 (1.89)	32.55 (1.33)	32.87 (1.61)
0.8	25.65 (1.51)	35.19 (1.50)	29.66 (1.43)
1.0	13.02 (0.40)	32.45 (4.37)	18.48 (0.36)

(b) Down-sampling paragraphs without alternative lexicalizations as a performance factor, range from no sampling at all to remove all negative samples.

Table 2: Experiments on hyper-parameter settings for optimizing recall during the first training phase.

τ	2500	5000	10000	40000
0.4	1973	3883	7751	123595
0.5	1423	2816	5690	90016
0.6	572	1110	2256	37472
0.7	308	605	1205	19805
0.8	148	282	607	10216
0.9	46	91	200	3495

Table 3: Number of training samples extracted from additional pseudo labeled corpus, per corpus sample size and per relation paragraph threshold.

C Numbers of Extracted Paragraphs

Table 3 summarizes the number of training samples that were extracted from a given corpus sample (limited by the number of documents) and a corresponding relation paragraph threshold that needs to be satisfied for positive training samples.

D Full Final Results

Table 4 summarizes our final experiments' results in full detail. Partial-Match and Exact-Match refer to 70% and 90% overlap, respectively. In contrast to the evaluation with previous work, for this evaluation, we split test data only once at the very beginning and stay with it throughout the evaluation. Results are averaged over different validation splits, though.

Model	Partial-Match			Exact-Match		
	Precision	Recall	F1	Precision	Recall	F1
Base	41.08 (4.95)	51.78 (3.58)	45.48 (2.26)	38.82 (5.10)	48.84 (2.90)	42.95 (2.52)
0.4	36.50 (1.50)	55.50 (1.74)	44.00 (0.90)	34.28 (1.62)	52.09 (1.24)	41.31 (0.98)
0.5	38.72 (3.44)	59.22 (3.01)	46.61 (1.50)	35.76 (3.01)	54.73 (3.05)	43.06 (1.29)
0.6	43.02 (1.49)	54.73 (3.27)	48.07 (0.77)	40.12 (1.84)	51.01 (3.00)	44.82 (1.18)
0.7	40.70 (5.78)	53.02 (4.48)	45.51 (1.86)	38.09 (6.12)	49.46 (3.51)	42.52 (2.36)
0.8	42.20 (2.87)	52.40 (2.23)	46.66 (1.67)	40.09 (2.79)	49.77 (1.79)	44.32 (1.52)
0.9	40.41 (3.33)	53.18 (3.49)	45.73 (1.83)	38.20 (3.51)	50.23 (3.19)	43.22 (2.06)

(a) NYT corpus (2500 documents).

Model	Partial-Match			Exact-Match		
	Precision	Recall	F1	Precision	Recall	F1
Base	41.08 (4.95)	51.78 (3.58)	45.48 (2.26)	38.82 (5.10)	48.84 (2.90)	42.95 (2.52)
0.4	34.97 (1.85)	58.29 (3.58)	43.59 (0.79)	32.69 (2.23)	54.42 (3.19)	40.72 (1.51)
0.5	38.45 (2.06)	56.74 (3.71)	45.71 (1.11)	36.29 (2.22)	53.49 (2.73)	43.12 (1.00)
0.6	40.51 (1.38)	58.29 (3.08)	47.79 (1.89)	37.49 (1.15)	53.95 (2.76)	44.23 (1.62)
0.7	38.78 (3.43)	54.57 (4.06)	45.08 (1.68)	36.66 (3.66)	51.47 (3.12)	42.57 (1.92)
0.8	39.58 (1.82)	55.50 (1.74)	46.16 (1.09)	36.19 (2.24)	50.70 (1.26)	42.19 (1.59)
0.9	42.54 (3.72)	53.64 (4.29)	47.12 (0.67)	38.77 (3.01)	48.99 (4.64)	42.99 (0.72)

(b) NYT corpus (5000 documents).

Model	Partial-Match			Exact-Match		
	Precision	Recall	F1	Precision	Recall	F1
Base	41.08 (4.95)	51.78 (3.58)	45.48 (2.26)	38.82 (5.10)	48.84 (2.90)	42.95 (2.52)
0.4	32.27 (1.87)	56.90 (3.42)	41.06 (0.82)	34.47 (2.06)	60.78 (3.56)	43.86 (0.90)
0.5	41.08 (4.95)	51.78 (3.58)	45.48 (2.26)	38.82 (5.10)	48.84 (2.90)	42.95 (2.52)
0.6	41.26 (2.75)	56.43 (2.75)	47.57 (1.99)	39.03 (3.03)	53.33 (2.37)	44.99 (2.24)
0.7	40.75 (1.83)	54.42 (2.57)	46.56 (1.51)	38.79 (1.80)	51.78 (2.05)	44.31 (1.31)
0.8	41.42 (3.25)	52.40 (2.48)	46.10 (1.23)	38.61 (3.10)	48.84 (2.25)	42.97 (1.32)
0.9	40.24 (3.44)	53.18 (2.11)	45.70 (2.21)	37.74 (4.16)	49.77 (2.37)	42.82 (3.11)

(c) NYT corpus (10000 documents).

Model	Partial-Match			Exact-Match		
	Precision	Recall	F1	Precision	Recall	F1
Base	41.08 (4.95)	51.78 (3.58)	45.48 (2.26)	38.82 (5.10)	48.84 (2.90)	42.95 (2.52)
0.4	38.29 (1.94)	**62.02** (4.33)	47.22 (1.42)	35.58 (2.18)	**57.52** (2.75)	43.85 (0.98)
0.5	42.51 (1.30)	60.31 (1.42)	49.85 (0.99)	39.35 (1.62)	55.81 (1.77)	46.14 (1.49)
0.6	44.13 (2.17)	58.60 (1.60)	**50.33** (1.80)	41.54 (1.53)	55.19 (1.42)	**47.38** (1.22)
0.7	43.68 (1.96)	55.81 (0.49)	48.98 (1.17)	41.52 (2.49)	53.02 (1.05)	46.55 (1.87)
0.8	**44.60** (3.03)	54.42 (1.14)	48.98 (2.05)	**42.32** (3.09)	51.63 (1.67)	46.47 (2.30)
0.9	43.54 (3.95)	55.19 (1.24)	48.55 (2.14)	41.00 (4.01)	51.94 (1.47)	45.70 (2.46)

(d) NYT corpus (40000 documents).

Table 4: Full results, partial and exact matching, of final model with varying paragraph threshold (0.4 to 0.9) trained on data including NYT corpus. All experiments run on the same test set, with varying training and validation splits, results are averaged over 5 repetitions.

Entity-based SpanCopy for Abstractive Summarization to Improve the Factual Consistency

Wen Xiao and Giuseppe Carenini
Department of Computer Science
University of British Columbia
Vancouver, BC, Canada, V6T 1Z4
{xiaowen3, carenini}@cs.ubc.ca

Abstract

Discourse-aware techniques, including entity-aware approaches, play a crucial role in summarization. In this paper, we propose an entity-based SpanCopy mechanism to tackle the entity-level factual inconsistency problem in abstractive summarization, i.e. reducing the mismatched entities between the generated summaries and the source documents. Complemented by a Global Relevance component to identify summary-worthy entities, our approach demonstrates improved factual consistency while preserving saliency on four summarization datasets, contributing to the effective application of discourse-aware methods summarization tasks. [1]

1 Introduction

Discourse-aware models play a crucial role in natural language processing applications, including machine translation (Guzmán et al., 2014) and text summarization (Xu et al., 2020). Among these applications, abstractive text summarization, the task of generating informative and fluent summaries of the given document(s), has attracted much attention in the NLP community. While early neural approaches focused more on designing customized architectures or training schema (Nallapati et al., 2016; Tan et al., 2017; Liu* et al., 2018), recent works have shown that both pre-trained generation models fine-tuned on in-domain datasets and zero-shot GPT-like decoder-only models generally have better performance (Lewis et al., 2020; Zhang et al., 2020; Raffel et al., 2020; Goyal et al., 2022).

However, even with state-of-the-art performance on standard automatic evaluation metrics such as ROUGE (Lin, 2004) and BERTScore (Zhang* et al., 2020), the generated summaries still suffer from the problem of factual inconsistency, which means the generated summaries may not be factually consistent with the content expressed in the source documents (Kryscinski et al., 2020; Bubeck et al., 2023). Inconsistencies may exist either at the entity, where summaries mention entities absent from source documents, or at the relation level, where summaries express relations between entities that differ from the source (Nan et al., 2021).

Entities in Source Doc: Royal Marine, Falklands, Portsmouth, Falklands War Memorial....
Ground Truth: Plans to move a statue depicting a Royal Marine in the Falklands conflict away from Portsmouth seafront have been criticised.
PEGASUS: A campaign has been launched to keep a statue of a Falklands War marine in Hampshire.
SpanCopy: A campaign to keep a statue of a Royal Marine marching across the Falklands in Portsmouth has been launched.
SpanCopy + GR: A statue of a Royal Marine marching across the Falklands during the Falklands War Memorial should remain in its current location, campaigners have said.

Table 1: An example of entity-level factual inconsistency from the XSum dataset. The summary generated by PEGASUS totally missed one entity (Royal Marine) and one entity indicates a larger area than the correct one (Hampshire).

In this paper, we focus on the entity-level inconsistency problem, i.e. to make the model generate summaries with less entities which do not appear in the source document(s) i.e., 'hallucinated' entities. Note however, that hallucinated entities are not necessarily 'unfaithful' or 'wrong' (Cao et al., 2021), so the goal is to reduce them without excluding entities that do appear in the reference summary i.e., without penalizing saliency. Table 1 shows an

[1]The code is available at https://github.com/Wendy-Xiao/Entity-based-SpanCopy

Proceedings of the 4th Workshop on Computational Approaches to Discourse (CODI 2023), pages 70–81
July 13-14, 2023 ©2023 Association for Computational Linguistics

example of entity-level factual inconsistency from the XSum dataset. Although the content of the summary generated by the SOTA summarizer PEGASUS (Zhang et al., 2020) is roughly similar that of the ground-truth summary, it does not accurately summarize the original documents with the *proper entities*. Specifically, the entity 'Hampshire' is 'hallucinated', as it does not appear in the source document. Despite the fact that the city 'Portsmouth' is located in 'Hampshire' county, the entity itself is still an instance of factual inconsistency (i.e., an unnecessary generalization).

Prior work (Dong et al., 2020; King et al., 2022) mainly address the entity-level inconsistency problem in the post-processing stage. However, those methods either requires additional sophisticated models, e.g. Dong et al. (2020) uses a pre-trained QA model to 'revise' the generated summaries, or being built on arguably brittle heuristics (King et al., 2022). Recent work (Nan et al., 2021) proposes two ways to directly improve the end-to-end summarization model, either by training with an auxiliary task, which is to recognize the summary-worthy entities in the source document using the hidden states from the encoder, or jointly generating the entities and the summaries, i.e. generating a chain of entities in the summary followed by the summary. The latter one is in-line with recently proposed entity-aware guided summarization methods (He et al., 2020; Narayan et al., 2021). Yet, both methods do not explicitly encourage the model to generate the summaries with more valuable entities, as both of them aim to guide the model to detect the summary-worthy entities without any changes in the summary generation process. Instead, aiming for a lean and modular solution, we propose the discourse-aware SpanCopy Mechanism to explicitly copy the matched entities[2] from the source documents when generating the summaries. One key advantage of our proposal is that it can be easily integrated into any pre-trained generative sequence-to-sequence model.

Since often only a few of the entities in the source documents can be included in the summary, which we call 'summary-worthy entities', we also explore an additional Global Relevance component to better recognize the summary-worthy entities by automatically generating a prior distribution over all the entities in the source documents.

We test our proposal on four summarization datasets in the news and scientific paper domain, comparing it with the established SOTA PEGASUS system (Zhang et al., 2020). In a first set of experiments, as a sanity check, we assess our models on arguably easier subsets of these datasets, where all the entities in the reference summaries belong to the source document. In these cases, SpanCopy should definitely dominate PEGASUS, which is confirmed by the results. In a second set of experiments, we fine-tune and test on the full datasets. On this realistic and more challenging task, we find that SpanCopy (without Global Relevance) can strongly improve the entity-level factual consistency ($+2.28$) on average across datasets, with essentially no change in saliency (-0.06).

2 Related Work

2.1 Abstractive Summarization

Early neural abstractive summarization models (Nallapati et al., 2016; Paulus et al., 2018; See et al., 2017) are mainly sequence-to-sequence models based on different variants of RNN, e.g. LSTM or GRU, with additional components targeting different properties of the summaries, like redundancy (Tan et al., 2017) and coverage (See et al., 2017). However, all the recurrent models suffer from serious weakness like long-term memory loss, and requiring excessive time to train.

To tackle these problems, researchers in the area of abstractive summarization started to use attention-based transformer models (Liu and Lapata, 2019a,b); recently reaching SOTA performance when pre-trained generative transformers are applied to the task, e.g. BART (Lewis et al., 2020), PEGASUS (Zhang et al., 2020) and PRIMERA (Xiao et al., 2022). The SpanCopy mechanism we propose in this paper can be advantageously injected into any pre-trained models.

2.2 Factual Consistency

Despite the large improvements with respect to automatic evaluation metrics, recent studies (Cao et al., 2018; Kryscinski et al., 2020) show that around 30% of the summaries generated by the SOTA summarization models contain factual inconsistencies. Ideally, the assessment of factual consistency should rely on human annotations (Maynez et al., 2020), but these are costly, time consuming and lack a unified standard. Thus promising automatic evaluation metrics for factual consisten-

[2]We particularly focus on the Named Entities in this paper, but our method can be easily applied to any kind of spans or entities.

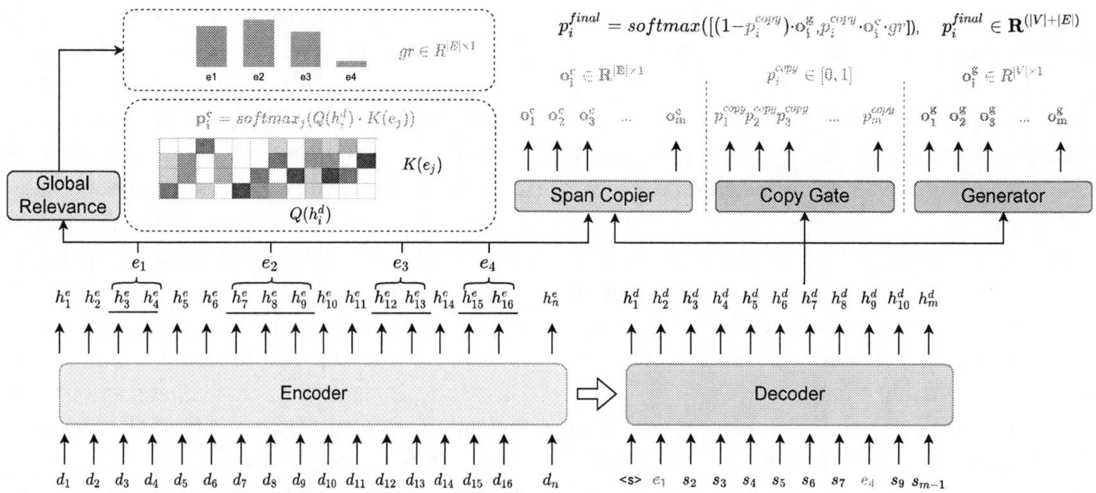

Figure 1: Structure of the model with Entity-based SpanCopy Mechanism, with five components: Encoder, Decoder, Span Copier, Copy Gate and Generator. The upper left bar plot shows the Global Relevance component, predicting the prior probability of all the entities $\{e_1, e_2, e_3, e_4\}$ to be copied to the summary.

cies of generated summaries have been explored in recent years. To assess relation-level factual consistency two kinds of metrics have been proposed: one based on classification (Kryscinski et al., 2020), and one based on Question-Answering (Maynez et al., 2020; Durmus et al., 2020). For entity-level factual consistency, the focus of this paper, Nan et al. (2021) propose a simple but effective evaluation metric, based on the matched named entities in both generated and ground-truth summaries. In our work, we use such metric to evaluate whether the generated summaries are consistent with both the source documents and the reference summaries at the entity-level.

2.3 Entity-aware Summarization

The use of entities as part of discourse-aware approaches has been shown to improve both saliency and factual consistency for the summarization task. Xiao et al. (2022) identify salient entities within document clusters and utilize them to select pseudo summaries during the pre-training phase, leading to superior performance on multiple datasets. Entities have also been employed in guided summarization, where researchers extract oracle entities from ground-truth summaries and use them to guide summary generation. For instance, Dou et al. (2021) introduce an additional encoder to encode guidance signals, sharing partial parameters with the original document encoder. In related research, He et al. (2020) propose a pre-training strategy that prepends source documents with oracle keywords as prefixes, and Narayan et al. (2021) train models to first predict an entity chain before generating the final summary. Diverging from prefix-based strategies, our approach enables the model to learn explicit copying of entities to specific positions in the generated summary, further advancing discourse-aware summarization techniques.

2.4 Copy Mechanism

See et al. (2017) first apply pointer-generator network in an abstractive summarization model, which facilitates copying words from the source documents by pointing, i.e., generating a distribution of probabilities to copy each word from the source. Following their work, Bi et al. (2020) propose PALM, in which the copy mechanism is applied on top of the transformer model, and with a novel pre-training schema, the model achieves SOTA on several generative tasks, such as abstractive summarization and generative QA. More recently, Li et al. (2021) further explores how to make use of the copy history to predict the copy distribution for the current step. However, all the aforementioned works focus on copying at the word level, which tends to be sparse and noisy. Instead, we aim to train the model to copy spans of text i.e., the named entities, in this paper.

Admittedly, some previous work has also investigated span-based copy mechanisms. Yet, those models either predict the start and end indices of a span (Zhou et al., 2018), or predict the BIO labels for each token (Liu et al., 2021). Even if such strategies can copy any kinds of spans (clauses, n-grams, entities, phrases or longest common sequence) from the source document, they may introduce unnecessary noise and break the coherence of the generated text. In this work, we focus on copying the spans of the Named Entities, extracted by a high-quality NER tool, aiming to improve factual consistency of the generated summary without negatively affecting saliency.

3 Our SpanCopy Method

3.1 Transformer-based Summarizers

Typically, transformer-based summarization(Lewis et al., 2020; Zhang et al., 2020) consists of two steps (i) The **Encoding Step** (by the Encoder shown in yellow in Fig.1), which encodes the source input(s) into an hidden space; (ii) the **Decoding Step**, which computes a probability distributions on the output vocabulary to generate each token of the resulting summary. In this paper, to better describe our methods in the context of a generic summarization models, we split the Decoding process into two components, the Decoder itself (shown in green in Fig.1), which outputs the representations of predicted tokens, and the Generator (shown in purple in Fig.1), an MLP layer mapping the representations to the final probability distribution on the output vocabulary.

More formally, for a document with n tokens $D = \{t_1^d, t_2^d, ..., t_n^d\}$, and the corresponding summary with m tokens, $S = \{t_1^s, t_2^s, ..., t_m^s\}$, the output of the Encoder is a sequence of hidden states of all the tokens, i.e. $\{h_1^e, h_2^e, ..., h_n^e\}$. And then the Decoder predicts a sequence of vector, $\{h_1^d, h_2^d, ..., h_m^d\}$, representing the tokens to be predicted. Finally, the Generator maps those vectors to the distributions over the vocabulary, i.e. $\{\mathbf{p}_1, \mathbf{p}_2, ..., \mathbf{p}_m\}$, where $\mathbf{p}_i \in R^{|V|}$.

There has been recent research on models with a decoder-only structure for summarization (Goyal et al., 2022), where the decoder is responsible for both the encoding and decoding steps. In this approach, the tokens in the source documents are represented using the output of the decoder, rather than relying on the encoder. Our proposed method specifically applies to the decoder, making it compatible with both encoder-decoder models and decoder-only models. However, in this paper, we primarily focus on exploring the application of our method to encoder-decoder models, while leaving the investigation of decoder-only models for future research.

3.2 SpanCopy Mechanism

A key problem with generic sequence-to-sequence transformer-based summarizers is that the decoding step is prone to generate factual inconsistencies, i.e. the model may make up entities or relations that are not entailed by the source documents. To address entity-level factual inconsistency, we introduce in the Decoding Step the SpanCopy mechanism, which can be conveniently plugged into any pre-trained models. Specifically, we first identify and match the entities in both source document and summary, and then instead of generating the entire summary word by word, we add an additional Span Copier to directly copy entities from the source document, with a Copy Gate predicting the likelihood of whether the model should generate the current token from the vocabulary or directly copy an entity from the source document.

Span Copier (shown in blue in Fig.1) is an attention module over all the entities in the input document. Suppose there are $|E|$ entities in the input document, with each entity j being a span over tokens $[d_{j_s}, d_{j_e}]$, then the entities can be simply represented as $e_j = \mathbf{avg}([h_{j_s}^e : h_{j_e}^e])$, where h_i^e represents the output of the encoder for each token d_i. At each decoding step i, we compute the logit vector of copying each entity at the current step as:

$$\mathbf{o_i^c} = Q(h_i^d) \cdot K(e_j), \mathbf{o_i^c} \in \mathbf{R}^{|E|} \quad (1)$$

indicating how likely it is to copy the entities from the source document at each step. Notice that to better balance the numeric difference caused by the size of selection space ($|V|$ and $|E|$), we generate and combine the raw logit vectors[3] from the Span Copier and Generator, and take softmax over the combined space to get the final probability.

Copy Gate (shown in red in Fig.1) is a classifier to map the hidden states to a singular value, i.e.

$$p_i^{copy} = \sigma(MLP(h_i^d)), p_i^{copy} \in [0, 1] \quad (2)$$

which indicates the probability of copying an entity at each step. On the contrary, $1 - p_i^{copy}$ represent the probability of generating a token from the vocabulary at step i.

[3]The vector of raw (non-normalized) predictions that the classification model generates

Then the final probability, combining both generation over the vocabulary and the copy mechanism over the entity space, is computed as

$$\mathbf{p_i^{final}} = softmax([(1 - p_i^{copy}) \cdot \mathbf{o_i^g}, p_i^{copy} \cdot \mathbf{o_i^c}]) \quad (3)$$

with $\mathbf{p_i^{final}} \in \mathbf{R}^{(|V|+|E|)}$, where $\mathbf{o_i^g} \in \mathbf{R}^{(|V|)}$ is the logit vector of token generation and $\mathbf{o_i^c} \in \mathbf{R}^{(|E|)}$ is the logit vector of entity copying. As a result, the first $|V|$ dimensions of the final probability represent the probability of generating all the tokens from the vocabulary, while the following $|E|$ dimensions contain the probabilities of copying the entities from the source document.

Note that the input of the original Decoder in the transformer model at each step is the embedding of the previous token (which is the ground-truth one during training, and the predicted one for inference), but a span of text longer than 1 does not naturally have an embedding to match. We simply use the average of the embedding of all the tokens in the entity, following previous work using average embedding to represent a span of text (Xiao and Carenini, 2019).

3.3 Loss

We use the standard loss for abstractive summarization, i.e. the cross entropy loss between the predicted probability and the ground truth labels,

$$L_1 = \sum_i L_s(\mathbf{p_i^{final}}, t_i) \quad (4)$$

However, notice that, since the predicted probability distribution is over the combined space of vocabulary size and entity size ($\mathbf{p_i^{final}} \in \mathbf{R}^{|V|+|E|}$), the corresponding ground truth labels can be either indices of words to be generated from the vocabulary, or the indices of entities to be copied from the source document, i.e. $t_i \in [0, |V| + |E|]$. Specifically, if $t_i < |V|$, then the t_i-th token should be generated, and if $t_i > |V|$, the $(t_i - |V|)$-th entity should be copied from the source document.

3.4 SpanCopy with Global Relevance

Among all the entities in the source documents, there are only a few summary-worthy entities that should be copied into the summary (e.g. around 10% in CNNDM and 1.5% in arXiv). To make the model better recognize such summary-worthy entities, we explore a Global Relevance (GR) component, which takes all the entities in the source document as inputs, and predicts how likely each entity is to appear in the final summary. We use the generated 'entity likelihood' as a prior distribution for the Span Copier component, with GR also trained as an auxiliary task.

Global Relevance is a classifier mapping the hidden state of a source document entity into a value within $[0, 1]$, indicating the probability that such entity should be included in the summary.

$$\mathbf{gr} = \sigma(MLP(\mathbf{e})), \mathbf{gr} \in \mathbf{R}^{|E|} \quad (5)$$

Then p_i^{final} in Eq.3 is updated with gr as

$$\mathbf{p_i^{final}} = softmax([(1 - p_i^{copy}) \cdot \mathbf{o_i^g}, p_i^{copy} \cdot \mathbf{o_i^c} \cdot \mathbf{gr}]) \quad (6)$$

New Loss As an auxiliary task, we also train the model with the ground-truth GR labels to make it more accurate. Specifically, the label $y_i^{gr} = 1$ if the i-th entity in the input document is included in the ground truth summary. Then we update the loss function with L_{gr} balanced by β:

$$\begin{aligned} L_2 =& (1 - \beta) \sum_i L_s(\mathbf{p_i^{final}}, t_i) \\ &+ \beta \sum_j L_{gr}(gr_j, y_j^{gr}) \end{aligned} \quad (7)$$

4 Experiments and Analysis

4.1 Settings

SpanCopy can be plugged into any pre-trained generation model. In this paper, we use PEGASUS(Zhang et al., 2020) as our base model, since it has delivered top performance on multiple summarization datasets. We recognize named entities with an off-the-shelf NER tool[4]. The balance factor β of GR is set by grid search on small subsets of each dataset (2k for training and 200 for validation).

4.2 Evaluation Metrics

To evaluate the saliency and entity-level factual consistency of the generated summaries, we apply the following metrics:

Saliency metrics assess the similarity of the generated summary with the reference summary.

ROUGE scores (Lin, 2004) measure the n-gram overlaps between generated and ground truth summaries. We apply the metrics R-1, R-2 and R-L.

Summary-precision, -recall and -f1 (sum_p, sum_r and sum_f) (Nan et al., 2021) measure the

[4]https://spacy.io/

Dataset	Original					Filtered				
	L_{doc}	L_{summ}	N_{doc}	N_{summ}	$src_p(gt)$	L_{doc}	L_{summ}	N_{doc}	N_{summ}	$src_p(gt)$
CNNDM	690.9	52.0	42.8	5.9	80.41	671.9	47.1	39.4	4.4	100
XSum	373.8	21.1	27.9	2.7	39.85	483.4	20.6	31.6	1.9	100
Pubmed	3049.0	202.4	71.1	6.4	70.93	3165.4	178.5	69.9	3.4	100
arXiv	6033.3	271.5	157.5	6.0	39.12	6478.9	164.1	161.9	2.3	100

Table 2: Statistics of all the datasets (original/filtered), on the lengths (L_{doc},L_{summ}) and number of entities (N_{doc}, N_{summ}) in the source documents and ground truth summaries, as well as $src_p(gt)$, the entity level source-precision of the ground-truth summary.

precision/recall/f1 score of the matched entities in the generated summaries and the reference summaries. we use $NE(S_{ref})$ and $NE(S_{gen})$ to represent the named entities in the reference summaries and generated summaries, respectively.

$$
\begin{aligned}
sum_p &= |NE(S_{ref}) \cap NE(S_{gen})|/|NE(S_{gen})| \\
sum_r &= |NE(S_{ref}) \cap NE(S_{gen})|/|NE(S_{ref})| \\
sum_f &= 2 * (sum_p + sum_r)/sum_p * sum_r
\end{aligned}
$$

These three metrics measure the entity-level saliency of the generated summaries, i.e. recognizing how many copied (and generated) entities are salient, and should be included in the summary.

Entity-level factual consistency metric: measures the named entity matching between the generated summaries and the source documents. (Nan et al., 2021) With $NE(D)$ and $NE(S_{gen})$ representing the named entities in the source document and generated summaries, respectively, *Source-precision*(src_p) measures how many entities in the generated summaries are from the source documents, i.e. $src_p = |NE(D) \cap NE(S_{gen})|/|NE(S_{gen})|$. It is an evaluation metric for entity-level factual consistency, as it directly measures how consistent the generated summaries are with the source.

4.3 Datasets

We test and compare our SpanCopy model with the original PEGASUS on four datasets, in the domains of news (CNNDM(Nallapati et al., 2016), XSum(Narayan et al., 2018)) and scientific papers (Pubmed and arXiv(Cohan et al., 2018)). As a sanity check, we initially assess our models on subsets of these datasets, where all the entities in the reference summaries belong to the source document (we call these filtered datasets). In these cases ($src_p(gt) = 1$), Span Copy and GR should dominate PEGASUS, because by design they tend to generate entities from the source document. [5]

The statistics of the filtered and original datasets, on the lengths and number of entities in the document and summaries, can be found in Table 2. $src_p(gt)$ measures the entity-level factual consistency between the source document and the ground-truth summary, with lower value meaning that there are more novel entities in the ground-truth summaries. The table shows that the datasets in the news domain have higher density of the entities with respect to the lengths (number of words) of both documents and ground-truth summaries, i.e. N_{doc}/L_{doc} and N_{summ}/L_{summ} are larger for the news articles. a possible explanation is that news articles tend to describe an event or a story, which may contain more names of people, organizations, locations, etc., as well as dates. Interestingly, CNNDM and Pubmed contain less novel than the other two datasets (with higher $src_p(gt)$), something that the proposed SpanCopy mechanism may benefit from. Comparing the filtered datasets with the original ones, we can see that the number of entities in the summaries drops for all the datasets, especially for arXiv, as the more entities in the summary, the less likely they can be all matched to the source documents.

4.4 Results and Analysis

The results on the filtered and original datasets are shown in Table 3 and Table 4.

Filtered Datasets We first evaluate our models, with the backbone model, PEGASUS on the filtered datasets, which is an easier task, and the results can be found in Table 3. All the models are fine-tuned and tested on the filtered datasets. Since we only keep the examples with all the entities in the summaries being matched with the entities in the source documents, the theoretical ceiling of

[5]Statistics of the (filtered/original) datasets can be found in Appendix.B

Model	ROUGE R-1	ROUGE R-2	ROUGE R-L	Entity(Summ) sum_r	Entity(Summ) sum_p	Entity(Summ) sum_f	Entity(Doc) src_p
CNNDM Filtered							
PEGASUS	44.70	22.23	32.52	50.80	45.32	45.03	92.85
SpanCopy	45.46	23.12	33.48	53.08	48.63	47.86	94.64
SpanCopy+GR	45.74	23.44	33.67	54.61	48.27	48.36	95.02
XSum Filtered							
PEGASUS	43.01	19.00	34.01	59.14	54.94	54.68	77.32
SpanCopy	44.23	19.90	35.50	61.34	59.15	58.16	84.30
SpanCopy+GR	43.78	19.12	34.97	60.69	60.50	58.36	83.75
Pubmed Filtered							
PEGASUS	46.99	21.46	42.57	42.63	33.28	33.16	73.59
SpanCopy	47.82	22.34	43.43	41.58	34.12	33.44	73.74
SpanCopy+GR	48.04	22.18	43.56	42.11	36.21	34.86	74.15
arXiv Filtered							
PEGASUS	46.23	18.02	41.02	37.65	35.98	33.48	68.13
SpanCopy	46.36	18.29	41.23	39.50	37.61	34.95	72.12
SpanCopy+GR	46.56	18.27	41.34	35.38	36.11	32.76	67.56

Table 3: Result of our models and the compared backbone model (PEGASUS) on the filtered datasets. ROUGE score and Entity(Summ) are mainly used to measure the word-level saliency and entity-level saliency, respectively. Entity(Doc) is used to measure the entity-level factual consistency. Red represents the lowest among all the three models, while Green represents the highest.

Model	ROUGE R-1	ROUGE R-2	ROUGE R-L	Entity(Summ) sum_r	Entity(Summ) sum_p	Entity(Summ) sum_f	Entity(Doc) src_p
CNNDM							
PEGASUS	44.62	20.82	31.05	46.87	42.25	42.29	89.92
SpanCopy	44.19	20.86	31.19	43.15	43.87	41.25	91.89
SpanCopy+GR	44.16	20.61	30.97	42.72	43.34	40.79	91.31
XSum							
PEGASUS	46.65	23.47	38.67	41.09	44.43	40.96	41.23
SpanCopy	46.23	22.76	37.96	39.90	42.97	39.70	41.89
SpanCopy+GR	46.02	22.36	37.58	40.12	42.66	39.67	42.79
Pubmed							
PEGASUS	46.11	19.43	41.22	22.12	24.81	20.61	67.03
SpanCopy	46.21	19.86	41.51	23.47	25.10	21.29	68.91
SpanCopy+GR	46.27	19.82	41.59	23.34	25.29	21.39	66.91
arXiv							
PEGASUS	44.23	16.55	39.15	20.98	25.42	20.56	52.70
SpanCopy	44.05	16.76	38.91	20.65	25.46	20.39	56.88
SpanCopy+GR	44.00	16.87	38.92	20.01	25.75	20.15	54.21

Table 4: Result of our models and the compared backbone model (PEGASUS) on the unfiltered datasets. See Table 3 for the details of the columns.

src_p is 100. Comparing SpanCopy and PEGASUS, SpanCopy performs better than PEGASUS regarding both saliency and entity-level factual consistency. Plausibly, this is because all the entities in the ground-truth summary can be copied from the source document, in which case the SpanCopy mechanism can better learn to copy. The SpanCopy model with the GR component performs better regarding the entity-level saliency on three out of all the four datasets. On arXiv, the performance of SpanCopy with the GR component regarding both entity-level saliency and factual consistency is quite low. One likely reason might be that it is a rather difficult task to identify the salient entities in the arxiv dataset, as there is a large amount of entities in the source documents, but only very

Model	R_{avg}	sum_f	src_p
CNNDM			
SpanCopy	-0.08	-1.04	+1.97
SpanCopy+GR	-0.25	-1.50	+1.39
XSum			
SpanCopy	-0.61	-1.26	+0.66
SpanCopy+GR	-0.94	-1.29	+2.16
Pubmed			
SpanCopy	+0.27	+0.68	+1.88
SpanCopy+GR	+0.31	+0.78	-0.12
arXiv			
SpanCopy	+0.20	+1.47	+3.99
SpanCopy+GR	+0.30	-0.72	-0.57
Overall (avg. across all datasets)			
SpanCopy	-0.06	-0.04	+2.13
SpanCopy+GR	-0.15	-0.68	+0.72

Table 5: The relative ROUGE score (avg of R-1, R-2 and R-L), the entity-level summary-f1 and source-precision of our models, compared with the PEGASUS model on the four datasets (original). The last block shows the overall performance for all the datasets.

few entities are summary-worthy (164.1 v.s. 2.3 as shown in Table 2), which might bring in excessive noise.

Original Datasets In a second set of experiments, we fine-tune and test on the full/original datasets. On this realistic and more challenging task results are encouraging. As shown in Table 4, when the SpanCopy model is compared to PEGASUS, it improves the factual consistency of generated summaries with the source documents (src_p) on all the datasets, maintaining a very similar performance on the saliency metrics, i.e. ROUGE and entity-level saliency. Comparing across the four datasets, SpanCopy outperforms PEGASUS on both the saliency and factual consistency metrics on the Pubmed dataset. For better comparison, we show the relative gains/loss regarding PEGASUS on all the datasets, as well as the overall average results in Table 5. It is clear that the SpanCopy model performs much better regarding entity-level factual consistency ($+2.13$) with essentially no change in saliency (-0.06 on average ROUGE and -0.04 on entity-level saliency). Admittedly, despite the success of the GR component on the filtered datasets on both word-level and entity-level saliency, it fails to deliver any gain on the original datasets. A plausible explanation is that GR makes the model focus excessively on the entities in the source document, therefore penalizing generation of new, potentially summary-worthy, entities.

Comparing the entity-level factual consistency on the filtered datasets and the original datasets, the filtered datasets always have higher src_p than the original ones, and the gain is especially larger on the XSum and arXiv datasets, as both of them contain more entity-level hallucinations in the original datasets. Remarkably, the performance gain of the SpanCopy model over PEGASUS on the filtered XSum dataset is much larger on the original XSum datasets (7.98 v.s. 0.66) , which might be because original XSum is more abstractive, the entity-level guidance is especially helpful for the abstractive examples with consistent entities in the summary.

4.5 Qualitative Analysis

For illustration, we examine a real example from the CNNDM dataset in Table 6, which is a news article on the evacuation of Americans during the time of the crossfire of warring parties in Yemen. While all of the three system generated summaries are able to capture the main statement that 'it's too dangerous to evacuate the Americans', the person 'Ivan Watson' mentioned by PEGASUS's summary does not exist in the source document, i.e., it is an 'hallucinated' entity. Most likely, PEGASUS is generating such hallucination because 'Ivan Watson' is a senior CNN correspondent several time associated with Yemen in other news article in the training set, and the model automatically 'picked the entity from the memory' to generate the summary without tightly adhering to the given document. In contrast, both of our models do not contain entities that are not in the source document, as the SpanCopy mechanism tend to guide the model to use more the entities in the source document. In addition, with the GR component, although the generated summary contains more matched entities with the source document, it pushes the model too far towards copying entities which are not salient (e.g. *The State Department*).

5 Conclusion and Future Work

In this paper, we tackle the problem of entity-level factual consistency for abstractive summarization through a discourse-aware approach, by guiding the model to directly copy the summary-worthy entities from the source document, through the novel SpanCopy mechanism (with the optional GR component). This mechanism can be integrated into

Entities in the Source Document: Yemen(0.28), Americans(0.25), Saudi Arabia(0.23), the State Department(0.23), CNN(0.20),..., U.S.(0.15), ...
Ground-truth Summary: No official way out for Americans stranded amid fighting in Yemen. U.S. Deputy Chief of Mission says situation is very dangerous so no mass evacuation is planned .
PEGASUS: CNN's Ivan Watson joins a mother and her grandchildren waiting to be evacuated from Yemen. The State Department has said it is too risky to evacuate Americans from the area. Watson meets Americans who were on a CNN ship that docked at a Yemeni port.
SpanCopy: Dozens of Americans are trapped in Yemen. The U.S. has said it is too dangerous to evacuate Americans.
SpanCopy+GR: The U.S. has said it is too dangerous to evacuate Americans from Yemen. The State Department said it is too risky to conduct an evacuation of citizens. A group of U.S. organizations have filed a lawsuit against the government's stance on evacuations.

Table 6: Example of the entity-level factual inconsistency, taken from the CNNDM dataset. The first block shows the entities in the source document with high GR scores (shown in parenthesis) from the SpanCopy + GR model.

any transformer-based generative frameworks, contributing to the advancement of discourse-aware neural summarization.

To validate the effectiveness of our approach, we conducted experiments on four diverse summarization datasets, including a sanity check on arguably easier subsets. The results confirmed that SpanCopy with GR performs better on both entity-level factual consistency and saliency. Notably, experiments on the original test sets demonstrated that the SpanCopy mechanism can effectively improve entity-level factual consistency while maintaining word-level and token-level saliency.

Despite the recent success of GPT-like decoder-only systems on the summarization task (Goyal et al., 2022), they still appear to suffer from hallucinations and inconsistencies in the generated text (Bubeck et al., 2023). As mentioned in Section 3, our method can be easily extended to the decoder-only models, we intend to investigate how the mechanism works with the models for addressing these limitations.

More long term, we plan to extend our discourse-aware approach towards controllable generation with given entities. Specifically, instead of using the learned GR scores, the model could generate summaries with desired entities provided by human users.

Limitation

In our method, we employ an existing NER tool (Spacy) to label the entities in both the source documents and the summaries, and the performance of the NER tool may have an influence on the results of the model. Thus a good in-domain NER tool may be required when the work is extended to some specific domains, e.g. medical text.

In addition, we use PEGASUS(Zhang et al., 2020) as our base model in all the experiments on different datasets, as it has delivered top performance on multiple summarization datasets. We follow the original paper on the length limits of all the datasets, however, the length of the source documents in both scientific paper datasets are much longer than the length limit (3k/6k v.s. 1024), which leaves the room for further improvement with sparse attention techniques applied (Xiao et al., 2022; Guo et al., 2022).

Ethics Consideration

Although we tackle the problem of factual inconsistency for abstractive summarization, and improve the entity-level factual consistency of the generated summaries by applying the entity-level span copy mechanism, the generated summaries still contain unfactual information. Therefore, caution must be exercised when the model is deployed in practical settings.

Acknowledgement

This research was supported by the Language & Speech Innovation Lab of Cloud BU, Huawei Technologies Co., Ltd.

References

Bin Bi, Chenliang Li, Chen Wu, Ming Yan, Wei Wang, Songfang Huang, Fei Huang, and Luo Si. 2020. PALM: Pre-training an autoencoding&autoregressive language model for context-conditioned generation. In *Proceedings of the 2020 Conference on Empirical Methods in Natural Language Processing (EMNLP)*, pages 8681–8691, Online. Association for Computational Linguistics.

Sébastien Bubeck, Varun Chandrasekaran, Ronen Eldan, Johannes Gehrke, Eric Horvitz, Ece Kamar, Peter Lee, Yin Tat Lee, Yuanzhi Li, Scott Lundberg, Harsha Nori, Hamid Palangi, Marco Tulio Ribeiro, and Yi Zhang. 2023. Sparks of artificial general intelligence: Early experiments with gpt-4.

Meng Cao, Yue Dong, and Jackie Chi Kit Cheung. 2021. Inspecting the factuality of hallucinated entities in abstractive summarization. *CoRR*, abs/2109.09784.

Ziqiang Cao, Furu Wei, Wenjie Li, and Sujian Li. 2018. Faithful to the original: Fact aware neural abstractive summarization. *Proceedings of the AAAI Conference on Artificial Intelligence*, 32(1).

Arman Cohan, Franck Dernoncourt, Doo Soon Kim, Trung Bui, Seokhwan Kim, Walter Chang, and Nazli Goharian. 2018. A discourse-aware attention model for abstractive summarization of long documents. In *Proceedings of the 2018 Conference of the North American Chapter of the Association for Computational Linguistics: Human Language Technologies, Volume 2 (Short Papers)*, pages 615–621, New Orleans, Louisiana. Association for Computational Linguistics.

Yue Dong, Shuohang Wang, Zhe Gan, Yu Cheng, Jackie Chi Kit Cheung, and Jingjing Liu. 2020. Multi-fact correction in abstractive text summarization. In *Proceedings of the 2020 Conference on Empirical Methods in Natural Language Processing (EMNLP)*, pages 9320–9331, Online. Association for Computational Linguistics.

Zi-Yi Dou, Pengfei Liu, Hiroaki Hayashi, Zhengbao Jiang, and Graham Neubig. 2021. GSum: A general framework for guided neural abstractive summarization. In *Proceedings of the 2021 Conference of the North American Chapter of the Association for Computational Linguistics: Human Language Technologies*, pages 4830–4842, Online. Association for Computational Linguistics.

Esin Durmus, He He, and Mona Diab. 2020. FEQA: A question answering evaluation framework for faithfulness assessment in abstractive summarization. In *Proceedings of the 58th Annual Meeting of the Association for Computational Linguistics*, pages 5055–5070, Online. Association for Computational Linguistics.

Tanya Goyal, Junyi Jessy Li, and Greg Durrett. 2022. News summarization and evaluation in the era of gpt-3.

Mandy Guo, Joshua Ainslie, David Uthus, Santiago Ontanon, Jianmo Ni, Yun-Hsuan Sung, and Yinfei Yang. 2022. LongT5: Efficient text-to-text transformer for long sequences. In *Findings of the Association for Computational Linguistics: NAACL 2022*, pages 724–736, Seattle, United States. Association for Computational Linguistics.

Francisco Guzmán, Shafiq Joty, Lluís Màrquez, and Preslav Nakov. 2014. Using discourse structure improves machine translation evaluation. In *Proceedings of the 52nd Annual Meeting of the Association for Computational Linguistics (Volume 1: Long Papers)*, pages 687–698, Baltimore, Maryland. Association for Computational Linguistics.

Junxian He, Wojciech Kryscinski, Bryan McCann, Nazneen Fatema Rajani, and Caiming Xiong. 2020. Ctrlsum: Towards generic controllable text summarization. *CoRR*, abs/2012.04281.

Daniel King, Zejiang Shen, Nishant Subramani, Daniel S. Weld, Iz Beltagy, and Doug Downey. 2022. Don't say what you don't know: Improving the consistency of abstractive summarization by constraining beam search.

Wojciech Kryscinski, Bryan McCann, Caiming Xiong, and Richard Socher. 2020. Evaluating the factual consistency of abstractive text summarization. In *Proceedings of the 2020 Conference on Empirical Methods in Natural Language Processing (EMNLP)*, pages 9332–9346, Online. Association for Computational Linguistics.

Mike Lewis, Yinhan Liu, Naman Goyal, Marjan Ghazvininejad, Abdelrahman Mohamed, Omer Levy, Veselin Stoyanov, and Luke Zettlemoyer. 2020. BART: Denoising sequence-to-sequence pre-training for natural language generation, translation, and comprehension. In *Proceedings of the 58th Annual Meeting of the Association for Computational Linguistics*, pages 7871–7880, Online. Association for Computational Linguistics.

Haoran Li, Song Xu, Peng Yuan, Yujia Wang, Youzheng Wu, Xiaodong He, and Bowen Zhou. 2021. Learn to copy from the copying history: Correlational copy network for abstractive summarization. In *Proceedings of the 2021 Conference on Empirical Methods in Natural Language Processing*, pages 4091–4101, Online and Punta Cana, Dominican Republic. Association for Computational Linguistics.

Chin-Yew Lin. 2004. ROUGE: A package for automatic evaluation of summaries. In *Text Summarization Branches Out*, pages 74–81, Barcelona, Spain. Association for Computational Linguistics.

Peter J. Liu*, Mohammad Saleh*, Etienne Pot, Ben Goodrich, Ryan Sepassi, Lukasz Kaiser, and Noam Shazeer. 2018. Generating wikipedia by summarizing long sequences. In *International Conference on Learning Representations*.

Yang Liu and Mirella Lapata. 2019a. Hierarchical transformers for multi-document summarization. In *Proceedings of the 57th Annual Meeting of the Association for Computational Linguistics*, pages 5070–5081, Florence, Italy. Association for Computational Linguistics.

Yang Liu and Mirella Lapata. 2019b. Text summarization with pretrained encoders. In *Proceedings of the 2019 Conference on Empirical Methods in Natural Language Processing and the 9th International Joint Conference on Natural Language Processing (EMNLP-IJCNLP)*, pages 3730–3740, Hong Kong, China. Association for Computational Linguistics.

Yi Liu, Guoan Zhang, Puning Yu, Jianlin Su, and Shengfeng Pan. 2021. BioCopy: A plug-and-play span copy mechanism in Seq2Seq models. In *Proceedings of the Second Workshop on Simple and Efficient Natural Language Processing*, pages 53–57, Virtual. Association for Computational Linguistics.

Joshua Maynez, Shashi Narayan, Bernd Bohnet, and Ryan McDonald. 2020. On faithfulness and factuality in abstractive summarization. In *Proceedings of the 58th Annual Meeting of the Association for Computational Linguistics*, pages 1906–1919, Online. Association for Computational Linguistics.

Ramesh Nallapati, Bowen Zhou, Cicero dos Santos, Çağlar Gulçehre, and Bing Xiang. 2016. Abstractive text summarization using sequence-to-sequence RNNs and beyond. In *Proceedings of The 20th SIGNLL Conference on Computational Natural Language Learning*, pages 280–290, Berlin, Germany. Association for Computational Linguistics.

Feng Nan, Ramesh Nallapati, Zhiguo Wang, Cicero Nogueira dos Santos, Henghui Zhu, Dejiao Zhang, Kathleen McKeown, and Bing Xiang. 2021. Entity-level factual consistency of abstractive text summarization. In *Proceedings of the 16th Conference of the European Chapter of the Association for Computational Linguistics: Main Volume*, pages 2727–2733, Online. Association for Computational Linguistics.

Shashi Narayan, Shay B. Cohen, and Mirella Lapata. 2018. Don't give me the details, just the summary! topic-aware convolutional neural networks for extreme summarization. In *Proceedings of the 2018 Conference on Empirical Methods in Natural Language Processing*, pages 1797–1807, Brussels, Belgium. Association for Computational Linguistics.

Shashi Narayan, Yao Zhao, Joshua Maynez, Gonçalo Simões, Vitaly Nikolaev, and Ryan McDonald. 2021. Planning with learned entity prompts for abstractive summarization. *Transactions of the Association for Computational Linguistics*, 9:1475–1492.

Romain Paulus, Caiming Xiong, and Richard Socher. 2018. A deep reinforced model for abstractive summarization. In *International Conference on Learning Representations*.

Colin Raffel, Noam Shazeer, Adam Roberts, Katherine Lee, Sharan Narang, Michael Matena, Yanqi Zhou, Wei Li, and Peter J. Liu. 2020. Exploring the limits of transfer learning with a unified text-to-text transformer. *Journal of Machine Learning Research*, 21(140):1–67.

Abigail See, Peter J. Liu, and Christopher D. Manning. 2017. Get to the point: Summarization with pointer-generator networks. In *Proceedings of the 55th Annual Meeting of the Association for Computational Linguistics (Volume 1: Long Papers)*, pages 1073–1083, Vancouver, Canada. Association for Computational Linguistics.

Jiwei Tan, Xiaojun Wan, and Jianguo Xiao. 2017. Abstractive document summarization with a graph-based attentional neural model. In *Proceedings of the 55th Annual Meeting of the Association for Computational Linguistics (Volume 1: Long Papers)*, pages 1171–1181, Vancouver, Canada. Association for Computational Linguistics.

Wen Xiao, Iz Beltagy, Giuseppe Carenini, and Arman Cohan. 2022. PRIMERA: Pyramid-based masked sentence pre-training for multi-document summarization. In *Proceedings of the 60th Annual Meeting of the Association for Computational Linguistics (Volume 1: Long Papers)*, pages 5245–5263, Dublin, Ireland. Association for Computational Linguistics.

Wen Xiao and Giuseppe Carenini. 2019. Extractive summarization of long documents by combining global and local context. In *Proceedings of the 2019 Conference on Empirical Methods in Natural Language Processing and the 9th International Joint Conference on Natural Language Processing (EMNLP-IJCNLP)*, pages 3011–3021, Hong Kong, China. Association for Computational Linguistics.

Jiacheng Xu, Zhe Gan, Yu Cheng, and Jingjing Liu. 2020. Discourse-aware neural extractive text summarization. In *Proceedings of the 58th Annual Meeting of the Association for Computational Linguistics*, pages 5021–5031, Online. Association for Computational Linguistics.

Jingqing Zhang, Yao Zhao, Mohammad Saleh, and Peter J. Liu. 2020. Pegasus: Pre-training with extracted gap-sentences for abstractive summarization. In *Proceedings of the 37th International Conference on Machine Learning*, ICML'20. JMLR.org.

Tianyi Zhang*, Varsha Kishore*, Felix Wu*, Kilian Q. Weinberger, and Yoav Artzi. 2020. Bertscore: Evaluating text generation with bert. In *International Conference on Learning Representations*.

Qingyu Zhou, Nan Yang, Furu Wei, and Ming Zhou. 2018. Sequential copying networks. *Proceedings of the AAAI Conference on Artificial Intelligence*, 32(1).

A Model and Training Details

We use PEGASUS as our backbone model, which contains 571M parameters, and the span copy mechanism has 2M additional parameters. We train the fine-tuned models from the huggingface model hub[6] for 100k steps (16 data per step) with early stopping based on the ROUGE scores on the validation set, which takes around 24 hours with single V100 GPU.

B Datasets

We compare the size of filtered and original datsets in Table 7.

Dataset	# Data (original)	# Data (filtered)
CNNDM	287,113/13,368/13,368	105,847/4,490/3,903
XSum	204,017/11,327/11,333	42,481/2,349/2,412
Pubmed	119,924/6,633/6,658	32,123/1,797/1,772
arXiv	202,914/6,436/6,440	66,360/2,365/2,324

Table 7: Number of data examples in all the datasets (original v.s. filtered).

C Software and Licenses

Our code is licensed under Apache License 2.0. Our framework dependencies are:

- HuggingFace Datasets[7], Apache 2.0
- NLTK [8], Apache 2.0
- Numpy[9], BSD 3-Clause "New" or "Revised"
- Spacy[10], MIT
- Transformers[11], Apache 2.0
- Pytorch[12], Misc
- Pytorch Lightning [13],Apache 2.0
- ROUGE [14], Apache 2.0

[6] https://huggingface.co/models
[7] https://github.com/huggingface/datasets/blob/master/LICENSE
[8] https://github.com/nltk/nltk
[9] https://github.com/numpy/numpy/blob/main/LICENSE.txt
[10] https://github.com/explosion/spaCy/blob/master/LICENSE
[11] https://github.com/huggingface/transformers/blob/master/LICENSE
[12] https://github.com/pytorch/pytorch/blob/master/LICENSE
[13] https://github.com/PyTorchLightning/pytorch-lightning/blob/master/LICENSE
[14] https://github.com/google-research/google-research/tree/master/rouge

Discourse Information for Document-Level Temporal Dependency Parsing

Jingcheng Niu[123], **Victoria Ng**[2], **Erin E. Rees**[2], **Simon de Montigny**[24], **Gerald Penn**[13]
{niu,gpenn}@cs.toronto.edu {victoria.ng,erin.rees}@phac-aspc.gc.ca
simon.de.montigny@umontreal.ca
University of Toronto[1], Public Health Agency of Canada[2], Vector Institute[3], University of Montreal[4]

Abstract

In this study, we examine the benefits of incorporating discourse information into document-level temporal dependency parsing. Specifically, we evaluate the effectiveness of integrating both high-level discourse profiling information, which describes the discourse function of sentences, and surface-level sentence position information into temporal dependency graph (TDG) parsing. Unexpectedly, our results suggest that simple sentence position information, particularly when encoded using our novel sentence-position embedding method, performs the best, perhaps because it does not rely on noisy model-generated feature inputs. Our proposed system surpasses the current state-of-the-art TDG parsing systems in performance.

Furthermore, we aim to broaden the discussion on the relationship between temporal dependency parsing and discourse analysis, given the substantial similarities shared between the two tasks. We argue that discourse analysis results should not be merely regarded as an additional input feature for temporal dependency parsing. Instead, adopting advanced discourse analysis techniques and research insights can lead to more effective and comprehensive approaches to temporal information extraction tasks.

1 Introduction

Temporal Information Extraction (TIE) is the task of modelling the relative and/or absolute temporal relations between all the temporal nodes in an article. A temporal node can be either an event or a time expression (timex). TIE is a core component task of text comprehension. Despite its importance, TIE remains one of the lowest performing natural language understanding tasks. It is a difficult task, and the challenge is further compounded when expanding it to the document level, as the number of temporal relations scales quadratically with the number of temporal nodes, and the requisite amount of reasoning must incorporate longer spans of text.

To address these challenges, Kolomiyets et al. (2012); Zhang and Xue (2018b); Yao et al. (2020) proposed the use of temporal dependency structures to represent the overall temporal relational structure within an article. This approach is based on the phenomenon of *temporal anaphora*, where the interpretation of the occurring time of one temporal node depends on knowing the occurring time of another temporal node. By modelling these temporal dependency relations, the overall temporal structure of an article can be obtained without the need for exhaustively labelling every pair of temporal nodes.

As a result, temporal dependency parsing not only models the temporal relations between events but also captures narrative and discourse structure. There are striking similarities between temporal dependency structures and the constituency discourse tree structures (Guz and Carenini, 2020) used for discourse parsing in the context of Rhetorical Structure Theory (RST; Mann and Thompson, 1988), and not just in their use of trees or graphs. More importantly, temporal dependency relations can be viewed as a specific type of anaphoric relation that discourse analysis models attempt to capture. This observation suggests a potential connection between dependency parsing and discourse analysis, warranting further investigation into their relationship and potential synergies.

This connection between document-level temporal structure and discourse structure was corroborated by Choubey and Huang (2022), who discovered that incorporating discourse profiling (DP) information, specifically the functional role of each sentence, could enhance the overall performance of temporal dependency graph parsing (TDG; Yao et al., 2020). Their evaluation may not have been sufficiently comprehensive, however. TDG parsing encompasses three distinct types of relation parsing:

Proceedings of the 4th Workshop on Computational Approaches to Discourse (CODI 2023), pages 82–88
July 13-14, 2023 ©2023 Association for Computational Linguistics

timex to timex (t2t), event to timex (e2t), and event to event (e2e), each requiring a different prediction mechanism. Upon a more detailed reexamination of Choubey and Huang's (2022) findings, DP information in fact does not consistently improve performance across all three relation types; it reliably enhances e2e, but may lead to a decline in performance for the other two.

We believe this is caused by two major limitations of Choubey and Huang's (2022) approach. First, DP is a hard problem in its own right. The state-of-the-art DP system (Choubey and Huang, 2021) only yields a 59.21% F1 performance. This means TIE systems following Choubey and Huang's (2022) guidance will only have access to noisy and inaccurate DP features. Second, sentence function is a relatively high-level, descriptive type of discourse structure. Temporal dependency structure, on the other hand, can also benefit from a lot of simple surface-level discourse information, such as precedence (Zhang and Xue, 2018a).

To address these issues, we have experimented with incorporating surface-level sentence-position information into a TIE system, and in two ways: encoding absolute sentence-position by appending the sentence number directly onto the context sentences, following Choubey and Huang (2022), and proposing a novel Sentence Position Embedding (SPE) using a sinusoid. Our experiments demonstrate that SPE could significantly enhance temporal dependency graph parsing performance across all relation types, with the performance increase being mostly greater or at least comparable to that provided by DP information. The resulting TDG parsing system[1] with SPE obtains the state-of-the art performance.

2 Temporal Dependency Parsing

TIE is the task of classifying the temporal relation between two temporal nodes. A temporal node can be either an event trigger (a.k.a. event mention) that represents an event that exists in the narrative of an article, or a timex that is a nominal description of a date or time. When treating a pair of temporal nodes as either intervals or points on the timeline, the temporal relation between temporal nodes can be described by Allen's (1983) temporal calculus. There are some variations between different TIE annotation standards, but generally

[1]The code and data are publicly available online: https://github.com/frankniujc/tdg-discourse.

"A 26 years [sic] old woman died early this week. She fell roughly 30m down the Bergisel mountain in Tyrol on Friday. Remaining conscious after the fall, she had alerted her family via telephone who in turn contacted emergency services."

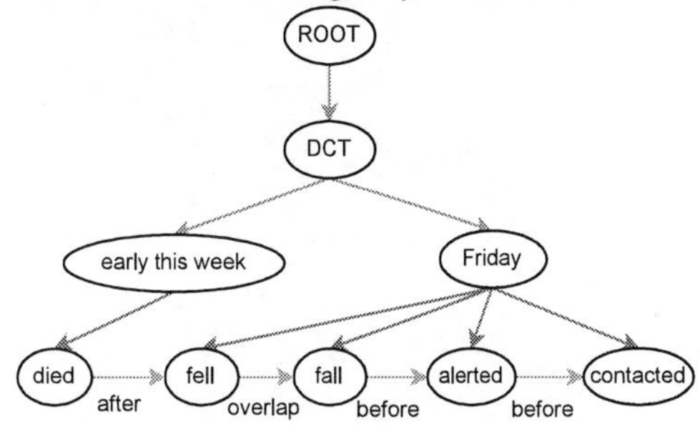

Figure 1: An example of a TDG from (Yao et al., 2020). In the example text (upper), event triggers are highlighted in green and timexes are highlighted in orange. In the TDG (lower), different types of dependency relations have different edge colours (t2t, e2t and e2e). Each arrow points from the parent node to the child node.

	Docs	Timex	Event	t2t	e2t	e2e
Train	400	1,952	12,047	2,352	15,369	8,725
Dev	50	325	1,717	375	2,136	1,298
Test	50	209	1,015	259	1,324	706
Total	500	2,486	14,779	2,986	18,829	10,729

Table 1: TDG corpus statistics.

speaking, temporal relations include links such as BEFORE, AFTER and OVERLAP.

This pairwise annotation scheme, however, fails to generalize to the document level. The number of temporal node pairs is quadratic in the number of temporal nodes (n), i.e., $\binom{n}{2} \in O(n^2)$. Yao et al. (2020) pointed out that this quadratic increase, together with the increase in the complexity and number of vague relation links for annotators to consider will, in practice, inevitably cause errors to annotation.

To address this issue, Kolomiyets et al. (2012); Zhang and Xue (2018b); Yao et al. (2020) have advocated for using dependency structures to represent document-level temporal relations. Kolomiyets et al. (2012) annotated a children's story with temporal dependency trees. Each event u only depends on one other event v iff the interpretation of when u occurred requires knowing when v occurred. Kolomiyets et al.'s (2012) temporal dependency tree structure only includes events, but this standard may yield disconnected structures. Zhang and Xue (2018b) refined temporal dependency tree structure to allow the inclusion of timex

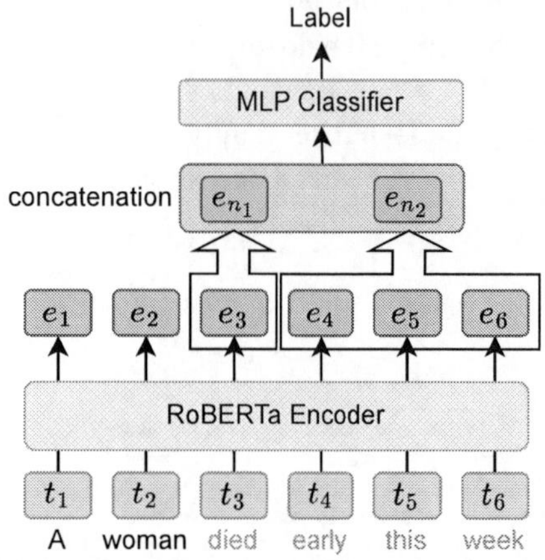

Figure 2: An overview of the pairwise classification model architecture.

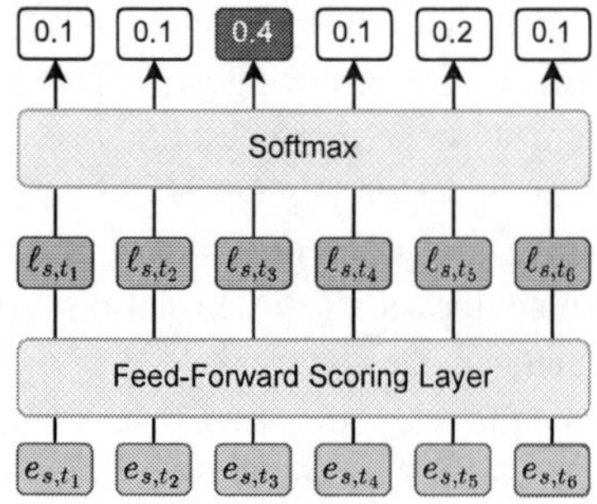

Figure 3: An overview of the joint ranking model architecture. Given a temporal node s in the article, the model predicts a scalar reference score for every candidate node ($t_1, \ldots, t_6$). This reference score can be considered as classification logits and later trained using the cross-entropy loss.

vertices as well as two special vertices: a document creation time (DCT) vertex and a ROOT vertex. The inclusion of timex vertices allows for capturing the missing events in timex (e2t) temporal dependencies and timex to timex (t2t) temporal dependencies. The addition of the DCT and ROOT vertices ensures each document is always parsed into a valid TDT.

Both Kolomiyets et al. (2012) and Zhang and Xue (2018b) assumed that each event or timex had exactly one reference temporal node (to which the dependency edge points), resulting in a tree structure. Yao et al. (2020), on the other hand, argued that this assumption is overly stringent, and that it is possible for an event to have both a reference timex and an reference event. They therefore proposed to characterise temporal structure with temporal dependency graphs (TDG), in which each event can have a timex parent, an event parent, or both. As depicted in Figure 1, the event *alerted* depends on both the timex *Friday* and the event *fall*. As a result, TDG is more expressive than the earlier TDTs. In this work, we used the TDG corpus released by Yao et al. (2020). Table 1 shows the statistics of this corpus.[2]

3 Model Architectures

3.1 Pairwise Classification Model

Typically, TIE is formulated as a classification task. Given a pair of temporal nodes (n_1, n_2), the sentences containing the nodes $([t_{11}, \ldots, t_{1m}], [t_{21}, \ldots, t_{2n}])$ are encoded into a context vector $\mathbf{e} = [e_{11}, \ldots, e_{1m}, e_{21}, \ldots, e_{2n}]$. Next, the event embedding pair $[e_{n_1}; e_{n_2}]$ are concatenated and the classification task is performed using a multilayer perceptron (MLP) layer. Where a temporal node spans multiple tokens, we utilize Lee et al.'s (2017) method for obtaining an attentive span representation. Figure 2 depicts an overview of this architecture. In this model, we deliberately avoid jointly learning the pairwise model to observe the effects of different discourse information on various relation types.

3.2 Joint Ranking Model

Neural ranking models (Zhang and Xue, 2018a; Ross et al., 2020; Choubey and Huang, 2022) formulate the task as a regression problem. For each temporal node, the model predicts a scalar reference score for every potential parent node and selects the edge with the highest reference score. Therefore, this edge selection process can be formulated as a classification task — the reference scores can be considered as classification logits, and the cross-entropy loss of the edge prediction can be calculated. The three relation types (t2t, e2t, and e2e) are trained jointly. Unlike the pairwise model that uses the concatenation of the two event embeddings, we follow Choubey and Huang (2022), who enclose both triggers in special symbols ($\$n_1\$$ and $\#n_2\#$) and use the embedding of the `[CLS]` token as the pair embedding $e_{n_1,n_2} = e_{\texttt{[CLS]}}$.

[2]There are some minor discrepancies between the statistics reported by Yao et al. (2020) and the final released corpus. We used the final version of the TDG corpus released at https://github.com/Jryao/temporal_dependency_graphs_crowdsourcing.

4 Discourse Analysis for TDG Parsing

Based on Dijk's (1986) schemata of news content, Choubey et al. (2020) proposed the task of discourse profiling (DP). The task is to classify each sentence into one of eight content types (see appendix B). There are two ways of encoding DP information, as proposed by Choubey and Huang (2022). The first (**DP Feature**) appends the content type label directly, marked with a special token #. For instance, if the sentence represents a *main event*, the label `#M1#` is appended to the sentence. We obtained the same model-generated content type labels from Choubey and Huang (2022). The second (**DP Distillation**) involves using model distillation. In this approach, the model is equipped with two decoders: one predicts the reference score, while the other performs DP classification. The training of both tasks occurs simultaneously, distilling the DP information into the underlying language model.

4.1 Sentence Position Information

Sentence position information has proven valuable in various tasks. For instance, the next sentence prediction (NSP) task played a crucial role in training BERT (Devlin et al., 2019), and similar techniques have been shown to be effective for discourse analysis (Yu et al., 2022). In temporal dependency parsing, previous work (Zhang and Xue, 2018a) employed hand-crafted precedence features to enhance performance. In this study, we also present two methods for encoding sentence position:

Sentence Position Feature (SPF) We experimented with directly incorporating sentence position information into the context sentence, in a manner similar to the DP feature. For each sentence, we prepend the context sentences with "`Sentence X:`," where `X` represents the sentence number.

Sentence Position Embedding Vaswani et al. (2017) utilized sine and cosine functions with varying frequencies for token position encoding. We extend this idea by proposing a sentence position encoding (SPE; Equation 1), where pos denotes the sentence number, i is the dimension, and d_{model} is the model's dimension.

$$
\begin{aligned}
SPE_{(pos,2i)} &= \sin(pos/10000^{2i/d_{\text{model}}}) \\
SPE_{(pos,2i+1)} &= \cos(pos/10000^{2i/d_{\text{model}}})
\end{aligned}
\tag{1}
$$

Since the SPE shares the same dimension as RoBERTa's word embeddings, they can be summed. For the pairwise model, we add the SPE of the event's sentence to its event embedding. For the joint ranking model, we directly add both SPEs of both sentences to the pooler's output. A *post-hoc* classifier on RoBERTa itself serves as our baseline.

5 Experimental Results

5.1 Pairwise Prediction Results

The left side of Table 2 displays the performance of the models with various types of discourse information. Among the results, we can emphasize two key comparisons. First, **the addition of all kinds of discourse information leads to a substantial performance increase in the e2e parsing task**; however, it may result in a decline in performance for the other two types. A contributing factor is that the e2e task not only models temporal dependency structure but also requires the model to learn a shortcut heuristic that takes sequence length into account. Upon closer examination, we discovered that Yao et al.'s (2020) assumption that each event can depend on at most one other event is not always valid. It is common for an event to have multiple parents. In such cases, the TDG annotation standard instructs the annotator to choose the event that is closer in time. If this is not feasible, the annotator should select the event that is closer in textual order. Therefore, discourse information offers extra benefits for e2e parsing, regardless of the DP encoding.

Second, **SPE is the only information that leads to performance improvements across all three relation types, and it also yields the most significant performance increase**. As previously discussed, DP information that is model-generated is noisy. Moreover, the discourse structure of TDG news articles is relatively simple. Surface-level sentence position can be considered a reliable proxy for the article's discourse structure. For instance, every news article in the TDG corpus begins with a timex indicating the publication date of the article. Additionally, the majority of the articles follow the publication time with the lead sentence of the article. Directly incorporating the sentence number into the article, however, does not produce the same level of performance improvement. This outcome is also expected, as a BERT-based language model struggles with representing numbers (Wallace et al., 2019).

Model	Pairwise Model			Joint Ranking Model			
Relation	t2t	e2t	e2e	t2t	e2t	e2e	overall
Baseline	94.72	74.07	60.59	93.82	78.72	70.37	77.94
DP-F	94.55	76.64	70.79	**94.59**	76.91	70.99	77.15
DP-D	92.87	73.71	67.72	91.12	77.97	**73.20**	78.07
SPF	94.53	71.41	70.74	92.66	76.83	71.78	77.05
SPE	**95.37**	**77.69**	**72.19**	91.12	**79.10**	72.73	**78.64**

Table 2: Performance on different settings. Top performance of each segment is highlighted in bold.

5.2 Ranking Model Results

The right side of Table 2 presents the performance of the ranking models. Once again, SPE achieves the highest overall performance, showcasing the effectiveness of this approach. Similar to the pairwise results, all models surpass the baseline for the e2e task. Interestingly, with only a few exceptions, the e2t and t2t performance of each model declines. In addition to the previously mentioned reasons, one contributing factor is the imbalanced distribution of the three relation types. The TDG corpus contains 2,486 timexes and 14,779 events, resulting in 20,862 t2t, 63,065 e2t, and 233,065 e2e potential pairs in the training set. When all three types are trained jointly, the model overfits on the e2t and e2e relations, leading to performance disparities across the three relation types.

Despite the issue of data imbalance, the benefits of joint learning are substantial. All models exhibit better performance on the e2t and e2e tasks compared to their pairwise counterparts. The three relation types are not disconnected; for instance, events that depend on the same timex are likely to depend on each other. Without joint learning, this valuable TDG structural information is lost. There are moreover several ways to better model structural information, such as the application of GNNs (Ji et al., 2019), as well as methods to address the data imbalance issue. We leave these topics for future research.

6 Discussion

Before Choubey and Huang (2022), the relationship between discourse and TIE had not been explored, and indeed our own experiments corroborate the value of their insight to incorporate discourse information into constructing document-level temporal structures. Merely using the output of a discourse system as an additional input feature for document-level TIE may not be the most effective strategy, however. A very superficial, but novel sentence position embedding effectively encodes surface-level sentence-order information, and seems to be more reliable as a proxy for the discourse structure of news articles. Incorporating this information leads to state-of-the-art performance in TDG parsing.

The success of sentence-position embedding offers a significant opportunity to bridge discourse analysis and document-level temporal dependency parsing. It suggests that we should not naïvely rely on discourse information as a separate, modular input source. Instead, the similarities between the two tasks indicate that various techniques and insights can be transferred and applied across both domains, leading to more effective models and a deeper understanding of the relationship between discourse analysis and temporal dependency parsing.

Acknowledgement

This study is funded by the Canadian Safety and Security Program (CSSP) from Defence Research and Development Canada (DRDC) awarded to the Public Health Agency of Canada (CSSP-2018-CP-2334: Incorporating Advanced Data Analytics into a Health Intelligence Surveillance System). We thank the Global Public Health Intelligence Network (GPHIN) and Epidemic Intelligence from Open Sources (EIOS) teams for their support. We would also like to thank Prafulla Kumar Choubey for sharing the DP data.

Limitations

In accord with Choubey and Huang (2022), our study focuses solely on the *unlabelled* performance of TDG parsing. This implies that our evaluation is limited to identifying reference temporal relations without considering the classification of relation types. We plan to explore the labelled TDG parsing task in future research.

Owing to resource constraints, our experiments were conducted using only one type of language model, RoBERTa-base. However, other models such as BERT (Devlin et al., 2019), DeBERTa (He et al., 2021), and ERNIE (Zhang et al., 2019) have demonstrated impressive performance across various natural language understanding benchmarks. We aim to evaluate these models in future research, and we encourage other researchers to reproduce our work using these alternative models.

References

James F. Allen. 1983. Maintaining knowledge about temporal intervals. *Communications of the ACM*, 26(11):832–843.

Prafulla Kumar Choubey and Ruihong Huang. 2021. Profiling News Discourse Structure Using Explicit Subtopic Structures Guided Critics. In *Findings of the Association for Computational Linguistics: EMNLP 2021*, pages 1594–1605, Punta Cana, Dominican Republic. Association for Computational Linguistics.

Prafulla Kumar Choubey and Ruihong Huang. 2022. Modeling Document-level Temporal Structures for Building Temporal Dependency Graphs. In *Proceedings of the 2nd Conference of the Asia-Pacific Chapter of the Association for Computational Linguistics and the 12th International Joint Conference on Natural Language Processing (Volume 2: Short Papers)*, pages 357–365, Online only. Association for Computational Linguistics.

Prafulla Kumar Choubey, Aaron Lee, Ruihong Huang, and Lu Wang. 2020. Discourse as a Function of Event: Profiling Discourse Structure in News Articles around the Main Event. In *Proceedings of the 58th Annual Meeting of the Association for Computational Linguistics*, pages 5374–5386, Online. Association for Computational Linguistics.

Jacob Devlin, Ming-Wei Chang, Kenton Lee, and Kristina Toutanova. 2019. BERT: Pre-training of Deep Bidirectional Transformers for Language Understanding. In *Proceedings of the 2019 Conference of the North American Chapter of the Association for Computational Linguistics: Human Language Technologies, Volume 1 (Long and Short Papers)*, pages 4171–4186, Minneapolis, Minnesota. Association for Computational Linguistics.

Teun A. Van Dijk. 1986. News Schemata. *Studying writing: linguistic approaches*, pages 155–186.

Grigorii Guz and Giuseppe Carenini. 2020. Coreference for Discourse Parsing: A Neural Approach. In *Proceedings of the First Workshop on Computational Approaches to Discourse*, pages 160–167, Online. Association for Computational Linguistics.

Pengcheng He, Xiaodong Liu, Jianfeng Gao, and Weizhu Chen. 2021. DeBERTa: Decoding-enhanced BERT with Disentangled Attention. In *International Conference on Learning Representations*.

Tao Ji, Yuanbin Wu, and Man Lan. 2019. Graph-based Dependency Parsing with Graph Neural Networks. In *Proceedings of the 57th Annual Meeting of the Association for Computational Linguistics*, pages 2475–2485, Florence, Italy. Association for Computational Linguistics.

Oleksandr Kolomiyets, Steven Bethard, and Marie-Francine Moens. 2012. Extracting Narrative Timelines as Temporal Dependency Structures. In *Proceedings of the 50th Annual Meeting of the Association for Computational Linguistics (Volume 1: Long Papers)*, pages 88–97, Jeju Island, Korea. Association for Computational Linguistics.

Kenton Lee, Luheng He, Mike Lewis, and Luke Zettlemoyer. 2017. End-to-end Neural Coreference Resolution. In *Proceedings of the 2017 Conference on Empirical Methods in Natural Language Processing*, pages 188–197, Copenhagen, Denmark. Association for Computational Linguistics.

William C. Mann and Sandra A. Thompson. 1988. Rhetorical structure theory: Toward a functional theory of text organization. *Text*, 8(3):243–281.

Hayley Ross, Jonathon Cai, and Bonan Min. 2020. Exploring Contextualized Neural Language Models for Temporal Dependency Parsing. In *Proceedings of the 2020 Conference on Empirical Methods in Natural Language Processing (EMNLP)*, pages 8548–8553, Online. Association for Computational Linguistics.

Ashish Vaswani, Noam Shazeer, Niki Parmar, Jakob Uszkoreit, Llion Jones, Aidan N Gomez, Łukasz Kaiser, and Illia Polosukhin. 2017. Attention is All you Need. In *Advances in Neural Information Processing Systems*, volume 30. Curran Associates, Inc.

Eric Wallace, Yizhong Wang, Sujian Li, Sameer Singh, and Matt Gardner. 2019. Do NLP Models Know Numbers? Probing Numeracy in Embeddings. In *Proceedings of the 2019 Conference on Empirical Methods in Natural Language Processing and the 9th International Joint Conference on Natural Language Processing (EMNLP-IJCNLP)*, pages 5307–5315, Hong Kong, China. Association for Computational Linguistics.

Jiarui Yao, Haoling Qiu, Bonan Min, and Nianwen Xue. 2020. Annotating Temporal Dependency Graphs via Crowdsourcing. In *Proceedings of the 2020 Conference on Empirical Methods in Natural Language Processing (EMNLP)*, pages 5368–5380, Online. Association for Computational Linguistics.

Nan Yu, Meishan Zhang, Guohong Fu, and Min Zhang. 2022. RST Discourse Parsing with Second-Stage EDU-Level Pre-training. In *Proceedings of the 60th Annual Meeting of the Association for Computational*

Linguistics (Volume 1: Long Papers), pages 4269–4280, Dublin, Ireland. Association for Computational Linguistics.

Yuchen Zhang and Nianwen Xue. 2018a. Neural Ranking Models for Temporal Dependency Structure Parsing. In *Proceedings of the 2018 Conference on Empirical Methods in Natural Language Processing*, pages 3339–3349, Brussels, Belgium. Association for Computational Linguistics.

Yuchen Zhang and Nianwen Xue. 2018b. Structured Interpretation of Temporal Relations. In *Proceedings of the Eleventh International Conference on Language Resources and Evaluation (LREC 2018)*, Miyazaki, Japan. European Language Resources Association (ELRA).

Zhengyan Zhang, Xu Han, Zhiyuan Liu, Xin Jiang, Maosong Sun, and Qun Liu. 2019. ERNIE: Enhanced Language Representation with Informative Entities. In *Proceedings of the 57th Annual Meeting of the Association for Computational Linguistics*, pages 1441–1451, Florence, Italy. Association for Computational Linguistics.

A Training Details

We follow Choubey and Huang's (2022) experiment setup. We first conducted a hyperparamter search on learning rate using the baseline models. In particular, we used 1e-5 for the t2t pairwise models, 3e-5 for the e2t and e2e pairwise models, and 8e-5 for the joint ranking models. We train each model for 15 epochs, and report the test set performance on the model with the highest development set performance. RoBERTa-base is used as the encoder for all the experiments. For the pairwise model, we down sampled e2e labels by a factor of 10.

B DP Content Types

Choubey et al. (2020) specified eight DP content types: Main event (M1), Consequence (M2), Previous Event (C1), Current Context (C2), Historical Event (D1), Anecdotal Event (D2), Evaluation (D3) and Expectation (D4).

Encoding Discourse Structure: Comparison of RST and QUD

Sara Shahmohammadi[1*], Hannah Seemann[2*], Manfred Stede[1], Tatjana Scheffler[2]
[1] Department of Linguistics, University of Potsdam, Germany
[2] Department for German Language and Literature, Ruhr-University Bochum, Germany
shahmohammadi@uni-potsdam.de hannah.seemann@rub.de
stede@uni-potsdam.de tatjana.scheffler@rub.de

Abstract

We present a quantitative and qualitative comparison of the discourse trees defined by the Rhetorical Structure Theory and Questions under Discussion models. Based on an empirical analysis of parallel annotations for 28 texts (blog posts and podcast transcripts), we conclude that both discourse frameworks capture similar structural information. The qualitative analysis shows that while complex discourse units often match between analyses, QUD structures do not indicate the centrality of segments.

1 Introduction

Rhetorical structure Theory (RST) (Mann and Thompson, 1988) and the Question under Discussion (QUD) model (e.g., Ginzburg, 1996; Roberts, 2012; Onea, 2019) are two accounts of discourse structure that stem from different research fields and aim to explain different phenomena (speaker intentions and rhetoric versus information structure). However, they share a fundamental formal assumption: that discourse structure is to be represented as a tree that is constructed by recursively combining adjacent "elementary units" of the discourse. For QUD, "discourse" originally meant primarily dialog, while RST was designed for monologue text. Nonetheless, researchers have occasionally explored ways to apply one theory also to the mode of the other.

In this paper, we systematically compare these two approaches to discourse structure, based on empirical observations in a novel multi-media corpus. While some researchers have previously noted the intuitive similarities of RST based trees and QUD based trees on a theoretical level, this work presents the first study where both frameworks are systematically applied to a corpus of both spoken and written data, and compared in a quantitative and qualitative manner.

*Equal contribution

We first present part of a novel corpus of German blog posts (monologue) and podcast transcripts (dialog). There is a loose 1:1 correspondence between the two, in that the blogs are descriptions of what is being discussed in the podcasts. To our knowledge, this is one of the first corpora that are annotated in parallel with RST and QUD structures. Our aim is to compare the annotated material so that insights into the descriptive and explanatory power of the two approaches can be gained from an empirical perspective of studying authentic data. We make the annotated corpus available to facilitate follow-up research.

To enable the quantitative comparison, we automatically map manually-annotated RST trees to Riester (2019)-style QUD trees. We make the conversion tool available as a web application (and will later release the code). Based on the common format, we perform a quantitative analysis of the similarity of RST and QUD discourse trees, for which we propose an evaluation measure. In addition, our thorough qualitative comparisons show that QUD trees do not indicate the centrality of segments, and often fail to cover relations such as concession and contrast. On the other hand, the topic progression and speaker change within a dialog is captured in QUD analyses but may be missing from RST.

2 Related Work

In annotating both media present in our corpus, we apply both discourse models outside of what they have been primarily designed for. While QUD has been applied to monologue texts before (Riester et al., 2018; Westera et al., 2020), it is most centrally applied to (short) dialogs. On the other hand, RST aims to capture the intentional structure constructed by the writer and is thus designed for monologue, but it has been occasionally applied to dialog, as well (e.g., Stent, 2000).

The QUD framework has been developed to capture aspects of the information structure of sen-

Proceedings of the 4th Workshop on Computational Approaches to Discourse (CODI 2023), pages 89–98
July 13-14, 2023 ©2023 Association for Computational Linguistics

tences and certain specific pragmatic phenomena (Ginzburg, 1996; Roberts, 2012). Only recently has it been used for annotating larger texts, and compared to models of the coherence structure of discourse.

Hunter and Abrusán (2017) compare QUD structures to those proposed by Segmented Discourse Representation Theory (SDRT). They argue that although there likely is no QUD corresponding to every discourse relation, "QUDs correspond to complex discourse units in a discourse graph" (p. 41), that is, topics that lead to grouping discourse units together.

Onea (2019) similarly starts by comparing QUD and SDRT and argues that formally analyzing the erotetic (i.e., question) structure of a discourse can be useful to understand its meaning and its relation structure, for example its SDRT representation. He develops a method for mapping (parts of) question graphs to SDRT representations, and takes a close look at the *Result* relation as a case study. He argues that QUD theories (in particular, models based on potential questions) have repercussions for the larger discourse structure of a text (as represented for example in SDRT).

Riester et al. (2018) offer the first detailed guidelines for segmenting discourse and annotating QUD trees in authentic text, discussing individual texts from English, French, and German and from three different genres. One claim is that the same guidelines apply to monologue (newspaper articles) and dialog (interviews) alike. In later work, Riester et al. (2021) compare QUD, RST, and the CCR approach to discourse structure for one text. Regarding segmentation rules in QUD and RST, they point out that QUD calls for smaller segments than RST when information-structural factors suggest a discourse contribution, e.g., for contrastive foci. Conversely, adjunct clauses can sometimes be separate segments in RST (e.g., in *Circumstance* relations) but not in QUD. As for the relations, the authors show how RST relations can be integrated into a QUD tree notation, and discuss some typical mappings.

Riester (2019) presents a proposal to include both sub- and coordinating relations in a tree that combines QUD and SDRT, based on the approach by Klein and von Stutterheim (1987). For example, the temporal progression of a discourse can be represented by questions asking about each point in time: *What happened at* $t_{1:n}$*?*

Finally, we mention that an early (but somewhat inconclusive) debate in the RST community on the interplay of "intentional" and "informational" coherence relations (e.g., (Moore and Pollack, 1992)) foreshadowed the kind of duality that RST and QUD embody.

3 Data and Method

We carry out an empirical comparison of QUD- and RST-based annotations of the same texts in two media. The idea is based on the assumption that while the QUD and RST frameworks cannot be directly mapped onto one another, both aim to capture the overall coherence of a discourse in a tree-like fashion. Thus, previous work such as (Hunter and Abrusán, 2017; Riester et al., 2021) has proposed to study the correspondences in these discourse trees by looking at the relation between rhetorical relations and question-based structures. Our study is the first, to our knowledge, which carries out a parallel annotation of both spoken and written texts in the two frameworks.

Our data and annotation process is described here.

3.1 Data

The corpus contains texts from two media: podcast transcripts and their corresponding blog posts, both in German. Furthermore, the corpus contains different domains: business podcasts that are produced by companies like DELL or Deutsche Telekom and science podcasts that cover topics from various fields of science and politics. For this analysis, we use 14 blog posts and chunks of 14 podcast transcripts. The blog posts are composed of 26 EDUs on average. The contiguous discourse chunks we annotated from the transcripts consist of 17 EDUs on average. Table 1 shows the size of the resulting sub-corpus.

medium	# episodes	# EDUs	# tokens
blog posts	14	364	4,204
transcripts	14	502	4,980
total	28	866	9,184

Table 1: Corpus overview, EDU and token count.

3.2 Annotation

The texts have been manually annotated in both frameworks, RST and QUD. To simplify the com-

```
[root]
└── [evaluations]
    ├── [summary]
    │   ├── [conjunction]
    │   │   ├── [concession]
    │   │   │   ├── Für alle anderen Meldungen , die davor reingekommen ist , musste man den Datendump vom Vortag kennen .
    │   │   │   └── Es gibt aber kein veröffentlichtes Archiv
    │   │   └── [reason]
    │   │       ├── und weil ich erst von der Woche damit angefangen habe ,
    │   │       └── [conjunction]
    │   │           ├── habe ich jetzt auch erst auch dank noch jemandem auf Twitter so , der mir noch zwei fehlende Dumps , dass ich jetzt eine woche habe an an Dumps
    │   │           └── und damit schon mal dann rechnen kann .
    │   └── S1 : Es gibt keinen ,
    └── [cause]
        ├── das macht mich jetzt noch ein bisschen fassungslos .
        └── [evaluations]
            ├── [summary]
            │   ├── [conjunction]
            │   │   ├── [conjunction]
            │   │   │   ├── Die daten sind immer nur tagesaktuell
            │   │   │   └── und ändern sich dann am laufenden Meter
            │   │   └── [concession]
            │   │       ├── und es gibt kein Archiv der letzten Daten ,
            │   │       └── [purpose]
            │   │           ├── obwohl man genau die bräuchte ,
            │   │           └── um die volle Information herauslesen zu können .
            │   └── S2 : So ist es so .
            └── S1 : Mann ey oh gott .
```

Figure 1: A QUD tree converted from an RST tree (UKW024-p3).

parison between the annotations, we use the RST segmentation according to the Potsdam Commentary Corpus guidelines (Stede, 2016) for both frameworks. For now, we assume EDUs as viable segments for QUD annotation, even though there are differences compared to the usual QUD segmentation, as discussed by Riester et al. (2021). Other than the segmentation, the QUD annotation follows the guidelines defined by Riester et al. (2018). The RST annotation mainly follows the guidelines proposed by Stede et al. (2017), with a few changes.[1]

The annotations were conducted by one person for each model, and revised by a second annotator (a co-author of this paper).[2] The annotated files can be found in the project's GitHub repository[3]. For reasons of space, not all examples referred to in our analysis are shown in the text, but they can be found under the file name given, e.g. CRE210_Transcript_p3. An example of the same file annotated with both discourse models is presented in Figure 2. The English translation of this example is given in (4).[4]

4 Converting RST to QUD Trees

Both RST structures and QUD trees encode discourse structure formally as trees that span over the entire discourse. In RST, intermediate nodes are discourse relations that group (typically) two segments, (typically) a nucleus and satellite. In QUD, intermediate nodes are explicit or implicit questions which guide the discourse; children are (partial) answers to these questions. Disregarding node labels for intermediate nodes, trees with the same yield can be mapped onto each other by comparing just the branching structure.

To evaluate the similarity of RST and QUD trees, we converted the RST trees to a format similar to the QUD trees that can be quantitatively compared to the QUD annotation. Figure 1 shows the converted version of the RST tree in Figure 2.

To convert an RST tree to the QUD format, we take a discourse relation in an RST tree as an intermediate node (implicit question) in a QUD structure. The satellite and nucleus of the relation are daughters of this intermediate node at the same level of nesting.[5] The details of the conversion will be made available in the project repository on GitHub.

5 Quantitative Analysis of RST and QUD Correspondence

We automatically evaluated the similarity of the RST and QUD discourse structures quantitatively

[1]To account for particularities of speech, we added a 'completion' relation that is used in podcast conversations, if a speaker says something that is not complete, e.g. does not have a verb, and then completes it later. In addition, we extended the 'restatement' relation to allow being used as a forward-looking relation. This way, it also covers cases of a speaker's self-correction. It is noteworthy to know that there is no "question" relation in these guidelines. Such a relation exists in some RST guidelines, for instance in the annotation guide proposed by Carlson and Marcu (2001).

[2]For future work, we will add a second annotation in each framework and inter-annotator-agreement.

[3]https://github.com/mohamadi-sara20/rst-qud-comparison

[4]All examples are our own translations of the original German data.

[5]It is also possible to convert an RST tree into a QUD tree where the satellite is nested one more level compared to the nucleus. That is, to consider the satellite a subtopic of the nucleus. This way, information on nuclearity will not be lost in the conversion. However, we found this less similar to a QUD structure, so it was not used for the final analysis.

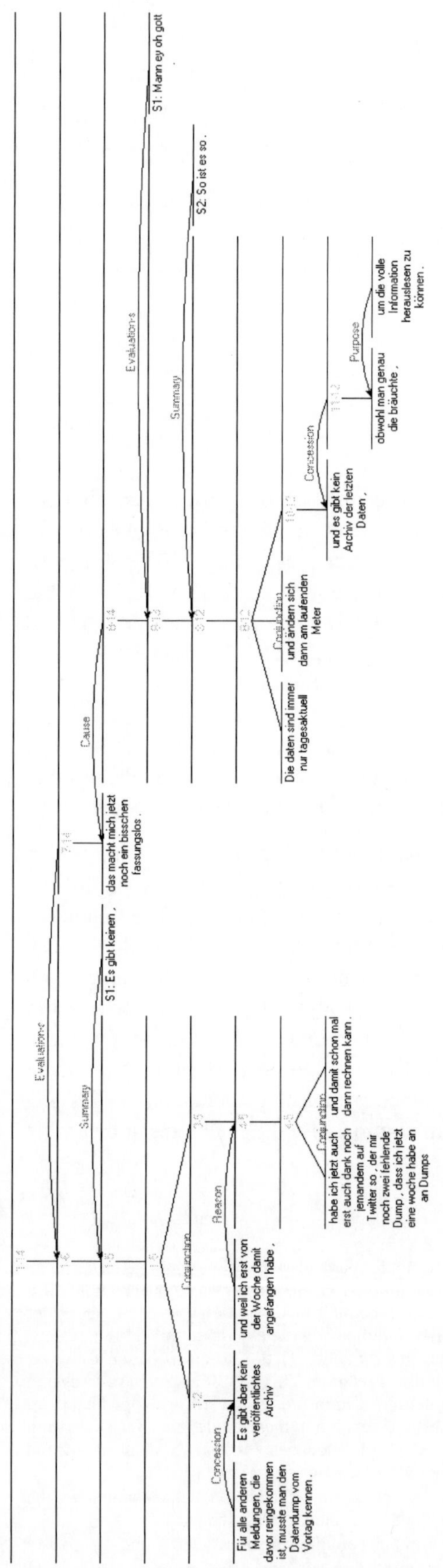

Figure 2: Representations of (4) in QUD (top/left) and RST (bottom/right) (UKW024-p3).

across the whole corpus. To do this, we computed a variant of the PARSEVAL measure known from evaluating (syntactic) constituency parse trees. This measure compares unlabelled trees A and B: First, for all nodes N_A in tree A, one determines whether tree B contains a node with the same yield (= concatenation of all the text dominated by a node) as N_A. In the case of comparing an automatic parse tree with a gold standard, this would reflect precision. Second, for all nodes N_B in B, the same is repeated ($\sim$ recall). We finally compute the harmonic mean of both directions to determine the similarity of RST and QUD structures.

We use unlabelled parseval scores because intermediate nodes are labelled with relations in the case of RST trees, and with questions in QUD trees.[6] Note that the standard parseval score includes leaf nodes in its computation (in the case of syntactic trees, POS tags), and that this practice typically leads to much higher scores than excluding leaves. In our computation, we also include leaves, not only because it is commonly done, but also because in our tree structures, certain error cases can only be reflected when including leaf nodes. This happens in particular, when an explicit text segment is used as an explicit question under discussion (i.e., internal node) in a QUD tree. For this reason, we also redefine the "yield" of a node to be all explicit text dominated by that node, both when it is represented in a leaf node and when it is in an intermediate node.

medium	Q→R	R→Q	f-score
blogs	0.87	0.68	0.76
transcripts	0.85	0.63	0.73
total	0.86	0.65	0.74

Table 2: (Micro-averaged) parseval scores comparing RST and QUD discourse trees.

The results of the quantitative comparison are shown in Table 2. It can be seen that there is a large amount of overlap in the tree structures between QUD and RST frameworks, with an average similarity (parseval) score of 0.74. In addition, we see that the blog posts show higher similarity across frameworks than the podcast transcripts. This is the case even though the blog posts annotated here are on average longer than the transcript snippets (in a longer discourse, there are more possibilities for mismatches in discourse structure annotations). However, we can observe that the similarity of discourse structure between QUD and RST trees is quite high, comparable to inter-annotator agreement within the same framework.

6 Qualitative Comparison of RST and QUD Trees

To further evaluate the correspondences between the analyses, we take a closer look at our annotations. First, we inspected the five pairs of trees that received the lowest matching scores in the quantitative comparison; here we note that a frequent source of mismatch is RST's tendency to build a complex discourse unit in cases where QUD attaches the material locally (see below). Then we turned also to the other pairs, trying to generalize sources of misalignment. Section 6.1 compares the way complex discourse units are constructed in both models.The overall structure of texts annotated with both models seems to often be similar, yet there are instances where the structures are quite different. Sections 6.2 and 6.3 compare how translatable different rhetorical relations are to QUD trees and whether RST trees are able to represent typical characteristics of dialog, like speaker changes.

6.1 Comparison of Complex Discourse Units

As discussed in the previous section, both RST trees and QUD trees seem to similarly cluster EDUs into groups, which is particularly beneficial in higher-level units. It is possible to decompose an RST tree into prominent sub-trees. EDUs in the same sub-tree or cluster are closer to each other than they are to other EDUs. In a QUD tree, EDUs grouped together are put under the same parent question and hence address the same topic or rather, answer sub-questions of an overarching question under discussion. One example can be seen in the RST tree in Figure 2: EDUs 1–6 make up one cluster, while EDUs 7–14 are grouped together.

The tendency for QUD and RST analyses to group discourse units similarly is noticeable in most of the trees of the corpus, but there are also exceptions. Figure 2 shows an example where QUD

[6] We cannot compute labelled parseval scores because the RST node labels are (a fixed set of) coherence relations and the QUD node labels are (totally free) natural language questions, some of which actually are part of the discourse and thus represented as leaf nodes in the RST trees. To compare QUD trees automatically in general, one would need to define an evaluation method that can rate the equivalence of natural language questions, a task we leave for future work.

and RST trees seem to capture different aspects of the functions of discourse unit 6. As evident in the figure, RST subtree 1-5 discusses the problem of the unavailability of public data archives. Unit 6 repeats the same idea, without the details. According to the guidelines, one possible relation holding between 6 and 1-5 is the Summary relation. On the other hand, unit 7 starts with the pronoun 'Das' ('that'), which expresses an evaluation of the current condition of the archives. Hence, the best attachment point for it is unit 6.

However, if the evaluation is attached to 6, the summary relation cannot be chosen to relate it to the prior discourse. On the other hand, if the evaluation is attached to 1-6 instead of only 6, it would mean ignoring the intention behind this repetition. This is where the difference between the two trees arises: The RST tree groups 6 with the previous discourse, and therefore loses the ideal attachment point for the evaluation. The QUD tree, on the other hand, groups 6 with the discourse following it, and hence fails to fully observe the function of this repetition.

This pattern is not limited to discourse management in dialogs but is also seen in monologues. In example (1), part (1-a) discusses the fact that there is a great difference between theory and practice in IT security, and brings some evidence to support this claim. Part (1-b) repeats this idea with fewer details and different wording, and (1-c) evaluates the situation.

(1) a. And what we actually see in crime out there is that the so-called cybercrime is working on a level way lower than, for example, academic research. In academic research, we invent amazing new procedures of cryptography, helping us against quantum computers. What I think, I think this research is important. But what really happens to us is that companies are being hacked because some recipients click on e-mail attachments.
  b. Meaning, there is a huge difference between the technically complex and artistic attacks in academic research and street crime.
  c. And it makes sense if you compare that to a purse thief.

(DELL001_Transcript)

The main reason for adding (1-b) is to bring attention back to the 'difference between theory and practice in IT security' in order to later evaluate it. If the evaluation is attached to (1-b), the summary relation cannot be chosen. If the evaluation is attached to Summary(a, b) instead of just (1-b), it would mean ignoring the intention behind this repetition. This is, again, the source of the difference between the two trees: The RST tree groups (1-b) with the previous discourse, and hence loses the ideal attachment point for the evaluation, while the QUD tree groups it with the discourse following it, neglecting the function of the repetition.

Another example of the two representations capturing different aspects of a conversation is shown in (2). In this example, the second sentence by speaker 2 (2-c) has two functions: It is an evaluation of the speaker's knowledge of the current topic but at the same time part of a turn-taking-mechanism, offering speaker 1 to evaluate on the net research.

(2) Context: The first human settlements, beginnings of agriculture, and domestication of animals.
  a. Speaker 1: I just looked it up, and it is not really well... It seems to be disputed when the dog really joined us, the process seems to have been over a very long time and gradually.
  b. Speaker 2: Yes, maybe it fluctuates, too, that is, how cultures reacted to it.
  c. Well, with your net research, you probably know more about it than I do.
  d. S1: Well, I'm not reading all of it now. There is a lot to say here about *canis lupus*, but sometime around 15,000 and 100,000 years. It really is vaguely defined.

(CRE210_Transcript_p5)

Double functions like these are not rare in our data, many utterances have a discourse-managing function on top of the propositional content. Thus, they may be interpreted differently by different annotators, leading to a different annotation of the same text independent of systematic differences between the two discourse models.

6.2 Comparison Between Relations

Restatement. Figure 4 shows an example of a 'restatement' relation in both QUD and RST trees.

```
[Q6 Which products contain fructose?]
├── Apples, juice, dairy products, cereal, and some sweets have one thing in common:
├── they contain fructose.
└── [Q7 What is the problem with fructose?]
    ├── What health-conscious and sweet teeth often don't know:
    ├── Excessive consumption of fructose can lead to stomach ache and diarrhea.
    └── [Q8 How much fructose do products contain?]
        ├── Some drinks, for example, contain up to 40g of fructose per liter.
        ├── [Q9 What amount of fructose is problematic?]
        │   └── But consuming more than 35g per meal is considered problematic.
        └── Even a cup of yogurt with low sugar content can contain up to 15g of fructose.
```

Figure 3: Concession represented in QUD tree, translated to English (VBZ011_Blog).

Instances of 'restatement' are all at the same level in a QUD tree (since they all answer the same question), while an RST tree does not represent this as a parallel structure; it forms a tree that is right-branching. Our RST annotation guidelines allow the restatement of adjacent units to be successfully modeled.[7]

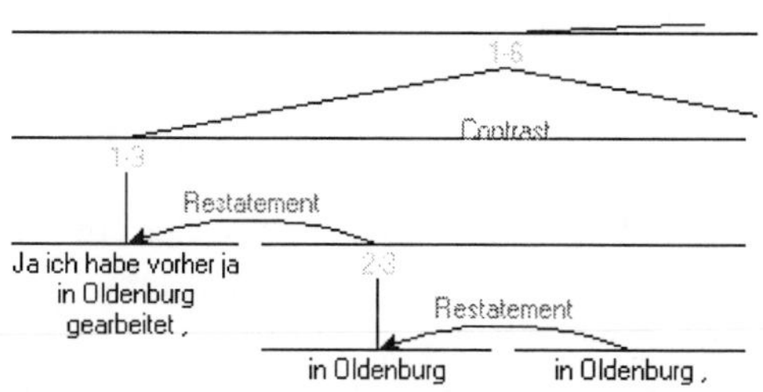


```
[Q1 Wie ist der Werdegang der Sprecherin?]
├── Ja ich habe vorher ja in Oldenburg gearbeitet ,
├── in Oldenburg
├── in Oldenburg ,
```

Figure 4: Restatement represented in RST tree (top) and QUD tree (bottom) (FG029-p2).

Although restating an idea does not introduce a new topic, there are definitely intentions behind it; sometimes the speaker needs time to think and so they buy time by repeating themselves, sometimes interlocutors want to make a topic more memorable and do so by restating it. It is also possible to restate a previous topic, which is not the current topic, in order to make it salient in current discourse. A QUD structure would not be concerned with these functions of a 'restatement' relation. In contrast, the fine-grained representation of discourse relations provided in RST or SDRT would distinguish such cases of 'restatement'.

[7]Our guidelines respect the adjacency constraint, so it is not possible to mark non-adjacent restatements. That is, if somewhere the fifth EDU restates the content of the first EDU, we cannot model that with a restatement relation according to our guidelines, as it would need a non-adjacent edge.

Background. A background relation in RST introduces background information in order to enable the reader to understand a more central claim. What is annotated with a 'background' relation in an RST tree has been modeled in different fashions in the QUD annotation. Sometimes it is represented in the QUD tree with a nested structure, with a series of nested questions and answers leading to the more central claim. But in different cases what is a 'background' satellite in the RST tree is annotated in the QUD tree to share the same immediate parent of the central claim – and therefore without a nested structure.

This is probably due to the QUD model being concerned with different aspects of discourse than the RST model. A QUD representation does not aim at presenting what is the most important or central claim of discourse but rather the series of sub-questions that are talked about.

Concession and Contrast. Since there is no question type that can be answered with a 'but'-statement (Scheffler, 2013), it may be expected that a QUD representation of a discourse is unable to model contrastive relations. Q9 in the QUD tree shown in Figure 3 is annotated with the 'concession' relation in the corresponding RST tree.

In the QUD tree, the concession is represented by an additional sub-question – as is also suggested by Riester et al. (2021). This way, concessions can, in principle, be modeled in a QUD representation. However, the QUD representation cannot explicitly show which part of the concession is the expectation or the violation of the expectation – the information conveyed by the nucleus and the satellite in an RST representation is lost.

A similar problem arises when dealing with 'contrast' relations. Even though contrasts can be modeled by a parallel structure in a QUD tree, see example (3) Q4.1 and Q4.2, the contrastive meaning is not explicitly represented due to the list character of this representation. Thus, it is not impossible to represent a tree that has contrastive relations in a QUD structure in general, but the resulting representation is not explicitly contrastive.

(3) A1: And then there seems to have been some shift in the climate,
{Q2: What did this shift in the climate cause?}
A2': causing Africa to dry in its center,
A2": that is changing more and more into a savannah landscape.
{Q3: What were the resulting changes in humanity?}
A3: and then there seems to have been a split in the evolution
{Q4: What was the result of this split?}
{Q4.1: What did the first half do?}
A4.1: one part further tried to eat vegetarian food
{Q4.2: What did the second half do?}
A4.2: and the others started to hunt.

(CRE210_Transcript_p2)

6.3 Comparison of Speaker Changes

While the QUD model is made to deal with explicit questions and speaker changes in dialog, RST is not. Still, in some examples, both representations deal with the speaker change in a similar way: A different speaker than the person before takes the turn, their utterance has its own subtree giving more information, elaboration, or repeating what has been said, then both models go back to a higher discourse level (see figure 5).

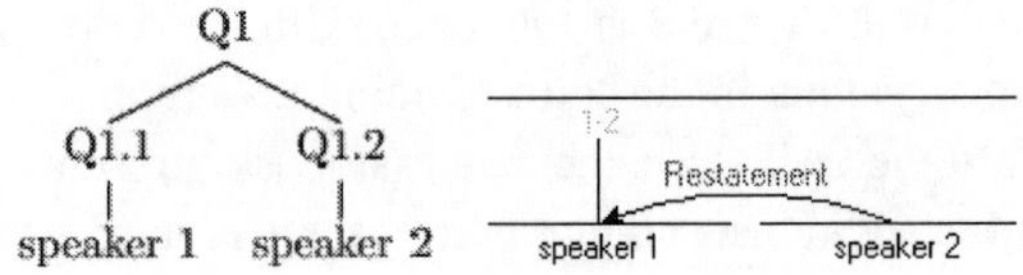

Figure 5: Representations of the same speaker change in QUD (left) and RST tree (right).

But in most cases of speaker changes, the utterances by each speaker are separate sub-trees connected on a higher level in the RST tree, while in the QUD, the second speaker's utterance does not form its own sub-tree. Since RST and QUD deal differently with topical progression, examples like (4) are represented in different ways.

(4) Context: Daily reports of COVID case numbers and the German government's archive infrastructure.

a. Speaker 2: For all the other reports that came in before, you have to know all the data dumps from the day before. But there is no public archive and because I only started this week, I now have only, thanks to someone on Twitter who gave me two missing dumps, so that I now have one week of dumps and do calculations with it.
b. Speaker 1: There is none, that really stuns me. The data is always only on a daily basis and changing constantly and there is no archive of the previous data, even though you would need exactly this to be able to extract all the information.
c. S2: That's how it is.
d. S1: Man that sucks.

(UKW024_Transcript_p2)

In the RST representation, an utterance containing a summary of the previous topic and a transition to the next topic will always be parts of two different sub-trees. On the other hand, in the QUD representation, the transition to the next topic will be a child of the previous topic, as long as both topics are closely connected to each other - see figure 2 for both representations of (4). This means that in the RST representation, the utterance by speaker 1 is split up between two different sub-trees while in the QUD representation, it is not. Unsurprisingly, example (4) has one of the lowest similarities (0.68) in our quantitative comparison between discourse annotations.

Another problem occurs if a speaker change is accompanied by an explicit question. While this is what QUD is meant to model and has no problem dealing with, an explicit question that has no other function than introducing a new topic cannot be appropriately represented in an RST tree without introducing an additional discourse relation.

7 Discussion

In this paper, we have carried out a systematic comparison of the discourse structures induced by RST and QUD frameworks for the same texts from two media, blog posts and podcast transcripts. Our annotations of the 28 texts show that both frameworks can be successfully applied to monologue texts as well as dialogs.

We compare the branching structure of the resulting RST and QUD trees by first providing a method that converts an RST tree into an equivalent QUD representation. We compare these representations to the manually annotated QUD trees and find an overall similarity of 0.74 – similar to or surpassing the agreement scores between human annotators for discourse structure annotation tasks. This shows that the two frameworks cover some of the same information for our corpus. The similarity between analyses is higher for the blog posts, indicating that the topic structure (QUD) and coherence/intentional structure (RST) are more closely related for monologue texts than for dialog (where two speakers have to agree on how the overall discourse progresses).

Finally, we provide a detailed qualitative comparison of the way complex discourse units are mapped across frameworks, about how certain discourse relations can be represented in QUD trees, and the effects of speaker changes in dialog. We discuss that while the overall structure of QUD and RST trees often matches approximately, QUD trees do not indicate the centrality of discourse segments and cannot represent certain types of relations easily, such as concession and contrast. In contrast, the topic progression within a discourse is captured in QUD analyses but may be missing from RST.

Limitations

We have carried out all analyses according to our best abilities. Nevertheless, it should be noted that RST structures and QUD structures were annotated by distinct researchers. While all annotations have been double-checked by at least one other expert for plausibility, in many cases there are alternative analyses of the texts which may also be applicable (as is usually the case for discourse structure). Since we do not have direct access to the discourse creators and their goals, this limitation is unavoidable in corpus studies.

Ethics Statement

The data reported on in this paper was collected within the research project named below. For all texts, explicit consent was obtained from the creators to use the data for annotation and scientific analysis. The data was automatically and manually preprocessed and reformatted, and manually annotated for discourse structure (among other levels). All annotations were carried out by researchers during their regular work time, either PhD students (authors of this paper) or student research assistants with regular work contracts. The data will be long-term archived and made available to other researchers according to the laws that apply. We see no other ethical issues with our data or research practices.

Acknowledgements

This work was funded by the Deutsche Forschungsgemeinschaft (DFG, German Research Foundation) – Project ID 317633480 – SFB 1287. We want to thank Elisa Lübbers for helping with RST annotation.

References

Lynn Carlson and Daniel Marcu. 2001. Discourse tagging reference manual. *ISI Technical Report ISI-TR-545*, 54(2001):56.

Jonathan Ginzburg. 1996. Dynamics and the semantics of dialogue. *Logic, language and computation*, 1:221–237.

Julie Hunter and Márta Abrusán. 2017. Rhetorical structure and QUDs. In *New Frontiers in Artificial Intelligence*, pages 41–57. Springer International Publishing.

Wolfgang Klein and Christiane von Stutterheim. 1987. Quaestio und referentielle Bewegung in Erzählungen. *Linguistische Berichte*, 109:163–183.

William Mann and Sandra Thompson. 1988. Rhetorical structure theory: Towards a functional theory of text organization. *TEXT*, 8:243–281.

Johanna Moore and Martha Pollack. 1992. A problem for RST: The need for multi-level discourse analysis. *Computational Linguistics*, 18(4):537–544.

Edgar Onea. 2019. Underneath rhetorical relations. The case of result. In Malte Zimmermann, Klaus von Heusinger, and Edgar Onea, editors, *Questions in Discourse: Volume 2: Pragmatics*, pages 194–250. Brill, Leiden, The Netherlands.

Arndt Riester. 2019. Constructing QUD trees. In Malte Zimmermann, Klaus von Heusinger, and Edgar Onea, editors, *Questions in Discourse: Volume 2: Pragmatics*, pages 164–193. Brill, Leiden, The Netherlands.

Arndt Riester, Lisa Brunetti, and Kordula De Kuthy. 2018. Annotation guidelines for questions under discussion and information structure. In *Information structure in lesser-described languages. Studies in prosody and syntax*, pages 403–443. John Benjamins.

Arndt Riester, Amalia Canes Nápoles, and Jet Hoek. 2021. Combined discourse representations: Coherence relations and Questions under Discussion. In *Proceedings of the First Workshop on Integrating Perspectives on Discourse Annotation*, pages 26–30, Tübingen, Germany. Association for Computational Linguistics.

Craige Roberts. 2012. Information structure in discourse: Towards an integrated formal theory of pragmatics. *Semantics and Pragmatics*, 5(6):1–69.

Tatjana Scheffler. 2013. *Two-dimensional semantics: Clausal adjuncts and complements*, volume 549 of *Linguistische Arbeiten*. Walter de Gruyter.

Manfred Stede, editor. 2016. *Handbuch Textannotation: Potsdamer Kommentarkorpus 2.0*. Number 8 in Potsdam cognitive science series. Universitätsverlag Potsdam, Potsdam.

Manfred Stede, Maite Taboada, and Debopam Das. 2017. Annotation guidelines for rhetorical structure. *Manuscript. University of Potsdam and Simon Fraser University*.

Amanda Stent. 2000. Rhetorical structure in dialog. In *INLG'2000 proceedings of the first international conference on natural language generation*, pages 247–252.

Matthijs Westera, Laia Mayol, and Hannah Rohde. 2020. TED-Q: TED talks and the questions they evoke. In *Proceedings of the Twelfth Language Resources and Evaluation Conference*, pages 1118–1127, Marseille, France. European Language Resources Association.

Exploiting Knowledge about Discourse Relations for Implicit Discourse Relation Classification

Nobel Jacob Varghese and **Frances Yung** and **Kaveri Anuranjana** and **Vera Demberg**
Language Science and Technology, Saarland University
nobeljacobv@gmail.com, {frances, kaveri, vera}@coli.uni-saarland.de

Abstract

In discourse relation recognition, the classification labels are typically represented as one-hot vectors. However, the categories are in fact not all independent of one another – on the contrary, there are several frameworks that describe the labels' similarities (by e.g. sorting them into a hierarchy or describing them in terms of features (Sanders et al., 2021)). Recently, several methods for representing the similarities between labels have been proposed (Zhang et al., 2018; Wang et al., 2018; Xiong et al., 2021). We here explore and extend the *Label Confusion Model* (Guo et al., 2021) for learning a representation for discourse relation labels. We explore alternative ways of informing the model about the similarities between relations, by representing relations in terms of their names (and parent category), their typical markers, or in terms of CCR features that describe the relations. Experimental results show that exploiting label similarity improves classification results.

1 Introduction

Discourse relations (DRs) are logical relations between units of text ("arguments 1 and 2") that make the whole text coherent, see e.g. the concession relation in (1).

(1) [John prepared for his final exam hoping to get at least a pass.]$_{Arg1}$ [He got an E.]$_{Arg2}$ (DR: COMPARISON.CONCESSION.ARG2-AS-DENIER)

The task of implicit DR recognition (IDRR) is particularly challenging because informative discourse connectives (DCs), such as *"however"* are missing. Implicit discourse relation classification tasks using the Penn Discourse Treebank (PDTB) framework (Prasad et al., 2008) typically distinguish between 11 different labels. However, these labels are not completely independent of one another – some relations tend to co-occur or be confused more than others. The similarities between relations are represented in the PDTB relation hierarchy, which groups the labels into four top-level classes, or by the CCR feature representation proposed in Sanders et al. (2021). However, these well-known similarities are typically not exploited for discourse relation classification tasks – instead, all labels are treated as if they were independent of one another.

Guo et al. (2021) recently proposed the Label Confusion Model (LCM), which seems well-suited for the characteristics of the IDRR task: Guo et al. (2021) showed that the method is particularly suitable for problems with many labels, classification problems in which labels are ambiguous and tend to be confused with each other, and/or when there is semantic overlap between the labels. They demonstrated the benefit of the method on several text classification tasks.

The goal of the present paper is to test whether the LCM approach is indeed helpful for IDRR and experiment with three different ways of capturing the label similarities. (1) We use label embeddings: DR labels are not random words but terms that lexically describe the meaning of the DRs, such as REASON, PRECEDENCE, CONDITION, and so on. Using label embeddings assumes that similar relations also tend to have names with similar lexical embeddings. However, some relation labels may additionally be associated with a quite different meaning in normal language use (e.g., "concession"), and their embedding may hence not capture the technical meaning well. (2) We characterize a DR by a set of prototypical connectives (e.g., *however* and *nevertheless* for a CONCESSION relation). (3) We encode DRs via their cognitive features (e.g., a concession relation would be described as a negative causal relation).

Proceedings of the 4th Workshop on Computational Approaches to Discourse (CODI 2023), pages 99–105
July 13-14, 2023 ©2023 Association for Computational Linguistics

2 Related work

2.1 Discourse Relation Classification

Our work is not the first to use information from typical connectives for enriching classification: For example, the implicit DCs that are annotated together with the sense labels in PDTB have been incorporated into the training objective (Kishimoto et al., 2020; Jiang et al., 2021a; Kurfalı and Östling, 2021; Jiang et al., 2021b). Several works also utilize the label hierarchy of the PDTB to train the model to learn the difference between the labels by contrastive learning (Long and Webber, 2022) or operate on the label hierarchy for learning sounder embeddings to direct the prediction (Wu et al., 2021). In this work, we operate on the label names to incorporate the information of the DCs and the PDTB hierarchy.

In addition, DRs can be described in terms of features. The Cognitive approach to Coherence Relations (CCR) (Sanders et al., 1992, 2021) characterizes the nature of DRs by "dimensions" such as *basic operation*, *source of coherence*, *order* and *polarity*. For example, a CONTRAST relation can be described as a *negative* relation of *addition* operation with *objective* source of coherence. We also explore the potential of encoding these unifying dimensions of DRs into the label names for IDRR.

2.2 Exploiting label Similarity

Text classification tasks typically distinguish between a large number of categories or labels. Various approaches have been proposed to model the relation between the semantics of the labels and the text to be classified. Zhang et al. (2018) compares the vectors of the inputs and labels in a multitask learning setting. Wang et al. (2018) use label-based attention scores to embed the label information. Xiong et al. (2021) append the labels to the inputs, such that the embeddings of the labels are learned using the self-attention mechanism of BERT.

Our work builds on the Label Confusion Model (LCM; Guo et al., 2021), which was proposed for learning about the similarity of instances and labels simultaneously during training and which can be expected to be particularly useful in classification tasks with many similar labels. The LCM generates an alternate semantically informed vector in place of one-hot vectors.

For every input to the base model, the LCM inputs all the labels of the corresponding classification tasks, i.e., the LCM is run in parallel with a base model, as seen on the right side of Figure 1. The LCM model consists of a label encoder and a Simulated Label Distribution (SLD) block. The encoder, which comprises an input layer, an embedding layer and a linear layer produces a representation for all the labels.

The representation produced by the base model before the soft-max layer and the representation generated by the LCM encoder is made compatible such that they have dimensions that enable a similarity calculation. A similarity calculation is performed in the SLD block between the representation produced by the base model and the label encoder to generate the SLD distribution in place of one-hot vectors. A controlling parameter is α modulates the balance between the original label one-hot vector and the generated SLD.

Then, KL-divergence loss is computed between the predicted label distribution (PLD) of the base model and the generated SLD. The final labels are predicted using the soft-max classifier of the base model. The LCM trains in parallel with the base model until the LCM-stop epoch, which is determined by a hyper-parameter.

Experiments and analyses on data sets like DBPedia[1], THUCNews[2], etc., show that the LCM can generate representations that capture the dependencies between the labels and assist the base model to better understand the obscure meaning of the target labels compared with one-hot representation. In this work, we train an IDRR model with the LCM to exploit the semantics of the DR labels.

3 Methodology

3.1 LCM for IDRR

We train an 11-way classification model which predicts one of the second-level DR labels defined in PDTB 2.0, as shown in the first column of Table 1, given the two spans of text (called *Arg 1* and *Arg 2*) the DR links. To do so, we trained the LCM with a state-of-the-art IDRR model, which is the Bilateral Matching and Gated Fusion (BMGF) RoBERTa model (Liu et al., 2020).

The BMGF-RoBERTa is a complex model that comprises six layers: a hybrid representation layer, a context representation layer, a matching layer, a fusion layer, an aggregation layer, and a prediction layer. As shown in Fig 1, the LCM runs concurrently with the BMGF-RoBERTa for each input

[1]https://www.dbpedia.org/

[2]http://thuctc.thunlp.org/

instance. We initialize the embedding layer of the LCM with pre-trained GloVe (Pennington et al., 2014) word embeddings of the labels and their variations as described in table 1. The learned representation generated by the prediction layer of the BMGF-RoBERTa is fed as the input to the SLD block of the LCM. KL-divergence loss is calculated between the predicted label distribution (PLD) of the BMGF-RoBERTa and the generated SLD. The final labels are predicted using the soft-max classifier of the BMGF-RoBERTa and the SLD produced by the LCM is utilized for optimizing the loss until the LCM-stop epoch, which is determined by a hyper-parameter. After the LCM-stop epoch, only the BMGF-RoBERTa is trained further and the LCM is inactive.

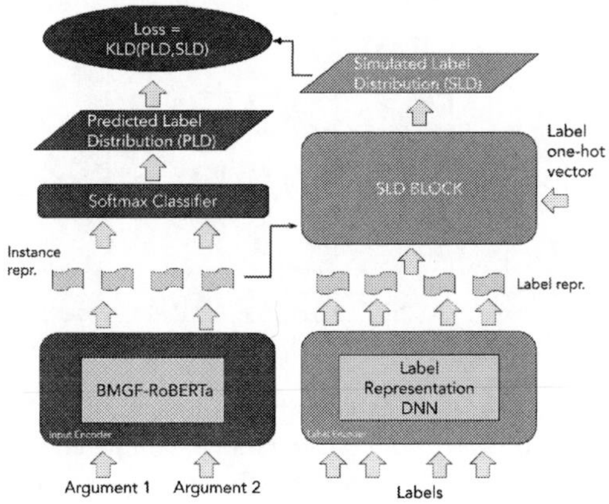

Figure 1: Combined architecture of the BMGF-RoBERTa and the LCM

3.2 Encoding other DR knowledge

Training with the LCM allows the IDRR model to learn the association between the input arguments and the semantics of the label tokens, such as CONJUNCTION and CAUSE. We hypothesize that more detailed relationships could be learned with more expressive label tokens. We explore three alternative ways of encoding label similarity: via label encodings, via encodings of prototypical connectives and via CCR features.

DR labels The PDTB 2.0 labels are arranged in a three-level hierarchical structure, where the 11-way labels, which are usually used in classification tasks, belong to the second level and are children of one of the four parent categories, namely TEMPORAL, COMPARISON, CONTINGENCY, and EXPANSION. Labels under the same parent category are more closely related than labels of different parent categories. In our experiments, we compare the use of only the level-2 labels with the combination of level-2 and level-1 "parent" labels.

Prototypical DCs DCs are used in both traditional and crowd-sourced annotations to facilitate the identification of the implicit DRs (Prasad et al., 2007; Yung et al., 2019). Most relations can be characterized by some prototypical DCs. For example, a CAUSAL relation is best represented by *because* and *therefore*. We define a subset of prototypical DCs for each label and replace the label tokens with the DC tokens. We do not include preposition tokens present in multi-word DCs in order not to dilute the overall semantic representation of the labels (e.g. *example* instead of *for example*).

Cognitive approach to Coherence Relations (CCR) Sanders et al. (2021) decompose each third-level DR in the PDTB 2.0 with five unifying dimensions. We specify each second-level relation by the dimension values shared by its children. Two or three dimensions are enough to specify the second-level relations. We use these CRR tokens in addition to the original DR tokens because certain second-level relations, such as CONJUNCTION and RESTATEMENT, have the same set of dimension values. We do not include value tokens that semantically overlap with the relation label. For example, we do not include the value of the *temporal order* dimension of the SYNCHRONOUS relation, because it is also *synchronous*.

Table 1 shows the lexical terms we use for each setting. We combine the representation of the multiple tokens per label by summing up the GloVe embeddings of the individual tokens[3].

3.3 Data and setting

We train and evaluate the proposed model on the PDTB 2.0 data set (Prasad et al., 2008). We use sections 2-20 for the training, 21-22 for testing, and 0-1 for validation, following e.g. Ji and Eisenstein (2015). The models are trained for the 11-way classification of the second-level sense labels.

We use the codes of the BMGF-RoBERTa released on GitHub[5], which was implemented in PyTorch, and re-implemented the original LCM from

[3]We also experimented with vector averaging. Similar results were obtained.

[4]For integrity, we use single tokens in the original labels. For the PRAGMATIC CAUSE relation, we used the token *pragmatic* instead of *cause* since there is already a CAUSE relation.

[5]https://github.com/HKUST-KnowComp/BMGF-RoBERTa

Original labels	Parent labels	Prototype DCs	CCR features
concession	comparison	despite, even, though, however	negative, causal
contrast	comparison	contrast, comparison, but	negative, addition, objective
cause	contingency	because, result, therefore	positive, causal, objective
pragmatic (cause)	contingency	considering, accordingly	positive, causal, subjective
alternative	expansion	alternatively, instead, rather	positive, addition
conjunction	expansion	addition, also, furthermore	positive, addition
instantiation	expansion	example, instance	positive, addition
list	expansion	firstly, secondly, thirdly	positive, addition
restatement	expansion	other, words, means	positive, addition
asynchronous	temporal	subsequently, afterwards, previously	positive, addition
synchrony	temporal	same, time, simultaneously, meanwhile	positive, addition

Table 1: Tokens used in each label representation strategy. The *prototype DC* tokens replace the original labels while the *CCR* and *parent* tokens are used in addition to the original labels [4].

TensorFlow to PyTorch in order to integrate the two models.

For training, we have utilized 3 $\times$ NVIDIA Tesla V100, with a batch size of 16. The pre-trained embedding utilized where GloVe (Pennington et al., 2014) common crawl with 42B tokens. Whenever we utilized the pre-trained word embeddings for the labels, the weights of the embedding layer were frozen and not updated during the training. The values of the hyper-parameters α is optimized to 4 using initialization in the range of 1–6. The LCM-stop parameter is set to 100, which is chosen based on the implementation of Guo et al. (2021). The results reported below are averaged over five runs.

4 Results

Table 2 compares the results of the models evaluated by accuracy and macro F1. It can be observed that all versions of the LCM improved the baseline model. In particular, the LCM model using prototype DCs outperforms the other models.

Model	Accuracy	macro F1
BL (Liu et al., 2020)	55.20 (.013)	36.07 (.010)
+ LCM (orig.)	57.20 (0.006)	38.92 (0.014)
+ LCM (orig.+parent)	57.55 (.010)	40.48 (.006)
+ LCM (orig.+CCR)	57.69 (.004)	39.45 (.015)
+ LCM (protyp. DC)	**57.80** (0.013)	**40.63** (0.025)

Table 2: 11-way classification results on PDTB 2.0[6]. The standard deviation of the five runs is shown in brackets respectively.

Figure 2 compares the distribution of the labels predicted by the baseline and the *LCM (protyp. DC)* models as well as the gold labels of the five most frequent DRs in the test set[7]. It shows that the baseline model over-predicts CONTRAST, CAUSAL, and CONJUNCTION. Inspection of the samples reveals that many of the over-predicted CONTRAST are actually CAUSAL, while the over-predicted CAUSAL and CONJUNCTION are mostly RESTATEMENT and these are correctly classified by the model with LCM. However, the LCM also leads to over-prediction of RESTATEMENT. We will look at some concrete examples in the next section.

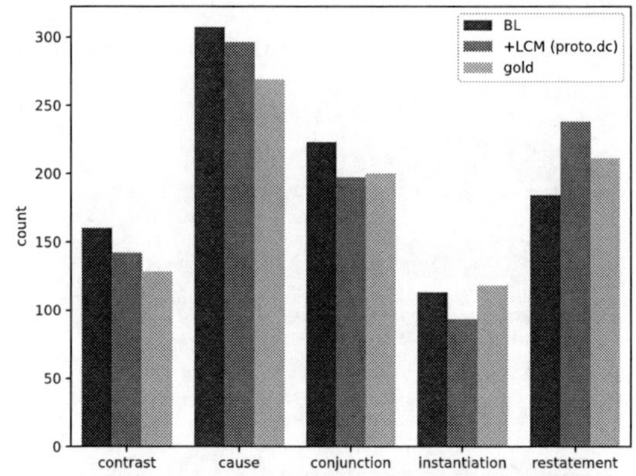

Figure 2: Distribution of the predictions produced by the *BL* and *LCM (protyp. DC)* model compared with gold on the five most frequent DR labels. The counts are the average values of the five runs of each model.

The predicted label distributions suggest that the LCM allows the IDRR model to learn the difference and similarity between COMPARISON and EXPANSION, but not among different types of EXPANSION. The parent relation and the CCR features of all EXPANSION relations are in fact the same. That could explain why the performances of these two versions on the EXPANSION items are similar, while LCM_{DC} performs slightly better.

[6]The published accuracy of the BMGF-RoBERTa is 58.13. We found that the discrepancy is because, according to the released codes, the result of the best **test** epoch has been reported. For fair evaluation, we report the results of all the models based on the best **validation** epoch (based on macro F1).

[7]These are the gold labels of 90% of the test set instances.

5 Qualitative Analysis

In this section, we analyze some examples that demonstrate that the LCM has better captured the implicit DRs between two arguments.

First, as mentioned in the previous section, the false positive CONTRAST relations predicted by the baseline model are mostly CAUSAL relations. In most of these cases, the *Arg2* contains the tokens *now* or *still*, which are often used to mark *contrast*, as in the following example.

(2) [Last week that company and union negotiations had overcome the major hurdle, ...]$_{Arg1}$ [Now only minor points remain to be cleaned up]$_{Arg2}$
(gold: : CONTINGENCY.CAUSE
LCM: CONTINGENCY.CAUSE
baseline: COMPARISON.CONTRAST)

In Example 2, the baseline model's prediction might have been based on the local markers *now* and the lexical pair *major* and *minor*, while the LCM model infers the positive relation between *overcome major hurdle* and *only minor points remain*.

Secondly, the LCM models overpredict RESTATEMENT relations, which are annotated as other relations in the PDTB. We found that for some of these cases, a restatement label could actually be justifiable as a secondary label.

(3) [Treating employees with respect is crucial for managers.]$_{Arg1}$ [It's in their top five work values.]$_{Arg2}$
(gold: : CONTINGENCY.CAUSE
LCM: EXPANSION.RESTATEMENT
baseline: CONTINGENCY.CAUSE)

(4) [Sotheby's defends itself and Mr. Paul in the matter.]$_{Arg1}$ [Mr. Wachter says Mr. Paul was a quick study who worked intensely and bought the best pictures available at the moment.]$_{Arg2}$
(gold: : EXPANSION.INSTANTIATION
LCM: EXPANSION.RESTATEMENT
baseline: EXPANSION.INSTANTIATION)

In Example (3), *respect being crucial* is the reason that it is counted as a *top value*, but these two arguments can also be viewed as different ways to state that it is important for managers to repect their employees. In Example (4), *Mr. Wachter's comment* could be an example of how *Sotheby's defends Mr. Paul*. However, depending on the context, Arg2 can also be interpreted as a RESTATEMENT. These cases suggest that the LCM tends to confuse relations most easily when they are similar or have semantic overlap.

However, we do note that there are cases where the LCM model indeed overpredicts restatement relations, see example (5).

(5) [It's no longer enough to beat the guy down the street.]$_{Arg1}$ [You have to beat everyone around the world.]$_{Arg2}$
(gold: : EXPANSION.ALTERNATIVE
LCM: EXPANSION.RESTATEMENT
baseline: EXPANSION.ALTERNATIVE)

Finally, comparing the different versions of the LCM models, the LCM$_{DC}$ model outperforms the other two models in predicting CAUSAL and CONJUNCTION relations. A possible explanation is that the DC tokens used to represent these relations are indeed strongly prototypical compared with other relations. This suggests that the choice of prototype DCs has a strong effect on the model performance. On the other hand, the LCM$_{parent}$ model has the highest recall of INSTANTIATION relations, but these are often co-occurring with RESTATEMENT, which is predicted by the other two variants.

6 Conclusion

We proposed to inform an IDRR model with knowledge about the DRs encoded in the classification labels using the LCM, instead of treating each class independently. In addition, we explored various strategies to encode different types of knowledge into the model and found that they are all beneficial. This approach is flexible and can also be applied to other base models. Furthermore, learning the lexical semantics of the label tokens allows a model to train on multiple datasets even if they do not share the same label set, and this is the direction of our future work.

7 Limitations

The encoder of the LCM which we have utilized for our experiments is a basic deep neural network. Replacing it with more robust and effective architectures could help achieve better performance. Furthermore, instead of using pre-trained GloVe embeddings for the encoder, using IDDR-specific embeddings could have been a more efficient approach. Lastly, our models have been trained and evaluated on PDTB 2.0, instead of the latest PDTB 3.0, which includes also intra-sentential implicit relations and has a more systematic sense hierarchy.

Acknowledgments

This project is supported by the German Research Foundation (DFG) under Grant SFB 1102 ("Information Density and Linguistic Encoding", Project-ID 232722074).

References

Biyang Guo, Songqiao Han, Xiao Han, Hailiang Huang, and Ting Lu. 2021. Label confusion learning to enhance text classification models. In *Proceedings of the AAAI Conference on Artificial Intelligence*, volume 35, pages 12929–12936.

Yangfeng Ji and Jacob Eisenstein. 2015. One vector is not enough: Entity-augmented distributed semantics for discourse relations. *Transactions of the Association for Computational Linguistics*, 3:329–344.

Congcong Jiang, Tieyun Qian, Zhuang Chen, Kejian Tang, Shaohui Zhan, and Tao Zhan. 2021a. Generating pseudo connectives with mlms for implicit discourse relation recognition. In *PRICAI 2021: Trends in Artificial Intelligence: 18th Pacific Rim International Conference on Artificial Intelligence, PRICAI 2021, Hanoi, Vietnam, November 8–12, 2021, Proceedings, Part II 18*, pages 113–126. Springer.

Feng Jiang, Yaxin Fan, Xiaomin Chu, Peifeng Li, and Qiaoming Zhu. 2021b. Not just classification: Recognizing implicit discourse relation on joint modeling of classification and generation. In *Proceedings of the 2021 Conference on Empirical Methods in Natural Language Processing*, pages 2418–2431.

Yudai Kishimoto, Yugo Murawaki, and Sadao Kurohashi. 2020. Adapting bert to implicit discourse relation classification with a focus on discourse connectives. In *Proceedings of the Twelfth Language Resources and Evaluation Conference*, pages 1152–1158.

Murathan Kurfalı and Robert Östling. 2021. Let's be explicit about that: Distant supervision for implicit discourse relation classification via connective prediction. In *Proceedings of the 1st Workshop on Understanding Implicit and Underspecified Language*, pages 1–10.

Xin Liu, Jiefu Ou, Yangqiu Song, and Xin Jiang. 2020. On the importance of word and sentence representation learning in implicit discourse relation classification.

Wanqiu Long and Bonnie Webber. 2022. Facilitating contrastive learning of discourse relational senses by exploiting the hierarchy of sense relations. In *Proceedings of the 2022 Conference on Empirical Methods in Natural Language Processing*, pages 10704–10716, Abu Dhabi, United Arab Emirates. Association for Computational Linguistics.

Jeffrey Pennington, Richard Socher, and Christopher Manning. 2014. GloVe: Global vectors for word representation. In *Proceedings of the 2014 Conference on Empirical Methods in Natural Language Processing (EMNLP)*, pages 1532–1543, Doha, Qatar. Association for Computational Linguistics.

Rashmi Prasad, Nikhil Dinesh, Alan Lee, Eleni Miltsakaki, Livio Robaldo, Aravind Joshi, and Bonnie Webber. 2008. The Penn Discourse TreeBank 2.0. In *Proceedings of the Sixth International Conference on Language Resources and Evaluation (LREC'08)*, Marrakech, Morocco. European Language Resources Association (ELRA).

Rashmi Prasad, Eleni Miltsakaki, Nikhil Dinesh, Alan Lee, and Aravind Joshi. 2007. The penn discourse treebank 2.0 annotation manual.

Ted JM Sanders, Vera Demberg, Jet Hoek, Merel CJ Scholman, Fatemeh Torabi Asr, Sandrine Zufferey, and Jacqueline Evers-Vermeul. 2021. Unifying dimensions in coherence relations: How various annotation frameworks are related. *Corpus Linguistics and Linguistic Theory*, 17(1):1–71.

Ted JM Sanders, Wilbert PM Spooren, and Leo GM Noordman. 1992. Toward a taxonomy of coherence relations. *Discourse processes*, 15(1):1–35.

Guoyin Wang, Chunyuan Li, Wenlin Wang, Yizhe Zhang, Dinghan Shen, Xinyuan Zhang, Ricardo Henao, and Lawrence Carin. 2018. Joint embedding of words and labels for text classification. In *Proceedings of the 56th Annual Meeting of the Association for Computational Linguistics (Volume 1: Long Papers)*, pages 2321–2331, Melbourne, Australia. Association for Computational Linguistics.

Changxing Wu, Liuwen Cao, Yubin Ge, Yang Liu, Min Zhang, and Jinsong Su. 2021. A label dependence-aware sequence generation model for multi-level implicit discourse relation recognition.

Yijin Xiong, Yukun Feng, Hao Wu, Hidetaka Kamigaito, and Manabu Okumura. 2021. Fusing label embedding into BERT: An efficient improvement for text classification. In *Findings of the Association for Computational Linguistics: ACL-IJCNLP 2021*, pages 1743–1750, Online. Association for Computational Linguistics.

Frances Yung, Vera Demberg, and Merel Scholman. 2019. Crowdsourcing discourse relation annotations by a two-step connective insertion task. In *Proceedings of the 13th Linguistic Annotation Workshop*, pages 16–25.

Honglun Zhang, Liqiang Xiao, Wenqing Chen, Yongkun Wang, and Yaohui Jin. 2018. Multi-task label embedding for text classification. In *Proceedings of the 2018 Conference on Empirical Methods in Natural Language Processing*, pages 4545–4553, Brussels, Belgium. Association for Computational Linguistics.

SAE-NTM: Sentence-Aware Encoder for Neural Topic Modeling

Hao Liu, Jingsheng Gao, Suncheng Xiang, Ting Liu, Yuzhuo Fu*
School of SEIEE, Shanghai Jiao Tong University, China
{liuh236, gaojingsheng, xiangsuncheng17, louisa_liu, yzfu}@sjtu.edu.cn

Abstract

Incorporating external knowledge, such as pre-trained language models (PLMs), into neural topic modeling has achieved great success in recent years. However, employing PLMs for topic modeling generally ignores the maximum sequence length of PLMs and the interaction between external knowledge and bag-of-words (BOW). To this end, we propose a sentence-aware encoder for neural topic modeling, which adopts fine-grained sentence embeddings as external knowledge to entirely utilize the semantic information of input documents. We introduce sentence-aware attention for document representation, where BOW enables the model to attend on topical sentences that convey topic-related cues. Experiments on three benchmark datasets show that our framework outperforms other state-of-the-art neural topic models in topic coherence. Further, we demonstrate that the proposed approach can yield better latent document-topic features through improvement on the document classification.

1 Introduction

Topic models have been widely used to identify human-interpretable topics and learn text representations, which have been applied for various tasks in Natural Language Processing (NLP) such as information retrieval (Lu et al., 2011), summarization (Nguyen et al., 2021), and semantic similarity detection (Peinelt et al., 2020). A typical topic models is based on the latent Dirichlet allocation (LDA) (Blei et al., 2003) and Bayesian inference. However, to avoid the complex and expensive iterative inference of conventional topic models, topic modeling with the deep neural network has been the leading research direction in this field (Miao et al., 2016; Srivastava and Sutton, 2017; Ding et al., 2018).

Neural topic models (NTMs) usually exploit the BOW representation as input, disregarding the syntactic and semantic relationships among the words in a document, thus leading to relatively inferior quality of topics. Recently, pre-trained language models (PLMs) (Kenton and Toutanova, 2019; Reimers and Gurevych, 2019) demonstrate their strong ability to capture sentential coherence by achieving state-of-the-art performance on many natural language processing tasks. Therefore, several approaches have been proposed to incorporate external knowledge into topic models to address the limitations of BOW. A typical method to take external knowledge as additional features (Bianchi et al., 2021; Jin et al., 2021) concentrates the outputs of PLMs with BOW data. Another way (Hoyle et al., 2020) is to distill the knowledge of the teacher PLMs to generate a smoothed pseudo-document, which guides the training of a student topic model.

However, there are still limitations to the above approaches. Firstly, the document-level sequences are too long to be modeled, since the token-level sequence in the context is usually considered as input to the PLMs. Extracting the document-level semantic embedding with PLMs as external knowledge ignores the restriction on sequence length, which loses massive semantic information from input text. Secondly, the difference in learning objectives between NTMs and PLMs makes it challenging to incorporate external knowledge. The encoder of NTMs is designed to handle the sparse BOW data, unable to take into account the dense contextual document embedding from PLMs.

To address these limitations, we build upon the framework of variational autoencoders (VAE) (Kingma and Welling, 2013) and propose a sentence-aware encoder for incorporating external semantic knowledge into topic models. The proposed approach integrates the advantages of NTMs and PLMs as encoders. Specifically, the encoder of the topic model is responsible for processing document-level BOW data like most NTMs, while the PLMs is used to encode sentence-

* Corresponding Author

Proceedings of the 4th Workshop on Computational Approaches to Discourse (CODI 2023), pages 106–111
July 13-14, 2023 ©2023 Association for Computational Linguistics

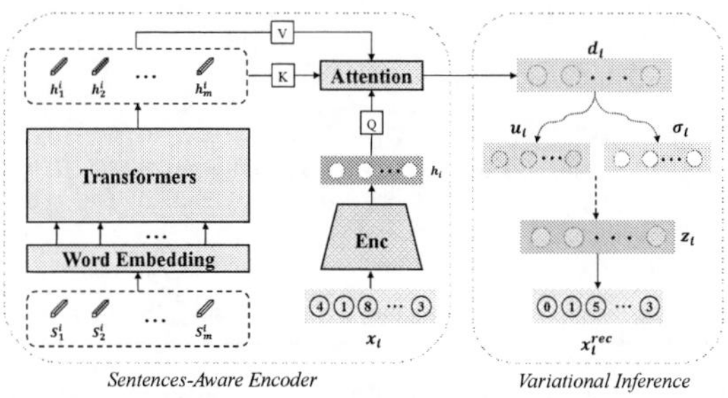

Figure 1: Basic Architecture of SAE-NTM. The sentence-aware encoder deals with the BOW data $\boldsymbol{x}_i$ and sentence sequences $\{\boldsymbol{s}_1^i, \cdots, \boldsymbol{s}_m^i\}$ of the ith document, while variational inference reconstructs the BOW data $\boldsymbol{x}_i^{rec}$ from document representation $\boldsymbol{d}_i$.

level semantic information as its original training objective. Different from previous approaches, our proposed framework considers cross-attention (Vaswani et al., 2017) between the BOW data and sentence embeddings, which leverages fine-grained semantic information for topic discovery.

To summarize, the main contributions of this paper are as followed: (1) We propose a novel framework **SAE-NTM**: **S**entences-**A**ware **E**ncoder for **N**eural **T**opic **M**odeling which leverages the cross-attention for incorporating external semantic knowledge in a sentence-aware manner. (2) Quantitative and qualitative experiments demonstrate that our proposed approach significantly outperforms the existing state-of-the-art topic models in topic coherence. (3) We show that the BOW-guided attention yields practical latent document-topic features, achieving better performance on the document classification task.

2 Methodology

2.1 SAE: Sentence-Aware Encoder

In this section, we introduce the sentence-level semantic information as external knowledge and propose a method to efficiently combine BOW data with external knowledge for document representations, as shown in Figure 1.

Encoder for bag-of-words and sentence sequences. Neural topic models with variational autoencoders usually take high-dimensional, sparse word counts $\boldsymbol{x}_i$ as input and transform it into a low-dimensional dense feature $\boldsymbol{h}_i$ to fit the variational autoencoders framework as formulated in Eq.1.

$$\boldsymbol{h}_i = Enc\left(\boldsymbol{x}_i\right) \tag{1}$$

Where $Enc : \mathbf{R}^V \to \mathbf{R}^L$ is usually a multi-layer perceptron (MLP) for the inference of the ith document representation.

Complementary to the orderless BoW, the context of the document carries more affluent and more sophisticated semantic information. And it can be represented as contextual embeddings by pre-trained language models (e.g., BERT (Kenton and Toutanova, 2019)) from large corpora, which have a fine-grained ability to capture aspects of linguistic context. In this paper, we employ sentence-transformers (Reimers and Gurevych, 2019) to encode each sentence in the document as follows:

$$\{\boldsymbol{h}_1^i, \cdots, \boldsymbol{h}_m^i\} = Trans\left(\{\boldsymbol{s}_1^i, \cdots, \boldsymbol{s}_m^i\}\right) \tag{2}$$

where s_j^i is a sequence of tokens and h_j^i is the aggregated contextual embedding from the pre-trained sentence-transformers for the jth sentence.

Sentence-aware Attention. The contextual embeddings $\{\boldsymbol{h}_1^i, \cdots, \boldsymbol{h}_m^i\}$ and BOW representation $\boldsymbol{h}_i$ jointly constitute the input of sentence-aware encoder. Then sentence-aware attention is employed to accomplish the interaction of word counts and semantic embeddings formulated in Eq.3.

$$\begin{aligned} \boldsymbol{d}_i &= \sum_{j=1}^{j=m} \alpha_j^i h_j^i \\ \alpha_j^i &= \frac{\exp(score(h_i, h_j^i))}{\sum_{k=1}^{k=m} \exp(score(h_i, h_k^i))} \end{aligned} \tag{3}$$

Where the representation $\boldsymbol{d}_i$ of the ith document is a weighted sum of contextual embeddings $\{\boldsymbol{h}_1^i, \cdots, \boldsymbol{h}_m^i\}$ and α_j^i is the normalized attention of the jth sentence. Typically, the scoring function *score* is scaled dot-product attention. Sentence embeddings as external knowledge provide rich textual information, while the BOW data guides topic model in the assignment of attention on topical sentences, which contributes to capturing the co-occurrence patterns of the words.

2.2 Variational inference

Starting with the document representation, variational inference (Kingma and Welling, 2013) consider Logistic-Normal distribution as the posterior distribution $q(\mathbf{z} \mid \mathbf{x})$, whose mean $\boldsymbol{\mu}_i$ and variance $\boldsymbol{\sigma}_i$ vectors are separately derived from the document representation through a linear layer. Then the reparameterization trick in Eq.4 is used to estimate the gradient.

$$\boldsymbol{z}_i = \mathrm{softmax}\left(\boldsymbol{\mu}_i + \boldsymbol{\sigma}_i \cdot \boldsymbol{\varepsilon}_i\right) \tag{4}$$

Method	K=50			K=200		
	20NG	Wiki	IMDb	20NG	Wiki	IMDb
W-LDA (Nan et al., 2019)	0.274 ± 0.012	0.492 ± 0.014	0.134 ± 0.003	0.159 ± 0.002	0.316 ± 0.007	0.090 ± 0.001
SCHOLAR (Chang et al., 2009)	0.322 ± 0.005	0.480 ± 0.009	0.166 ± 0.004	0.262 ± 0.003	0.416 ± 0.005	0.140 ± 0.002
CLNTM (Nguyen and Luu, 2021)	0.327 ± 0.002	0.486 ± 0.013	0.167 ± 0.002	0.267 ± 0.002	0.425 ± 0.003	0.144 ± 0.001
CTM (Bianchi et al., 2021)	0.329 ± 0.003	0.484 ± 0.016	0.176 ± 0.002	0.283 ± 0.005	0.432 ± 0.004	0.163 ± 0.004
SCHOLAR + BAT (Hoyle et al., 2020)	0.343 ± 0.006	0.501 ± 0.007	0.170 ± 0.004	0.301 ± 0.002	0.437 ± 0.003	0.160 ± 0.002
SAE-NTM (Ours)	**0.352 ± 0.006**	**0.511 ± 0.011**	**0.196 ± 0.001**	**0.314 ± 0.002**	**0.472 ± 0.004**	**0.174 ± 0.002**

Table 1: Results of average NPMI scores with 50 and 200 topics on three datasets. For each group of results, we repeat the experiment five times with different random initialization and report the standard deviation.

where $\varepsilon_i \sim \mathcal{N}(0,1)$ denotes samples from the normal distribution and z_i is the latent document-topic vector. Next, it attempts to reconstruct the original BOW data x_i by modeling the words distributions of topics ϕ as follows:

$$x_i^{rec} \sim \text{Multi}\left(\text{softmax}\left(z_i \phi^T\right), N\right) \quad (5)$$

where $\phi \in \mathbf{R}^{V \times K}$ is the word-topic matrix and $\mathbf{N}$ is a vector of document lengths.

Finally, SAE-NTM are trained by maximizing the Evidence Lower Bound (ELBO) of the marginal likelihood of the BoW data:

$$\mathcal{L}(\mathbf{x}) = -\mathbf{E}_q [\log p(\mathbf{x} \mid \mathbf{z})] + \mathbf{KL}[q(\mathbf{z} \mid \mathbf{x}) \| p(\mathbf{z})] \quad (6)$$

where $\log p(\mathbf{x} \mid \mathbf{z})$, $q(\mathbf{z} \mid \mathbf{x})$ and $p(\mathbf{z})$ are respectively the reconstructed data likelihood, the posterior distribution and prior Dirichlet distribution.

3 Experiments

In this section, we design empirical experiments to answer the following questions of concern in topic modeling. First, how effectively does SAE-NTM perform quantitatively and qualitatively in terms of topic quality? Second, how does SAE-NTM perform in automated document-topic inference for downstream tasks? Besides, more details about the impact of external knowledge on topic modeling can be found in Appendix A.

3.1 Experimental Settings

Datasets. We evaluate our proposed SAE-NTM on three benchmark datasets, which differ significantly in the domain, vocabulary size, and document length: 20Newsgroups (20NG, Lang, 1995) [1], Wikitext-103 (Wiki, Merity et al., 2016) [2], IMDb movie reviews (IMDb, Maas et al., 2011) [3]. For consistency with prior work, we adopt the same preprocessing steps and train/dev/test split from the original papers for 20NG (i.e., 48/12/40), Wiki (i.e., 70/15/15), IMDb (i.e., 50/25/25).

Baselines. We compare our model with existing state-of-the-art neural topic models: W-LDA (Nan et al., 2019) is a neural model with wassestein autoencoder, which approximates the Dirichlet prior by minimizing Maximum Mean Discrepancy. SCHOLAR (Card et al., 2018) is a VAE-based neural topic model with a logistic normal prior to facilitate approximate Bayesian inference and provide a flexible way to incorporate document metadata. SCHOLAR+BAT (Hoyle et al., 2020) is a knowledge-distilled neural topic model where a BERT-based autoencoder as a teacher provides contextual knowledge for the student model. CTM (Bianchi et al., 2021) is a combined topic model with the incorporation of contextualized document embeddings in neural topic models. CLNTM (Nguyen and Luu, 2021) is a contrastive learning version of the neural topic model through a word-based sampling strategy.

3.2 Evaluation in topic coherence

Since topic models aim to discover a set of latent topics that are meaningful and useful for humans (Chang et al., 2009), we evaluate topic coherence using the Normalized Mutual Pointwise Information (NPMI) which is significantly correlated with human judgments on topic quality (Aletras and Stevenson, 2013; Lau et al., 2014). Specifically, we first select the top 10 words under each topic generated by topic models, and then estimate NPMI scores with reference co-occurrence counts from the held-out corpus, e.g. the dev or test split.

As shown in Table 1, we report the results of the average NPMI over 5 runs with different random seeds for initialization for robustness. It can be observed that our model yields the most coher-

[1] qwone.com/~jason/20Newsgroups

[2] s3.amazonaws.com/research.metamind.io/wikitext/wikitext-103-v1

[3] ai.stanford.edu/Ëœamaas/data/sentiment

Dataset	Model	NPMI	Topic Words
20NG	SCHOLAR	0.234	encryption enforcement privacy conversation *industry manufacturer* protect *administration* device
	Our Model	0.434	encryption enforcement clipper agency wiretap privacy escrow protect security secure
Wiki	SCHOLAR	0.379	opera composer repertory theatre conductor *libretto* operatic *painting* orchestral *painter*
	Our Model	0.632	cantata bach recitative oboe continuo soloist chorale viola soprano violin
IMDb	SCHOLAR	0.161	religious beliefs christian *society* christ *views* portray *racist issues* jesus
	Our Model	0.333	christ christian religion church jesus religious bible faith god beliefs

Table 2: Some example topics on three datasets, where the italic words are less relevant to the topic.

ent topics across all baselines for three benchmark datasets in NPMI scores. This demonstrates that our method promotes the overall quality of generated topics. More importantly, our model not only significantly outperforms the baseline without external knowledge such as SCHOLAR, but also surpasses other state-of-the-art neural topic models that incorporate external knowledge, such as CTM, SCHOLAR+BAT. It suggests that our approach is more efficient than others for incorporating external knowledge into neural topic models.

In addition to the quantitative evaluation, we also randomly extract sample topics from three datasets to gain an intuitive view on the quality of generated topics, as shown in Table 2. Obviously, the topic words generated by our model capture the concept of topics in the document rather than the baseline model. For example, it can be noticed that in the 20NG dataset our words are closely related to encryption (*agency, wiretap, etc.*), rather than some common words (*industry, manufacturer, etc.*) from SCHOLAR. The words generated by our model in Wiki are more focused on *cantata* and *opera*, while SCHOLAR drifts gradually away from the music topic to *paintings*. Similarly in the IMDb dataset, the topic words generated by our model reflect religion-related themes, which is different from SCHOLAR including off-topic words such as *views, racist, etc.*

3.3 Document Classification

Since the latent vectors inferred by neural topic models can be applied as text features (Nan et al., 2019), we employ the downstream task of document classification to compare the predictive performance of the models in addition to the evaluation of topic coherence. Specifically, we collect latent document-topic features from the trained neural topic models setting number of topics to 50 and use these vectors as inputs to train a Random Forest classifier on the training split separately.

Model	20NG	IMDb
W-LDA	52.3	80.3
SCHOLAR	62.8	82.7
CLNTM	58.4	79.5
CTM	62.4	84.5
SCHOLAR + BAT	65.2	83.1
SAE-NTM (Ours)	**66.1**	**85.9**

Table 3: Test Accuracy between different topic models on document classification.

We report classification accuracy on the test split of 20NG and IMDb in Table 3. It is worth noting that we aim to evaluate the predictive capability of topic models by the performance in document classification, rather than training the model to obtain higher accuracy. The document-topic features provided by our proposed model achieve best accuracy for all the datasets with a significant improvement. It demonstrates that the proposed sentence-aware encoder not only discovers topics that are more meaningful to humans, but also learns better latent document features.

4 Conclusions

In this paper, we propose a Sentence-Aware Encoder for Neural Topic Modeling framework: SAE-NTM to incorporate external knowledge into neural topic models. The proposed method can capture document information by performing attention on sequential sentences in a bag-of-words guided manner. Extensive experiments have shown that our framework can achieve state-of-the-art performance in topic coherence and encode better latent document-topic features. In the future, we would like to explore the possibility of integrating our approach with neural topic models built on other frameworks, such as generative adversarial training (Nan et al., 2019; Wang et al., 2020).

Limitations

The proposed model with sentence-aware encoder aims to efficiently incorporate external knowledge and bag-of-words for topic modeling, which means that in this work we are mainly interested in how documents should be encoded for topic inference. However, the decoder of topic models can also be coupled with word embeddings through factorization, such as embedded topic models (Dieng et al., 2020). It is worth exploring how hierarchical semantic embeddings can be employed for topic modeling with our model.

In this paper, we do not conduct any fine-tuning for the pre-trained language model. Our approach reveals how the frozen pre-trained language model can be effectively used to improve the performance of the topic model with limited computational overhead, given that the parameter size of the pre-trained language model is much larger than that of the topic model. Moreover, fine-tuning pre-trained language models for topic modeling as an unsupervised learning task (Mueller and Dredze, 2021) is challenging.

References

Nikolaos Aletras and Mark Stevenson. 2013. Evaluating topic coherence using distributional semantics. In *Proceedings of the 10th International Conference on Computational Semantics (IWCS 2013)–Long Papers*, pages 13–22.

Federico Bianchi, Silvia Terragni, and Dirk Hovy. 2021. Pre-training is a hot topic: Contextualized document embeddings improve topic coherence. In *ACL*, pages 759–766.

David M Blei, Andrew Y Ng, and Michael I Jordan. 2003. Latent dirichlet allocation. *Journal of machine Learning research*, 3(Jan):993–1022.

Dallas Card, Chenhao Tan, and Noah A Smith. 2018. Neural models for documents with metadata. In *ACL*, pages 2031–2040.

Jonathan Chang, Sean Gerrish, Chong Wang, Jordan Boyd-Graber, and David Blei. 2009. Reading tea leaves: How humans interpret topic models. *Advances in neural information processing systems*, 22.

Adji B Dieng, Francisco JR Ruiz, and David M Blei. 2020. Topic modeling in embedding spaces. *Transactions of the Association for Computational Linguistics*, 8:439–453.

Ran Ding, Ramesh Nallapati, and Bing Xiang. 2018. Coherence-aware neural topic modeling. *arXiv preprint arXiv:1809.02687*.

Alexander Miserlis Hoyle, Pranav Goel, and Philip Resnik. 2020. Improving neural topic models using knowledge distillation. In *EMNLP*, pages 1752–1771.

Yuan Jin, He Zhao, Ming Liu, Lan Du, and Wray Buntine. 2021. Neural attention-aware hierarchical topic model. In *EMNLP*, pages 1042–1052.

Jacob Devlin Ming-Wei Chang Kenton and Lee Kristina Toutanova. 2019. Bert: Pre-training of deep bidirectional transformers for language understanding. In *Proceedings of naacL-HLT*, pages 4171–4186.

Diederik P Kingma and Max Welling. 2013. Auto-encoding variational bayes. *arXiv preprint arXiv:1312.6114*.

Ken Lang. 1995. Newsweeder: Learning to filter netnews. In *Machine Learning Proceedings 1995*, pages 331–339. Elsevier.

Jey Han Lau, David Newman, and Timothy Baldwin. 2014. Machine reading tea leaves: Automatically evaluating topic coherence and topic model quality. In *EACL*, pages 530–539.

Jianhua Lin. 1991. Divergence measures based on the shannon entropy. *IEEE Transactions on Information theory*, 37(1):145–151.

Yue Lu, Qiaozhu Mei, and ChengXiang Zhai. 2011. Investigating task performance of probabilistic topic models: an empirical study of plsa and lda. *Information Retrieval*, 14(2):178–203.

Andrew Maas, Raymond E Daly, Peter T Pham, Dan Huang, Andrew Y Ng, and Christopher Potts. 2011. Learning word vectors for sentiment analysis. In *ACL*, pages 142–150.

Stephen Merity, Caiming Xiong, James Bradbury, and Richard Socher. 2016. Pointer sentinel mixture models. *arXiv preprint arXiv:1609.07843*.

Yishu Miao, Lei Yu, and Phil Blunsom. 2016. Neural variational inference for text processing. In *International conference on machine learning*, pages 1727–1736. PMLR.

Aaron Mueller and Mark Dredze. 2021. Fine-tuning encoders for improved monolingual and zero-shot polylingual neural topic modeling. In *Proceedings of the 2021 Conference of the North American Chapter of the Association for Computational Linguistics: Human Language Technologies*, pages 3054–3068.

Feng Nan, Ran Ding, Ramesh Nallapati, and Bing Xiang. 2019. Topic modeling with wasserstein autoencoders. In *ACL*, pages 6345–6381.

Thong Nguyen and Anh Tuan Luu. 2021. Contrastive learning for neural topic model. *Advances in Neural Information Processing Systems*, 34:11974–11986.

Thong Nguyen, Anh Tuan Luu, Truc Lu, and Tho Quan. 2021. Enriching and controlling global semantics for text summarization. *arXiv preprint arXiv:2109.10616*.

Nicole Peinelt, Dong Nguyen, and Maria Liakata. 2020. tbert: Topic models and bert joining forces for semantic similarity detection. In *ACL*, pages 7047–7055.

Nils Reimers and Iryna Gurevych. 2019. Sentence-bert: Sentence embeddings using siamese bert-networks. In *Proceedings of the 2019 Conference on Empirical Methods in Natural Language Processing and the 9th International Joint Conference on Natural Language Processing (EMNLP-IJCNLP)*, pages 3982–3992.

Akash Srivastava and Charles Sutton. 2017. Autoencoding variational inference for topic models. *arXiv preprint arXiv:1703.01488*.

Ashish Vaswani, Noam Shazeer, Niki Parmar, Jakob Uszkoreit, Llion Jones, Aidan N Gomez, Łukasz Kaiser, and Illia Polosukhin. 2017. Attention is all you need. *Advances in neural information processing systems*, 30.

Rui Wang, Xuemeng Hu, Deyu Zhou, Yulan He, Yuxuan Xiong, Chenchen Ye, and Haiyang Xu. 2020. Neural topic modeling with bidirectional adversarial training. *arXiv preprint arXiv:2004.12331*.

Andrew KC Wong and Manlai You. 1985. Entropy and distance of random graphs with application to structural pattern recognition. *IEEE transactions on pattern analysis and machine intelligence*, (5):599–609.

A Analysis on individual topics

To evaluate whether our improvements are meaningful on individual topics, we directly compare each of the aligned topics generated by the baseline SCHOLAR without external knowledge and our model. Follow previous works (Hoyle et al., 2020; Nguyen and Luu, 2021), we align the topics by using a variation of competitive linking to greedily approximate the optimal weight of the bipartite graph matching. And the weight of each link is calculated based on the similarity between their word distributions as measured Jenson-Shannon (JS) divergence (Wong and You, 1985; Lin, 1991). We iteratively select the topic pair with the lowest score based on JS divergence, separate the two topics from the topic list, and repeat until the rest JS score exceeds a certain threshold.

Figure 2 shows the JS-divergences for aligned topic pairs for three benchmark corpora. Based on visual inspection, we choose the most aligned 44 topic pairs to conduct the comparison, since there is no conceptual relationship between topic pairs beyond this point and employ the same threshold across all three datasets for simplicity. Considering these aligned topic pairs conceptually related, we explore the impact of external knowledge on the baseline topic model on a topic-by-topic basis as shown in Figure 3. It can be observed that the number of topics with high NPMI scores from our model is apparently more than that of the baseline model. This means that the overall promotion achieved by our approach can be interpreted as identifying the topic space generated by the baseline models and in most cases, improving the coherence of individual topics.

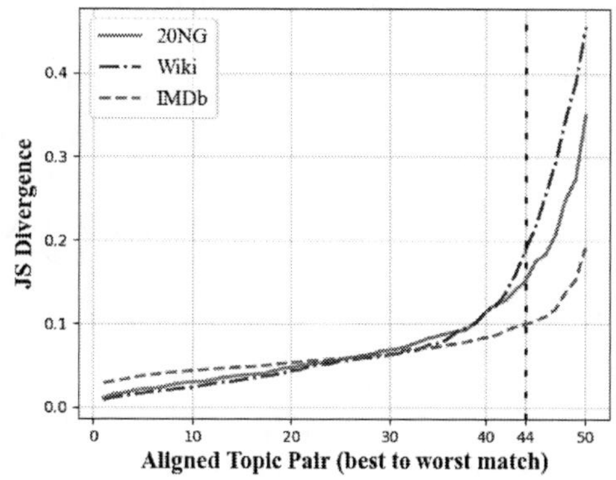

Figure 2: Jensen-Shannon divergence for aligned topic pairs of SCHOLAR and our model.

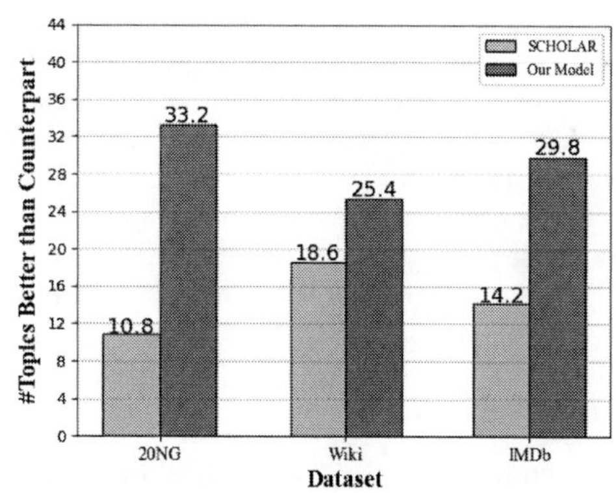

Figure 3: The number of aligned topic pairs which our model improves upon SCHOLAR model.

Improving Long Context Document-Level Machine Translation

Christian Herold **Hermann Ney**
Human Language Technology and Pattern Recognition Group
Computer Science Department
RWTH Aachen University
D-52056 Aachen, Germany
{herold|ney}@cs.rwth-aachen.de

Abstract

Document-level context for neural machine translation (NMT) is crucial to improve the translation consistency and cohesion, the translation of ambiguous inputs, as well as several other linguistic phenomena. Many works have been published on the topic of document-level NMT, but most restrict the system to only local context, typically including just the one or two preceding sentences as additional information. This might be enough to resolve some ambiguous inputs, but it is probably not sufficient to capture some document-level information like the topic or style of a conversation. When increasing the context size beyond just the local context, there are two challenges: (i) the memory usage increases exponentially (ii) the translation performance starts to degrade. We argue that the widely-used attention mechanism is responsible for both issues. Therefore, we propose a constrained attention variant that focuses the attention on the most relevant parts of the sequence, while simultaneously reducing the memory consumption. For evaluation, we utilize targeted test sets in combination with novel evaluation techniques to analyze the translations in regards to specific discourse-related phenomena. We find that our approach is a good compromise between sentence-level NMT vs attending to the full context, especially in low resource scenarios.

1 Introduction

Machine translation (MT) is the task of mapping some input text onto the corresponding translation in the target language. MT systems typically operate on the sentence-level and utilize neural networks trained on large amounts of bilingual data (Bahdanau et al., 2014; Vaswani et al., 2017). These neural machine translation (NMT) systems perform remarkably well on many domains and language pairs, sometimes even on par with professional human translators. However, when the automatic translations are evaluated on the document-level (e.g. the translation of a whole paragraph or conversation is evaluated), they reveal shortcomings regarding consistency in style, entity-translation or correct inference of the gender, among other things (Läubli et al., 2018; Müller et al., 2018; Thai et al., 2022). The goal of document-level NMT is to resolve these shortcomings by including context information as additional input when translating a sentence.

In recent years, many works have been published on the topic of document-level NMT. However, most of these works focus only on including a few surrounding sentences as context. When the context size is increased beyond that, typically a degradation of overall translation performance is reported. Additionally, the transformer architecture as the quasi standard in NMT seems sub optimal to handle long sequences as input/output, since the memory complexity increases quadratically with the sequence length. This is due to the attention mechanism, where each token in a sequence needs to attend to all other tokens.

In this work, we propose a constrained attention variant for the task of document-level NMT. The idea is to reduce the memory consumption while at the same time focusing the attention of the system onto the most relevant parts of the sequence. Our contributions are two-fold:

1. We observe that the attention patterns become less focused on the current sentence when increasing the context-size of our document-level NMT systems. Therefore we propose a constrained attention variant that is also more memory efficient.

2. We utilize a targeted evaluation method to assess automatic translations in regards to consistency in style and coreference resolution. We find that our document-level NMT approach performs among the best across all language-pairs and test scenarios.

Proceedings of the 4th Workshop on Computational Approaches to Discourse (CODI 2023), pages 112–125
July 13-14, 2023 ©2023 Association for Computational Linguistics

2 Related Work

Many works have been published on the topic of document-level NMT. The widely used baseline approach consists of simply concatenating a few adjacent sentences and feeding this as an input to the MT system, without modifying the system architecture in any way (Tiedemann and Scherrer, 2017; Bawden et al., 2018; Agrawal et al., 2018; Talman et al., 2019; Nguyen et al., 2021; Majumde et al., 2022). Also, several modifications to this baseline concatenation approach have been proposed. Ma et al. (2020) introduce segment embeddings and also partially constrain the attention to the tokens of the current sentence. Zhang et al. (2020) propose to calculate the self-attention both on the sentence- and on the document-level and then combine the two representations. Fernandes et al. (2021) and Lei et al. (2022) both mask out tokens in the current sentence to increase context utilization while Yang et al. (2023) remove tokens from the context if they are not attended. Typically, slight improvements in BLEU are reported as well as more significant improvements on targeted test sets e.g. for coreference resolution.

Apart from the simple concatenation method, there exist other approaches to document-level NMT. They include using a single document-embedding vector (Macé and Servan, 2019; Stojanovski and Fraser, 2019; Jiang et al., 2020; Huo et al., 2020), multiple encoders (Jean et al., 2017; Bawden et al., 2018; Wang et al., 2017; Voita et al., 2018; Zhang et al., 2018), hierarchical attention (Miculicich et al., 2018; Maruf et al., 2019; Tan et al., 2019; Wong et al., 2020), translation caches (Maruf and Haffari, 2018; Tu et al., 2018; Kuang et al., 2018) or dynamic evaluation (Mansimov et al., 2021). However, these approaches are less versatile and require significant changes to the model architecture, often introducing a significant amount of additional parameters. Furthermore, recent works have concluded that the baseline concatenation approach first proposed by Tiedemann and Scherrer (2017) performs as good - if not better - than these more complicated approaches (Lopes et al., 2020; Sun et al., 2022).

While the concatenation approach works well for short context sizes, when used with a larger number of context sentences, typically performance degradation is reported: Scherrer et al. (2019) saw a severe performance degradation when using input sequences with a length of 250 tokens. Liu et al. (2020) could not get their system to converge when using context sizes of up to 512 tokens. They improve training stability by adding additional monolingual data via pre-training. Bao et al. (2021) also report that their systems with context length of more than 256 tokens fail to converge. They propose to partially constrain the attention to the current sentence, similar to Zhang et al. (2020). Sun et al. (2022) try to translate full documents with the concatenation approach but could not get their system to converge during training. Their solution is to mix document- and sentence-level data, which reportedly improves system convergence. Li et al. (2022) report severe performance degradation for context sizes longer than 512 tokens. They argue this is due to insufficient positional information and improve performance by repeatedly injecting this information during the encoding process. However, increasing the context size seems to not always result in performance degradation. In their works, Junczys-Dowmunt (2019) and Saleh et al. (2019) train systems with a context size of up to 1000 tokens without degradation in translation quality, which stands in contrast to the works mentioned above and which we will discuss again in the context of our own results. We want to point out that all of the approaches mentioned above still have the problem of quadratically increasing resource requirements, which poses a big challenge even on modern hardware.

Since our proposed approach consists of modifying the attention matrix in the model architecture, we give a brief overview of previous works related to this concept. The works of Ma et al. (2020), Zhang et al. (2020) and Bao et al. (2021) are most closely related and were already mentioned above. All three papers restrict the attention (partially) to the current sentence and combine sentence- and document-level attention context vectors for the final output. However, this means all approaches still suffer from the quadratic dependency on the number of input tokens. Luong et al. (2015) were among the first to propose using the attention concept for the task of MT. They also proposed using a sliding-window with target-to-source alignment for attention similar to us. However, they only work on sentence-level NMT and to the best of our knowledge, this approach was never before transferred to document-level NMT. Shu and Nakayama (2017) and Chen et al. (2018) both extend the approach of Luong et al. (2015) while still working solely on sentence-level NMT. Our approach is also related to the utilization of relative positional encoding, which was introduced by Shaw et al. (2018) and later extended by Yang et al. (2018) to be applicable for cross-attention. The work by Indurthi et al. (2019) should also be mentioned, where they pre-select a subset of source tokens on which to perform attention on. Again, all of the above mentioned works only perform experiments on sentence-level NMT. The works of Child et al. (2019), Sukhbaatar et al. (2019) and Guo et al. (2020) are also related, since they use attention windows similar to us for tasks other than MT.

Finally, we briefly want to touch on the subject of automatic evaluation of document-level MT systems. Many works only report results on general MT metrics like BLEU (Papineni et al., 2002), sometimes matching n-grams across sentence-boundaries. However, it has been argued that these metrics do not capture well the very specific improvements that could be expected by including document-level context and that the reported improvements rather come from regularization effects and comparing to sub optimal baseline performance (Kim et al., 2019; Li et al., 2020; Nguyen et al., 2021). Several targeted test suites have been released to better assess the improvements gained by document-level NMT (Müller et al., 2018; Bawden et al., 2018; Voita et al., 2019; Jwalapuram et al., 2019). These test suites have some limitations, for example they are language-specific and they are based on just scoring predefined contrastive examples without scoring the actual translations. More recently, Jiang et al. (2022) and Currey et al. (2022) have released frameworks that allow to score the actual MT hypotheses in regards to their consistency regarding specific aspects of the translation.

3 Methodology

Here, we explain the baseline concatenation approach (Section 3.1), the more refined method that we are comparing ourselves against (Section 3.2) as well as our own approach (Section 3.3). We also discuss our different evaluation approaches in Section 3.5.

3.1 The Baseline Concatenation Approach

The baseline concatenation approach is very simple and follows Tiedemann and Scherrer (2017) using the vanilla transformer architecture (Vaswani et al., 2017). Assume we are given a document $\mathcal{D} = (F_n, E_n)_1^N$ consisting of N source-target sentence-pairs (F_n, E_n). If we want our model to have a context length of k sentences, we simply concatenate the current input sentence with its $k-1$ predecessor sentences and the input to the model would be

F_{n-k} <sep> F_{n-k+1} ... <sep> F_n <eos>

while on the target side we include the preceding sentences as a prefix

E_{n-k} <sep> E_{n-k+1} ... <sep> E_{n-1} <sep>.

We use a special token <sep> as a separator between adjacent sentences and <eos> denotes the end of the sequence. This is done to make it easier for the model to distinguish between the sentence that needs to be translated and the context. Furthermore, we use a special token $F_0 = E_0 =$ <bod> to denote the start of a document. Since we use the vanilla transformer architecture with self-attention and cross-attention components, the memory usage is $\mathcal{O}(L^2)$ with L being the sequence length.

When we train full document-level systems, we simply concatenate all sentences in the document using again the special <sep> token. Due to hardware limitations, if the length of the target-side of the document exceeds 1000 tokens, we split the document into smaller parts of roughly equal length (i.e. a document of length 1500 tokens would be split into two parts with ca. 750 tokens each).

Model	Context	Attn. [%]	BLEU
sent.-level	0 sent.	100.0	32.8
concat adj.	1 sent.	76.0	33.1
	1000 tok.	46.6	29.5

Table 1: Percentage of attention on the n-th source sentence during decoding the n-th target sentence, as well as overall translation quality measured in BLEU, for the newstest2018 test set of the *NEWS* task.

In a preliminary study, we train systems using no context (sentence-level), just a single sentence as context as well as the maximum context size of 1000 tokens. When looking at the percentage of attention that is payed to the n-th source sentence F_n when decoding the n-th target sentence E_n (extracted from cross-attention module, see Table 1) we find that this percentage becomes lower as the context size increases. This finding motivates us to explore approaches that bias the attention towards the current sentence.

3.2 LST-attention

This method was proposed by Zhang et al. (2020) and is called Long-Short Term (LST) attention. The authors find that their approach outperforms the baseline concatenation approach but they only use a maximum of 3 sentences as context. Nevertheless we deem this approach promising, since it also focuses the attention onto the current sentence. The input to the system is augmented in the same way as described in Section 3.1. Given some queries $Q \in \mathbb{R}^{I \times d}$, keys $K \in \mathbb{R}^{J \times d}$ and values $V \in \mathbb{R}^{J \times d}$, Zhang et al. (2020) formulate their restricted version of the attention as[1]

$$\mathrm{A}(Q, K, V) = \mathrm{softmax}\left(\frac{Q \cdot K^{\intercal}}{\sqrt{d}} + M\right) V$$

with d being the hidden dimension of the model and $M \in \mathbb{R}^{I \times J}$ being the masking matrix. This masking matrix is defined as

$$M_{i,j} = \begin{cases} 0 & , s(i) = s(j) \\ -\inf & , \text{otherwise} \end{cases}$$

where $s(\cdot) \in 1, .., N$ is a function that returns the sentence index that a certain position belongs to. This means we are restricting the attention to be calculated only within the current sentence. For self-attention in the encoder and the decoder, Zhang et al. (2020) calculate both the restricted and the non-restricted variant and then combine the output context-vectors via concatenation and a linear transformation. The cross-attention between encoder and decoder remains unchanged in this approach and the memory consumption remains $\mathcal{O}(L^2)$.

3.3 window-attention

This method is proposed by us. We can use the same formulation as above to describe this approach by simply changing the definition of the attention mask to

$$M_{i,j} = \begin{cases} 0 & , b_i - w \leq j \leq b_i + w \\ -\inf & , \text{otherwise} \end{cases} \quad (1)$$

where w is the window size and $b_i \in 1, ..., J$ is a target-source alignment. This means a certain query vector q_i is only allowed to attend to the key vectors k_j that surround the position b_i that this query vector is aligned to. We replace all self-attention and cross-attention modules in our network with this window-attention variant. Please note that in practice we do not calculate this mask, but instead we first select the corresponding key-vectors for each query and then calculate attention only between these subsets which reduces the memory consumption from $\mathcal{O}(L^2)$ to $\mathcal{O}(L \cdot w)$. We also want to point out that with this approach, the context is not as restricted as it seems on first glance. For any individual attention module, the context is restricted to $2 \cdot w$ or w for self-attention in the encoder and decoder respectively. However, since in the transformer architecture we stack multiple layers, we get a final effective context size of $2 \cdot w \cdot num\_enc\_layers + w \cdot num\_dec\_layers$.

This approach requires us to define an alignment function $b_i : [1, I] \rightarrow [1, J]$. For self-attention, we assume a 1-1 alignment so the alignment function is the identity function $b_i = i$. For cross-attention, during training we use a linear alignment function

$$b_i = \mathrm{round}(\frac{J}{I} \cdot i)$$

where J is the number of tokens in the source document and I is the number of tokens in the target document. This is not possible during decoding, as we do not know the target document length beforehand. Therefore, we propose three different ways to approximate the alignment during decoding:

1. 1-1 alignment: $b_i = i$
2. linear alignment: $b_i = \mathrm{round}(train\_ratio \cdot i)$ where we define $train\_ratio$ as the average source-target ratio over all documents in the training data.
3. sent-align: assume we have already produced N' full target sentences (i.e. we have produced N' <sep> tokens) up to this point, then

$$b_i = \begin{cases} \sum_{n=1}^{N'} J_n + 1 & , e_{i-1} == \texttt{<sep>} \\ b_{i-1} + 1 & , \text{otherwise} \end{cases}$$

with J_n being the length of the n-th source sentence in the input document. In simple terms, when starting to decode a new sentence, we always force-align to the beginning of the corresponding source sentence.

We also test the *window-attention* approach with relative positional encoding in the self-attention

[1] In practice we use multi-head attention in all our architectures, but we omit this in the formulas for sake of simplicity. Also, for all methods, causal masking is applied in the decoder self-attention just like in the vanilla transformer.

instead of absolute positional encoding, which in this framework only requires a small modification to Equation 1:

$$M_{i,j} = \begin{cases} r_{i-j} & , b_i - w \leq j \leq b_i + w \\ -\inf & , \text{otherwise} \end{cases}$$

where $r_{i-j} \in \mathbb{R}^d$ are additional learnable parameters of the network.

3.4 Decoding

During decoding, given a document F_1^N, we want to find the best translation $\hat{E}_1^N$ according to our model. We can not perform exact search due to computational limitations, therefore we have to use approximations. There exist multiple approaches for decoding with a document-level NMT system and since we could not determine a single best approach from the literature, we describe and compare two competing approaches.

Full Segment Decoding (FSD) (Liu et al., 2020; Bao et al., 2021; Sun et al., 2022): we split the document into non-overlapping parts $F_1^k, F_{k+1}^{2k}, ..., F_{N-k}^N$ and translate each part separately using

$$\hat{E}_{i-k}^i = \operatorname*{argmax}_{E_{i-k}^i} \left\{ p(E_{i-k}^i | F_{i-k}^i) \right\},$$

which is approximated using standard beam search on the token level (we use beam size 12 for all experiments). For the full document-level systems, we simply use

$$\hat{E}_1^N = \operatorname*{argmax}_{E_1^N} \left\{ p(E_1^N | F_1^N) \right\}.$$

Sequential Decoding (SD) (Miculicich et al., 2018; Voita et al., 2019; Garcia et al., 2019; Fernandes et al., 2021): we generate the translation sentence by sentence, using the previously generated target sentences as context:

$$\hat{E}_i = \operatorname*{argmax}_{E_i} \left\{ p(E_i | \hat{E}_{i-k}^{i-1}, F_{i-k}^i) \right\}.$$

3.5 Evaluation

For all tasks we report BLEU (Papineni et al., 2002) and TER (Snover et al., 2006) using the SacreBLEU (Post, 2018) toolkit. In addition, for the two En-De tasks (*NEWS* and *OS*) we analyze the translations in regards to ambiguous pronouns and style. For pronouns, the goal is to measure how well a system can translate the English 3rd person pronoun 'it' (and its other forms) into the correctly gendered German form (which can be male, female or neuter depending on the context). For style, the goal is to measure, how well a system can translate the 2nd person pronoun 'you' (and its other forms) into the correct style in German. For example, 'you' (singular) can be translated into 'sie' or 'du' in German, depending if the setting is formal or informal. We employ several strategies to determine the systems ability to disambiguate these phenomena.

We utilize the ContraPro test suite (Müller et al., 2018) and report the contrastive scoring accuracy for pronoun resolution. The test suite contains 12,000 English sentences, each with the correct German reference as well as 2 contrastive German references where the pronoun has been changed to a wrong gender. We score all test cases with the NMT system and each time the system gives the best score to the true reference, it gets a point. In the end we report the scoring accuracy, i.e. the number of points the system has gathered divided by 12,000.

Additionally we also report F1 scores for pronoun and style translation, the method for which is inspired by Jiang et al. (2022). We use parts of speech (POS) taggers as well as language-specific regular expressions to identify ambiguous pronouns/formality in the test sets. We then compare the occurrences in the reference against the occurrences in the hypothesis, calculate precision and recall and then finally the F1 score for both pronoun as well as formality translation. The exact algorithm as well as detailed data statistics for the test sets are given in Appendix A.1. We report pronoun translation F1 score for both *NEWS* and *OS* tasks and the formality translation F1 score only for the *OS* task, since in the *NEWS* test set there are not enough examples of ambiguous formality cases. Our extension to the work of Jiang et al. (2022) can be found here: `https://github.com/christian3141/BlonDe`.

4 Experiments

We perform experiments on three document-level translation benchmarks. We call them **NEWS** (En→De) with `newstest2018` as test set, **TED** (En→It) with `tst2017` as test set and **OS** (En→De) where the test set is simply called `test`. *NEWS* is a collection of news articles, *TED* is a collection of transcribed TED talks and their respective translations and *OS* consists of subtitles for movies and TV shows. Especially the latter holds many examples for discourse between different entities. For the details regarding data conditions, preparation and training, we refer to Appendix A.2.

4.1 GPU Memory efficiency

First, we compare the GPU memory consumption of the baseline *concat-adj.* approach against the *window-attention* approach for various input sequence lengths. The results are shown in Table 2. As expected, the memory usage increases at a much higher rate for the *concat-adj.* approach, while the *window-attention* approach scales roughly linearly, the slope being a function of the window-size w.

# target tokens	concat-adj.	window-attn	
		$w = 10$	$w = 20$
736	2.3 GB	2.4 GB	3.5 GB
1472	5.8 GB	3.9 GB	5.9 GB
2208	10.9 GB	5.2 GB	8.5 GB

Table 2: GPU-memory consumption for the different approaches when training on a single document of specified number of target tokens.

4.2 Comparison of Decoding Strategies

After training all models on the *NEWS* task according to Appendix A.2, we test the different search strategies for each of the systems, the result of which can be found in Table 3. For the baseline *concat-adj.* approach as well as the *LST-attn* approach, *FSD* works best. However, we still see significant performance degradation for the systems using long context information. For *concat-adj.* and *LST-attn* with 1000 tokens context size, *SD* performs very poorly. This is because when beginning translating a document, the input sequences are very short and the systems can not appropriately handle that. However, *FSD* sometimes leads to sentence-misalignment while translating a document, resulting in a lower BLEU score as well. For the *window-attention* approach (rel. pos. enc., sent-align, window-size 20) we find that the *SD* decoding strategy works best. Since this approach seems to be able to better handle short input sequences, *SD* performs better than *FSD*, since it seems more robust to sentence-misalignment. Moving forward, all numbers reported will be generated with the best respective decoding approach, i.e. *SD* for *window-attention* and *FSD* for all other approaches.

Model	Context	Search Strategy	BLEU
sent.-level	0 sent.	-	32.8
concat-adj.	2 sent.	*FSD*	33.4
		SD	33.0
	1000 tok.	*FSD*	29.5
		SD	23.1
LST-attn	1000 tok.	*FSD*	30.0
		SD	22.2
window-attn	1000 tok.	*FSD*	31.5
		SD	33.1

Table 3: Results for employing the different search strategies for translating the `newstest2018` test set of the *NEWS* task.

4.3 Hyperparameter Tuning

Our *window-attention* approach has three hyperparameters that need to be tuned: (i) positional encoding variant (ii) alignment variant during search (iii) window size. Again, we use the *NEWS* task for tuning and the results for the different variants can be found in Table 4.

In terms of positional encoding, *relative* works significantly better than *absolute* for the *window-attention* system. We also test relative positional encoding (window-size 20) for the baseline *concat-adj.* method, but here the training did not converge. This is, because for long input sequences the system without explicit target-source alignment can no longer distinguish the token ordering on the source side (on the target side it is still possible due to the causal attention mask). The only way to resolve this would be to drastically increase the window-size for the relative positions, however, this would add a significant amount of additional parameters to the network so we decide against this. In terms of alignment, using the *sent-align* variant significantly outperforms the other approaches. For the *window-size*, 20 works best. An important finding is, that if we make the window too large, we start losing performance, probably due to the less focused attention problem discussed in Section 3.1.

4.4 Final Performance Comparison

In Table 5 we report the translation performance of the different document-level approaches on all three translation benchmarks measured in terms of BLEU and TER. None of the document-level systems can consistently outperform the sentence-

Model	pos. enc.	Alignment	window-size	BLEU	TER
concat-adj.	abs.	-	-	29.5	53.7
	rel.	-	-	N/A	N/A
window-attn	abs.	1-1	20	29.7	51.7
		train avg.	20	28.1	55.3
		sent-align	10	28.3	53.7
			20	30.3	50.9
			30	29.4	52.2
	rel.	1-1	20	31.9	49.8
		train avg.	20	30.5	53.2
		sent-align	10	30.6	51.8
			20	33.1	48.1
			30	32.8	48.4

Table 4: Results for the different hyperparameter settings of the *window-attention* system reported on the `newstest2018` test set of the *NEWS* task. All systems have context size 1000 tokens.

Model	Context	NEWS newstest2018		TED tst2017		OS test	
		BLEU	TER	BLEU	TER	BLEU	TER
sent.-level (external)	0 sent.	†32.3	-	‡33.4	-	*37.3	-
sent.-level (ours)		32.8	49.0	34.2	46.3	37.1	**43.8**
concat adj.	2 sent.	**33.4**	48.6	34.3	46.3	38.2	43.9
	1000 tok.	29.5	53.7	32.1	48.4	38.1	46.0
LST-attn	1000 tok.	30.0	53.1	29.8	54.5	**38.5**	45.1
window-attn	1000 tok.	33.1	**48.1**	**34.6**	**45.8**	38.3	44.4

Table 5: Results for the different document-level approaches in terms of BLEU and TER on the three translation benchmarks. Best results for each column are highlighted. External baselines are from † Kim et al. (2019), ‡ Yang et al. (2022) and *Huo et al. (2020).

level baseline on all tasks. On the *OS* test set, there is a disagreement between BLEU and TER which we think comes from the fact that the average sentence-length on this test set is quite short. The hypothesis of the sentence-level system is the shortest of all hypotheses and also shorter than the reference which gets punished more heavily by BLEU than TER. Out of all full-document approaches, *window-attention* performs best and is on par with the sentence-level baseline and the document-level system using only 2 sentences as context. For full-document translation, *LST-attn* performs better than the baseline concatenation approach but still falls behind the sentence-level system especially on the *NEWS* and *TED* tasks. One possible reason for why these approaches work better on *OS* is, that for this task we have much more training data available than for *NEWS* and *TED*. We argue that this could also be the reason for the conflicting results reported by Junczys-Dowmunt (2019) and Saleh et al. (2019) compared to the other works who report performance degradation for longer context sizes (see Section 2). However, we leave a detailed analysis of this for future work.

Next, we analyze the ability of the systems to translate ambiguous pronouns and to translate in a consistent style using the methods explained in Section 3.5. The results for the two En→De tasks can be found in Table 6. For both *NEWS* and *OS*, all document-level systems can significantly improve over the sentence-level baseline in terms of pronoun translation. We also find that a context longer than two sentences does not seems to help for the pronoun task. This is actually to be expected since typically the distance between noun and pronoun is not that large and according to Müller et al. (2018), the overwhelming majority of ContraPro test cases do not require more than two sentences as context. For the correct translation of the style however, the larger context size is clearly beneficial,

Model	Context	NEWS			OS			
		ContraPro			ContraPro			test
		BLEU	Scoring Acc. Pronoun	Pronoun Trans. F1	BLEU	Scoring Acc. Pronoun	Pronoun Trans. F1	Formality Trans. F1
sent.-level	0 sent.	18.4	48.2	44.5	29.7	45.8	40.3	59.4
concat adj.	2 sent.	**19.6**	**67.9**	**54.1**	31.2	81.8	63.2	61.7
	1000 tok.	15.4	61.9	47.8	29.9	83.1	64.6	70.1
LST-attn	1000 tok.	16.8	61.4	51.3	29.1	83.3	64.8	**70.9**
window-attn	1000 tok.	**19.6**	63.0	51.9	**31.4**	**83.9**	**66.5**	67.9

Table 6: Results for the different document-level approaches in terms of pronoun and formality translation. Best results for each column are highlighted.

source	reference
What's between you and Dr. Webber - is none of my business...	Was zwischen dir und Dr. Webber ist, geht mich nichts an...
- You don't owe me an apology.	Du schuldest mir keine Entschuldigung.
You owe Dr. Bailey one.	Du schuldest Dr. Bailey eine.
We were taking a stand for Dr. Webber.	Wir haben uns für Dr. Webber eingesetzt.
I don't understand why...	Ich verstehe nicht wieso...
Dr. Webber doesn't need you to fight his battles.	Dr. Webber braucht dich nicht, um seine Schlachten zu kämpfen.
What you did stands to hurt this entire hospital.	Was du getan hast, hat dem ganzen Krankenhaus geschadet.
Your first priority needs to be this place and its patients.	Deine oberste Priorität muss diesem Haus und seinen Patienten gelten.

sentence-level-hypothesis	window-mask-hypothesis
Was zwischen Ihnen und Dr. Webber ist, geht mich nichts an...	Was zwischen dir und Dr. Webber ist, geht mich nichts an...
- Du schuldest mir keine Entschuldigung.	- Du schuldest mir keine Entschuldigung.
Sie schulden Dr. Bailey etwas.	- Du schuldest Dr. Bailey eine.
Wir haben für Dr. Webber Partei ergriffen.	Wir haben für Dr. Webber Stellung bezogen.
Ich verstehe nicht, warum...	Ich verstehe nicht, warum...
Dr. Webber braucht Sie nicht, um seine Schlachten zu schlagen.	Dr. Webber braucht dich nicht, um seine Schlachten zu kämpfen.
Was du getan hast, verletzt das gesamte Krankenhaus.	Was du getan hast, könnte das ganze Krankenhaus verletzen.
Ihre oberste Priorität muss dieser Ort und seine Patienten sein.	Deine oberste Priorität muss dieser Ort und seine Patienten sein.

Table 7: Example translation of a snippet from the OpenSubtitles `test` set. Formal 2nd person pronouns are marked in red and informal ones are marked in blue.

as the system with just 2 sentences as context can barely outperform the sentence-level baseline. To correctly infer the style of a conversation, ideally the whole dialog should be part of the context, especially the beginning of the conversation. In Table 7, we show a snippet of the `test` set of the *OS task* together with the translations of the sentence-level system and the *window-attention* system. This example highlights the need for long-context NMT systems especially for the task of dialogue translation, since there we need to stay consistent in terms of style, which the sentence-level system can not manage. Overall, the *LST-attn* approach performs best for the task of formality translation, but the other full-document systems are not far behind.

5 Conclusion

In this work, we focus on methods to increase the context-size for document-level NMT systems. We point out the shortcomings of the baseline approaches to long-context document-level NMT and in turn propose to modify the attention component to be more focused and also to be more memory efficient. We compare our approach against approaches from literature on multiple translation tasks and using different targeted evaluation methods. We confirm the improved memory efficiency of the proposed method. We find that for some discourse phenomena like pronoun translation, the longer context information is not necessary. For other aspects, like consistent style translation, the longer context is very beneficial. It seems that the baseline concatenation approach needs large amounts of training data to perform well for larger context sizes. We conclude that our approach performs among the best across all tasks and evaluation methods, with the additional benefit of reduced memory consumption for long input sequences.

Acknowledgements

This work was partially supported by the project HYKIST funded by the German Federal Ministry of Health on the basis of a decision of the German Federal Parliament (Bundestag) under funding ID ZMVI1-2520DAT04A, and by NeuroSys which, as part of the initiative "Clusters4Future", is funded by the Federal Ministry of Education and Research BMBF (03ZU1106DA).

Limitations

This work is about document-level NMT, we focus specifically on methods that improve the model performance for long input sequences. Due to constrained resources, this work has several limitations. To be able to train all methods including the inefficient baseline approach, we have to limit the context size to 1000 tokens. While we do a comparison to existing approaches, other approaches have been proposed to improve the performance of systems with long context information, which we do not compare against. We run experiments on three different tasks, but two of them are low resource and two of them translate into German, which was necessary because we only had access to German language experts for preparing the evaluation.

References

Ruchit Rajeshkumar Agrawal, Marco Turchi, and Matteo Negri. 2018. Contextual handling in neural machine translation: Look behind, ahead and on both sides. In *21st Annual Conference of the European Association for Machine Translation*, pages 11–20.

Dzmitry Bahdanau, Kyunghyun Cho, and Yoshua Bengio. 2014. Neural machine translation by jointly learning to align and translate. *arXiv preprint arXiv:1409.0473*.

Guangsheng Bao, Yue Zhang, Zhiyang Teng, Boxing Chen, and Weihua Luo. 2021. G-transformer for document-level machine translation. In *Proceedings of the 59th Annual Meeting of the Association for Computational Linguistics and the 11th International Joint Conference on Natural Language Processing (Volume 1: Long Papers)*, pages 3442–3455.

Rachel Bawden, Rico Sennrich, Alexandra Birch, and Barry Haddow. 2018. Evaluating discourse phenomena in neural machine translation. In *Proceedings of the 2018 Conference of the North American Chapter of the Association for Computational Linguistics: Human Language Technologies, Volume 1 (Long Papers)*, pages 1304–1313.

Mauro Cettolo, Marcello Federico, Luisa Bentivogli, Jan Niehues, Sebastian Stüker, Katsuitho Sudoh, Koichiro Yoshino, and Christian Federmann. 2017. Overview of the iwslt 2017 evaluation campaign. In *Proceedings of the 14th International Workshop on Spoken Language Translation*, pages 2–14.

Kehai Chen, Rui Wang, Masao Utiyama, Eiichiro Sumita, and Tiejun Zhao. 2018. Syntax-directed attention for neural machine translation. *Proceedings of the AAAI Conference on Artificial Intelligence*, 32(1).

Rewon Child, Scott Gray, Alec Radford, and Ilya Sutskever. 2019. Generating long sequences with sparse transformers.

Anna Currey, Maria Nădejde, Raghavendra Pappagari, Mia Mayer, Stanislas Lauly, Xing Niu, Benjamin Hsu, and Georgiana Dinu. 2022. Mt-geneval: A counterfactual and contextual dataset for evaluating gender accuracy in machine translation. *arXiv preprint arXiv:2211.01355*.

Akhbardeh Farhad, Arkhangorodsky Arkady, Biesialska Magdalena, Bojar Ondřej, Chatterjee Rajen, Chaudhary Vishrav, Marta R Costa-jussa, España-Bonet Cristina, Fan Angela, Federmann Christian, et al. 2021. Findings of the 2021 conference on machine translation (wmt21). In *Proceedings of the Sixth Conference on Machine Translation*, pages 1–88. Association for Computational Linguistics.

Patrick Fernandes, Kayo Yin, Graham Neubig, and André FT Martins. 2021. Measuring and increasing context usage in context-aware machine translation. In *Proceedings of the 59th Annual Meeting of the Association for Computational Linguistics and the 11th International Joint Conference on Natural Language Processing (Volume 1: Long Papers)*, pages 6467–6478.

Eva Martínez Garcia, Carles Creus, and Cristina España-Bonet. 2019. Context-aware neural machine translation decoding. In *Proceedings of the Fourth Workshop on Discourse in Machine Translation (DiscoMT 2019)*, pages 13–23.

Qipeng Guo, Xipeng Qiu, Pengfei Liu, Xiangyang Xue, and Zheng Zhang. 2020. Multi-scale self-attention for text classification. *Proceedings of the AAAI Conference on Artificial Intelligence*, 34(05):7847–7854.

Jingjing Huo, Christian Herold, Yingbo Gao, Leonard Dahlmann, Shahram Khadivi, and Hermann Ney. 2020. Diving deep into context-aware neural machine translation. In *Proceedings of the Fifth Conference on Machine Translation*, pages 604–616.

Sathish Reddy Indurthi, Insoo Chung, and Sangha Kim. 2019. Look harder: A neural machine translation model with hard attention. In *Proceedings of the 57th Annual Meeting of the Association for Computational Linguistics*, pages 3037–3043, Florence, Italy. Association for Computational Linguistics.

Sebastien Jean, Stanislas Lauly, Orhan Firat, and Kyunghyun Cho. 2017. Does neural machine translation benefit from larger context? *arXiv preprint arXiv:1704.05135*.

Shu Jiang, Hai Zhao, Zuchao Li, and Bao-Liang Lu. 2020. Document-level neural machine translation with document embeddings.

Yuchen Jiang, Tianyu Liu, Shuming Ma, Dongdong Zhang, Jian Yang, Haoyang Huang, Rico Sennrich, Ryan Cotterell, Mrinmaya Sachan, and Ming Zhou. 2022. BlonDe: An automatic evaluation metric for document-level machine translation. In *Proceedings of the 2022 Conference of the North American Chapter of the Association for Computational Linguistics: Human Language Technologies*, pages 1550–1565, Seattle, United States. Association for Computational Linguistics.

Marcin Junczys-Dowmunt. 2019. Microsoft translator at WMT 2019: Towards large-scale document-level neural machine translation. In *Proceedings of the Fourth Conference on Machine Translation (Volume 2: Shared Task Papers, Day 1)*, pages 225–233, Florence, Italy. Association for Computational Linguistics.

Prathyusha Jwalapuram, Shafiq Joty, Irina Temnikova, and Preslav Nakov. 2019. Evaluating pronominal anaphora in machine translation: An evaluation measure and a test suite. In *Proceedings of the 2019 Conference on Empirical Methods in Natural Language Processing and the 9th International Joint Conference on Natural Language Processing (EMNLP-IJCNLP)*, pages 2964–2975.

Yunsu Kim, Duc Thanh Tran, and Hermann Ney. 2019. When and why is document-level context useful in neural machine translation? In *Proceedings of the Fourth Workshop on Discourse in Machine Translation (DiscoMT 2019)*, pages 24–34.

Shaohui Kuang, Deyi Xiong, Weihua Luo, and Guodong Zhou. 2018. Modeling coherence for neural machine translation with dynamic and topic caches. In *Proceedings of the 27th International Conference on Computational Linguistics*, pages 596–606, Santa Fe, New Mexico, USA. Association for Computational Linguistics.

Taku Kudo. 2018. Subword regularization: Improving neural network translation models with multiple subword candidates. In *Proceedings of the 56th Annual Meeting of the Association for Computational Linguistics, ACL 2018, Melbourne, Australia, July 15-20, 2018, Volume 1: Long Papers*, pages 66–75. Association for Computational Linguistics.

Samuel Läubli, Rico Sennrich, and Martin Volk. 2018. Has machine translation achieved human parity? a case for document-level evaluation. In *Proceedings of the 2018 Conference on Empirical Methods in Natural Language Processing*, pages 4791–4796.

Yikun Lei, Yuqi Ren, and Deyi Xiong. 2022. CoDoNMT: Modeling cohesion devices for document-level neural machine translation. In *Proceedings of the 29th International Conference on Computational Linguistics*, pages 5205–5216, Gyeongju, Republic of Korea. International Committee on Computational Linguistics.

Bei Li, Hui Liu, Ziyang Wang, Yufan Jiang, Tong Xiao, Jingbo Zhu, Tongran Liu, and Changliang Li. 2020. Does multi-encoder help? a case study on context-aware neural machine translation. *arXiv preprint arXiv:2005.03393*.

Yachao Li, Junhui Li, Jing Jiang, Shimin Tao, Hao Yang, and Min Zhang. 2022. P-transformer: Towards better document-to-document neural machine translation.

Pierre Lison, Jörg Tiedemann, and Milen Kouylekov. 2018. Opensubtitles2018: Statistical rescoring of sentence alignments in large, noisy parallel corpora. In *Proceedings of the Eleventh International Conference on Language Resources and Evaluation (LREC 2018)*.

Yinhan Liu, Jiatao Gu, Naman Goyal, Xian Li, Sergey Edunov, Marjan Ghazvininejad, Mike Lewis, and Luke Zettlemoyer. 2020. Multilingual Denoising Pre-training for Neural Machine Translation. *Transactions of the Association for Computational Linguistics*, 8:726–742.

António V Lopes, M Amin Farajian, Rachel Bawden, Michael Zhang, and André FT Martins. 2020. Document-level neural mt: A systematic comparison. In *22nd Annual Conference of the European Association for Machine Translation*, pages 225–234.

Thang Luong, Hieu Pham, and Christopher D. Manning. 2015. Effective approaches to attention-based neural machine translation. In *Proceedings of the 2015 Conference on Empirical Methods in Natural Language Processing*, pages 1412–1421, Lisbon, Portugal. Association for Computational Linguistics.

Shuming Ma, Dongdong Zhang, and Ming Zhou. 2020. A simple and effective unified encoder for document-level machine translation. In *Proceedings of the 58th Annual Meeting of the Association for Computational Linguistics*, pages 3505–3511.

Valentin Macé and Christophe Servan. 2019. Using whole document context in neural machine translation. In *Proceedings of the 16th International Conference on Spoken Language Translation*, Hong Kong. Association for Computational Linguistics.

Suvodeep Majumde, Stanislas Lauly, Maria Nadejde, Marcello Federico, and Georgiana Dinu. 2022. A baseline revisited: Pushing the limits of multi-segment models for context-aware translation. *arXiv preprint arXiv:2210.10906*.

Elman Mansimov, Gábor Melis, and Lei Yu. 2021. Capturing document context inside sentence-level neural machine translation models with self-training. In *Proceedings of the 2nd Workshop on Computational Approaches to Discourse*, pages 143–153, Punta Cana, Dominican Republic and Online. Association for Computational Linguistics.

Sameen Maruf and Gholamreza Haffari. 2018. Document context neural machine translation with memory networks. In *Proceedings of the 56th Annual Meeting of the Association for Computational Linguistics (Volume 1: Long Papers)*, pages 1275–1284.

Sameen Maruf, André FT Martins, and Gholamreza Haffari. 2019. Selective attention for context-aware neural machine translation. In *Proceedings of the 2019 Conference of the North American Chapter of the Association for Computational Linguistics: Human Language Technologies, Volume 1 (Long and Short Papers)*, pages 3092–3102.

Lesly Miculicich, Dhananjay Ram, Nikolaos Pappas, and James Henderson. 2018. Document-level neural machine translation with hierarchical attention networks. *arXiv preprint arXiv:1809.01576*.

Mathias Müller, Annette Rios Gonzales, Elena Voita, and Rico Sennrich. 2018. A large-scale test set for the evaluation of context-aware pronoun translation in neural machine translation. In *Proceedings of the Third Conference on Machine Translation: Research Papers*, pages 61–72.

Toan Q. Nguyen, Kenton Murray, and David Chiang. 2021. Data augmentation by concatenation for low-resource translation: A mystery and a solution. In *Proceedings of the 18th International Conference on Spoken Language Translation (IWSLT 2021)*, pages 287–293, Bangkok, Thailand (online). Association for Computational Linguistics.

Myle Ott, Sergey Edunov, Alexei Baevski, Angela Fan, Sam Gross, Nathan Ng, David Grangier, and Michael Auli. 2019. fairseq: A fast, extensible toolkit for sequence modeling. In *Proceedings of the 2019 Conference of the North American Chapter of the Association for Computational Linguistics (Demonstrations)*, pages 48–53.

Kishore Papineni, Salim Roukos, Todd Ward, and Wei-Jing Zhu. 2002. Bleu: a method for automatic evaluation of machine translation. In *Proceedings of the 40th annual meeting of the Association for Computational Linguistics*, pages 311–318.

Matt Post. 2018. A call for clarity in reporting bleu scores. In *Proceedings of the Third Conference on Machine Translation: Research Papers*, pages 186–191.

Fahimeh Saleh, Alexandre Berard, Ioan Calapodescu, and Laurent Besacier. 2019. Naver labs Europe's systems for the document-level generation and translation task at WNGT 2019. In *Proceedings of the 3rd Workshop on Neural Generation and Translation*, pages 273–279, Hong Kong. Association for Computational Linguistics.

Yves Scherrer, Jörg Tiedemann, and Sharid Loáiciga. 2019. Analysing concatenation approaches to document-level NMT in two different domains. In *Proceedings of the Fourth Workshop on Discourse in Machine Translation (DiscoMT 2019)*, pages 51–61, Hong Kong, China. Association for Computational Linguistics.

Rico Sennrich, Barry Haddow, and Alexandra Birch. 2016. Neural machine translation of rare words with subword units. In *Proceedings of the 54th Annual Meeting of the Association for Computational Linguistics (Volume 1: Long Papers)*, pages 1715–1725.

Peter Shaw, Jakob Uszkoreit, and Ashish Vaswani. 2018. Self-attention with relative position representations. In *Proceedings of the 2018 Conference of the North American Chapter of the Association for Computational Linguistics: Human Language Technologies, Volume 2 (Short Papers)*, pages 464–468, New Orleans, Louisiana. Association for Computational Linguistics.

Raphael Shu and Hideki Nakayama. 2017. An empirical study of adequate vision span for attention-based neural machine translation. page 1.

Matthew Snover, Bonnie Dorr, Richard Schwartz, Linnea Micciulla, and John Makhoul. 2006. A study of translation edit rate with targeted human annotation. In *Proceedings of the 7th Conference of the Association for Machine Translation in the Americas: Technical Papers*, pages 223–231.

Dario Stojanovski and Alexander Fraser. 2019. Combining local and document-level context: The LMU Munich neural machine translation system at WMT19. In *Proceedings of the Fourth Conference on Machine Translation (Volume 2: Shared Task Papers, Day 1)*, pages 400–406, Florence, Italy. Association for Computational Linguistics.

Sainbayar Sukhbaatar, Edouard Grave, Piotr Bojanowski, and Armand Joulin. 2019. Adaptive attention span in transformers. In *Proceedings of the 57th Annual Meeting of the Association for Computational Linguistics*, pages 331–335, Florence, Italy. Association for Computational Linguistics.

Zewei Sun, Mingxuan Wang, Hao Zhou, Chengqi Zhao, Shujian Huang, Jiajun Chen, and Lei Li. 2022. Rethinking document-level neural machine translation. In *Findings of the Association for Computational Linguistics: ACL 2022*, pages 3537–3548.

Aarne Talman, Umut Sulubacak, Raúl Vázquez, Yves Scherrer, Sami Virpioja, Alessandro Raganato, Arvi Hurskainen, and Jörg Tiedemann. 2019. The University of Helsinki submissions to the WMT19 news translation task. In *Proceedings of the Fourth Conference on Machine Translation (Volume 2: Shared Task Papers, Day 1)*, pages 412–423, Florence, Italy. Association for Computational Linguistics.

Xin Tan, Longyin Zhang, Deyi Xiong, and Guodong Zhou. 2019. Hierarchical modeling of global context for document-level neural machine translation. In *Proceedings of the 2019 Conference on Empirical Methods in Natural Language Processing and the 9th International Joint Conference on Natural Language Processing (EMNLP-IJCNLP)*, pages 1576–1585, Hong Kong, China. Association for Computational Linguistics.

Katherine Thai, Marzena Karpinska, Kalpesh Krishna, Bill Ray, Moira Inghilleri, John Wieting, and Mohit Iyyer. 2022. Exploring document-level literary machine translation with parallel paragraphs from world literature. *arXiv preprint arXiv:2210.14250*.

Jörg Tiedemann and Yves Scherrer. 2017. Neural machine translation with extended context. In *Proceedings of the Third Workshop on Discourse in Machine Translation*, pages 82–92.

Zhaopeng Tu, Yang Liu, Shuming Shi, and Tong Zhang. 2018. Learning to remember translation history with a continuous cache. *Transactions of the Association for Computational Linguistics*, 6:407–420.

Ashish Vaswani, Noam Shazeer, Niki Parmar, Jakob Uszkoreit, Llion Jones, Aidan N Gomez, Ł ukasz Kaiser, and Illia Polosukhin. 2017. Attention is all you need. In *Advances in Neural Information Processing Systems*, volume 30. Curran Associates, Inc.

Elena Voita, Rico Sennrich, and Ivan Titov. 2019. When a good translation is wrong in context: Context-aware machine translation improves on deixis, ellipsis, and lexical cohesion.

Elena Voita, Pavel Serdyukov, Rico Sennrich, and Ivan Titov. 2018. Context-aware neural machine translation learns anaphora resolution. *arXiv preprint arXiv:1805.10163*.

Longyue Wang, Zhaopeng Tu, Andy Way, and Qun Liu. 2017. Exploiting cross-sentence context for neural machine translation. *arXiv preprint arXiv:1704.04347*.

KayYen Wong, Sameen Maruf, and Gholamreza Haffari. 2020. Contextual neural machine translation improves translation of cataphoric pronouns. *arXiv preprint arXiv:2004.09894*.

Baosong Yang, Zhaopeng Tu, Derek F. Wong, Fandong Meng, Lidia S. Chao, and Tong Zhang. 2018. Modeling localness for self-attention networks. In *Proceedings of the 2018 Conference on Empirical Methods in Natural Language Processing*, pages 4449–4458, Brussels, Belgium. Association for Computational Linguistics.

Jian Yang, Yuwei Yin, Shuming Ma, Liqun Yang, Hongcheng Guo, Haoyang Huang, Dongdong Zhang, Yutao Zeng, Zhoujun Li, and Furu Wei. 2023. Hanoit: Enhancing context-aware translation via selective context.

Jian Yang, Yuwei Yin, Liqun Yang, Shuming Ma, Haoyang Huang, Dongdong Zhang, Furu Wei, and Zhoujun Li. 2022. Gtrans: Grouping and fusing transformer layers for neural machine translation. *IEEE/ACM Transactions on Audio, Speech, and Language Processing*.

Jiacheng Zhang, Huanbo Luan, Maosong Sun, Feifei Zhai, Jingfang Xu, Min Zhang, and Yang Liu. 2018. Improving the transformer translation model with document-level context. In *Proceedings of the 2018 Conference on Empirical Methods in Natural Language Processing*, pages 533–542.

Pei Zhang, Boxing Chen, Niyu Ge, and Kai Fan. 2020. Long-short term masking transformer: A simple but effective baseline for document-level neural machine translation. In *Proceedings of the 2020 Conference on Empirical Methods in Natural Language Processing (EMNLP)*, pages 1081–1087, Online. Association for Computational Linguistics.

A Appendix

A.1 Pronoun and Formality Translation Evaluation

Here, we explain how we calculate the pronoun translation and formality translation F1 scores.

Pronouns

For each triplet (F_n, E_n, $\hat{E}_n$) (source, hypothesis, reference) of our test data we first check if it contains a valid ambiguous pronoun. That means, in the source sentence there must be an English 3rd person pronoun in the neutral form and it also must be labeled as a pronoun by the English POS-tagger. We also check if a 2nd or 3rd person plural pronoun is present in the source and if that is the case, we do not consider female pronouns on the target side, since we could not distinguish if e.g. 'sie' is the translation of 'it' or 'they'. This would require a word alignment between source and hypothesis/reference which we do not have. If we found the example to be valid, we then check for occurrences of 3rd person pronouns in the male, female and neuter forms, in both reference and hypothesis using a German POS-tagger as well as language-specific regular expressions. After going through the complete test data (F_n, E_n, $\hat{E}_n$) sentence-by-sentence we calculate an F1 score for pronoun translation:

$$F1_{pro} = \frac{2 \cdot \text{P}_{pro} \cdot \text{R}_{pro}}{\text{P}_{pro} + \text{R}_{pro}}$$

with precision $\text{P}_{pro} =$

$$\frac{\sum_{n=1}^{N} \sum_x \min\Big(\text{CP}(F_n, E_n, x), \text{CP}(F_n, \hat{E}_n, x)\Big)}{\sum_n \sum_x \text{CP}(F_n, E_n, x)}$$

and recall $\text{R}_{pro} =$

$$\frac{\sum_{n=1}^{N} \sum_x \min\Big(\text{CP}(F_n, E_n, x), \text{CP}(F_n, \hat{E}_n, x)\Big)}{\sum_n \sum_x \text{CP}(F_n, \hat{E}_n, x)}$$

where $\text{CP}(\cdot, \cdot, \cdot)$ counts the number of valid pronoun occurrences and $x \in \{male, female, neuter\}$.

Formality

We follow almost exactly the same steps as for detecting the pronoun translations described above. The only differences are that we check for validity slightly differently and instead of pronouns we check for occurrences of formal/informal style. For sentence-pairs where 3rd person female/neuter or 3rd person plural pronouns are present, we do not count the formal occurrences, since we might not be able distinguish the German translations in these cases. We calculate an F1 score for formality translation using

$$F1_{for} = \frac{2 \cdot \text{P}_{for} \cdot \text{R}_{for}}{\text{P}_{for} + \text{R}_{for}}$$

with precision $\text{P}_{for} =$

$$\frac{\sum_{n=1}^{N} \sum_x \min\Big(\text{CP}(F_n, E_n, x), \text{CP}(F_n, \hat{E}_n, x)\Big)}{\sum_n \sum_x \text{CP}(F_n, E_n, x)}$$

and recall $\text{R}_{for} =$

$$\frac{\sum_{n=1}^{N} \sum_x \min\Big(\text{CP}(F_n, E_n, x), \text{CP}(F_n, \hat{E}_n, x)\Big)}{\sum_n \sum_x \text{CP}(F_n, \hat{E}_n, x)}$$

where $\text{CP}(\cdot, \cdot, \cdot)$ counts the number of valid pronoun occurrences and $x \in \{formal, informal\}$.

The POS-taggers we use are `en_core_web_sm`[2] for English and `de_core_news_sm`[3] for German. For both languages, spaCy claims an accuracy of 97% for POS-tagging and in our testing we did not find even a single error in pronoun-tagging. For calculating the Pronoun Translation F1 score we use the same ContraPro test set as described in Section 3.5 with the correct references. For calculating the Formality Translation F1 score, we use the test set from the *OS* En-De task. The statistics for both test sets are reported in Table 8. In the ContraPro test set, for each gender class we have exactly 4,000 examples. The fact that we identify more than 4,000 valid examples for the pronoun case means, that in some cases we identify multiple pronouns per sentence. All in all, we find the classes to be relatively balanced for these test sets.

A.2 Dataset Statistics and Experimental Setups

For the **NEWS En→De** task, the parallel training data comes from the `NewsCommentaryV14` corpus[4]. As validation/test set we use the WMT `newstest2015`/`newstest2018` test sets from the WMT news translation tasks (Farhad et al., 2021). For the **TED En→It** task, the parallel training data comes from the IWSLT17 Multilingual Task (Cettolo et al., 2017). As validation set we

[2]`https://spacy.io/models/en`

[3]`https://spacy.io/models/de`

[4]`https://data.statmt.org/news-commentary/v14/`

	Pronoun Trans. F1 score			Formality Trans. F1 score	
	neuter	male	female	formal	informal
# examples	4565	4688	4001	416	605

Table 8: Number of valid examples for specific ambiguous pronoun/style translation in the reference of our test sets.

use the concatenation of `IWSLT17.TED.dev2010` and `IWSLT17.TED.tst2010` and as test set we use `IWSLT17.TED.tst2017.mltlng`. For the **OS En→De** task, the parallel training data comes from the `OpenSubtitlesV2018` corpus (Lison et al., 2018). We use the same train/validation/test splits as Huo et al. (2020) and additionally remove all segments that are used in the ContraPro test suite (Müller et al., 2018) from the training data. The data statistics for all tasks can be found in Table 9.

task	dataset	# sent.	# doc.
NEWS	train	330k	8.5k
	valid	2.2k	81
	test	3k	122
	ContraPro	12k	12k
TED	train	232k	1.9k
	valid	2.5k	19
	test	1.1k	10
OS	train	22.5M	29.9k
	valid	3.5k	5
	test	3.8k	5
	ContraPro	12k	12k

Table 9: Data statistics for the different document-level translation tasks.

Since in the original release of ContraPro only left side context is provided, we extract the right side context ourselves from the `OpenSubtitlesV2018` corpus based on the meta-information of the segments. For translation of the ContraPro test set, as well as for scoring the contrastive references, we take both the left- and the right-side context into account. For the full-document systems, we cap the context size for the ContraPro test set to 4 sentences for computational reasons.

We tokenize the data using byte-pair-encoding (Sennrich et al., 2016; Kudo, 2018) with 15k joint merge operations (32k for *OS* En→De). The models are implemented using the fairseq toolkit (Ott et al., 2019) following the transformer base architecture (Vaswani et al., 2017) with dropout 0.3 and label-smoothing 0.2 for **NEWS En→De** and **TED En→It** and dropout 0.1 and label-smoothing 0.1 for **OS En→De**. This resulted in models with ca. 51M parameters for *NEWS* and *TED* and ca. 60M parameters for *OS* for both the sentence-level and the document-level systems.

Let us assume that the training data $\mathcal{C}$ consists of M documents $\mathcal{D}_m$ and each document consists of source-target sentence pairs $(F_{n,m}, E_{n,m})$. The goal of training is to find the optimal model parameters $\hat{\theta}$ which minimize the loss function:

$$\hat{\theta} = \arg\min_{\theta} L(\theta)$$

When training the local context models, we define the loss function:

$$L(\theta) = -\frac{1}{|\mathcal{C}|} \sum_{m=1}^{M} \sum_{n=1}^{N_m} \log p_\theta(E_{n-k,m}^{n,m} | F_{n-k,m}^{n,m}).$$

When we take full documents as input to the model, the loss function simply becomes

$$L(\theta) = -\frac{1}{M} \sum_{m=1}^{M} \log p_\theta(E_{1,m}^{N_m,m} | F_{1,m}^{N_m,m}).$$

All systems are trained until the validation perplexity does no longer improve and the best checkpoint is selected using validation perplexity as well. Training took around 24h for *NEWS* and *TED* and around 96h for *OS* on a single NVIDIA GeForce RTX 2080 Ti graphics card. Due to computational limitations, we report results only for a single run. For the generation of segments (see Section 3.4), we use beam-search on the token level with beam-size 12 and length normalization.

Unpacking Ambiguous Structure: A Dataset for Ambiguous Implicit Discourse Relations for English and Egyptian Arabic

Ahmed Ruby[1] **Sara Stymne**[1] **Christian Hardmeier**[2]

[1]Uppsala University, Department of Linguistics and Philology
[2]IT University of Copenhagen, Department of Computer Science
{ahmed.ruby, sara.stymne}@lingfil.uu.se, chrha@itu.dk

Abstract

In this paper, we present principles of constructing and resolving ambiguity in implicit discourse relations. Following these principles, we created a dataset in both English and Egyptian Arabic that controls for semantic disambiguation, enabling the investigation of prosodic features in future work. In these datasets, examples are two-part sentences with an implicit discourse relation that can be ambiguously read as either causal or concessive, paired with two different preceding context sentences forcing either the causal or the concessive reading. We also validated both datasets by humans and language models (LMs) to study whether context can help humans or LMs resolve ambiguities of implicit relations and identify the intended relation. As a result, this task posed no difficulty for humans, but proved challenging for BERT/CamelBERT and ELECTRA/AraELECTRA models.

1 Introduction

Coherence is essential for effective communication in written or spoken language (Adornetti, 2015), and discourse connectives play a crucial role in achieving it by helping readers or listeners to infer the intended discourse relation holding between two text spans (Asr and Demberg, 2020). Listeners generally have little difficulty recovering the intended meanings with implicit connectives which are inferred between two juxtaposed independent sentences. They evidence this by combining lexical cues, general reasoning, and prosodic cues to effectively identify the implicit discourse relation. When interpreting ambiguous implicit relations, prosodic cues can be used for disambiguation in spoken language (Tyler, 2014; Jasinskaja, 2009), while semantics is essential in both speech and writing, ensuring effective communication and understanding. Consider for instance the following examples:

(a) John is tall, *so* she will ask him out.

(b) John is tall, *but* she will ask him out.

(c) John is tall. She will ask him out.

The discourse relations in both (a) and (b) can be understood by listeners and readers because the connectives "*so*" and "*but*", respectively, explicitly indicate the discourse relation. Although the implicit discourse relation is ambiguous in (c), listeners might be able to infer it through prosody. However, it is still an open question whether specific prosodic cues are helpful for disambiguation in this case. Moreover, disambiguation can also be achieved in written and spoken language using semantic cues (e.g., additional context), such as adding different preceding context sentences that can enforce either the causal or the concessive reading. For instance, the preceding context for the casual and concessive reading can be:

(1) *She prefers tall men.* John is tall. She will ask him out.

(2) *She prefers short men.* John is tall. She will ask him out.

The additional context can influence the ambiguous structure, suggesting a likely interpretation in (1) that her preference for tall men implies a causal relation, while her preference for short men indicates a concessive interpretation in (2).

We observed that the ambiguous structure of implicit relations arises when the first argument (Arg1) does not provide specific details about the event being described and can be influenced by additional context information. However, for some ambiguous examples or structures, there is a clearly preferred reading even without any context, unless there is extremely strong evidence for a different reading. Consider for instance the following example (adapted from (Carston, 1993))

(a) Max fell. John pushed him.

Proceedings of the 4th Workshop on Computational Approaches to Discourse (CODI 2023), pages 126–144
July 13-14, 2023

The preferred reading for this example is that the pushing caused the falling. However, there is another possible reading where Max fell first and was later pushed by John, but it needs extremely strong evidence to force this interpretation. This means that it is hard to figure out if other aspects than semantics contribute to inferring the intended reading.

In order to explore how ambiguous implicit relations can be successfully resolved by the listener, we plan to conduct, in future work, a controlled experiment on the impact of prosody without being disambiguated by the semantic component. To support this, this study presents a small dataset of "truly" ambiguous examples for implicit discourse relations for both English and Egyptian Arabic, which cannot be resolved in the absence of any context, so that it enables a future investigation of prosodic features. We create a set of sentences with an implicit discourse relation that can be ambiguously read as either causal or concessive with two different preceding context sentences forcing either the causal or the concessive reading. The dataset is validated by humans who read these sentences and filled in the intended implicit discourse connective by choosing the most appropriate option from the provided list of connectives.

We were able to identify the ambiguous structure of implicit discourse relations and propose a new set of principles to construct ambiguity in implicit discourse relations. This process led to the creation of a small dataset for English and Egyptian Arabic that was validated by human participants. As far as we are aware, this is the first dataset that addresses ambiguous implicit discourse relations.

Since human participants were able to identify the intended implicit connectives in a set of examples, we investigate whether language models like BERT (Devlin et al., 2019) and ELECTRA (Clark et al., 2020) can also fill in the implicit connectives in the examples correctly, which is a challenging task, as context barely influenced the choice made by these models.

2 Related Work

2.1 Discourse relation datasets

Although discourse relations have been extensively studied over the last two decades, leading to elaborate taxonomies and inventories of varying scope and levels of abstraction, it is still challenging to provide a general definition for implicit discourse relations (Jasinskaja, 2009). However, there are some inferred relation types that are considered in Wolf and Gibson (2004); Miltsakaki et al. (2005); Prasad et al. (2008); Lavid and Hovy (2010) and annotated implicit relations were covered in the Penn Discourse Tree Bank 2.0 (PDTB 2.0) (Prasad et al., 2008), which is the most popular resource. Moreover, there are discourse-annotated corpora that cover implicit relations in multiple languages, such as TED Multilingual Discourse Bank, or TED-MDB, which contains transcribed TED talks in English, German, Russian, European Portuguese, Polish, and Turkish (Zeyrek et al., 2020), as well as in individual languages following the PDTB approach, such as the Hindi Discourse Relation Bank (Oza et al., 2009) and the Chinese Discourse Treebanks for Chinese. (Yuping et al., 2014; Long et al., 2020).

2.2 Discourse relations and ambiguity

Ambiguous structures can signal multiple potential interpretations of implicit discourse relations, and the intended relation can be inferred by context or by drawing on one's background assumption (Verhagen, 2000). Our study focuses on ambiguous implicit discourse relations, where a two-part sentence implies various potential relations, and must be inferred by context. Considering the distribution of discourse connectives in both PDTB and LADTB as reported by (Alsaif, 2012), the connectives 'but' and 'so' are commonly used in English and Arabic (Pitler et al., 2008; Alsaif, 2012). This observation has inspired the present study to explore the implicit relations that can be expressed by these particular connectives.

3 Ambiguity in inferring implicit relations

Each discourse relation involves two arguments, which are typically expressed as two clauses or phrases (Cabrio et al., 2013). Muskens (2000) argues that underspecified representations must be ambiguous. Drawing from this notion, we have shaped our own study's approach to examining the first argument with ambiguity in mind. The results of the validation confirm that if Argument 1 does not provide information that is relevant to inferring a specific discourse relation, it is not possible to make an inference about that relation unless there are underlying assumptions or presuppositions. In this case, it may be necessary to look for additional information from context to infer the implicit discourse relation.

The meaning of Argument 1 can be shaped and influenced by context if it carries a neutral connotation, and Argument 2 gives additional information or detail based on the event influenced by context. Consider the example in Figure 1, where Argument 1 "John is tall" in both sentences is unspecified and needs to be interpreted in the context of the sentence to determine the intended information conveyed by Argument 2 "she will ask him out". In the first sentence, the context helped Argument 1 convey a positive meaning to infer that she has a preference for tall men, and because John fits this preference, she will ask him out, while in the second sentence, the context helped Argument 1 convey a negative meaning to infer that she does not have a preference for tall men, but she will still ask John out, even though he fits this preference.

While there is a lot of evidence that the context can disambiguate the discourse relation structure (Nowak and Michaelson, 2020; Lichao, 2010), we still do not have a thorough understanding of how ambiguity in implicit relations is structured, and how they can be interpreted only by context. In this regard, this study examines whether different preceding context influence whether the causal or concessive reading is elicited. A dataset was created and validated to investigate this question in two languages (English and Egyptian Arabic).

4 Constructing data for ambiguous implicit discourse relations

Creating a dataset for implicit discourse relations that involve ambiguity can be a challenging task. This is because the ambiguous structure is not linguistically defined in a way that influences meaning. Furthermore, inferring implicit discourse relations can be difficult, since it requires a nuanced understanding of language and discourse. Therefore, we aim to investigate this gap by identifying the ambiguous structure of implicit discourse relations and proposing a method to build a dataset for inferring relations by context.

4.1 Principles of constructing ambiguity in discourse relations

The initial validation findings, which are detailed in Section 4.4, reveal several principles that can be used when constructing ambiguity in implicit discourse relations, such as:

1. The discourse relation between sentences or Arg 1 and Arg 2 should be implicit, where:
   (a) *Arg 1* and *Arg 2* are not connected by any structural connective, such as "so", "but", "because", etc., but the connective can still be inferred.
   (b) *Arg 2* should not contain a lexical item e.g., "this" or "that" which implies a presupposition already established by *Arg 1*. This is because these anaphoric pronouns refer to the fact expressed by the first sentence, so the second sentence presents an evaluation of that fact, due to the lexical semantics of the verb that follows these pronouns. (Jasinskaja, 2009)
   (c) *Arg 2* should provide supplementary information or clarification for *Arg 1*.
2. Arg 1 should convey a neutral meaning[1], and be influenced by context. For instance, "The apple is red" can be influenced and shaped by context to be positive or negative.
3. The discourse relation can only be inferred by context.

4.2 Data and design

We create a set of contrastive sentences pairs that deliberately contain discourse relation ambiguities, with their preceding context, where both Arg1 and Arg2 are identical, with "but" versus "so", depending on if the context makes Arg 2 expected or unexpected. As shown in Table 1.

Context	Target_sentence
The car is very cheap	It's 100,000, __ I'll buy it.
The car is very expensive	It's 100,000, __ I'll buy it.

Table 1: Paired example with ambiguous implicit relations with two different preceding context sentences forcing either the causal or the concessive reading.

As you can see in Table 1, the preceding context sentence guides the speaker to the intended meaning of the target sentence whether the discourse relation between adjacent sentence is a causal or concessive relation, and thus the speaker can fill in the connective in these sentences depending on the context.

[1]Arg 1 can also contain contronyms, which have opposite or contradictory meanings such as "crazy prices" can have opposite meanings depending on the context, it could refer to the low prices, or it could refer to the high prices. However, when testing this principle, we realized that it may be inferred by drawing on one's background assumption.

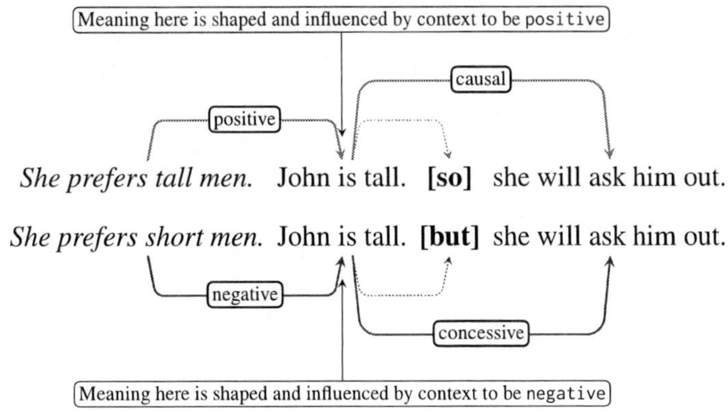

Figure 1: An example of inferring by context of the causal and concessive relation.

4.2.1 Arabic translation

There are five levels of Arabic used in Egypt as stated by Badawi (1973) in his socio-linguistic analysis of contemporary Arabic in Egypt: 1) Classical Arabic of the heritage, 2) Modern Standard Arabic, 3) Colloquial of the educated, 4) Colloquial of the enlightened, and 5) Colloquial of the illiterate. The "Colloquial of the educated" is a form of Arabic spoken by educated individuals that balance regional informality and linguistic proficiency. We opted for this level in our study, as opposed to Modern Standard Arabic (MSA) or "Colloquial of the enlightened," because it represents the prevalent form of spontaneous spoken communication. While MSA is widely understood, it is mainly used in formal written contexts or speeches, whereas "Colloquial of the enlightened" is characterized by its localized nature, which might limit understanding across regions or social groups.

By choosing the "Colloquial of the educated" level, we translated our English examples into Egyptian Arabic. In order to ensure consistency with the common writing style in Egyptian Arabic, two linguists, who are native Arabic-speaking, were asked to provide their feedback and suggestions about the writing style of the examples. This process helped to enhance the quality of the translation. After the first round of validation on translated examples, we decided to eliminate certain examples and introduce new ones. This implies that the English data is not entirely equivalent to the Arabic data.

4.3 Data validation method

In order to examine our data, we utilize human validation with the aim of ensuring the reliability and confidence of examples. This involves a number of procedures:

4.3.1 Distractors

To distract the respondents from the purpose of the study, and reinforce the impression that participants were reading the sentences naturally, we randomly interleave a number of distractors/ fillers with the target examples, which reflect the other implicit discourse relations: expansion and temporal according to the PDTB relations hierarchy (Prasad et al., 2008). Since distractors should be fitted syntactically in all examples, we created 5 examples with implicit 'in fact' connective for expansion relation, and also 5 examples with implicit 'when' connective for temporal relation. These distracted examples are similar to the target examples in terms of design and construction, where contain two discourse units, e.g. clauses or sentences, with proceeding context such as:

(a) *Writing on walls is illegal.* The teacher arrived early in the morning, _ we were painting on the wall.

(b) *Many people were thankful for the experience of traveling by car to Sharm El-Sheikh.* We tried to travel there by car, _ it was a very wonderful experience.

For Arabic, we used the same procedures as those applied in English, but we found that the equivalent of the "when" connective, *lámma*, can convey both causal and synchronous relations simultaneously, which means that this equivalent can be fitted in with both relations. As a result, we decided to eliminate it and use the "at the time/sāʕithā" connective instead for the temporal relation.

4.3.2 Questionnaire design

To achieve our aim of distraction, we added additional connectives, resulting in a balanced distribution of fillers and actual test connectives. As a result, the selection list comprises four connectives: "when", "so", "but", and "in fact", as illustrated in Figure 2.

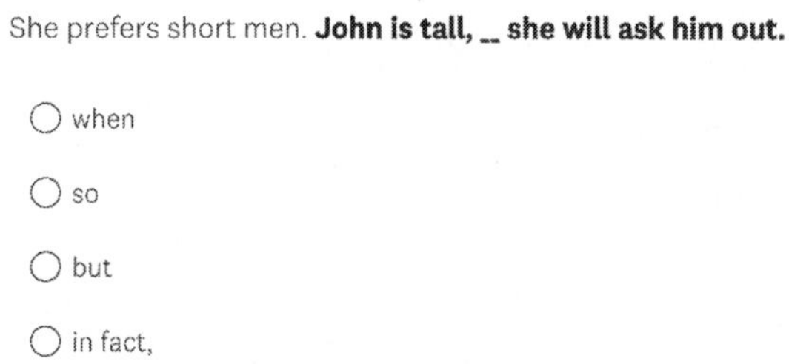

Figure 2: selection list

Regarding Arabic, there are more equivalent words for these connectives in Egyptian Arabic, such as "so" has three equivalents, and "but" has two equivalents as shown below.

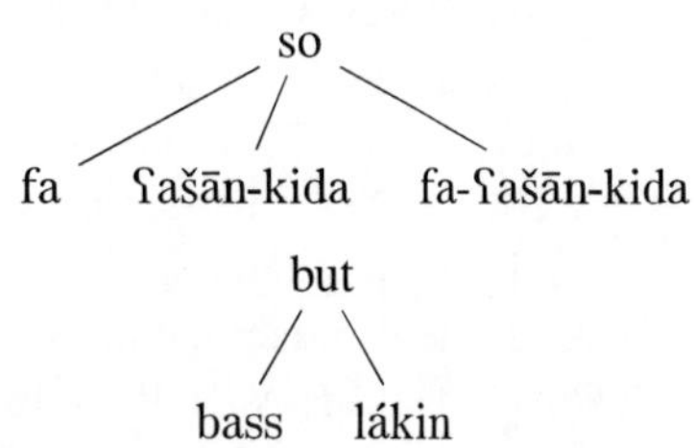

For the "so" connective, (fa) the first equivalent can also be used as a filler, so we exclude it in this experiment, as it can be fitted in with other connectives, and the second and the third equivalent are similar in use, but the second is more widely used. We decided to use the second equivalent *ʕašān-kida* in the experiment.

The first equivalent of the "but/bass" connective is more commonly used, but the results of the first iteration showed that it can also be used as a filler, whereas the second one is mainly used in Modern Standard Arabic and among the educated in colloquial language. Therefore, we decided to use "lákin" as the equivalent of "but" connective in the second iteration.

We also found that the "in fact" connective has two equivalents, the first one is *fil-ħqīqa*, which can be also used as a filler, and the second one is *bil-fiʕl*, which is more commonly used among the educated in colloquial language. we ultimately decided to use the latter.

We use the same ratio of test items and fillers as that used in the English experiment in both validation iterations. In the first iteration, we used the Arabic equivalents of distractors/fillers used in the English experiment: "when/*lámma*", "so/*ʕašān-kida*", "but/*bass*" and "in fact/*fil-ħqīqa*". while in the second iteration, we replaced the "when" connective with "at the time/sāʕithā" and used another Arabic equivalent of "in fact" connective and "but" connective: "at the time/sāʕithā", "so/*ʕašān-kida*", "but/*lákin*" and "in fact/*bil-fiʕl*".

4.3.3 Participants

In order to investigate whether humans are able to identify implicit discourse connectives for these examples, we designed a questionnaire in English and invited volunteers with diverse native languages to answer the questionnaire by selecting the most appropriate connective from the provided list of options to fill in the blanks. In the first and second iterations, 24 and 21 participated in this validation, respectively.

We used the same process to create a questionnaire in Egyptian Arabic and invited Egyptian Arabic speakers to answer the questionnaire by selecting the most appropriate connective from the provided list of options to fill in the blanks as well. In the first and second iterations, 19 and 28 native speakers of Egyptian Arabic participated, respectively.

4.3.4 Procedure

To perform the validation process, we utilized the SurveyMonkey platform and enabled the randomization feature to randomize the two context sentences across participants so that each participant will only see one variant of each example. We distributed the survey link via an email list to gather responses from volunteers. In this task, we marked the main sentence in boldface, which contained the missing connective and preceded by context, and added a list of connectives under each sentence, as illustrated in Figure 2. The task was organized into three blocks of questions and was followed by a few language-related questions presented in Appendix C. However, these questions were not used for analysis. The entire validation task took approximately 10 minutes to complete.

The validation of the Egyptian Arabic dataset was also run by using SurveyMonkey. To collect responses from Egyptian people, we used Facebook to distribute the survey link and request their participation in answering the questions. Following the same processes of the English validation, where

Dataset	Validation	> 80% both	> 80% concessive	> 80% causal	< 80% both
English	1st iteration	1	3	13	14
	2nd iteration	19	3	8	1
Arabic	1st iteration	10	5	8	5
	2nd iteration	22	7	2	1

Table 2: The summary of human validation results on So/But groups of English and Egyptian Arabic datasets

each participant can only see one variant of each example and is not allowed to do the validation twice.

4.4 Results and Analysis

This section presents the summary of validation results on both English and Egyptian Arabic examples, showing the results of the So/But grouping that was conducted to compare the performance of the pair examples. Two validation iterations were conducted in both English and Egyptian Arabic. After analyzing problematic cases and refining our principles from the first English iteration, we created significantly improved examples for the second English iteration. Similarly, by examining the results of the first Egyptian Arabic iteration and adjusting the corresponding connective words in Egyptian Arabic, we achieved much better outcomes in the second Egyptian Arabic iteration. To ensure the validity and reliability of the validation process, a minimum threshold of 80% agreement between participants was established, meaning that only paired examples with a high level of agreement were included. Table 2 shows the summary of the validation results for both languages within each iteration. Detailed validation results can be found in AppendixA. We also employ Krippendorff's alpha to determine the degree of agreement or reliability among annotators/participants for each variant of an example. More detailed results of the inter-annotator agreement can be found in Appendix B.

In the first iteration of the English validation, which was performed on 31 paired examples, only one example in both cases: causal and concession met the threshold, while 14 examples in both cases did not meet the threshold. However, in the second iteration, the findings reveal that the participants were relatively successful in selecting the appropriate connective, with 19 examples in both cases meeting the threshold and only one example in both cases failing to meet the threshold.

In the first iteration of the Egyptian Arabic validation conducted on 28 paired examples, only 10 examples in both cases met the threshold, while 5 examples in both cases did not meet the threshold. However, in the second iteration, which involved 32 paired examples, the findings reveal that the participants were relatively successful in selecting the appropriate connective, with 22 examples in both cases meeting the threshold and only one example in both cases failing to meet the threshold.

To maintain consistency, we followed our principles and added three more examples to the existing set in English, so that both datasets contain a total of 22 examples.

For our preliminary dataset, the findings reveal that the participants were relatively successful in selecting the appropriate connective in the 'so' group. However, the results for the 'but' group were less promising, indicating that the participants struggled to identify the correct connective in these instances. This could be attributed to a range of factors, such as difficulties in understanding the intended meaning, or Arg 1 carries underlying assumptions or presuppositions. For instance, instead of considering the contextual cues in the examples below, several participants relied on their presuppositions about how to interpret the meaning of Arg 1. Here is the phrase "the weather changed" that can carry presuppositions as it can be to the better or to the worse:

(a) *One day it was nice and sunny so my family and I decided to go on a trip.* Suddenly the weather changed, **[...]** we decided not to go.

(b) *On the morning of the game, it was cloudy and rainy.* Suddenly the weather changed, **[...]** we decided not to go.

Here is also the phrase "The time was short" typically implies a negative outcome rather than a positive one, especially when the second argument indicates the result of the event:

(a) *The guest lecturer we had this week was much less long-winded than our usual professor.* The time was short, **[...]** I had fun.

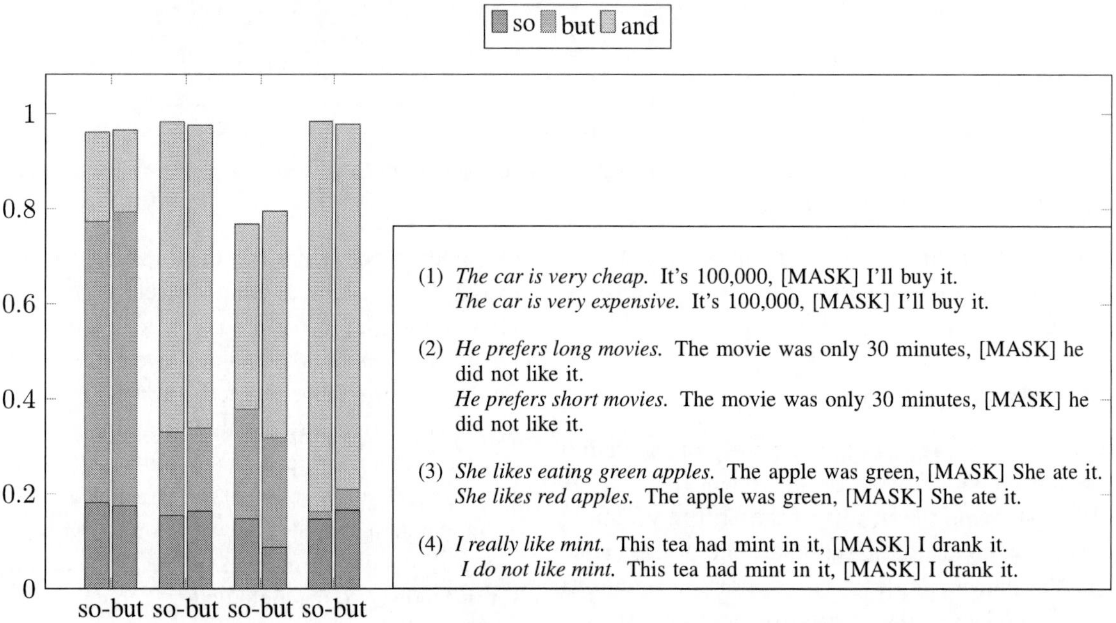

Figure 3: Sample of results from the pilot experiment showing four examples of So/But groups in English along with their respective scores

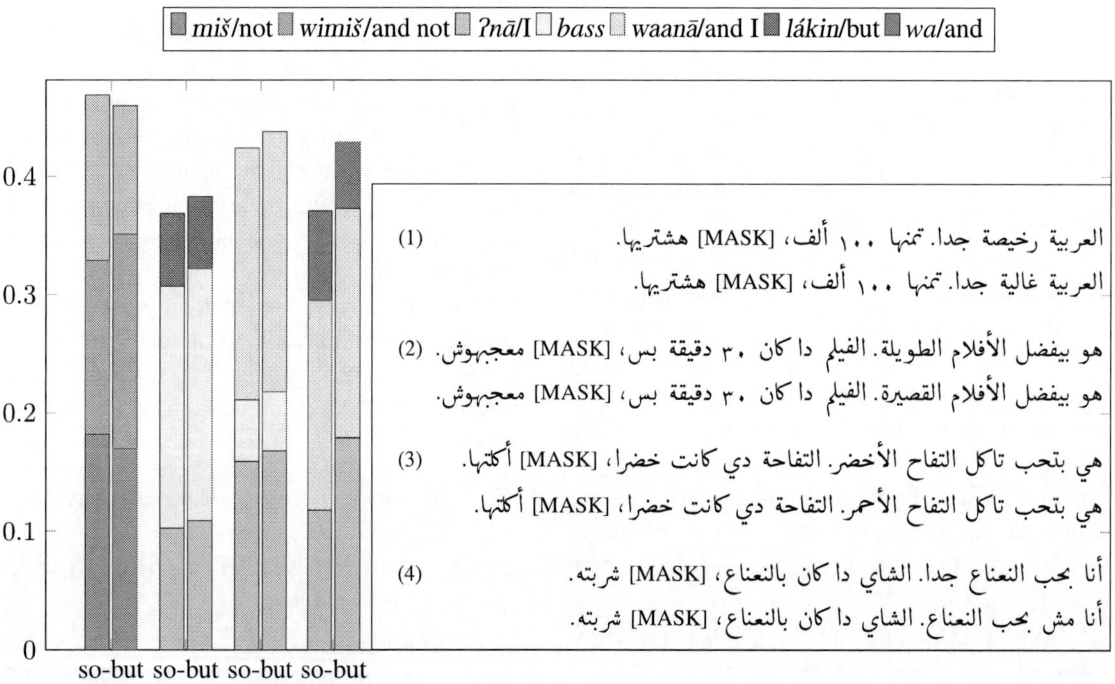

Figure 4: Sample of results from the pilot experiment showing four examples of So/But groups in Egyptian Arabic, which are the translations from English in the same order, and their respective scores

(b) *I spent a great time with my family.* The time was short, [...] I had fun.

Consequently, we removed instances with confusing or inconsistent results, modified some phrases to improve clarity, and added new instances. These changes led to a second iteration of human validation.

5 Pilot experiment

Since human participants were able to identify the intended implicit connectives in a set of examples, we now investigate whether language models like

BERT and ELECTRA will also be able to correctly fill in the implicit connectives within the provided examples.

5.1 English version

For English examples, we use the uncased version of the bert-base and electra-base models from Hugging Face[2] by inserting a mask between Arg 1 and Arg 2 to fill in the missing word, with setting up the topk parameter to 3 to obtain the top 3 predicted words.

5.2 Arabic version

We use CAMeLBERT-Mix (bert-base-arabic-camelbert-mix) model (Inoue et al., 2021) from Hugging Face as well, which is trained on a mixture of Modern Standard Arabic (MSA), Dialectal Arabic (DA) and classical Arabic (CA) variants, to fill in the implicit words for Arabic examples by inserting a mask between Arg 1 and Arg 2, with setting up the topk parameter to 3 to obtain the top 3 predicted words. we also use AraELECTRA-base-generator (Antoun et al., 2021) from Hugging Face, with the same setting.

5.3 Results and Analysis

The outcomes for the top three predicted words by BERT and ELECTRA on paired English examples are detailed in Appendix D. Figure 3 displays here the top predictions and their corresponding scores from BERT for 4 paired English examples with masked connectives.

These results indicate that identifying implicit discourse connectives is quite challenging for language models due to not capturing the influence of context on Arg 1 as there are small differences in the predictions for both So/But groups.

The results of the top three predicted words for Arabic examples, which encompass 25 and 33 different words in BERT and ELECTRA respectively, are also illustrated in Appendix D. Figure 4 presents here the top predictions and their corresponding scores from BERT for 4 paired Egyptian Arabic examples that include masked connectives. These examples are translations of the examples in Figure 3, following the same order.

These results indicate that identifying implicit discourse connectives for Arabic examples is quite challenging as well, as context barely influenced the choice made by these models. Furthermore, the performance of the models on Arabic examples is extremely poor, as many of the predicted words do not function as connectives. As shown in the legend entries of the figures, the words enclosed in **black squares** are connectives, while others are not. This can be interpreted for several reasons:

1. There are potentially systematic differences in the prevalence of implicit discourse relations in spoken data compared to written texts (Rehbein et al., 2016).

2. A discourse relation can be communicated by a pair of clauses conjoined by "and", but the sentences are not connected asyndetically(Jasinskaja, 2009; Rohde et al., 2018), For example, the Result relation can be communicated implicitly both with or without and, such as (Jasinskaja, 2009):

   (a) She fed him poisoned stew *and so* he died.

   (b) She fed him poisoned stew *and* he died.

   (c) She fed him poisoned stew. He died.

The connective "so" in (a) explicitly indicates a causal connection, but the same relation is successfully conveyed in (b) and (c), despite the absence of "so" or even "and".

This can explain the appearance of "and" in both the legend entries of English and Arabic results. Since “wa/and” is proclitic in Arabic, which is usually attached to the word (Habash, 2010), it may provide an explanation for the appearance of the words enclosed in **red squares** within legend entries of the Arabic results.

6 Conclusion and Future Work

In this paper, we introduced principles of constructing and inferring ambiguity in implicit discourse relations, and created a dataset for ambiguous implicit discourse relations, specifically causal and concessive relations for both English and Egyptian Arabic. We also validated both datasets by humans and language models (LMs) to study whether context can help humans or LMs resolve ambiguities of implicit relations and identify the intended relation. For future work, we plan to conduct a controlled experiment on the impact of prosody to figure out whether specific prosodic features correlate with the disambiguation of implicit discourse relations. We also intend to construct more examples to build a classification model to identify the two implicit discourse relations.

[2]https://huggingface.co/bert-base-uncased

Acknowledgements

We extend our thanks to Hannah Rohde for her valuable insights, and to Rima Haddad for her feedback on our Arabic texts.

References

Ines Adornetti. 2015. The phylogenetic foundations of discourse coherence: A pragmatic account of the evolution of language. *Biosemiotics*, 8:421–441.

Amal Alsaif. 2012. *Human and automatic annotation of discourse relations for Arabic*. Ph.D. thesis, University of Leeds, UK.

Wissam Antoun, Fady Baly, and Hazem Hajj. 2021. AraELECTRA: Pre-training text discriminators for Arabic language understanding. In *Proceedings of the Sixth Arabic Natural Language Processing Workshop*, pages 191–195, Kyiv, Ukraine (Virtual). Association for Computational Linguistics.

Fatemeh Torabi Asr and Vera Demberg. 2020. Interpretation of discourse connectives is probabilistic: Evidence from the study of but and although. *Discourse Processes*, 57(4):376–399.

El-Said Badawi. 1973. *Mustawayat al- arabiyya al-mu asira fi misr (Levels of Contemporary Arabic in Egypt)*. Dar almaarif-cairo, Cairo, Egypt.

Elena Cabrio, Sara Tonelli, and Serena Villata. 2013. From discourse analysis to argumentation schemes and back: Relations and differences. In *Computational Logic in Multi-Agent Systems*, pages 1–17, Berlin, Heidelberg. Springer Berlin Heidelberg.

Robyn Carston. 1993. Conjunction, explanation and relevance. *Lingua*, 90(1):27–48.

Kevin Clark, Minh-Thang Luong, Quoc V. Le, and Christopher D. Manning. 2020. ELECTRA: Pre-training text encoders as discriminators rather than generators. In *ICLR*.

Jacob Devlin, Ming-Wei Chang, Kenton Lee, and Kristina Toutanova. 2019. BERT: Pre-training of deep bidirectional transformers for language understanding. In *Proceedings of the 2019 Conference of the North American Chapter of the Association for Computational Linguistics: Human Language Technologies, Volume 1 (Long and Short Papers)*, pages 4171–4186, Minneapolis, Minnesota. Association for Computational Linguistics.

Nizar Y. Habash. 2010. *Introduction to Arabic natural language processing*, 1 edition, volume 3 of *Synthesis Lectures on Human Language Technologies*. Morgan and Claypool Publishers.

Go Inoue, Bashar Alhafni, Nurpeiis Baimukan, Houda Bouamor, and Nizar Habash. 2021. The interplay of variant, size, and task type in Arabic pre-trained language models. In *Proceedings of the Sixth Arabic Natural Language Processing Workshop*, pages 92–104, Kyiv, Ukraine (Virtual). Association for Computational Linguistics.

Ekaterina Jasinskaja. 2009. *Pragmatics and Prosody of Implicit Discourse Relations: The Case of Restatement*. Ph.D. thesis, Universität Tübingen, Germany.

Julia Lavid and Eduard Hovy. 2010. Towards a science of corpus annotation: a new methodological challenge for corpus linguistics. *International Journal of Translation*, 22:13–36.

Song Lichao. 2010. The role of context in discourse analysis. *Journal of Language Teaching and Research*, 1:876–879.

Wanqiu Long, Bonnie Webber, and Deyi Xiong. 2020. TED-CDB: A large-scale Chinese discourse relation dataset on TED talks. In *Proceedings of the 2020 Conference on Empirical Methods in Natural Language Processing (EMNLP)*, pages 2793–2803, Online. Association for Computational Linguistics.

Eleni Miltsakaki, Nikhil Dinesh, Rashmi Prasad, Aravind Joshi, and Bonnie Webber. 2005. Experiments on sense annotations and sense disambiguation of discourse connectives. In *Proceedings of the Fourth Workshop on Treebanks and Linguistic Theories (TLT 2005)*, Barcelona, Spain.

Reinhard Muskens. 2000. Underspecified semantics. In Klaus von Heusinger and Urs Egli, editors, *Reference and Anaphoric Relations*, pages 311–338. Springer Netherlands, Dordrecht.

Ethan Nowak and Eliot Michaelson. 2020. Discourse and method. *Linguistics and Philosophy*, 43:119–138.

Umangi Oza, Rashmi Prasad, Sudheer Kolachina, Dipti Misra Sharma, and Aravind Joshi. 2009. The Hindi discourse relation bank. In *Proceedings of the Third Linguistic Annotation Workshop (LAW III)*, pages 158–161, Suntec, Singapore. Association for Computational Linguistics.

Emily Pitler, Mridhula Raghupathy, Hena Mehta, Ani Nenkova, Alan Lee, and Aravind Joshi. 2008. Easily identifiable discourse relations. In *Coling 2008: Companion volume: Posters*, pages 87–90, Manchester, UK. Coling 2008 Organizing Committee.

Rashmi Prasad, Nikhil Dinesh, Alan Lee, Eleni Miltsakaki, Livio Robaldo, Aravind Joshi, and Bonnie Webber. 2008. The Penn Discourse TreeBank 2.0. In *Proceedings of the Sixth International Conference on Language Resources and Evaluation (LREC'08)*, Marrakech, Morocco. European Language Resources Association (ELRA).

Ines Rehbein, Merel Scholman, and Vera Demberg. 2016. Annotating discourse relations in spoken language: A comparison of the PDTB and CCR frameworks. In *Proceedings of the Tenth International*

Conference on Language Resources and Evaluation (LREC'16), pages 1039–1046, Portorož, Slovenia. European Language Resources Association (ELRA).

Hannah Rohde, Alexander Johnson, Nathan Schneider, and Bonnie Webber. 2018. Discourse coherence: Concurrent explicit and implicit relations. In *Proceedings of the 56th Annual Meeting of the Association for Computational Linguistics (Volume 1: Long Papers)*, pages 2257–2267, Melbourne, Australia. Association for Computational Linguistics.

Joseph Tyler. 2014. Prosody and the interpretation of hierarchically ambiguous discourse. *Discourse Processes*, 51(8):656–687.

Arie Verhagen. 2000. Concession implies causality, though in some other space. In Elizabeth Couper-Kuhlen and Bernd Kortmann, editors, *Cause - Condition - Concession - Contrast*, pages 361–380. De Gruyter Mouton, Berlin, Boston.

Florian Wolf and Edward Gibson. 2004. Representing discourse coherence: A corpus-based analysis. COLING '04, pages 134–140, USA. Association for Computational Linguistics.

Zhou Yuping, Lu Jill, Zhang Jennifer, and Xue Nianwen. 2014. Chinese discourse treebank 0.5.

Deniz Zeyrek, Amália Mendes, Yulia Grishina, Murathan Kurfalı, Samuel Gibbon, and Maciej Ogrodniczuk. 2020. TED Multilingual Discourse Bank (TED-MDB): A Parallel Corpus Annotated in the PDTB Style. *Language Resources and Evaluation*, 54:587–613.

A Human validation details

Figure 5 shows the results of the first iteration of human validation on English examples. This figure consists of two vertically stacked plots, each with four lines representing different categories: "When" (green stars), "so" (red circles), "but" (blue squares), and "in fact" (yellow triangles). The x-axis corresponds to the number of paired examples, labeled 1 to 31, while the y-axis represents the degree of agreement in responses. Each example has plotted points for each category.

In the first plot, the red "so" line has the highest values overall, with many points above 50. The green "When" line has some points above 20, but the majority of its points are below 20 or at 0. The blue "but" line has a few points above 10, but most of its points are at 0. The yellow "in fact" line is mostly below 20, with some points reaching above 20 or 30. On the other hand, the second plot shows the blue "but" with the highest values, featuring several points above 40 and the majority above 20. The red "so" line has several points above 20, but it is mostly below 40. The green "When" line is mostly below 20, with some points reaching above 20 or 30. The yellow "in fact" line has a few points above 20, but most of its points are at or near 0.

The results of the second iteration of human validation on English examples are shown in Figure6.

In the first plot, the red "so" line has the highest values overall, with many points ranging from 80 to 100. The green "When" line remains at 0 for all data points. The blue "but" line has a few points above 10, but most of its points are at 0. The yellow "in fact" line is mostly below 20, with some points reaching above 20. On the other hand, the second plot shows the blue "but" line with the highest values, featuring many points ranging from 80 to 100. The red "so" line is mostly below 40. The green "When" line is mostly at 0. The yellow "in fact" line has a few points above 10, but most of its points are at 0.

There is a significant improvement in both the "so" and "but" groups. As a result, we decided to select the example pairs that scored above 80% and translate them into Egyptian Arabic for further validation.

Figure 7 shows the results of the first iteration of human validation on Arabic examples. In the first plot, the red "so" line has the highest values overall, with many points ranging from 80 to 100. The green "When" line has a few points, but most of its points are at 0. The blue "but" line has some points above 10, and the majority of its points are below 20. The yellow "in fact" line is mostly below 20, with a few points reaching above 20. On the other hand, the second plot shows the blue "but" line with the highest values overall, featuring many points ranging from 80 to 100. The red "so" line is mostly below 40. The green "When" line is mostly at 0. The yellow "in fact" line has a few points above 10, but most of its points are at 0.

The findings indicate that using some Arabic equivalents as fillers led to confusion, making it challenging for participants to identify the correct connective in these cases. Therefore, we tried to avoid using ambiguous equivalents and proposed alternative equivalents of the selection list. These changes also led to a second iteration of human validation.

The results of the second iteration of human validation on Egyptian Arabic examples are shown in Figure8, indicating a significant improvement in both the "so" and "but" groups. In the first plot, the

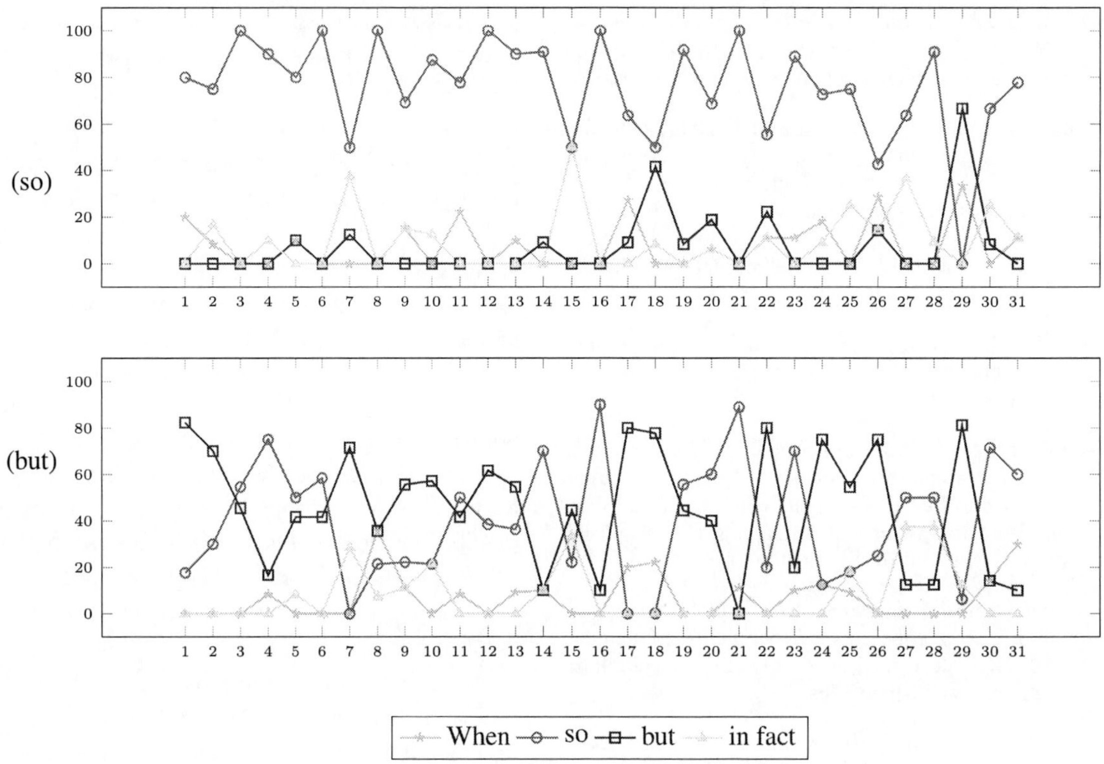

Figure 5: The validation results of the first iteration on So/But groups of English examples

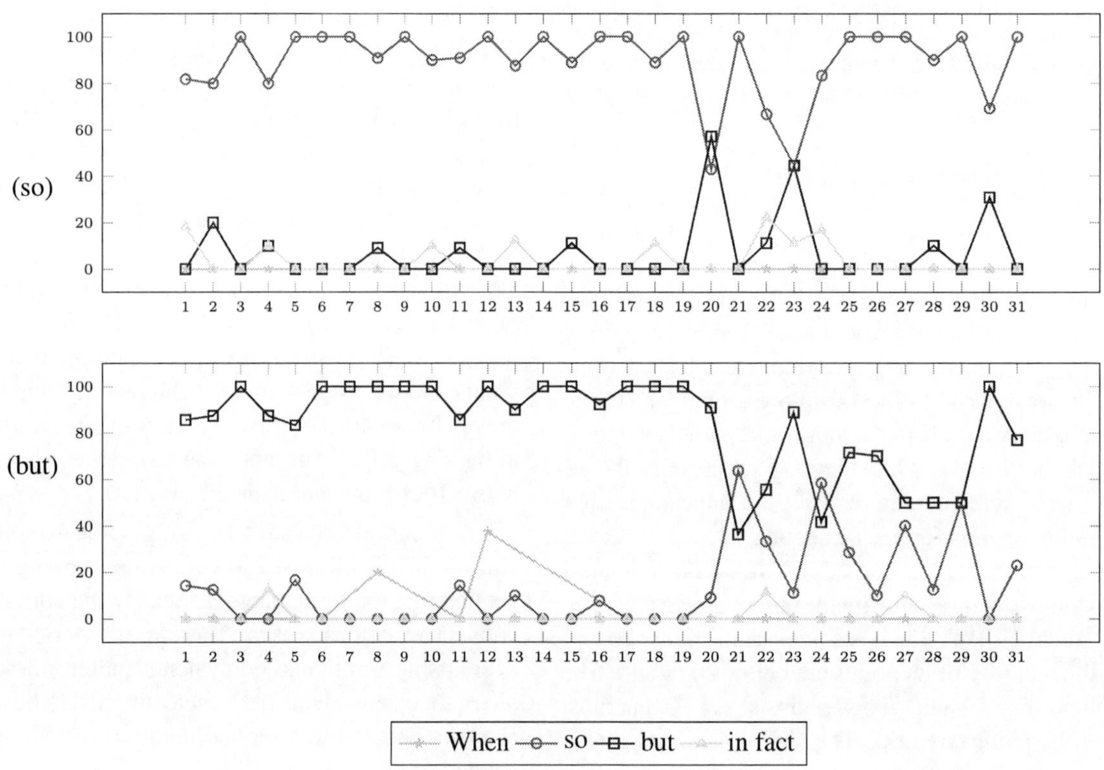

Figure 6: The validation results of the second iteration on So/But groups of English examples

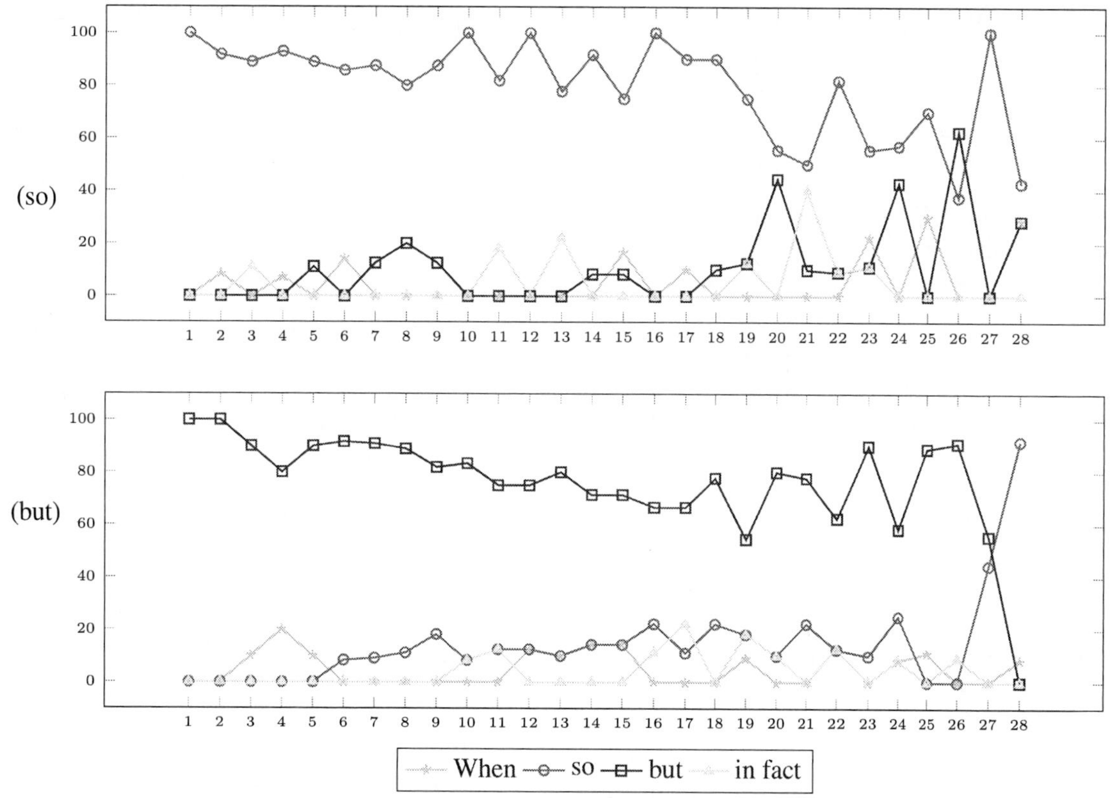

Figure 7: The validation results of the first iteration on So/But groups of Egyptian Arabic examples

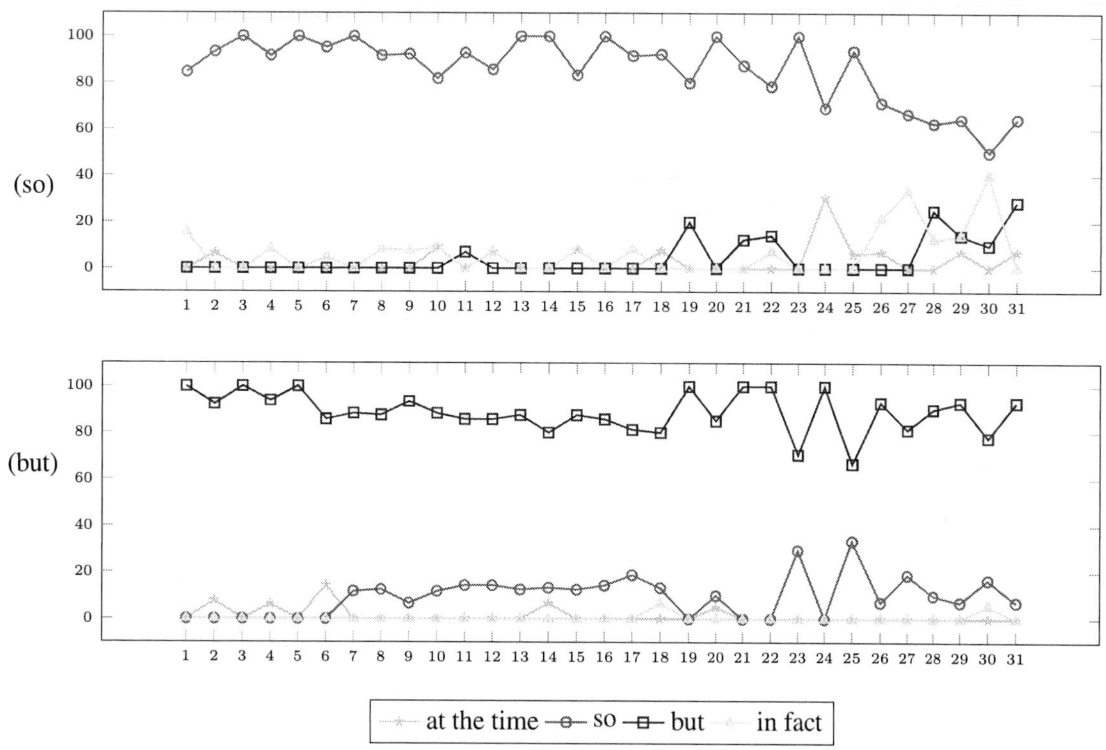

Figure 8: The validation results of the second iteration on So/But groups of Egyptian Arabic examples

Dataset	concessive	causal	concessive-causal pairs
English	22	22	22
Arabic	22	22	22

Table 3: Summary of the final examples for each discourse relation in each language

red "so" line has the highest values overall, with many points ranging from 80 to 100. The green "When" line has a few points, but most of its points are at 0. The blue "but" line has some points above 10, and the majority of its points are below 20. The yellow "in fact" line is mostly below 20, with a few points reaching above 20. On the other hand, the second plot shows the blue "but" line with the highest values overall, featuring many points above 40 and the majority above 20. The red "so" line has a few points above 20, but it is mostly below 40. The green "When" line has a few points above 10, but most of its points are at 0. The yellow "in fact" line has a few points above 10, but most of its points are at 0.

As a result, we obtained 19 (to which we later added 3 more, totaling 22) and 22 examples of pairs scoring above 80% for English and Egyptian Arabic, respectively. Table 3 provides a summary of the final examples count for each discourse relation in each language.

B Agreement Evaluation among Annotators

We use Krippendorff's alpha, which is a statistical measure to determine the degree of agreement or reliability among annotators/participants, by calling `krippendorff.alpha` function from the krippendorff Python package. Since each variant was only scored by a subset of all participants, we calculate it separately for each variant of each question, based only on the choice given by the subset of participants.

Table 8 shows the evaluation of inter-rater reliability using Krippendorff's Alpha calculation on the final English examples. It provides insights into the level of agreement among participants for each variant of an example, the concessive and causal relations. We observe that there are high agreement levels among the participants for most of the Causal and Concessive variants.

Table 9 illustrates the evaluation of inter-annotator agreement using Krippendorff's Alpha calculation on the final Egyptian Arabic dataset. The findings also reveal a substantial degree of agreement among the participants for the majority of the Causal and Concessive variants.

C Language-related questions

There were four language-related questions:

(1) *What was the first language you learned as an infant?* Table 4 displays a summary of the responses.

Dataset	Validation	en	sv-SE	ar-EG	other
English	1st iteration	6	7	0	7
	2nd iteration	7	5	0	12
Arabic	1st iteration	1	0	20	0
	2nd iteration	1	0	27	0

Table 4: The summary of answers for this question

(2) *Were any other languages spoken by your cares at home before you were 6?* Table 5 provides a summary of the responses.

Dataset	Validation	Yes	No
English	1st iteration	8	13
	2nd iteration	11	13
Arabic	1st iteration	0	21
	2nd iteration	0	28

Table 5: The summary of answers for this question

(3) *Did you attend daycare where a different language was spoken before the age of 6?* Table 6 shows a summary of the responses.

Dataset	Validation	Yes	No	en	ar-EG
English	1st iteration	4	17	1	0
	2nd iteration	6	14	4	0
Arabic	1st iteration	1	20	1	0
	2nd iteration	3	25	3	0

Table 6: The summary of answers for this question

(4) *What other languages do you speak fluently?* Table 7 shows a summary of the responses.

Dataset	Validation	No	en	fr	other
English	1st iteration	2	15	2	2
	2nd iteration	6	10	4	4
Arabic	1st iteration	9	12	0	0
	2nd iteration	13	15	0	0

Table 7: The summary of answers for this question

Dataset	Sentence Pair No	Causal		Concessive	
		No. of Participants	Agreement	No. of Participants	Agreement
English	1	11	0.57	10	0.74
	2	12	0.67	9	0.71
	3	6	1.00	15	1.00
	4	13	0.63	8	0.67
	5	6	1.00	15	0.67
	6	13	1.00	8	1.00
	7	12	1.00	9	0.71
	8	13	0.79	8	1.00
	9	13	0.79	8	1.00
	10	12	0.78	9	1.00
	11	13	0.79	8	0.67
	12	11	1.0	10	1.00
	13	11	0.76	10	0.74
	14	15	1.00	6	0.57
	15	6	1.00	15	0.55
	16	11	0.70	10	1.00
	17	7	1.00	14	0.81
	18	7	1.00	14	1.00
	19	11	0.76	10	1.00
	20	2	1.00	2	1.00
	21	2	1.00	2	1.00
	22	2	1.00	2	1.00

Table 8: Evaluation of Inter-Rater Reliability: Krippendorff's Alpha Calculation on the Final English Dataset Using the Nominal Measurement Level

Dataset	Sentence Pair No	Causal		Concessive	
		No. of Participants	Agreement	No. of Participants	Agreement
Arabic	1	8	0.67	7	1.00
	2	8	0.67	7	1.00
	3	15	1.00	2	1.00
	4	13	0.79	2	1.00
	5	5	0.67	10	0.74
	6	8	1.00	7	1.00
	7	8	1.00	7	0.63
	8	7	0.63	8	0.67
	9	8	0.67	7	1.00
	10	8	0.67	7	1.00
	11	8	0.67	7	0.63
	12	9	0.71	6	0.57
	13	6	1.00	9	0.71
	14	7	1.00	8	0.67
	15	7	0.63	8	0.67
	16	6	1.00	9	0.71
	17	7	0.63	8	1.00
	18	8	0.67	7	0.63
	19	8	1.00	7	1.00
	20	4	1.00	11	0.54
	21	10	1.00	5	1.00
	22	3	1.00	3	1.00

Table 9: Evaluation of Inter-Rater Reliability: Krippendorff's Alpha Calculation on the Final Egyptian Arabic Dataset Using the Nominal Measurement Level

D BERT and ELECTRA Validation

Figure 9 below shows the results of the top 3 predicted words on paired examples that scored above 80% in both cases in human validation for English. The figure presents the results of BERT on grouped examples through a pair of vertically aligned stacked bar charts. Each group represents the top predictions for masked connectives and their scores, which are the same in both groups (So, But, and And). In the first bar chart, the values of "so," "but," and "and" are distributed across the 22 bars/examples, with some bars showing a higher proportion of "so" or "but," and others displaying a higher proportion of "and." The second bar chart exhibits a similar distribution pattern. This means that identifying implicit discourse connectives is quite challenging for language models due to not capturing the influence of context on Arg 1 as there are no differences in the predictions for both So/But groups.

The results of the top 3 predicted words for Arabic examples are illustrated in Figure 9. The figure presents the outcomes of BERT on grouped examples in Egyptian Arabic, utilizing a pair of vertically aligned stacked bar charts. Each group signifies the top three predictions for masked connectives along with their respective scores, which differ between the two groups. These predictions cover a total of 25 categories, with only 8 of them recognized as connectives.

In both plots, the highest values occur in categories 1, 4, and 19. Category 1 has the maximum value of 0.544, followed by category 4 with 0.482, and category 19 with 0.337. The results indicate that the model's performance on Arabic examples is extremely poor since a considerable number of the predicted words do not function as connectives. In the Results and Analysis section, I presented some interpretations for these results.

Figure 10 shows the results of the top 3 predicted words, which are "so", "but", "and", "because" and "where", by ELECTRA on paired examples for English. The figure shows the results of ELECTRA on grouped examples through a pair of vertically aligned stacked bar charts as well. The plot reveals that the outcomes for ELECTRA didn't differ much from the results of BERT. This observation further confirms that this task remains a substantial challenge for ELECTRA as well, primarily due to its limitations in capturing context.

The results of the top 3 predicted words for Arabic examples by AraELECTRA are illustrated in Figure 12. The figure shows the outcomes of AraELECTRA on grouped examples in Egyptian Arabic, utilizing a pair of vertically aligned stacked bar charts as well. These predictions cover a total of 33 categories, with only 11 of them recognized as connectives.

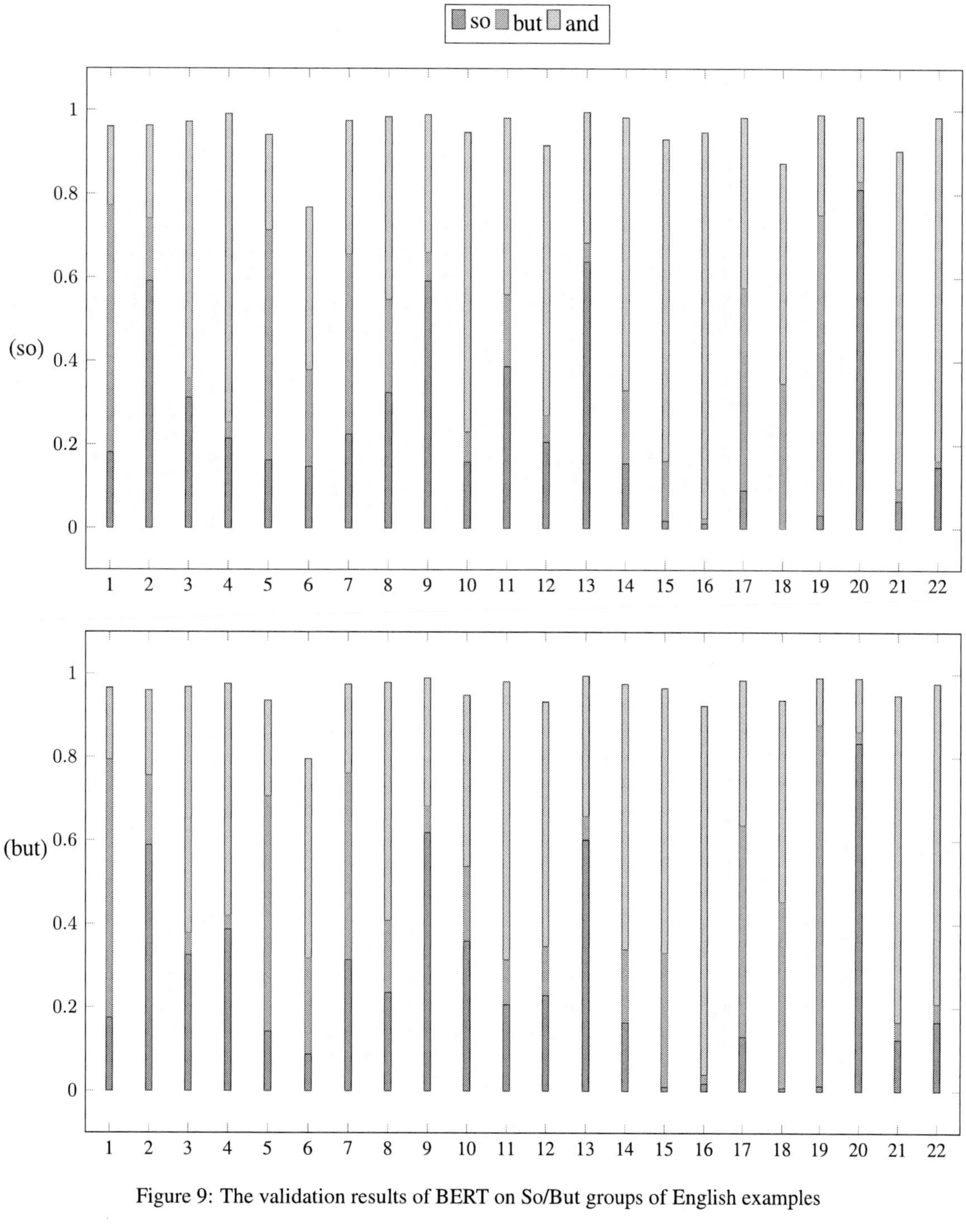

Figure 9: The validation results of BERT on So/But groups of English examples

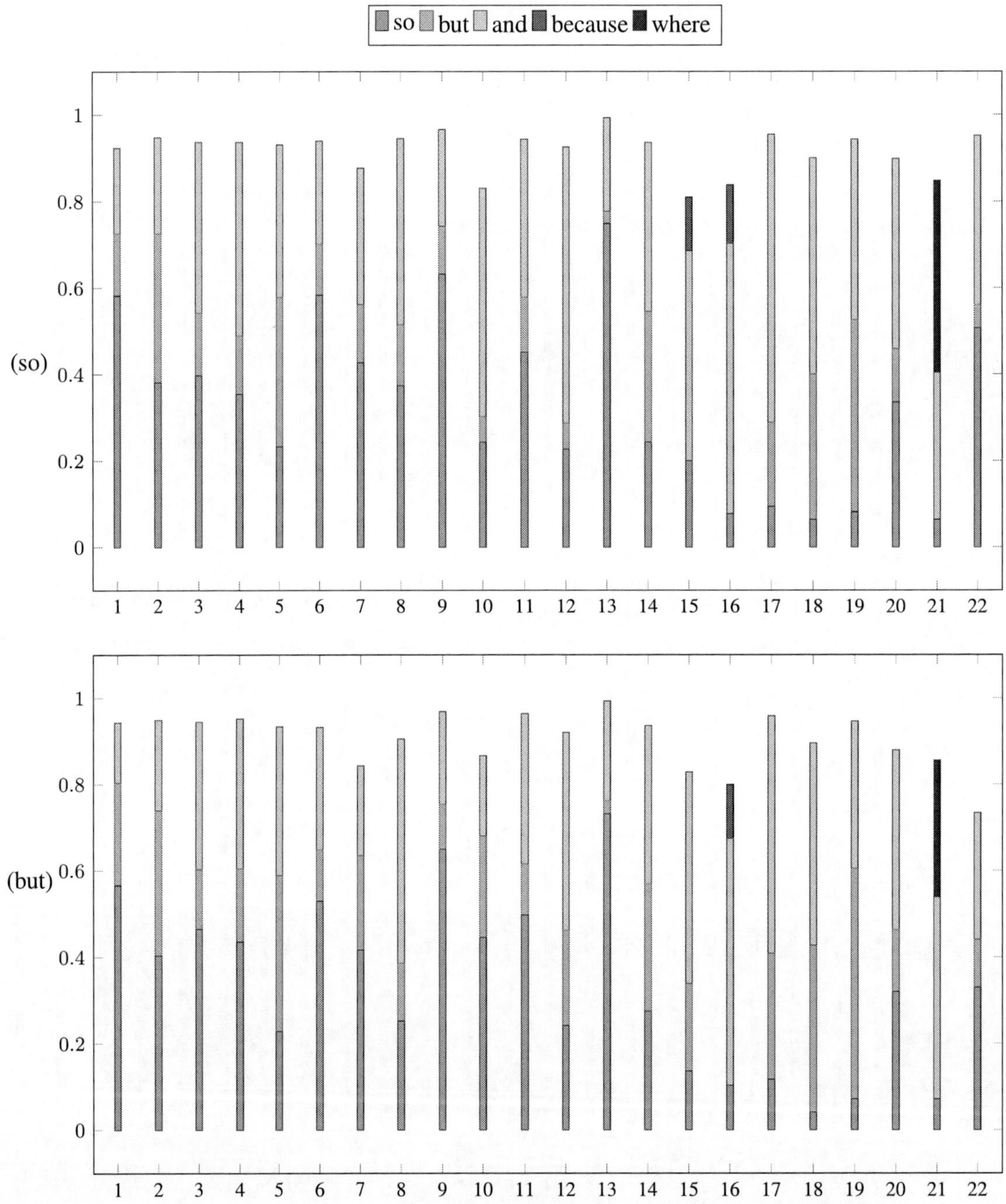

Figure 10: The validation results of ELECTRA on So/But groups of English examples

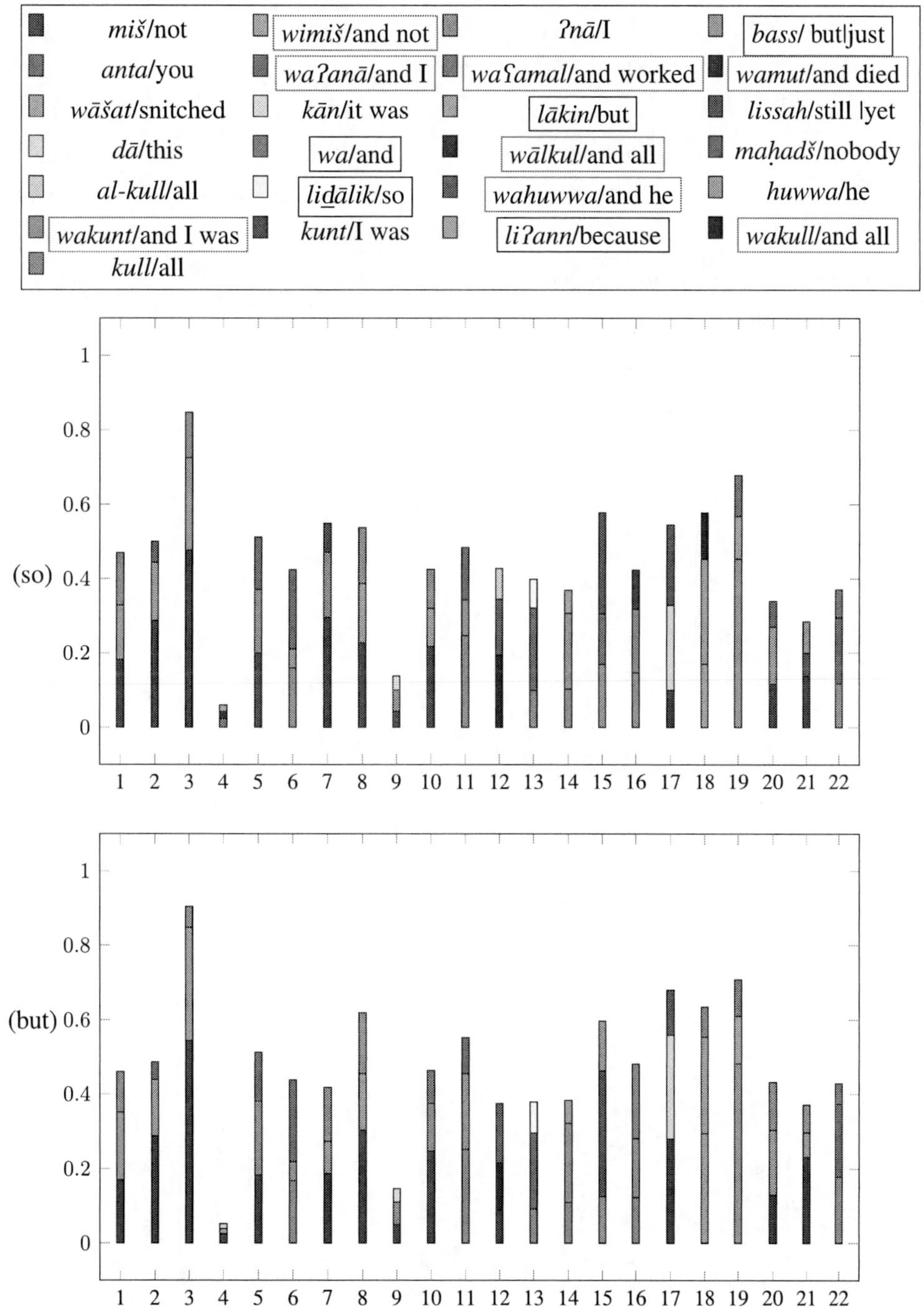

Figure 11: The validation results of BERT on So/But groups of Egyptian Arabic examples

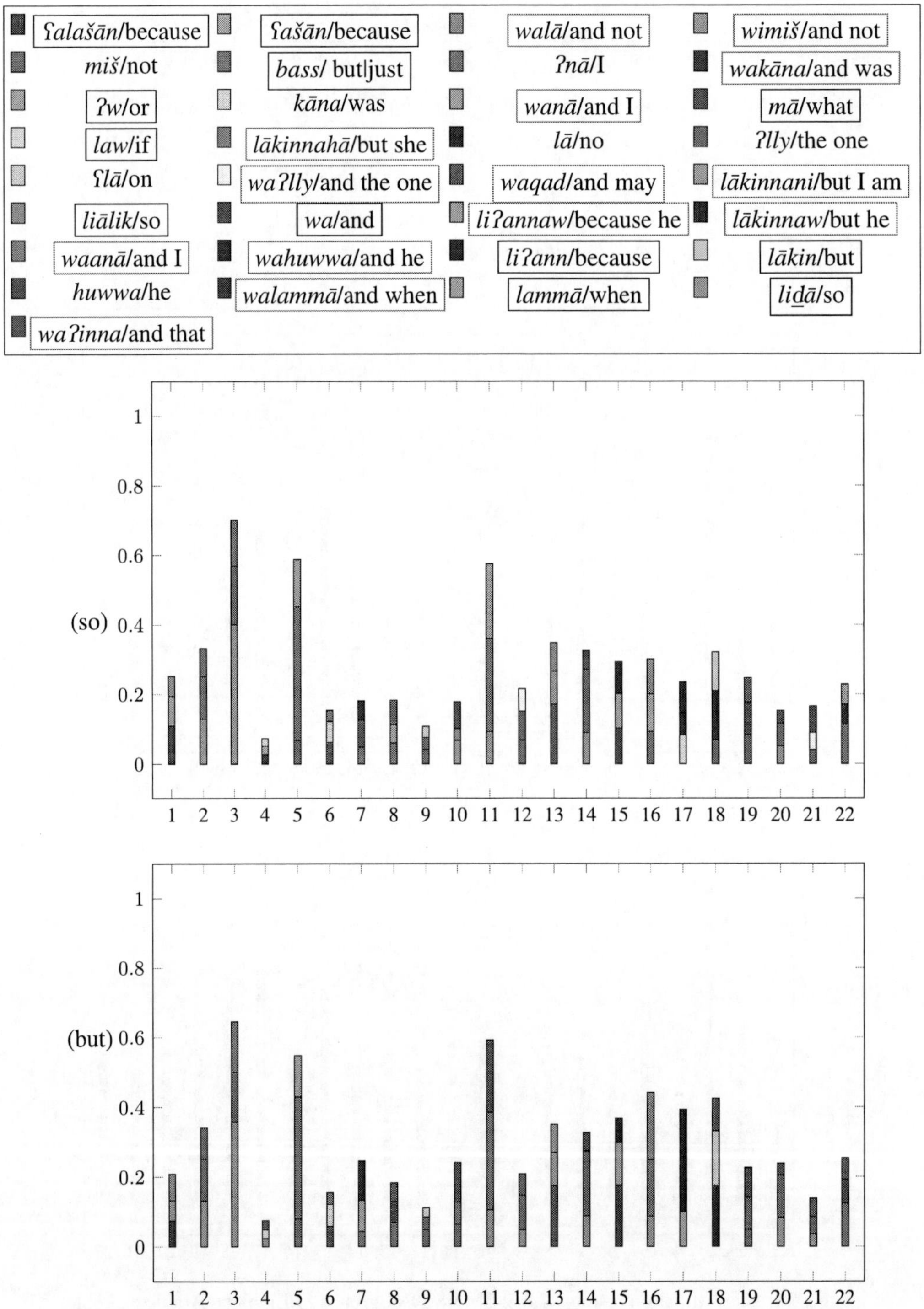

Figure 12: The validation results of AraELECTRA on So/But groups of Egyptian Arabic examples

Two-step Text Summarization for Long-form Biographical Narrative Genre

Avi Bleiweiss
BShalem Research
Sunnyvale, CA, USA
avibleiweiss@bshalem.onmicrosoft.com

Abstract

Transforming narrative structure to implicit discourse relations in long-form text has recently seen a mindset shift toward assessing generation consistency. To this extent, summarization of lengthy biographical discourse is of practical benefit to readers, as it helps them decide whether immersing for days or weeks in a bulky book turns a rewarding experience. Machine-generated summaries can reduce the cognitive load and the time spent by authors to write the summary. Nevertheless, summarization faces significant challenges of factual inconsistencies with respect to the inputs. In this paper, we explored a two-step summary generation aimed to retain source-summary faithfulness. Our method uses a graph representation to rank sentence saliency in each of the novel chapters, leading to distributing summary segments in distinct regions of the chapter. Basing on the previously extracted sentences we produced an abstractive summary in a manner more computationally tractable for detecting inconsistent information. We conducted a series of quantitative analyses on a test set of four long biographical novels and showed to improve summarization quality in automatic evaluation over both single-tier settings and external baselines.

1 Introduction

Text summarization is a principal tool for reasoning about narrative structure and foretell the content of a literary novel in a succinct form. Dated four decades back, the earlier seminal work by Lehnert (1981) pursued analytical summarization of narratives, and offered a graphical representation of human-generated plot units. In this graph, plot units are defined as conceptual elements referring to propositions or states that are linked by character relations. To produce a distilled version of the original discourse, a vast amount of information are selectively ignored by the reader. Similarly, traversing the graph identifies complex elements that are central to the story, and thus points of high relevance for summaries, and ones considered peripheral details.

e-summary: (1) It was committed in the presence of slaves, and they of course could neither institute a suit, nor testify against him; and thus the guilty perpetrator of one of the bloodiest and most foul murders goes unwhipped of justice, and uncensured by the community in which he lives. (2) He was, of all the overseers, the most dreaded by the slaves. (3) He was just proud enough to demand the most debasing homage of the slave, and quite servile enough to crouch, himself, at the feet of the master. [...]
a-summary: The guilty perpetrator of one of the bloodiest and most foul murders goes unwhipped of justice, and uncensured by the community in which he lives . He was cruel enough to inflict the severest punishment, artful enough to descend to the lowest trickery.

Table 1: An example of text generation in our two-stage summarization. In the first step, we extract top-ranked sentences from an extended source chapter of a biographical novel with an average length of over 15K tokens. Then, we produce from the extracted summary (e-summary) an order-of-magnitude compressed abstractive summary (a-summary) that faithfully rephrases its predecessor. Shown are the leading three out of ten top ranked relevant sentences for the e-summary.

Recently, the domain of narrative understanding has gained interest of the research community (Piper et al., 2021). A wide array of computational models developed by language technology professionals provided for expressive generative textual-summaries. Presently, the prevailing approach to natural language generation (NLG) tasks, including summarization, is data driven and uses a sequence-to-sequence neural model pretrained on large text

Proceedings of the 4th Workshop on Computational Approaches to Discourse (CODI 2023), pages 145–155
July 13-14, 2023

corpora. Our work centers on evaluating the quality of producing summaries from chapters of long-form biographical novels. Unlike fictional narratives that require concatenating chapter summaries due to an inherit progressive plot nature, biographical chapters are relatively context independent and thus more readily manageable individually. Automatic generation of fluent summaries in the literary domain can be useful to complement the short description of a book provided by the author and to a certain extent assist in constructing expert critiques. The work by Berov (2019) demonstrated that a functional unit approach to summarizing computational storytelling can perform at around human level and contribute to better framing. We note that the narrative summarization task— while a rich source of innovation— is by and large untapped.

Pretrained language models based on the Transformer network (Vaswani et al., 2017) have achieved state-of-the-art performance generating fluent summaries from short input text. However, for long documents, model efficiency and summary quality characterized by remaining faithful to the respectful source present a challenge to natural language generation practitioners (Huang et al., 2021; Zhang et al., 2022). To mitigate the severity, NLG research applied both topical and generic approaches to the task of summary generation, distinguishing extractive summarization that produces high lexical overlap between a summary and the source document, and hence tends to be factually consistent. While abstractive summaries are prone to unaligned content that is not obviously inferable from the original text.

One of the more constraining facet of current neural models tasked with producing abstractive summarizations is that the generated text can contain factually incorrect information with respect to the grounding text they are conditioned on. Summary inconsistencies are diverse and may include inversion, also known as negation, incorrect use of an entity that transpires as object swapping, or the introduction of an entity not in the original document, recognized as hallucination. Maynez et al. (2020) conducted a large-scale study and concluded that hallucination is the most critical to the coherence of abstractive summaries, while Cao et al. (2022) developed a detection approach that separates factual from non-factual hallucinations.

The complexity of the summarization task made automatic evaluation particularly challenging. In their recent line of work, Deng et al. (2021) proposed the intuition of information alignment between input and output text, and developed unified and interpretable metrics across a multitude of diverse NLG tasks. Distinctly for generative summaries, they offered effective definitions of relevance and consistency, widely identified as key aspects to characterize generation quality. Supported by robust theoretical grounds, their prevailing definitions strongly correlate with human judgment on how to concisely describe the most salient content in the input document. We adopted their interpretations in our empirical analysis and extended the consistency measure to a chapter-level rather than book-level over our test set of literary novels.

In Table 1, we present an overview of our two-step framework for summary generation. Distinguishing our work from prior research on extract-then-abstract methods, the approach we propose uses Transformer language models end-to-end, and experiments we conducted were run on exceptionally long-form chapters drawn from biographical literary novels. Our main contribution is twofold: (1) a high-quality and sustainable biographical literary dataset with each chapter consisting of its source text paired with both the extractive and abstractive summary constructs, and (2) through extensive experiments on a diverse biographical literary dataset, we demonstrate the effectiveness of our proposed approach and show similarity and consistency results that are exceeding or comparable to external baseline performance. Our biographical dataset is publicly accessible online. [1]

2 Related Work

We briefly survey existing methods that propose multi-stage text summarization systems evaluated on datasets from a broad range of domains.

Ling and Rush (2017) introduced a coarse-to-fine attention model that reads a document hierarchically, using coarse attention to select top-level blocks of text and fine attention to read the tokens of the chosen blocks. Their proposed summarizer scales linearly with the number of top-level chunks and effectively handles long sequences. However, their model performance lagged behind the standard instantiation baseline of the attention function on ROUGE similarity metrics.

Xu and Lapata (2020) proposed a coarse-to-fine modeling framework for extractive summarization

[1] https://github.com/bshalem/bns

applied to query focused multi-document. Their system incorporates a relevance estimator for retrieving textual segments– such as sentences or longer passages associated with a query—an evidence estimator which further isolates segments likely to contain answers to the query, and a centrality estimator which finally selects which segments to include in the summary. Our extractive summary component is resemblant in spirit to their centrality estimator, however we use a Sentence Transformers (SBERT; Reimers and Gurevych, 2019) model to generate contextual sentence embeddings that follows producing a sentence similarity matrix for computing graph centrality based ranking.

Pilault et al. (2020) explored Transformer language models and proposed an extract-then-summarize computational pipeline for long documents. Their model consists of an extractive element comprising a hierarchical neural encoder that outputs sentence representations of either a pointer to input sentences or to the result of sentence classification; and a Transformer language model conditioned on the extracted sentences as well as on either a part of or the entire input document to generate the summary. Their system was shown to outperform several baselines on similarity metrics, however, a discussion on factual correctness and consistency analyses of experimental results appears relatively sparse.

Gidiotis and Tsoumakas (2020) proposed a divide-and-conquer method by splitting the input into multiple segments, summarizing them separately, and combining the summary pieces. Basing on smaller source and target summary pairs that are focused on a specific aspect of the text, results in better alignment and considerable reduction of computation complexity. They used a basic sequence-to-sequence model and incorporated a rotational unit of memory (Dangovski et al., 2019) in its decoder that led to a more stable training and slightly improved F1 similarity scores. Content quality of their generated summaries relies entirely on ROUGE similarity metrics and could benefit from a broader evaluation framework such as offered by Deng et al. (2021).

More recently, Zhang et al. (2022) proposed a multi-stage split-then-summarize framework to generate summaries from long-form documents. Each source text divides into segments, matching each with a subset of target text. A coarse summary is generated for each segment and further concatenated as input to the next stage. After multiple stages of compression and summarization, a final stage produces a fine-grained summary. Their improved performance across baselines renders relatively low bi-gram scores, most likely owing to over-compression of source text.

An effective abstractive text summarization approach that first compresses long input text into a relatively short input sequence, and follows with efficient long-form document finetuning demonstrated comparable performance at a significantly lower computational cost (Choi et al., 2019; Su et al., 2020). Keen on a specific application, Pu et al. (2022) generate movie plots given movie scripts, by applying heuristic evaluation to extract actions and essential dialogues, a representation that reduces the average length of input movie scripts by 66%. Their system outperforms baselines on various automatic metrics.

3 Chapter Summarization

Our summarization task commences with producing an extractive summary from the source text of a book chapter, and follows with generating an abstractive summary from the salient extractive content (Table 1).

3.1 Importance Extraction

Extractive summarization generates text by selecting a subset of sentences in the original document. To this task we applied LexRank (Erkan and Radev, 2004) that computes sentence importance based on eigenvector centrality in a graph representation of sentences. The graph uses a cosine similarity matrix where each entry in the matrix is the similarity between the corresponding sentence pair. Formally, given n sentences in a novel chapter, we use a colon notation $s_{1:n} = (s_1, \ldots, s_n)$ to denote the collection of sentences. We used bag-of-words to represent each sentence as a $|V|$-dimensional vector p, where V is the chapter vocabulary. Hence, the similarity matrix $M \in \mathbb{R}^{n \times n}$ contains elements $m_{ij} = \text{sim}(p_i, p_j)$, where $1 \leq i, j \leq n$ and *sim* a similarity function. LexRank hypothesizes that sentences more similar to many other sentences in the book chapter are more central, or salient to the topic. The algorithm further emits the degree centrality of a node in the similarity graph— the count of similar sentences for each sentence.

Our extractive summarization task uses SBERT

(Reimers and Gurevych, 2019). [2] SBERT derives semantically meaningful sentence embeddings that can be compared using cosine-similarity. We chose the distilled RoBERTa (Liu et al., 2019) variant of the BERT (Devlin et al., 2019) model, a pretrained Transformer network (Vaswani et al., 2017) on a paraphrase dataset. This model generates a dense embedding vector for each input sentence, of which we construct a similarity adjacency matrix M that stores a weighted graph of all sentence-pairs. Matrix M is further provided to LexRank for sentence importance ranking. The chapter extractive summary produced thus comprises a collection of top-ranked sentences with a sentence count that is proportional to the chapter text length, and commonly defaults to a defined maximal saliency.

3.2 Factual Abstraction

Extractive summary generation contrasts with abstractive summarization, where the information in the text is rephrased. Consistent with the Transformer architecture, BART (Lewis et al., 2020), considered a state-of-the-art model for the task of abstractive summarization, introduced denoising autoencoding objectives to pretrain sequence-to-sequence models. As a result, input texts are corrupted in two ways: (1) Text Infilling, where sampled token spans are replaced with a sequence of mask tokens [MASK], and (2) Sentence Permutation that splits a document into declarative sentences thereafter shuffled in random order.

Abstractive summary generation can be cast as a typical sequence-to-sequence learning problem. The pretraining objective of the core transformer model is to minimize the negative log-likelihood of the original document over corrupted text

$$\mathcal{L}_G(\theta) = -\frac{1}{|Y|}\log p(Y|X;\theta),$$

where X is our extractive generated summary rendered as a set of sentences, $|Y|$ is the number of tokens in summary Y, and θ denotes the model parameters. In our experiments, we used the distilled version of BART, [3] from which we drew sentence level representation for our automatic evaluation.

4 Information Alignment

The goal of a summarization task is to concisely describe the most salient information of the input text. Thus, the summary generated should be consistent and only contain content from the input, and the included content must be relevant. Using the intuition of information alignment, defined as the extent to which the information in one generative component is grounded in another, we can evaluate summary consistency and relevance (Deng et al., 2021).

More formally, let $x_{1:n}$ and $y_{1:m}$ be our respective extractive and abstractive summary text-sequences for each book chapter. Summary tokens are each represented with contextual embeddings we extracted from pretrained BERT (Devlin et al., 2019). Using embedding matching, the alignment vector $align(y \to x)$ consists of scores $\in [0,1]$ for each token in y, and amount to the maximum cosine similarity with the tokens in x

$$(i,j) = \underset{i \in 1:n,j}{\operatorname{argmax}} \operatorname{cossim}(x_i, y_j),$$

where (i,j) is a pair of token indices pointing each to a distinct summary text sequence, and $1 \leq j \leq m$. The consistency metric that measures faithfulness thus follows naturally as the average of the alignment vector scores: $\operatorname{mean}(align(y \to x))$. On the other hand, relevance is implicit in our two-step model that commences with ranking source sentences by their importance.

Individual	Chapters	Tokens	FRE
Frederick Douglass	11	154,293	77.5
Mark Twain	60	620,312	75.1
Ulysses Grant	70	1,269,660	65.3
Napoleon Bonaparte	115	2,238,248	65.5

Table 2: Metadata for our test set of biographical novels.

Individual	Sentences	Min	Max	Mean
Frederick Douglass	1,812	69	703	164.7
Mark Twain	6,614	10	711	110.2
Ulysses Grant	12,139	67	301	173.4
Napoleon Bonaparte	20,514	19	861	178.4

Table 3: Chapter sentence distribution across our test set of biographical novels.

5 Evaluation

Our proposed two-step summarization method is evaluated on our curated biographical literary test-set. Automatic evaluation results are reported using

[2]https://huggingface.co/sentence-transformers

[3]https://huggingface.co/sshleifer/distilbart-cnn-12-6

	e-summary					a-summary				
Individual	Tokens	Min	Max	Mean	STD	Tokens	Min	Max	Mean	STD
Frederick Douglass	14,989	197	510	314.2	86.9	1,835	38	45	41.1	2.2
Mark Twain	98,059	63	744	369.9	144.7	9,458	21	46	38.1	4.3
Ulysses Grant	121,865	269	731	387.1	80.4	12,206	29	46	41.0	4.0
Napoleon Bonaparte	248,878	35	835	477.5	104.8	20,209	23	46	39.0	3.7

Table 4: Token-length distribution of e-summary and a-summary across our biographical narrative test set.

the canonical ROUGE measure (Lin, 2004), and we have also experimented with the recently developed BARTScore metric (Yuan et al., 2021), more suitable to NLG tasks. We compared our performance with a handful of external baselines set to reach similar objectives like ours, and analyzed the newly proposed information alignment concept and consistency metric (Deng et al., 2021). Unless otherwise noted, we report novel-level summary quality using the average of chapter scores.

Novel Test Set We obtained unicode encoding of the literature text from Project Gutenberg, and carried our work on four biographies including `Narrative of the Life of Frederick Douglass, An American Slave` by Frederic Douglass (2006), [4] `Life on the Mississippi` by Mark Twain (2004), [5] `Personal Memoirs of U. S. Grant` by Ulysses S. Grant (2004), [6] and `Memoirs of Napoleon Bonaparte` by Louis Antoine Fauvelet de Bourrienne (2006). [7] These texts total 256 chapters and over four million words (Table 2). We also post for the literary set the Flesch Reading Ease (FRE) score that identifies a difficulty level range from standard to fairly easy.

In Table 3, we present chapter sentence distribution across our narrative literary set. Per book chapter there are on average 15,491 tokens (Table 2), and about 150 sentences with a little over 100 tokens per sentence. Chapter text is notably long in form and present a challenge to generate fluent and faithful summaries in a single computational pass.

Generated Summaries Our model provides two user-settable parameters to control summary generation: (1) the number of top-ranked sentences in a chapter ordered by their relevance to the input source text and concatenated to construct the e-summary. This number is set to ten by default; (2) the maximum token-length of the predicted abstractive summary set by the user to either fifty or one hundred words. We conducted ablation experiments and analyzed the impact of the bound token-length parameter on the a-summary generation quality. In Table 4, we provide token-length distribution of both e-summary and a-summary across our literary test set. On average, e-summaries consist of 387 tokens, while a-summaries, set to a maximum length of 50 tokens, have a mean of close to 40 words. Thus, the first stage of our summarization system presents a compression ratio of roughly 40 between source chapter text and e-summaries. In the second step, generated a-summaries are more concise than their respective e-summaries by an almost order of magnitude.

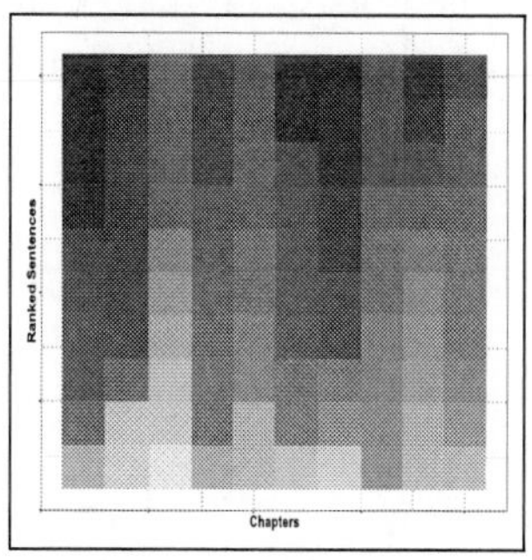

Figure 1: Chapter sentence ranking for the biography of Napoleon Bonaparte. Showing ten randomly sampled chapters and for each we highlight its respective ten top-ranked sentences in descending order. The brighter the tile, the higher the rank.

In Figure 1, we provide visualization of ten top-ranked sentences extracted from ten randomly sampled chapters in the Napoleon Bonaparte novel. We formulate extractive summaries as a matrix $\in \mathbb{R}^{m \times n}$, where m is the number of chapters in a book and n the number of top-ranked sentences that are concatenated to found an extractive summary. In our setup, LexRank is set to return a fixed number of n most relevant sentences, noting that the extracted list may contain ties. Over our experiments, we observed on average a fairly low— a slight over six percentage points— duplicated sentence salience across our test set. Most ties were an occurrence

[4]https://www.gutenberg.org/files/23/23-0.txt
[5]https://www.gutenberg.org/files/245/245-0.txt
[6]https://www.gutenberg.org/cache/epub/4367/pg4367.txt
[7]https://www.gutenberg.org/cache/epub/3567/pg3567.txt

Individual	maxlen=50						maxlen=100					
	ROUGE-2			ROUGE-L			ROUGE-2			ROUGE-L		
	r	p	f	r	p	f	r	p	f	r	p	f
Frederick Douglass	0.13	0.95	<u>0.23</u>	0.18	0.97	<u>0.30</u>	0.18	0.94	<u>0.29</u>	0.24	0.97	**0.38**
Mark Twain	0.11	0.91	0.19	0.16	0.96	0.26	0.17	0.91	0.27	0.22	0.96	0.35
Ulysses Grant	0.10	0.92	0.18	0.15	0.97	0.27	0.15	0.92	0.25	0.21	0.97	0.34
Napoleon Bonaparte	0.08	0.91	0.15	0.13	0.96	0.22	0.13	0.91	0.22	0.18	0.96	0.30

Table 5: ROUGE scores of a-summary generation (r - recall, p - precision, and f - F measure).

of two and a handful were of three sentences. Operating as a modular component, we applied the distilled RoBERTa-based pretrained SBERT model to generate contextual sentence embeddings. This model renders about 82 million trained parameters.

In our automatic evaluation we used the distilled checkpoint of BART, DistilBART-CNN-12-6, pretrained and finetuned on the CNN/Daily Mail news corpus (Nallapati et al., 2016) that comprises multi-sentence summaries, and on the extreme summarization dataset (XSUM; Narayan et al., 2018), both sustain a strong abstractive property. To generate a-summaries, we used the BART checkpoint model with a neural network of over 305 million parameters and ran inference on our biographical narrative test set.

ROUGE Scores We compute an a-summary from a reference e-summary. Rather than sentence-level that could potentially result in overlapping content and thus redundant summaries, we report summary-level ROUGE scores (Lin, 2004). [8] Following standard practice, we chose F1 ROUGE as our evaluation metric to estimate the generation quality of summaries. Concretely, we used bi-gram ROUGE (ROUGE-2) that is a proxy for assessing informativeness and the longest common subsequence (ROUGE-L) to represent fluency. In Table 5, we show recall, precision, and F1 scores of produced a-summaries bound to a maximum token-length (maxlen) of 50 and 100 over our biographical literary set. Consistently ROUGE-L scores are higher than the respective bi-gram performance by about twenty five percentage points, on average. As expected, summary quality reduces proportionally to the e-summary token count (Table 4). Although limited to only two settings, our results support the conjecture that the longer the summary text sequence produced the higher the performance by up to 36%.

[8]https://pypi.org/project/rouge/

Individual	ROUGE-2	ROUGE-L
Frederick Douglass	0.06	0.11
Mark Twain	<u>0.07</u>	**0.12**
Ulysses Grant	0.04	0.08
Napoleon Bonaparte	0.03	0.07

Table 6: ROUGE F1 scores for a single-tier setting. Summary maximum token-length is set to 500.

In Table 6, we report F1 ROUGE scores for a single-tier setting. This method collapses our summarizer stages and generates a-summary directly from the grounded source text of a chapter in a single computation pass. The summary maximum token length is implicitly set to 500 to account for the excessively long chapter document. Compared to our two-step summarization method, single-tier ROUGE-2 and ROUGE-L scores are shown to decline quadruply and triply, respectively.

We compared our summary generative performance with the quality of a half dozen of external baselines, presenting top F1 scores for both ROUGE-2 and ROUGE-L metrics in Table 7. At 0.29 F1, our ROUGE-2 measure exceeded state-of-the-art Gidiotis and Tsoumakas (2020) by 0.11 F1, while for ROUGE-L we came closely second with 0.38 F1 behind their best score of 0.41 F1. At an average of 15,491 words per novel chapter our dataset exceeded the token complexity of the baselines by at least 1.7X.

BARTScore We leveraged BARTScore (Yuan et al., 2021), [9] a recently introduced evaluation metric for generated text that is unsupervised and does not require human judgments to train. Owing to its ability to utilize the entirety of the BART pretrained parameters, BARTScore can better support evaluation from a factual perspective. BARTScore relies on contextual word embeddings extracted

[9]We obtained code to calculate BARTScore from https://github.com/neulab/BARTScore

System	Domain	Tokens	Model	ROUGE-2	ROUGE-L
Ling and Rush (2017)	News	804	Finetuned	0.15	0.29
Xu and Lapata (2020)	QA	400	Finetuned	0.12	0.17
Pilault et al. (2020)	News	3,615	Pretrained	0.12	0.34
Gidiotis and Tsoumakas (2020)	Sci,Med	5,069	Finetuned	0.18	**0.41**
Zhong et al. (2021)	Meetings	9,070	Pretrained	0.11	0.31
Zhang et al. (2022)	TV,Reports	8,883	Pretrained	0.09	0.29
Ours	News	**15,491**	Pretrained	**0.29**	0.38

Table 7: Token complexity and ROUGE F1 scores comparison with external baselines. Neural models are at least pretrained on a large text corpus and optionally finetuned on the target dataset.

from pretrained sequence-to-sequence models and explores weighted conditional log-probabilities of a summary sequence given source tokens. In Table 8, we report BARTScore figures in average log-likelihood of probabilities $\in [0, 1]$. The calculated scores are less than zero, thus the higher the log-likelihood, the higher the probability. BARTScore appears far less affected by varying the maximum token-length of the produced a-summary, suggesting BARTScore captures aspects complementary to ROUGE. Consistent with ROUGE, BARTScore performance decreases with a higher e-summary word count.

Individual	BARTScore maxlen=50	BARTScore maxlen=100
Frederick Douglass	**-10.89**	<u>-11.01</u>
Mark Twain	-11.07	-11.04
Ulysses Grant	-11.12	-11.10
Napoleon Bonaparte	-11.17	-11.19

Table 8: BARTScore metric in log-likelihood for our biographical test set. The higher the measure the better the performance.

Individual	Pearson	Kendall	Spearman
Frederick Douglass	0.13	0.09	0.13
Mark Twain	<u>0.24</u>	<u>0.19</u>	**0.27**
Ulysses Grant	0.23	0.17	0.24
Napoleon Bonaparte	0.14	0.11	0.15

Table 9: BARTScore correlation between a-summary generation of 50 and 100 limited token-length.

We also measured the BARTScore correlation between a-summaries confined to 50 and 100 token-length, respectively. The strength of association between the two measures and the direction of the relationship are outlined in Table 9. We present Pearson, Kendall, and Spearman correlation types, all indicating a stronger positive relation for the books on Mark Twain and Ulysses Grant that share a similar token complexity per chapter.

6 Discussion

Individual	Min	Max	Mean	SD
Frederick Douglass	0.41	0.75	0.61	0.11
	0.62	0.92	**0.81**	0.11
Mark Twain	0.27	0.85	0.59	0.12
	0.43	0.94	0.76	0.11
Ulysses Grant	0.42	0.89	0.63	0.10
	0.49	0.94	0.77	0.12
Napoleon Bonaparte	0.48	0.89	<u>0.67</u>	0.07
	0.43	0.96	0.77	0.10

Table 10: Factual consistency distribution across our test set of biographical novels. The figures for each title show consistency measures for generated a-summaries, contrasting their alignment with the source text (grayed) and to their respective e-summary.

Factual Consistency In this section, we offer qualitative analysis of factual consistency as it relates to biographical literary using embedding-matching alignment estimation. To extract contextual embeddings we used a pretrained BERT model that has nearly 109 million parameters. Our extractive summarization step warrants textually grounded generation of a summary, thus the following discussion pertains exclusively to the abstractive-summary computational stage. In Table 10, we show the distribution of factual correctness for aligning both (a-summary $\rightarrow$ e-summary) and (a-summary $\rightarrow$ source) across our biographical literary test set. The Frederick Douglass narrative scored the highest consistency of 0.81, along with the rest of the novels slightly behind, however, we contend that the three novels uphold a more faithful score of 0.77 owing to a larger sample of chapters. Using a comparable metric for compression tasks,

Deng et al. (2021) report consistency performance at 0.33 on the CNN/Daily Mail news corpus.

The impact on consistency performance gained by contrasting alignment of a-summaries with the source text and aligning a-summaries with e-summaries is a considerable 25% on average (Table 10). Evidently accurate automatic evaluation of generated summaries from long-form literary narratives is a multi-dimensional problem and pose a key challenge for optimization.

We note that extending the maximal generative token-length is not indefinite or else the summarizer aim to effectively balance both fluency and succinctness will be adversely affected.

Individual	Finetuned Train	Finetuned Test	Finetuned F1	Pretrained F1
Frederick Douglass	9	2	<u>0.17</u>	**0.30**
Mark Twain	48	12	0.14	0.26
Ulysses Grant	56	14	0.17	0.27
Napoleon Bonaparte	92	23	0.15	0.22
Unified	205	51	0.15	0.26

Table 11: Contrasting ROUGE-L F1 scores for finetuned and pretrained BART models across our biographical novels. Finetuned narrative chapter allocations are shown for train and test subsets in individual and consolidated datasets.

Finetuning We explored finetuning the BART checkpoint on our biographical literary set and looked at the model ability to generalize across datasets. To this end, we built a distinct model for each and all novels unified, and applied an 80/20 percent chapter split for training and testing, respectively. We trained the BART model for three epochs using a cross-entropy loss, the Adam optimizer, a batch size of 32, and a learning rate of 1e-3. In Table 11, we present finetuned ROUGE-L F1 scores using a generation not to exceed a length of 50 tokens, and contrast them with the pretrained model (Table 5). Both finetuned and pretrained results follow a similar performance decline with a growing chapter token complexity. Finetuned scores are lower than the pretrained measures by about 1.75X on average, because the BART model weights are fitting to a much smaller dataset that is genre-different from the pretrained domain. Results of finetuning on the unified dataset appear commensurate with the rates obtained on individual novel data.

Human Evaluation Perceived as the best practice to evaluate auto-generated summaries, human judgment of long-form content similar to our scale remains challenging, time consuming, and often delivers only moderately reliable results. In a more recent study, Krishna et al. (2023) conducted a survey to understand best practices for applying human evaluation to summarization of large-scale documents. Their findings concluded that summaries derived from greater length articles are rarely evaluated by humans and the results obtained are often irreproducible.

Individual	ROUGE-2	ROUGE-L
Frederick Douglass	0.56	0.61
Mark Twain	0.63	0.67
Ulysses Grant	<u>0.66</u>	**0.72**
Napoleon Bonaparte	0.63	0.69

Table 12: ROUGE F1 scores for a human evaluation. Summary maximum token-length is set to 100.

To ameliorate these shortfalls, our text generation process for human evaluation of summaries offers a span-based approach that resembles evidence annotation in question answering systems. A summary is thus a set of non-overlapping spans of contiguous text snippets from the chapter source. The total number of tokens across the spans is bound to the summary maximal token-length parameter. We considered twenty five readers from a book club as expert annotators, each assigned between ten to eleven distinct chapters for span labeling. We were less concerned about bias and avoided allocating more than one reader to a chapter.

In Table 12, we outline ROUGE F1 scores for human evaluation of span-based summaries. Top human scoring is at 0.72 ROUGE-L exceeding machine generation performance (Table 5) by up to about 2X. Given the current pace for developing state-of-the-art NLG systems, this apparent performance gap is expected to diminish rather precipitously, as research continues to reason the trade-off between cost and reward for conducting human annotation.

Method Generalization To evaluate the generalizability of our proposed two-step summarization method to other text genres or domains, we explored NarrativeQA (Kočiský et al., 2018). Destined for the reading comprehension (RC) problem space, NarrativeQA is a large-scale question answering dataset constructed from a collection of large documents in the form of full-length books and movie scripts. Learning to understand books through effective summarization modeling become key to a successful RC system.

NarrativeQA comprises full-length books with an average of slightly over 60K tokens per story. While its human-curated abstractive summaries has a token complexity of about 650 on average. This suggests an end-to-end compression ratio of roughly 100 from source to summary. In contrast to our automatic method that yields a data compaction rate of close to 400 across the two computational steps on our biographical test set. We note that a NarrativeQA book is represented as a cohesive long sequence of text, rather than a collection of chapter entities like ours, the result of performing a data preprocessing step on each of our novels to improve model scalability.

The authors of NarrativeQA performed question answering quality experiments comparing the use of a book in its entirety to its labor-intensive human-created summary for retrieving an answer. Using the ROUGE-L metric they achieved 0.37 for summaries and 0.14 on full length stories. Although for a different goal, these results highly resemble our automatic evaluation scores of 0.38 and 0.12 for two-step and single-tier configurations, respectively.

7 Conclusion

In this paper, we presented a summarization approach that ensures hallucination-free text generation in its first step, and follows by a more regulated and manageable production of a final abstractive summary. On a biographical literary dataset with doubled to quadrupled chapter token complexity, our method achieved superior or similar performance compared to six baseline models. Empirical results show that our fact-unaware summarization can produce abstractive summaries with compelling factual consistency. Noting that author-created book descriptions are often of less than adequate quality, we encourage not only span-based but also free-form reader-written chapter summaries that are factually faithful and benefit a plausible load sharing for curating annotations.

Limitations

Our proposed summarization model is pretrained exclusively on news datasets, however, our experiments and analysis were conducted on biographical narratives. We only studied English summarization and our processes and in particular relevance findings are likely not entirely applicable to long multi-lingual documents. Moreover, single-domain trained models may propagate inductive biases rooted in the data they were pretrained on. This was evidenced in finetuning on our target dataset as the model demonstrated a moderate degree of transferability in adapting the newswire domain to our biographical discourse genre.

Our work studies generated summaries for long narrative text. While our taxonomy appears generalizable to other domains, investigating summarization quality of large-scale datasets, such as scientific articles, patent documents, government reports or meeting discourses was confined to the scope of baseline performance comparison.

Ethics Statement

We assembled our biographical dataset for the grounded source consistent with Project Gutenberg permissions and terms of use. Emanating personal identifiable information of the individual history is unavoidable when obtained from biographical literary. However, improving the faithfulness of automatically generated summaries is essential to ensure reliable and trusted factual accuracy. To the extent of our judgment, produced narrative summaries are free of harmful or offensive content, yet we plan to restrict our dataset for research use only.

Acknowledgements

We would like to thank the anonymous reviewers for their insightful suggestions and feedback.

References

Leonid Berov. 2019. Summaries can frame - but no effect on creativity. In *International Conference on Computational Creativity (ICCC)*, pages 164–171, Charlotte, North Carolina. Association for Computational Creativity (ACC).

Meng Cao, Yue Dong, and Jackie Cheung. 2022. Hallucinated but factual! inspecting the factuality of hallucinations in abstractive summarization. In *Annual Meeting of the Association for Computational Linguistics (ACL)*, pages 3340–3354, Dublin, Ireland. Association for Computational Linguistics.

Hyungtak Choi, Lohith Ravuru, Tomasz Dryjański, Sunghan Rye, Donghyun Lee, Hojung Lee, and Inchul Hwang. 2019. VAE-PGN based abstractive model in multi-stage architecture for text summarization. In *Proceedings of the 12th International Conference on Natural Language Generation*, pages 510–515, Tokyo, Japan. Association for Computational Linguistics.

Rumen Dangovski, Li Jing, Preslav Nakov, Mićo Tatalović, and Marin Soljačić. 2019. Rotational unit of memory: A novel representation unit for RNNs with scalable applications. *Transactions of the Association for Computational Linguistics*, 7:121–138.

Mingkai Deng, Bowen Tan, Zhengzhong Liu, Eric Xing, and Zhiting Hu. 2021. Compression, transduction, and creation: A unified framework for evaluating natural language generation. In *Empirical Methods in Natural Language Processing (EMNLP)*, pages 7580–7605, Online and Punta Cana, Dominican Republic. Association for Computational Linguistics.

Jacob Devlin, Ming-Wei Chang, Kenton Lee, and Kristina Toutanova. 2019. BERT: Pre-training of deep bidirectional transformers for language understanding. In *North American Chapter of the Association for Computational Linguistics: Human Language Technologies (NAACL)*, pages 4171–4186, Minneapolis, Minnesota. Association for Computational Linguistics.

Günes Erkan and Dragomir R. Radev. 2004. LexRank: Graph-based lexical centrality as salience in text summarization. *Journal Artificial Intelligence Research (JAIR)*, 22(1):457–479.

Alexios Gidiotis and Grigorios Tsoumakas. 2020. A divide-and-conquer approach to the summarization of long documents. *IEEE/ACM Transactions on Audio, Speech, and Language Processing*, 28.

Luyang Huang, Shuyang Cao, Nikolaus Parulian, Heng Ji, and Lu Wang. 2021. Efficient attentions for long document summarization. In *North American Chapter of the Association for Computational Linguistics: Human Language Technologies (NAACL)*, pages 1419–1436, Online. Association for Computational Linguistics.

Tomáš Kočiský, Jonathan Schwarz, Phil Blunsom, Chris Dyer, Karl Moritz Hermann, Gábor Melis, and Edward Grefenstette. 2018. The NarrativeQA reading comprehension challenge. *Transactions of the Association for Computational Linguistics*, 6:317–328.

Kalpesh Krishna, Erin Bransom, Bailey Kuehl, Mohit Iyyer, Pradeep Dasigi, Arman Cohan, and Kyle Lo. 2023. LongEval: Guidelines for human evaluation of faithfulness in long-form summarization. In *European Chapter of the Association for Computational Linguistics (EACL)*, Dubrovnik,Croatia. Association for Computational Linguistics.

Wendy G. Lehnert. 1981. Plot units and narrative summarization. *Cognitive Science*, 5(4):293–331.

Mike Lewis, Yinhan Liu, Naman Goyal, Marjan Ghazvininejad, Abdelrahman Mohamed, Omer Levy, Veselin Stoyanov, and Luke Zettlemoyer. 2020. BART: Denoising sequence-to-sequence pre-training for natural language generation, translation, and comprehension. In *Annual Meeting of the Association for Computational Linguistics (ACL)*, pages 7871–7880, Online. Association for Computational Linguistics.

Chin-Yew Lin. 2004. ROUGE: A package for automatic evaluation of summaries. In *Text Summarization Branches Out*, pages 74–81, Barcelona, Spain. Association for Computational Linguistics.

Jeffrey Ling and Alexander Rush. 2017. Coarse-to-fine attention models for document summarization. In *New Frontiers in Summarization*, pages 33–42, Copenhagen, Denmark. Association for Computational Linguistics.

Yinhan Liu, Myle Ott, Naman Goyal, Jingfei Du, Mandar Joshi, Danqi Chen, Omer Levy, Mike Lewis, Luke Zettlemoyer, and Veselin Stoyanov. 2019. Roberta: A robustly optimized BERT pretraining approach. *CoRR*, abs/1907.11692.

Joshua Maynez, Shashi Narayan, Bernd Bohnet, and Ryan McDonald. 2020. On faithfulness and factuality in abstractive summarization. In *Annual Meeting of the Association for Computational Linguistics (ACL)*, pages 1906–1919, Online. Association for Computational Linguistics.

Ramesh Nallapati, Bowen Zhou, Cicero dos Santos, Çağlar Gçehre, and Bing Xiang. 2016. Abstractive text summarization using sequence-to-sequence RNNs and beyond. In *Computational Natural Language Learning (SIGNLL)*, pages 280–290, Berlin, Germany. Association for Computational Linguistics.

Shashi Narayan, Shay B. Cohen, and Mirella Lapata. 2018. Don't give me the details, just the summary! topic-aware convolutional neural networks for extreme summarization. In *Empirical Methods in Natural Language Processing (EMNLP)*, pages 1797–1807, Brussels, Belgium. Association for Computational Linguistics.

Jonathan Pilault, Raymond Li, Sandeep Subramanian, and Chris Pal. 2020. On extractive and abstractive neural document summarization with transformer language models. In *Empirical Methods in Natural Language Processing (EMNLP)*, pages 9308–9319, Online. Association for Computational Linguistics.

Andrew Piper, Richard Jean So, and David Bamman. 2021. Narrative theory for computational narrative understanding. In *Empirical Methods in Natural Language Processing (EMNLP)*, pages 298–311, Online.

Dongqi Pu, Xudong Hong, Pin-Jie Lin, Ernie Chang, and Vera Demberg. 2022. Two-stage movie script summarization: An efficient method for low-resource long document summarization. In *Proceedings of The Workshop on Automatic Summarization for Creative Writing*, pages 57–66, Gyeongju, Republic of Korea. Association for Computational Linguistics.

Nils Reimers and Iryna Gurevych. 2019. Sentence-BERT: Sentence embeddings using Siamese BERT-networks. In *Empirical Methods in Natural Language Processing and the 9th International Joint Conference on Natural Language Processing (EMNLP-IJCNLP)*, pages 3982–3992, Hong Kong, China. Association for Computational Linguistics.

Ming-Hsiang Su, Chung-Hsien Wu, and Hao-Tse Cheng. 2020. A two-stage transformer-based approach for variable-length abstractive summarization. *IEEE/ACM Transactions on Audio, Speech, and Language Processing*, 28:2061–2072.

Ashish Vaswani, Noam Shazeer, Niki Parmar, Jakob Uszkoreit, Llion Jones, Aidan N Gomez, Ł ukasz Kaiser, and Illia Polosukhin. 2017. Attention is all you need. In *Advances in Neural Information Processing Systems (neurIPS)*, volume 30. Curran Associates, Inc.

Yumo Xu and Mirella Lapata. 2020. Coarse-to-fine query focused multi-document summarization. In *Empirical Methods in Natural Language Processing (EMNLP)*, pages 3632–3645, Online. Association for Computational Linguistics.

Weizhe Yuan, Graham Neubig, and Pengfei Liu. 2021. Bartscore: Evaluating generated text as text generation. In *Advances in Neural Information Processing Systems*, volume 34, pages 27263–27277. Curran Associates, Inc.

Yusen Zhang, Ansong Ni, Ziming Mao, Chen Henry Wu, Chenguang Zhu, Budhaditya Deb, Ahmed Awadallah, Dragomir Radev, and Rui Zhang. 2022. Summ^n: A multi-stage summarization framework for long input dialogues and documents. In *Annual Meeting of the Association for Computational Linguistics (ACL)*, pages 1592–1604, Dublin, Ireland. Association for Computational Linguistics.

Ming Zhong, Da Yin, Tao Yu, Ahmad Zaidi, Mutethia Mutuma, Rahul Jha, Ahmed Hassan Awadallah, Asli Celikyilmaz, Yang Liu, Xipeng Qiu, and Dragomir Radev. 2021. QMSum: A new benchmark for query-based multi-domain meeting summarization. In *North American Chapter of the Association for Computational Linguistics: Human Language Technologies (NAACL)*, pages 5905–5921, Online. Association for Computational Linguistics.

The distribution of discourse relations within and across turns in spontaneous conversation

S. Magalí López Cortez **Cassandra L. Jacobs**
Department of Linguistics
University at Buffalo
Buffalo, NY, USA
solmagal;cxjacobs@buffalo.edu

Abstract

Time pressure and topic negotiation may impose constraints on how people leverage discourse relations (DRs) in spontaneous conversational contexts. In this work, we adapt a system of DRs for written language to spontaneous dialogue using crowdsourced annotations from novice annotators. We then test whether discourse relations are used differently across several types of multi-utterance contexts. We compare the patterns of DR annotation within and across speakers and within and across turns. Ultimately, we find that different discourse contexts produce distinct distributions of discourse relations, with single-turn annotations creating the most uncertainty for annotators. Additionally, we find that the discourse relation annotations are of sufficient quality to predict from embeddings of discourse units.

1 Introduction

Discourse relations (DRs) such as Elaboration, Background and Explanation, hold between discourse units contributing to the coherence of a text. Annotation of discourse relations has received attention for its relevance to discourse parsers, with applications in question answering systems (e.g. Jansen et al., 2014), text summarization (e.g. Liu and Chen, 2019), sentiment classification (e.g. Kraus and Feuerriegel, 2019), and machine translation (e.g. Meyer and Popescu-Belis, 2012). However, most of the annotated data and systems have focused on written language, with a few exceptions (e.g., Tonelli et al., 2010; Zeldes, 2017; Scholman et al., 2022). In spoken dialogue or multiparty conversation, participants must quickly juggle a variety of tasks, such as responding to another person to solve a problem (Levinson and Torreira, 2015) or negotiating the question under discussion (Roberts, 2012), often under considerable time pressure that is less present in written production. In addition to these time demands, it is unclear whether spontaneous conversation demonstrates the same patterns of discourse relations as observed in written language (see Crible and Cuenca, 2017, for a discussion of spoken vs. written use of discourse markers).

Perhaps unsurprisingly, the vast majority of work on discourse relations has focused either on written texts, especially news text (Carlson et al., 2003; Prasad et al., 2008, 2018), or highly structured conversations that are constrained by a particular game (Afantenos et al., 2015; Asher et al., 2016). Some recent corpora contain spoken monologues (Scholman et al., 2022), and spoken conversations (Tonelli et al., 2010; Zeldes, 2017), but the field still largely lacks annotated corpora of spontaneous dialogue.

Thus, our goal is to present the first efforts towards an annotated corpus of DRs for spontaneous spoken conversation, with particular attention to relations across different contexts within a conversation. We analyze the patterns of DR annotation within and across speakers and within and across turns and test the coherence of annotators' decisions.

2 Related Work

Most currently available corpora annotated with DRs have focused on written language or spoken monologues. An exception is the Georgetown University Multilayer (GUM) corpus (Zeldes, 2017), which has a set of conversations annotated within Rhetorical Structure Theory (RST, Mann and Thompson, 1987), following the guidelines of the RST Discourse Treebank (RST-DT, Carlson et al., 2003). But it is an open question whether the DRs that have been identified for news texts are appropriate for conversational data. Tonelli et al. (2010) adapt the PDTB framework to annotate a subset of a corpus of Italian conversations about software and hardware troubleshooting, and suggest modifications to the framework to account for

Proceedings of the 4th Workshop on Computational Approaches to Discourse (CODI 2023), pages 156–162
July 13-14, 2023 ©2023 Association for Computational Linguistics

spoken data.

Discourse relations corpora have usually been annotated by experts, but some recent corpora have been annotated by novice annotators, such as university students, in the case of the GUM corpus (Zeldes, 2017), or crowdsourced workers, in the case of the DiscoGEM corpus (Scholman et al., 2022). GUM was annotated using RST as part of a Corpus Linguistics class, while DiscoGEM was annotated following the Penn Discourse Treebank (PDTB, Prasad et al., 2008, 2018) framework, using a method for crowdsourcing annotations introduced in Yung et al. (2019), and using a multi-label approach. The present work deviates from prior work in its focus on conversational data and the use of Segmented Discourse Representation Theory (SDRT, Asher and Lascarides, 2003) alongside the STAC corpus (Asher et al., 2016) guidelines.

3 Discourse relation annotation

In this work, we focus on a subset of 19 dialogues from the Switchboard Corpus (Godfrey et al., 1992). This corpus contains informal language and has been the subject of study of numerous analyses of dialogue within linguistics (Jaeger and Snider, 2013; Reitter and Moore, 2014). In it, two strangers are presented with a topic (e.g., childcare) that they must discuss with each other, but the dialogues are otherwise not tightly constrained. Annotating Switchboard will provide us with a more complete understanding of the use and generality of discourse relations across linguistic contexts and genres.

Following the annotation procedure in the STAC corpus (Asher et al., 2016), we identified a subset of suitable elementary discourse units (EDUs) for annotation by parsing each turn into a dependency structure and included only those turns with at least two roots or verbs. Then, we segmented each of these turns into their respective EDUs. Using these segmentations, we identified EDU candidates for discourse relations that were either within-turn (same speaker) or across two turns (different speakers, or the same speaker), where the two turns were adjacent in the case of different speakers, or only interrupted by one turn, in the case of same speaker. We provide a representative set of these pair types in Table 1 under the Explanation, Comment, and Result examples, respectively.

3.1 Elementary Discourse Units

Elementary discourse units (EDUs) are typically defined as non-overlapping text spans (Mann and Thompson, 1987), which perform some basic discourse function (Asher and Lascarides, 2003), typically at the level of clauses. However, conversational EDUs may not necessarily contain a main verb (e.g., clarification questions: "Saginaw?") or may be incomplete or interrupted (e.g., "and so–"). So, we define EDUs in Switchboard similarly to written text, with some modifications to account for variability due to spoken language. In particular, our modifications account for noise; non-linguistic communication (e.g., laughter); restarts; and disfluencies (e.g., "uh" or "um"). Additionally, we use complex discourse units (CDUs), which are combinations of EDUs which function together as an argument to a DR (Asher and Lascarides, 2003).

3.2 Relation categories

Discourse relations (DRs) were selected from Segmented Discourse Representation theory (SDRT, Asher and Lascarides, 2003), following the annotation manual for the STAC corpus (Asher et al., 2012). 11 out of 16 relation labels used in Asher et al. (2012) were selected, based on a pilot annotation. We selected the most common relations in an attempt to minimize the number of choices presented to annotators, but the set is non-exhaustive. An "Other" category was added for cases in which none of the selected labels applied. Table 1 shows the list of DRs together with representative examples.

3.3 Annotators

The present study recruited 114 students enrolled in a computational linguistics course grouped into 19 teams consisting of approximately 5 members who annotated the dyads. Each team received a conversation for annotation. Annotations were performed individually, but groups then discussed their work and submitted a report as a team. One team was excluded because they completed their annotations together and submitted a single set of labels. Students were trained to identify discourse relations using a short quiz and live training with the instructor of the course. Annotators were provided with guidelines to which they could refer back, and they had read and annotated the conversation in three previous tasks before annotating discourse relations, to ensure that they were familiar with the

Relation	Discourse Units
Acknowledgement	A: ‖ *it starts recording now.* ‖ B: ‖ **Okay.** ‖
Background	A: ‖ *I'm, we're originally from another state* ‖ **and I know** ‖ **in the state we were from that they did that t-, similar type thing.** ‖
Clarification Question	A: ‖ *We live in the Saginaw area.* ‖ B: ‖ **Saginaw?**‖
Comment	B: ‖ *They seem to be having a real good response.* ‖ A: ‖ **That's pretty good.** ‖
Continuation	A: ‖ *I work off and on just temporarily* ‖ **and usually find friends to babysit,** ‖
Contrast	A: ‖ *I don't work, though,* ‖ **but I used to work and,** ‖
Elaboration	A: ‖ *in the state we were from that they did that t-, similar type thing.* ‖ **The city brought ought,** ‖ **you know,** ‖ **set tr-, separate trash cans** ‖ **and you separated your stuff** ‖
Explanation	A: ‖ *and they discontinued them* ‖ **because people were coming and dumping their trash in them.** ‖
Narration	A: ‖ *and you put it in there* ‖ **and they took it,** ‖
Question-Answer Pair	B: ‖ *Saginaw?* ‖ A: ‖ **Uh-huh.**‖
Result	B: ‖ *No,* ‖ *I just, I noticed* ‖ *it Iowa and other cities like that, it's a nickel per aluminum can.* ‖ A: ‖ Oh. ‖ B: ‖ **So you don't see too many thrown out around the** ‖ **[laughter]** ‖ **streets.** ‖
Other	None of the labels applies

Table 1: Representative discourse unit pairs for annotated discourse relations. The first argument to the discourse relation is shown in *italics* and the second one in **bold**. A and B correspond to speakers, and double pipes (‖) represent boundaries between elementary discourse units.

topics and speakers in each dyad.

3.4 Annotation procedure

Annotators were presented with pairs representing either an EDU or CDU (π_1) and another EDU or CDU (π_2). Annotators were shown two spans of text π_1 and π_2 with π_1 presented in italics and π_2 presented in bold face font in the annotation software Prodigy (Montani and Honnibal, 2018), with two preceding and two subsequent turns for context. Annotators were asked to determine the relation between π_1 and π_2 from a list of the DR categories in Table 1. If annotators thought that no relation was present, they were told to reject the item and move on to the next pair. Critically for our research question, annotators could mark several relations for a pair of EDUs simultaneously. In addition to labeling discourse relations, annotators were also asked to provide a confidence rating on a scale from 1-5, but we leave these analyses for future work. In total, each annotator provided judgments for an average of 25 EDU pairs across 464 total pairs.

In the next section, we test whether annotators show greater uncertainty about discourse relations in different discourse contexts. We analyze the distribution of their labels to assess whether discourse relations in conversation vary in their contexts of use.

4 Uncertainty in the annotation of discourse relations

Different EDU pairs in the present annotation task were drawn either from the same turn, or across turns but within or across speakers. Thus, we can assess how much discourse relations vary by the placement of an utterance in a dialogue. Given the complex dynamics in dialogue, we expect to find significant differences in discourse relation use across different discourse contexts. We visualize the distribution of the relations in Figure 1.

Annotators generally selected more discourse relations per EDU pair in the single-turn case, with an average of 8.16 relations per team or 1.60 per annotator. When EDUs spanned turns within a single speaker, groups selected significantly fewer relations (average = 7.29, $t(302) = -2.16$, $p < .05$). Groups likewise selected even fewer relations for EDUs between two speakers (average = 6.51, $t(314) = -2.54$, $p < .05$). On its face, this pattern appears surprising, because it suggests that annotators find more relations appropriate for single-speaker productions. However, an alternative interpretation of these results is that annotators may instead have been uncertain about the distinctions between the different discourse relations. This second interpretation is corroborated by post-hoc poll data from 35 annotators, of whom 32 (91.4%) stated that the selection of discourse relations was best suited to annotating cross-speaker

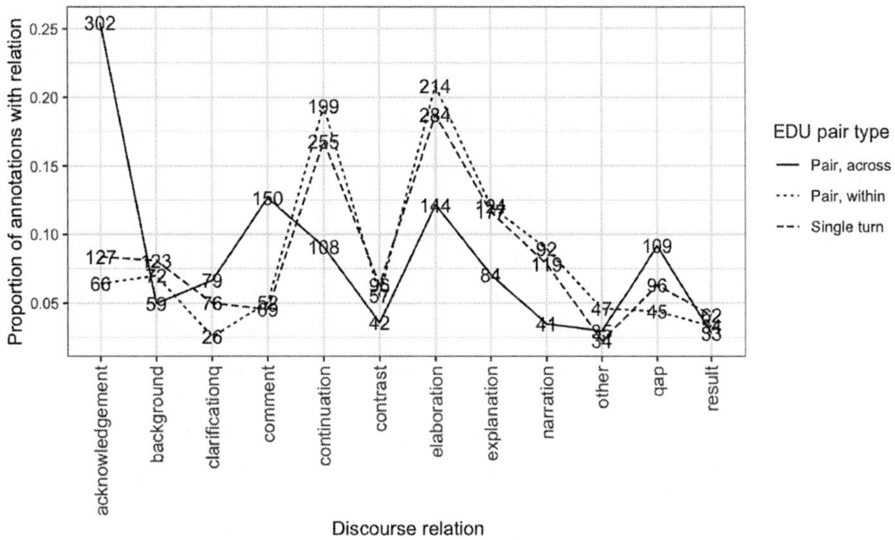

Figure 1: Distribution of discourse relations across three EDU pair types. y axis represents proportions of EDU pairs with a given label; numbers represent the count of a label within a discourse context category.

EDU pairs. Future work will require recruiting greater numbers of annotators to be able to distinguish between these two hypotheses.

4.1 Inter-annotator agreement

We computed measures of inter-annotator agreement for multilabel tasks using Marchal et al. (2022). This approach uses bootstrap sampling to estimate the chance frequencies of DRs in a multilabel dataset to provide a baseline for agreement between annotators.

We summarize the results of this analysis in Table 2. Following Marchal et al. (2022), we computed observed, expected and adjusted agreement for six measures. Soft-match agreement uses the intersection of labels selected by two annotators; boot-match corrects the expected agreement by using the bootstrapping method (as opposed to ignoring non-intersecting labels); augmented kappa uses DR labels weighted according to the number of labels annotated for each item; precision and recall are calculated as the proportion of intersecting DR labels over the set of labels selected by the first and second annotator, respectively; F1 is the usual harmonic mean between precision and recall.

Both observed and adjusted agreement metrics were well above chance using the bootstrapping method proposed by Marchal et al. (2022). Agreement is in general modest (Landis and Koch, 1977), which may be partly due to the challenging nature of the DRs annotation task (Spooren and Degand, 2010), and partly due to annotators' uncertainty on DR labels across different context types.

	observed	expected	adjusted kappa
`soft-match`	0.43	0.11	0.36
`augmented`	0.27	0.11	0.18
`boot-match`	0.43	0.21	0.27
`boot-rec.`	0.33	0.14	0.22
`boot-prec.`	0.36	0.17	0.23
`boot-F1`	0.32	0.13	0.21

Table 2: Outputs of Marchal et al. (2022) inter-annotator agreement analysis.

Relation	**Intercept**	**Different speaker**	**Within turn**
Background	-2.73	1.96	0.24
Clarification Q.	0.02	0.41	-0.43
Comment	-1.69	0.84	0.46
Continuation	-1.60	2.35	0.31
Contrast	-2.23	2.07	0.17
Elaboration	-0.78	1.95	0.13
Explanation	-1.40	2.00	0.09
Narration	-3.29	2.68	0.53
Other	-3.54	2.20	1.12
Q-A Pair	-0.81	0.64	-0.01
Result	-2.35	1.63	-0.00

Table 3: Coefficient estimates from a multiclass logistic regression predicting each annotation label.

4.2 Predicting relation selection

We use a model comparison approach to understand the contributions of discourse context (within/across speakers and within/across turns) to relation annotation by first constructing a null model that estimates the base rates of each discourse relation. Then, we constructed a multiclass logistic regression model containing the discourse context variables of interest, which significantly improved fit to the annotation data ($X^2(22) = 447.98$, $p < .001$). This improvement in fit suggests that the distribution of discourse relations that are identified by annotators is distinct across contexts. Adding the annotator group/topic also significantly improved fit beyond the model containing the contextual variables alone ($X^2(198) = 900.06$ $p < .001$). We summarize the results of this final model in Table 3.[1]

An informal evaluation of the coefficients suggests that discourse relations are not uniformly distributed across contexts. Intuitively, Acknowledgements, Clarification Questions, Comments, and Question-Answer Pairs are more likely across speakers than within. Additionally, Continuations, Elaborations, Explanations, and Narrations are more likely to occur within a single speaker. The pattern of results is more unclear when comparing EDUs that are produced by a single speaker but which occur either within or across turns. For example, relations such as Clarification Questions are less likely to occur within a turn than across turns.

4.3 Classifier for relations

To validate the quality of the annotations, we built a model to classify EDU pairs into discourse relations. We reasoned that if annotators are following the guidelines and use information about the EDU pairs, then a classifier should be able to predict DR labels. We encoded the first EDU or CDU (π_1) and the second (π_2) as the two "sentences" in the next sentence prediction architecture of BERT (Devlin et al., 2019). This enables the classifier to represent the π_1 and π_2 components somewhat separately.

We built a classifier head trained on the resulting embeddings without fine-tuning to predict each individual annotator label. We chose to model each annotator label individually to learn agreement/majority class implicitly because prior studies have shown that this improves generalization (Yung et al., 2022). We use a leave-one-conversation-out training procedure, in which we test a ridge regression classifier on all of the annotations from a single conversation while we train it on all other annotations across the other conversations. This ensures minimal memorization of specific turns within a conversation, which is critical given our multilabel annotation approach.

Strict annotation-level accuracy to predict each selected label from all annotators was quite poor, with macro average precision at .21, recall at .19, and F1 at .19. However, recall was substantially higher when considering whether the top guess belonged to the set of all labels provided by annotators, at .76 overall and .71 averaged by group.

To quantify the uncertainty of the annotators across different contexts, we leverage the classifier to produce a label distribution for a given (π_1, π_2) pair. We then compute the cross-entropy between the model's predictions and annotators' gold label distributions, collapsing across all annotations for an EDU pair. Overall, cross entropy between model predictions and annotator labels was highest for the single-turn case, with (mean $= 0.43$), but lowest for EDUs between two speakers (mean $= 0.38$), suggesting greater uncertainty in label assignment.

5 Discussion

In two experiments, we demonstrated that novice DR label annotations in a single turn are more difficult than across turns. We showed that including discourse context (within/across speaker and within/across turn) to a logistic regression model significantly improves fit to our annotation data. A classifier trained to predict DR labels from embeddings of (π_1, π_2) pairs showed modest success for recall of any of the annotations, but poor precision and recall overall. A comparison of this classifier's predictions and annotators' gold label distributions revealed greater uncertainty for the annotation of discourse relations within a single turn.

These results demonstrate that different conversational contexts are associated with different distributions of discourse relations. The uncertainty of choice of discourse relations within a turn may be due to several factors. DRs that typically occur across adjacent turns and across speakers (e.g., Acknowledgements) might have clearer signals. At the same time, DRs that occur more frequently within speakers, and, in particular, within a turn, might be more ambiguous, or might co-occur with other relations. More work is necessary to disentangle uncertainty about the identity of the best fit relation from whether multiple relations are appropriate.

[1] Due to the multilabel nature of the annotation task and the one-versus-rest training for the multiclass model, coefficients for each DR are not independent, were not estimated jointly, and should be interpreted broadly as representing separate logistic regressions.

Limitations

The current work is limited by the size of the dataset and the nature of spontaneous conversation. While the discourse relations proposed as part of this work were selected to be general and build on categories from the literature, the list is not exhaustive and it is likely that these relations may be culturally, linguistically, and situationally specific. Future work in this area should validate the generality of the discourse relation system used in this work.

The selection of EDUs and CDUs for annotation is also non-exhaustive; additional segments could be included in future work.

Annotation quality is also a practical limitation. Annotation for discourse relations typically results in low-agreement data, even among expert annotators (e.g., DiscoGEM; Scholman et al., 2022). Even though our research questions focus on this disagreement as a positive, other researchers may require greater numbers of annotations in order to obtain a gold label.

Ethics Statement

We are not aware of ethical issues associated with the texts used in this work. Students participated in the annotation task as part of course credit but annotation decisions were not associated with their performance in the course.

Acknowledgements

We would like to thank Jürgen Bohnemeyer and three anonymous reviewers for feedback on a previous version of this paper.

References

Stergos Afantenos, Eric Kow, Nicholas Asher, and Jérémy Perret. 2015. Discourse parsing for multiparty chat dialogues. In *Proceedings of the 2015 Conference on Empirical Methods in Natural Language Processing*, pages 928–937, Lisbon, Portugal. Association for Computational Linguistics.

Nicholas Asher, Julie Hunter, Mathieu Morey, Benamara Farah, and Stergos Afantenos. 2016. Discourse structure and dialogue acts in multiparty dialogue: the STAC corpus. In *Proceedings of the Tenth International Conference on Language Resources and Evaluation (LREC'16)*, pages 2721–2727, Portorož, Slovenia. European Language Resources Association (ELRA).

Nicholas Asher and Alex Lascarides. 2003. *Logics of conversation*. Cambridge University Press.

Nicholas Asher, Vladimir Popescu, Philippe Muller, Stergos Afantenos, Anais Cadilhac, Farah Benamara, Laure Vieu, and Pascal Denis. 2012. Manual for the analysis of settlers data. *Strategic Conversation (STAC). Université Paul Sabatier*.

Lynn Carlson, Daniel Marcu, and Mary Ellen Okurowski. 2003. Building a discourse-tagged corpus in the framework of rhetorical structure theory. In *Current and new directions in discourse and dialogue*, pages 85–112. Springer.

Ludivine Crible and Maria-Josep Cuenca. 2017. Discourse markers in speech: distinctive features and corpus annotation. *Dialogue and Discourse*, 8(2):149–166.

Jacob Devlin, Ming-Wei Chang, Kenton Lee, and Kristina Toutanova. 2019. BERT: Pre-training of deep bidirectional transformers for language understanding. In *Proceedings of the 2019 Conference of the North American Chapter of the Association for Computational Linguistics: Human Language Technologies, Volume 1 (Long and Short Papers)*, pages 4171–4186, Minneapolis, Minnesota. Association for Computational Linguistics.

John J. Godfrey, Edward C. Holliman, and Jane McDaniel. 1992. Switchboard: Telephone speech corpus for research and development. In *Proceedings of the 1992 IEEE International Conference on Acoustics, Speech and Signal Processing - Volume 1*, ICASSP'92, page 517–520, USA. IEEE Computer Society.

T Florian Jaeger and Neal E Snider. 2013. Alignment as a consequence of expectation adaptation: Syntactic priming is affected by the prime's prediction error given both prior and recent experience. *Cognition*, 127(1):57–83.

Peter Jansen, Mihai Surdeanu, and Peter Clark. 2014. Discourse complements lexical semantics for non-factoid answer reranking. In *Proceedings of the 52nd Annual Meeting of the Association for Computational Linguistics (Volume 1: Long Papers)*, pages 977–986.

Mathias Kraus and Stefan Feuerriegel. 2019. Sentiment analysis based on rhetorical structure theory: Learning deep neural networks from discourse trees. *Expert Systems with Applications*, 118:65–79.

J Richard Landis and Gary G. Koch. 1977. The measurement of observer agreement for categorical data. *Biometrics*, 33 1:159–74.

Stephen C. Levinson and Francisco Torreira. 2015. Timing in turn-taking and its implications for processing models of language. *Frontiers in Psychology*, 6.

Zhengyuan Liu and Nancy Chen. 2019. Exploiting discourse-level segmentation for extractive summarization. In *Proceedings of the 2nd Workshop on New*

Frontiers in Summarization, pages 116–121, Hong Kong, China. Association for Computational Linguistics.

William C Mann and Sandra A Thompson. 1987. *Rhetorical Structure Theory: A theory of text organization*. University of Southern California, Information Sciences Institute Los Angeles.

Marian Marchal, Merel Scholman, Frances Yung, and Vera Demberg. 2022. Establishing annotation quality in multi-label annotations. In *Proceedings of the 29th International Conference on Computational Linguistics*, pages 3659–3668, Gyeongju, Republic of Korea. International Committee on Computational Linguistics.

Thomas Meyer and Andrei Popescu-Belis. 2012. Using sense-labeled discourse connectives for statistical machine translation. In *EACL 2012: Proceedings of the Joint Workshop on Exploiting Synergies between Information Retrieval and Machine Translation (ESIRMT) and Hybrid Approaches to Machine Translation (HyTra)*, CONF, pages 129–138.

Ines Montani and Matthew Honnibal. 2018. Prodigy: A new annotation tool for radically efficient machine teaching. *Artificial Intelligence*.

Rashmi Prasad, Nikhil Dinesh, Alan Lee, Eleni Miltsakaki, Livio Robaldo, Aravind Joshi, and Bonnie Webber. 2008. The Penn Discourse TreeBank 2.0. In *Proceedings of the Sixth International Conference on Language Resources and Evaluation (LREC'08)*, Marrakech, Morocco. European Language Resources Association (ELRA).

Rashmi Prasad, Bonnie Webber, and Alan Lee. 2018. Discourse annotation in the PDTB: The next generation. In *Proceedings 14th Joint ACL - ISO Workshop on Interoperable Semantic Annotation*, pages 87–97, Santa Fe, New Mexico, USA. Association for Computational Linguistics.

D. Reitter and Johanna D. Moore. 2014. Alignment and task success in spoken dialogue. *Journal of Memory and Language*, 76:29–46.

Craige Roberts. 2012. Information structure: Towards an integrated formal theory of pragmatics. *Semantics and pragmatics*, 5:6–1.

Merel Scholman, Tianai Dong, Frances Yung, and Vera Demberg. 2022. DiscoGeM: A crowdsourced corpus of genre-mixed implicit discourse relations. In *Proceedings of the Thirteenth Language Resources and Evaluation Conference*, pages 3281–3290, Marseille, France. European Language Resources Association.

Wilbert Spooren and Liesbeth Degand. 2010. Coding coherence relations: Reliability and validity. *Corpus Linguistics and Linguistic Theory*, 6(2):241–266.

Sara Tonelli, Giuseppe Riccardi, Rashmi Prasad, and Aravind Joshi. 2010. Annotation of discourse relations for conversational spoken dialogs. In *Proceedings of the Seventh International Conference on Language Resources and Evaluation (LREC'10)*, Valletta, Malta. European Language Resources Association (ELRA).

Frances Yung, Kaveri Anuranjana, Merel Scholman, and Vera Demberg. 2022. Label distributions help implicit discourse relation classification. In *Proceedings of the 3rd Workshop on Computational Approaches to Discourse*, pages 48–53, Gyeongju, Republic of Korea and Online. International Conference on Computational Linguistics.

Frances Yung, Vera Demberg, and Merel Scholman. 2019. Crowdsourcing discourse relation annotations by a two-step connective insertion task. In *Proceedings of the 13th Linguistic Annotation Workshop*, pages 16–25, Florence, Italy. Association for Computational Linguistics.

Amir Zeldes. 2017. The GUM corpus: Creating multilayer resources in the classroom. *Language Resources and Evaluation*, 51(3):581–612.

Embedding Mental Health Discourse for Community Recommendation

Hy Dang*, **Bang Nguyen***, **Noah Ziems**, **Meng Jiang**
University of Notre Dame
{hdang, bnguyen5, nziems2, mjiang2}@nd.edu

Abstract

Our paper investigates the use of discourse embedding techniques to develop a community recommendation system that focuses on mental health support groups on social media. Social media platforms provide a means for users to anonymously connect with communities that cater to their specific interests. However, with the vast number of online communities available, users may face difficulties in identifying relevant groups to address their mental health concerns. To address this challenge, we explore the integration of discourse information from various subreddit communities using embedding techniques to develop an effective recommendation system. Our approach involves the use of content-based and collaborative filtering techniques to enhance the performance of the recommendation system. Our findings indicate that the proposed approach outperforms the use of each technique separately and provides interpretability in the recommendation process.

1 Introduction

The rise of social media as a platform has allowed people all over the world to connect and communicate with one another. Further, these communities that exist online are able to keep their members anonymous from one another, allowing new communities to form which would have a hard time existing without anonymity.

Specifically, this new and robust anonymity has allowed an explosion of online communities with a focus on giving each other advice on health issues. While being involved in seeking peer support in a community with people that have experienced similar issues can provide a significant positive impact on someone's ability to navigate their personal problems (Richard et al., 2022), finding communities with relevant discourse is not trivial. Often, the platforms which host these communities have a very large quantity of them. There are over 100,000 different communities on Reddit alone. Further, some communities are not easily found due to their inherently anonymous nature, so the only way a user can decide if they fit within the community is by spending time reading through the discourse happening within the community.

For these reasons, new users seeking others who have experienced similar situations may have a very hard time finding communities that would help them the most, even if they are familiar with the platform which hosts the communities.

Recently, embedding long sequences of text has received lots of interest both from the research community and from practitioners. A number of studies have shown embeddings can be useful for measuring the similarity both between document pairs and between question-document pairs (Karpukhin et al., 2020; Xiong et al., 2020; Qu et al., 2021), allowing for retrieval of the most similar documents given a new question or document. However, little work has been done investigating how the discourse within a community, which represents the meaning of that community, can be represented in a single embedding. The discourse of a community in this context can be all users' posts in that specific community or represented community's description. This poses a unique challenge as discourse within these communities is often in the form of threads that, unlike documents, are not naturally represented as a single block of text.

The goal of this work is to develop a system to recommend support groups to social media users who seek help regarding mental health issues using embeddings to represent the communities and their discourse. Specifically, we aim to leverage the text of a given user's posts along with the description and posts in each subreddit community to help recommend support groups that the user could consider joining.

Our main research questions are as follows:

*These authors contributed equally to this work

Proceedings of the 4th Workshop on Computational Approaches to Discourse (CODI 2023), pages 163–172
July 13-14, 2023

1. In representing online communities through discourse embeddings, what type of information can be used?

2. To what degree do these representations improve the accuracy of predicting users' behaviors regarding their involvement in sharing experiences within groups or communities?

3. Do different discourse embedding methods change the prediction capacity of our community recommendation model?

In exploring these research questions, we propose a hybrid recommendation approach that leverages both content-based and collaborative filtering to construct our community recommendation model. As shown in Fig. 1, the content-based filtering component investigates different methods of embedding discourse within a community to recommend similar communities to users. It is then combined with a matrix factorization model that learns user engagement behavior in a community to improve recommendation decisions. Utilizing users' past interactions as well as text-based information about the communities, we show that our model achieves promising accuracy while offering interpretability.

2 Related Work

There are a number of studies related to our work.

Son et al. (2022) and Balusu et al. (2022) constructed discourse embeddings to find relations between short text segments. While the two studies were similar in concept, they focused on short text segments where this work instead focused on constructing discourse embeddings for entire social media communities.

Garriga et al. (2022) showed NLP techniques could be used with electronic health records to predict mental health crises 4 weeks in advance. While online communities were no replacement for professional medical help, this suggested many who had looming mental health problems seek help before a crisis.

Low et al. (2020) experimented on the same dataset we used with Natural Language Processing techniques such as TF-IDF and sentiment analysis to understand the effects of COVID-19 on mental health. Although working on the same dataset, our work studies a different task: to recommend mental health-related support community to Reddit users.

Musto et al. (2016) adopted a similar approach to ours in content-based filtering for recommendation. Specifically, they mapped a Wikipedia page to each item and generate its corresponding vector representation using three feature-extraction methods - Latent Semantic Indexing, Random Indexing, and Word2Vec. We extended this method by exploring more recent representations of text such as BERT (Devlin et al., 2019) and OpenAI embeddings.

Halder et al. (2017) recommended threads in health forums based on the topics of interest of the users. Specifically, self-reported medical conditions and symptoms of treatments were used as additional information to help improve thread recommendations (Wang et al., 2020; Jiang et al., 2012). While our work is also situated in the health domain, we are interested in recommending a broader support group to users rather than a specific thread.

Ghazarian et al. (2022) used sentiment and other features to automatically evaluate dialog, showing NLP techniques could be used to evaluate quality of discourse. In doing so, they leveraged weak supervision to train a model on a large dataset without needing quality annotations.

3 Problem Definition

Suppose we have a Reddit's "*who-posts-to-what*" graph, which is denoted by $G = (U, V, E)$ where U is the set of users, V is the set of subreddit communities, and E, a subset of $U \times V$, is the set of edges. The number of user nodes is $m = |U|$ and the number of subreddit communities is $n = |V|$. So, $U = \{(u_1, P_1), (u_2, P_2), ..., (u_m, P_m)\}$ where P_i is the set of posts by user u_i and $V = \{(v_1, P'_1), ..., (v_n, P'_n)\}$ where P'_j is the set of all posts in subreddit v_j. If a user u_i posts to subreddit v_j, there is an edge that goes from u_i to v_j, which is denoted by $e_{ij} = e(u_i, v_j)$. The problem is that given G, predict if $e_{ij} = e(u_i, v_j)$ exists. In other words, will user u_i post to subreddit v_j?

4 Methodology

Figure 1 illustrates our recommendation pipeline, which adopts a hybrid approach by incorporating both content-based filtering (CBF) and collaborative filtering, specifically matrix factorization (MF) strategies. The CBF model recommends new subreddits based on the average of a user's previous interactions, weighted by how similar the previous subreddits are to the new ones. Meanwhile, users and subreddits are represented in a k-dimensional

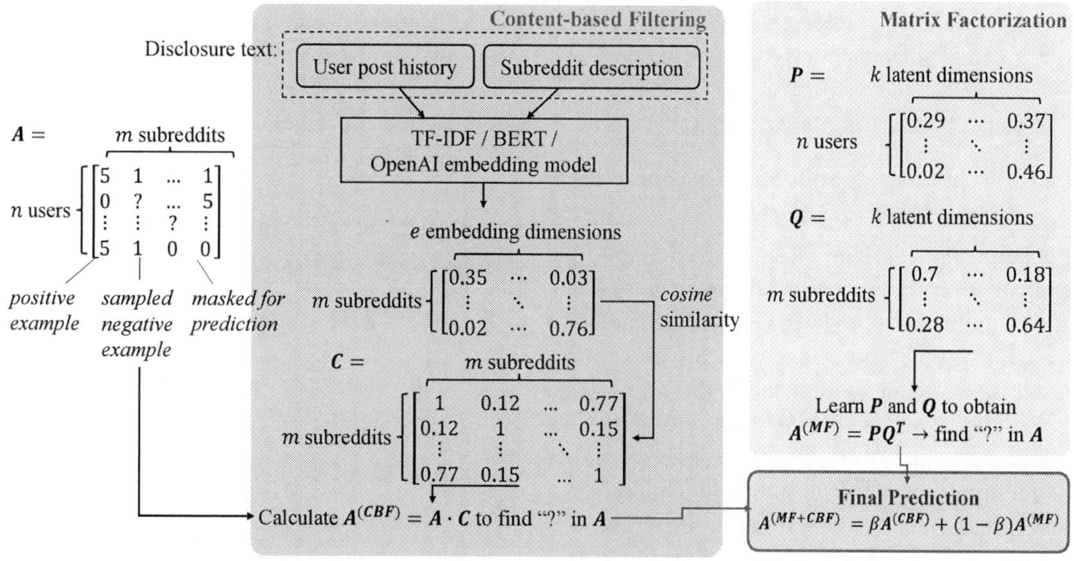

Figure 1: Our recommendation pipeline, which linearly combines the prediction of a content-based filtering (CBF) and a matrix factorization (MF) model. In the CBF model, recommendations of new subreddits are made through the average of a user's past interaction, weighted by how similar the past subreddits are to the new ones. In the MF model, users and subreddits are represented in a joint latent space of k dimensions. Recommendations of new subreddits are made based on the distance between users and subreddits in this latent space.

joint latent space in the MF model. The distance between users and subreddits in this latent space is used to provide recommendations for new subreddits. The predictions from these two components are linearly combined to obtain the final recommendation of subreddits to users.

The collaborative filtering component of our solution leverages nonnegative matrix factorization to represent our users and subreddits in lower-dimensional latent space. In this sense, we redefine the adjacency matrix $\mathbf{A}$ in our problem definition so that it works with nonnegative factorization. More specifically, users' past interactions with items are represented by the adjacency matrix $\mathbf{A} \in \{5, 1, 0\}^{m \times n}$. $A_{ij} = 5$ if the user u_i has posted to subreddit j, $A_{ij} = 1$ if the user u_i has NOT posted to the subreddit v_j, and $A_{ij} = 0$ is the missing connection that needs predicting. Given this adjacency matrix $\mathbf{A}$, the task is to predict the missing elements $A_{ij} = 0$. In the following sections, we elaborate on each component of our recommendation model and then discuss how they are combined to obtain our final solution.

4.1 Content-based Filtering

In recommending items to users based on their past interactions and preferences, content-based filtering methods represent each item with a feature vector, which can then be utilized to measure the similarity between items (Linden et al., 2003). If an item is similar to another item with which a user interacted in the past, it will be recommended to that same user. Thus, in addition to the adjacency matrix $\mathbf{A}$, we utilize another matrix $\mathbf{C}$ of size $m \times m$, where $\mathbf{C}_{ab}$ is the similarity between the embeddings for two subreddits with embedding vectors $\mathbf{a}$ and $\mathbf{b}$. In this paper, we use cosine similarity as the similarity measure:

$$\mathbf{C}_{ab} = \frac{\mathbf{a} \cdot \mathbf{b}}{\|\mathbf{a}\| \, \|\mathbf{b}\|},$$

To predict the value of the missing element where $A_{ij} = 0$ (whether user u_i will post to subreddit v_j), we compute the average of user u_i's past interactions (which subreddits user u_i posted and did not post to), weighted by the similarity of these subreddits to subreddit v_j. Mathematically,

$$A'_{ij} = \frac{\sum_{k=1}^{n} A_{ik} C_{kj}}{\sum_{k=1}^{n} C_{kj}}.$$

We can generalize the above formula to obtain the new predicted adjacency matrix using matrix-level operations:

$$\mathbf{A}^{(\mathrm{CBF})} = (\mathbf{AC}) \odot \mathbf{D},$$

where

- $\mathbf{D} = 1./(\mathbf{I} \cdot \mathbf{C})$ (element-wise),
- $\mathbf{I}$ is an indicator matrix such that $I_{ij} = 1$ if $A_{ij} \neq 0$, otherwise $I_{ij} = 0$,
- and $\odot$ is the Hadamard product.

4.1.1 Representing Subreddit Discourse with Description and Posts

It is helpful to consider the specific domain of the application to represent each item as an embedding. In the context of our subreddit recommendation problem, we take advantage of two types of text-based information about a subreddit to construct the similarity matrix: (1) the posts within the subreddit itself and (2) the general description about the reddit provided by the subreddit moderators.

We then use a feature extraction method to obtain two embeddings of a subreddit, one based on its description and the other based on its posts. As a subreddit contains many posts, each of which has a different embedding given the same feature-extraction method, we take the average of the embeddings across all posts within a subreddit to obtain one embedding for the subreddit.

4.1.2 Feature Extraction

In this paper, we consider three feature-extraction methods: Term Frequency-Inverse Document Frequency (TF-IDF), Bidirectional Encoder Representations from Transformers (BERT) (Devlin et al., 2019), and OpenAI.*

TF-IDF: The TF-IDF algorithm represents a document as a vector, each element of which corresponds to the TF-IDF score of a word in that document. The TF-IDF score for each word in the document is dictated by (1) the frequency of the word in the document (Sparck Jones, 1972), and (2) the rarity of the word in the entire text corpus (Luhn, 1957). That is, a term is important to a document if it occurs frequently in the document but rarely in the corpus. We use the implementation from scikit-learn (Pedregosa et al., 2011) to obtain the TF-IDF representations of our subreddits.

BERT: We employ BERT to generate sentence embeddings as another feature extraction technique (Devlin et al., 2019). BERT takes a sentence as input and generates a fixed-length vector representation of the sentence. This representation is meant to capture the syntactic and semantic meaning of the input sentence in a way that can be used for various natural language processing tasks, such as sentence classification or semantic similarity comparison. In the context of our problem, we can treat each subreddit description or each post as a sentence and feed it to a pre-trained BERT model to generate the embeddings that represent the subreddit. Long posts are truncated to fit within the context limits of pre-trained models. We experiment with 4 different variations of BERT embeddings:

- BERT base and large (Devlin et al., 2019)
- Sentence-BERT, or SBERT (Reimers and Gurevych, 2019)
- BERTweet (Nguyen et al., 2020)

OpenAI: Similar to BERT embeddings, OpenAI embeddings take in a string of text and output an embedding that represents the semantic meaning of the text as a dense vector. To do this, the input string is first converted into a sequence of tokens. The tokens are then fed to a Large Language Model (LLM), which generates a single embedding vector of fixed size. OpenAI's text-embedding-ada-002 can take strings of up to 8191 tokens and returns a vector with 1536 dimensions.

4.2 Nonnegative Matrix Factorization for Collaborative Filtering

Matrix factorization (MF) approaches map users and items (subreddits in this case) to a joint latent factor space of a lower dimension k (Koren et al., 2009). The goal of this method is to recommend to a user the subreddits that are close to them in the latent space. More formally, MF involves the construction of user matrix $\mathbf{P}$ of dimension $n \times k$ and subreddit matrix $\mathbf{Q}$ of dimension $m \times k$. In this sense, the resulting term, $\mathbf{p}_i{}^\top \mathbf{q}_j$, captures user u_i's interest in item v_j's characteristics, thereby approximating user u_i's rating of item v_j, or denoted by A_{ij}.

This modeling approach learns the values in $\mathbf{P}$ and $\mathbf{Q}$ through the optimization of the loss fuction

$$\min_{\mathbf{P},\mathbf{Q}} \sum_{A_{ij} \in \mathbf{A}} (A_{ij} - \mathbf{p}_i^\top \mathbf{q}_j)^2 + \lambda(\|\mathbf{p}_i\|^2 + \|\mathbf{q}_j\|^2).$$

Matrix factorization offers the flexibility of accounting for various data and domain-specific biases that may have an effect on the interaction between user u_i and subreddit v_j. In this paper, we consider three types of biases: global average μ,

*OpenAI API Embeddings: https://platform.openai.com/docs/guides/embeddings

user bias $b_i^{(p)}$, and subreddit bias $b_j^{(q)}$. The updated loss function is given by:

$$\min_{\mathbf{P},\mathbf{Q}} \sum_{A_{ij} \in \mathbf{A}} (A_{ij} - \mu - b_i^{(p)} - b_j^{(q)} - \mathbf{p}_i^\top \mathbf{q}_j)^2 + \lambda(\|\mathbf{p}_i\|^2 + \|\mathbf{q}_j\|^2 + b_i^{(p)^2} + b_j^{(q)^2}). \quad (1)$$

After optimization, each element in the new predicted adjacency matrix $\mathbf{A}^{\text{MF}}$ is given by:

$$\mathbf{A}_{ij}^{(\text{MF})} = \mathbf{p}_i^\top \mathbf{q}_j + \mu + b_i + b_j$$

4.3 Final Model: Hybrid Approach

Our main model leverages insights from both content-based filtering and matrix factorization by taking a linear combination of their predicted adjacency matrix. Specifically, the new adjacency matrix is given by:

$$\mathbf{A}^{(\text{MF+CBF})} = \beta \mathbf{A}^{(\text{CBF})} + (1 - \beta)\mathbf{A}^{(\text{MF})},$$

where β is a hyperparameter that controls how much the CBF model (vs MF model) contributes to the final prediction.

5 Data and Experimental Setup

For the experimental setup, we use the data from Low et al. (2020) working on Reddit platforms in mental health domains, particularly health anxiety.

5.1 Data Description

The dataset is collected from 28 mental health and non-mental health subreddits. The dataset is suitable for studying how subreddits and social media platforms correlated with individuals' mental health and behavior. The original data comprises 952,110 Reddit posts from 770,176 unique users across 28 subreddit communities, which include 15 mental health support groups, 2 broad mental health subreddits, and 11 non-mental health subreddits. We also manually collect descriptions of the 28 subreddits and use that information along with the posts to conduct the content similarity matrix.

5.2 Data Preprocessing

Although the original dataset has a large number of unique users, the majority of them only contribute posts to one or two different communities. This presents a challenge when evaluating our specific task. As our objective is to examine users' behavior over time and provide recommendations for engaging in suitable subreddits, we have implemented a filter to exclude users who post to fewer than three subreddits. After filtering, the remaining users and posts are 16,801 and 69,004, respectively, while the number of subreddits remains to be 28. We also seek to understand the distribution of interactions between users and different subreddits. The detailed distribution of post frequency across subreddits is visualized in Figure 2.

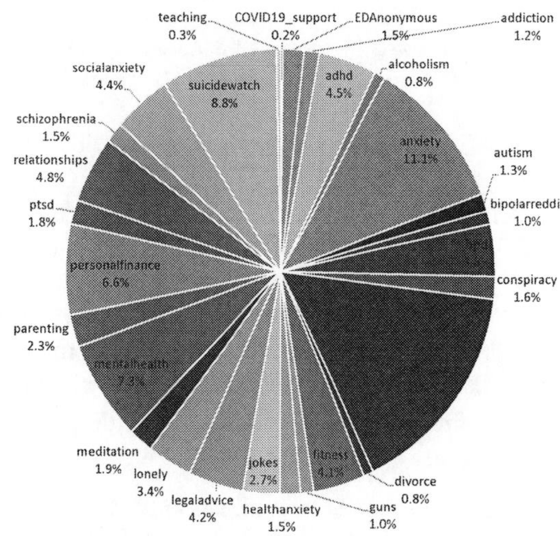

Figure 2: Distribution of post frequency across subreddits: r/depression, r/anxiety, and r/suicidewatch are the three most popular subreddits.

5.3 Experimental Setup

5.3.1 Data Splits

To construct our data splits, for each user in our dataset, we choose the most recent subreddit that the user first posted to as the test example. For example, if the user post history is [*subreddit1, subreddit2, subreddit3, subreddit1, subreddit2*], then *subredddit3* will be used as the test example. For each positive training example, we pair it with a negative example randomly sampled from the list of subreddits where the user has not posted to.

5.3.2 Evaluation Metrics

In assessing the performance of our recommendation method and the baseline, we use the following evaluation metrics: *Recall@K* and *Mean Reciprocal Rank (MRR)*.

5.4 Results

Table 1 presents the performance of our hybrid recommendation system as well as its individual

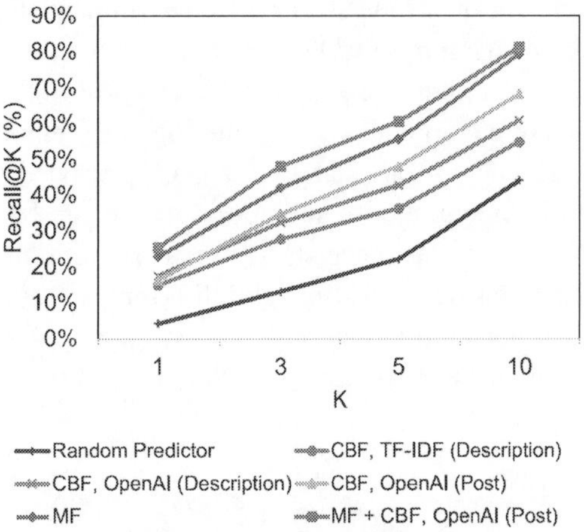

Figure 3: Model Performance on Recall@K

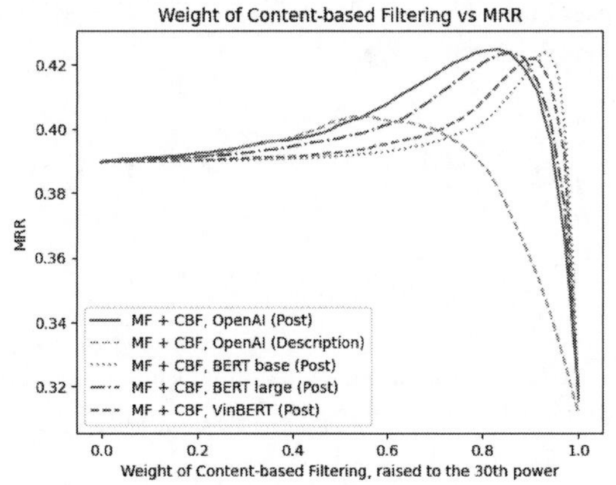

Figure 4: Hybrid Model Performance (MRR) across different values of β

components (MF or CBF). For CBF, we report its performance on different types of embeddings constructed using different information (posts or description) and different feature extraction methods (TF-IDF, BERT, or OpenAI). Figure 3 visualizes the results of exemplary models in a diagram for better analysis using Recall@K.

According to Table 1, all variants of our recommendation method outperform the random predictor. Among all the variants, the hybrid solution using the content similarity matrix generated from OpenAI embeddings achieves the highest performance in MRR (0.4244) and average Recall@K.

For CBF, operating a feature-extraction method on subreddit posts results in higher performance than operating the same method on description. For example, the MRR for CBF - BERT base is 0.3140 when using posts and 0.3024 when using description. It can also be observed that given the same information (either posts or information), deep-learning-based feature extraction methods like OpenAI and BERT bring about better performance for CBF than TF-IDF.

As our recommendation model combines both MF and CBF, we investigate the effect of hyperparameter β, which dictates how much CBF contributes to the final prediction. Figure 4 illustrates the performance of the hybrid models on varying β. When $\beta = 0$, the hybrid model's performance is the same as that of MF. When $\beta = 1$, the hybrid model's performance is the same as that of CBF. It can be seen from the peak of these curves that this way of linearly combining MF and CBF brings about significant improvement in MRR.

5.5 Case Studies

We perform a series of case studies to understand why certain information and methods are more helpful than others in recommending subreddits to users. We present our findings by comparing the behavior of the following models: (1) CBF models using TF-IDF and OpenAI Embedding on Subreddit Descriptions, (2) CBF models using OpenAI Embeddings on Subreddit Descriptions and Posts, and (3) MF model and Hybrid model.

5.5.1 CBF models using TF-IDF and OpenAI Embedding on Subreddit Descriptions

The objective of the first case study is to investigate the impact of different types of embedding methods on the performance of recommendations. To achieve this, we employ TF-IDF and OpenAI Embedding approaches to analyze subreddit descriptions and compare their predictions using content-based filtering (CBF) approaches, as illustrated in Figure 5. Specifically, we consider User A's historically interacted subreddits, which relate to *depression*, *loneliness*, and *anxiety*, respectively, with the ground truth of *socialanxiety*. For CBF models, the content similarity C between historically interacted and ground truth subreddits is crucial for accurate predictions. Hence, we evaluate the similarity scores between them. According to the result, the OpenAI Embedding technique outperforms TF-IDF in learning the representation of subreddits. Based on the analysis of content similarity matrices of the two approaches, we observe that TF-IDF has low similarity scores among subreddits due to its bag-of-words (BOW) approach, which fails to capture semantic relationships in short texts (Naseem et al., 2021), such as subreddit descrip-

Approach	MRR	Recall@1	Recall@3	Recall@5	Recall@10
Random Predictor	0.1631	0.0429	0.1318	0.2221	0.4409
Matrix Factorization (MF)	0.3895	0.2300	0.4197	0.5585	0.7946
CBF - TF-IDF (Description)	0.2751	0.1503	0.2777	0.3634	0.5494
CBF - BERT base (Description)	0.3024	0.1807	0.3050	0.3799	0.5668
CBF - OpenAI (Description)	0.3113	0.1761	0.3233	0.4266	0.6093
CBF - SBERT (Post)	0.2865	0.1317	0.3109	0.4281	0.6545
CBF - BERT base (Post)	0.3140	0.1598	0.3446	0.4776	0.6651
CBF - BERT large (Post)	0.3168	0.1637	0.3436	0.4795	0.6674
CBF - BERTweet base (Post)	0.3154	0.1570	0.3516	0.4918	0.6700
CBF - OpenAI (Post)	0.3195	0.1642	0.3484	0.4815	0.6823
MF + CBF OpenAI (Description)	0.4039	0.2405	0.4491	0.5790	0.8093
MF + CBF BERT base (Post)	0.4114	0.2449	0.4613	0.5966	0.8023
MF + CBF BERTweet base (Post)	0.4221	0.2570	0.4809	0.6022	0.8056
MF + CBF BERT large (Post)	0.4237	**0.2593**	0.4832	0.6000	0.8059
MF + CBF OpenAI (Post)	**0.4244**	0.2571	**0.4841**	**0.6063**	**0.8154**

Table 1: Model Performance with different content similarity matrices generated by embedding methods evaluated on MRR and $Recall@K$

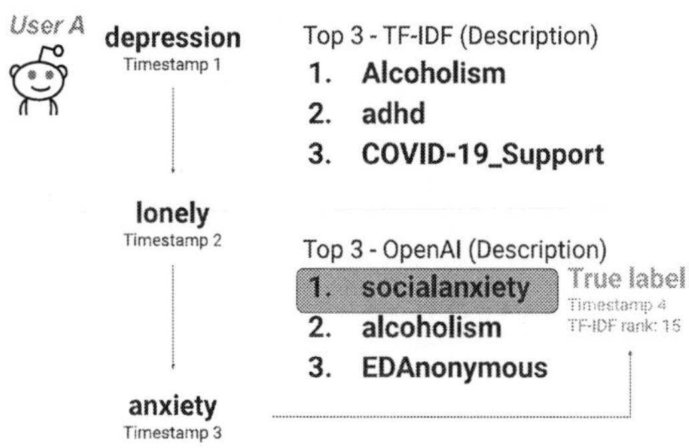

Figure 5: Case Study 1: Top 3 TFIDF Predictions vs. OpenAI Predictions. The higher the timestamp, the more recent the interactions between the user under study and the subreddits they engaged with.

tions. In contrast, OpenAI Embeddings, which can capture semantic meanings, performs better for encoding the meanings of subreddit descriptions for recommendation tasks.

5.5.2 CBF models using OpenAI Embeddings on Subreddit Descriptions and Posts

The second case study aims to investigate the impact of different types of information on the performance and recommendations of CBF models. To achieve this goal, we evaluate OpenAI Embeddings approaches on two types of information, subreddit descriptions, and posts. Figure 6 illustrates the predictions using CBF approaches utilizing OpenAI Embeddings on posts and descriptions. Specifically, we examine User B's historical posts, which are in *depression* and *personalfinance*, and the ground truth label is *legaladvice*. To understand the behavior of CBF on these two types of information, we analyze the similarities between historical subreddit interactions of User B and how the ground truth label is correlated with these subreddits. Our analysis shows that using OpenAI Embeddings on subreddit posts can capture strong relationships between *personalfinance* and *legaladvice*, where many *legaladvice* posts are related to financial information. However, when only using subreddit descriptions of *legaladvice*, which is "A place to ask simple legal questions, and to have legal concepts explained.", the model fails to capture this relationship. Furthermore, as shown in Table 1, the use of subreddit posts as representations for communities generally exhibits higher performance across most metrics when compared to using community descriptions. The reason is that subreddit descriptions contain less information than posts describing only the general purpose of the subreddit. In contrast, using subreddit posts can accurately learn the representations of the subreddits. Therefore, among the two types of information, using subreddit posts to represent subreddits helps models achieve better performance.

Figure 6: Case Study 2: Top 3 OpenAI Description Predictions (Left) vs. OpenAI Post Predictions (Right). The higher the timestamp, the more recent the interactions between the user under study and the subreddits they engaged with. *Post content has been paraphrased to protect user's privacy.*

5.5.3 MF vs MF + CBF model using OpenAI Embeddings on Subreddit Discourses

The objective of the third study is to investigate the performance improvement achieved by combining MF and CBF. Specifically, we aim to explore how the use of discourse embeddings to generate content similarity matrices among subreddits can address challenges encountered by the MF approach. To this end, we evaluate the MF and MF + CBF approaches using OpenAI Embeddings on posts. The predictions generated by the two models are presented in Figure 7.

We further examine the construction of scores using MF for this case study. The scores values are generated using latent features P, Q, μ, $b^{(p)}$, and $b^{(q)}$, representing user, item features, global average, user, and item biases, respectively. However, due to the imbalance in the dataset, there are more posts in some subreddits than others, leading to a cold start problem for the MF approach to accurately learn communities with a small number of examples. In this case study, MF fails to generate correct predictions for the *divorce* community due to the limited number of posts available. Additionally, MF is biased towards subreddits with more posts, as reflected by the $b^{(q)}$ values that have strong correlations with the number of posts in the subreddit communities, as depicted in Figure 8.

We demonstrate that the top three predictions generated by MF are the subreddits with the highest item biases compared to other subreddits, which are also the ones with the most posts. However, as *divorce* only accounts for 0.78% of the dataset, the performance of MF is limited. By utilizing

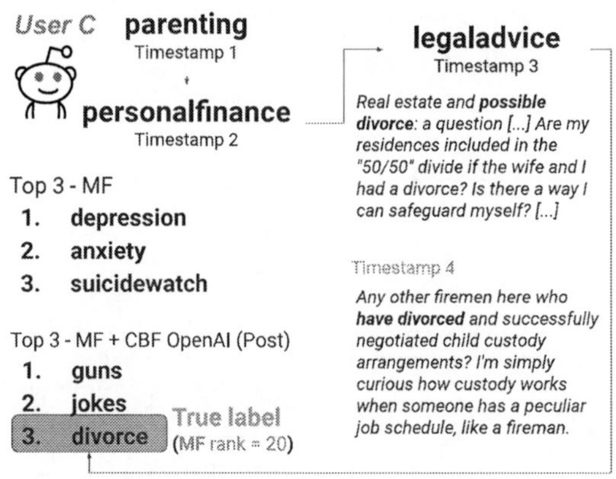

Figure 7: Case Study 3: Top 3 MF Predictions vs. Top 3 MF + CBF Post Predictions. The higher the timestamp, the more recent the interactions between the user under study and the subreddits they engaged with. *Post content has been paraphrased to protect user's privacy.*

OpenAI Embeddings on Subreddit Discourses to represent subreddit communities, we can integrate semantic information into the prediction process, thereby overcoming the cold start problem encountered by MF. Furthermore, this approach captures the relationships between the target recommended subreddit, historically interacted communities and semantic similarities. In this case, the most similar subreddits to *personalfinance* are *legaladvice* and *divorce*, while the most similar subreddits to *parenting* are *autism* and *divorce*.

Overall, we showcase that integrating semantic information into MF can address the cold start problem, and combining MF with CBF using discourse embeddings can make better recommendations.

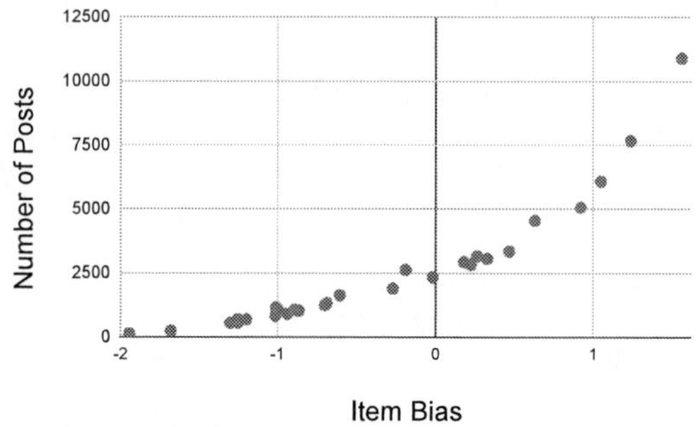

Figure 8: Item Biases values learned from MF vs. Subreddits' number of posts

6 Conclusion

This study aimed to investigate the effectiveness of different types of discourse embeddings when integrated into content-based filtering for recommending support groups, particularly in the mental health domain. Our findings showed that the hybrid model, which combined content-based filtering and collaborative filtering, yielded the best results. Moreover, we conducted an extensive case study to demonstrate the interpretability of our approach's predictions.

Previous studies have brought to light the use of past behaviors to make more accurate recommendations in mental health (Valentine et al., 2022). They also emphasize effective communication between the recommender system and the user as an essential factor for users' proper understanding of mental health in general as well as in their own journey (Valentine et al., 2022). Through promising prediction accuracy and interpretability, we believe that this method can serve as a valuable tool to support individuals, particularly those with mental health concerns, to share and seek help regarding their issues.

Limitations

In our current project, we have not taken into account the temporal information that treats the historical behavior of users as a sequence of actions. Thus, the model may not capture how user behaviors change over time. To ensure full support to users in need, we recommend that future work should address this limitation by considering users' historical behaviors as a sequence of actions. Moreover, although our pre-trained models achieved significant results without fine-tuning discourse embeddings, we suggest that fine-tuning these models can enhance performance by capturing the nuances of the datasets' distribution and contexts. Furthermore, conducting a detailed comparison of additional open-source Large Language Models (LLMs) would provide more comprehensive insights into their performance. Additionally, in addition to analyzing the efficiency of different models, it is crucial to evaluate the cost associated with implementing these models. Therefore, future work should consider both fine-tuning and evaluating additional LLMs, while also taking into account the costs of utilizing these models.

Acknowledgement

This work was supported by NSF IIS-2119531, IIS-2137396, IIS-2142827, CCF-1901059, and ONR N00014-22-1-2507.

References

Murali Raghu Babu Balusu, Yangfeng Ji, and Jacob Eisenstein. 2022. Pre-trained sentence embeddings for implicit discourse relation classification.

Jacob Devlin, Ming-Wei Chang, Kenton Lee, and Kristina Toutanova. 2019. BERT: Pre-training of deep bidirectional transformers for language understanding. In *Proceedings of the 2019 Conference of the North American Chapter of the Association for Computational Linguistics: Human Language Technologies, Volume 1 (Long and Short Papers)*, pages 4171–4186, Minneapolis, Minnesota. Association for Computational Linguistics.

Roger Garriga, Javier Mas, Semhar Abraha, Jon Nolan, Oliver Harrison, George Tadros, and Aleksandar Matic. 2022. Machine learning model to predict mental health crises from electronic health records. *Nature medicine*, 28(6):1240–1248.

Sarik Ghazarian, Behnam Hedayatnia, Alexandros Papangelis, Yang Liu, and Dilek Hakkani-Tur. 2022. What is wrong with you?: Leveraging user sentiment for automatic dialog evaluation. In *Findings of the Association for Computational Linguistics: ACL 2022*, pages 4194–4204, Dublin, Ireland. Association for Computational Linguistics.

Kishaloy Halder, Min-Yen Kan, and Kazunari Sugiyama. 2017. Health forum thread recommendation using an interest aware topic model. In *Proceedings of the 2017 ACM on Conference on Information and Knowledge Management*, CIKM '17, page 1589–1598, New York, NY, USA. Association for Computing Machinery.

Meng Jiang, Peng Cui, Rui Liu, Qiang Yang, Fei Wang, Wenwu Zhu, and Shiqiang Yang. 2012. Social contextual recommendation. In *Proceedings of the 21st*

ACM international conference on Information and knowledge management, pages 45–54.

Vladimir Karpukhin, Barlas Oguz, Sewon Min, Patrick Lewis, Ledell Wu, Sergey Edunov, Danqi Chen, and Wen-tau Yih. 2020. Dense passage retrieval for open-domain question answering. In *Proceedings of the 2020 Conference on Empirical Methods in Natural Language Processing (EMNLP)*.

Yehuda Koren, Robert Bell, and Chris Volinsky. 2009. Matrix factorization techniques for recommender systems. *Computer*, 42(8):30–37.

G. Linden, B. Smith, and J. York. 2003. Amazon.com recommendations: item-to-item collaborative filtering. *IEEE Internet Computing*, 7(1):76–80.

Daniel M Low, Laurie Rumker, Tanya Talkar, John Torous, Guillermo Cecchi, and Satrajit S Ghosh. 2020. Natural language processing reveals vulnerable mental health support groups and heightened health anxiety on reddit during covid-19: Observational study. *Journal of medical Internet research*, 22(10):e22635.

Hans Peter Luhn. 1957. A statistical approach to mechanized encoding and searching of literary information. *IBM Journal of research and development*, 1(4):309–317.

Cataldo Musto, Giovanni Semeraro, Marco de Gemmis, and Pasquale Lops. 2016. Learning word embeddings from wikipedia for content-based recommender systems. In *Advances in Information Retrieval*, volume 9626, pages 729–734.

Usman Naseem, Imran Razzak, Shah Khalid Khan, and Mukesh Prasad. 2021. A comprehensive survey on word representation models: From classical to state-of-the-art word representation language models. *Transactions on Asian and Low-Resource Language Information Processing*, 20(5):1–35.

Dat Quoc Nguyen, Thanh Vu, and Anh Tuan Nguyen. 2020. BERTweet: A pre-trained language model for English Tweets. In *Proceedings of the 2020 Conference on Empirical Methods in Natural Language Processing: System Demonstrations*, pages 9–14.

Fabian Pedregosa, Gaël Varoquaux, Alexandre Gramfort, Vincent Michel, Bertrand Thirion, Olivier Grisel, Mathieu Blondel, Peter Prettenhofer, Ron Weiss, Vincent Dubourg, Jake Vanderplas, Alexandre Passos, David Cournapeau, Matthieu Brucher, Matthieu Perrot, and Édouard Duchesnay. 2011. Scikit-learn: Machine learning in python. *J. Mach. Learn. Res.*, 12(null):2825–2830.

Yingqi Qu, Yuchen Ding, Jing Liu, Kai Liu, Ruiyang Ren, Wayne Xin Zhao, Daxiang Dong, Hua Wu, and Haifeng Wang. 2021. Rocketqa: An optimized training approach to dense passage retrieval for open-domain question answering. In *Procs. of NAACL*.

Nils Reimers and Iryna Gurevych. 2019. Sentence-bert: Sentence embeddings using siamese bert-networks. In *Proceedings of the 2019 Conference on Empirical Methods in Natural Language Processing and the 9th International Joint Conference on Natural Language Processing (EMNLP-IJCNLP)*, pages 3982–3992.

Jérémie Richard, Reid Rebinsky, Rahul Suresh, Serena Kubic, Adam Carter, Jasmyn EA Cunningham, Amy Ker, Kayla Williams, and Mark Sorin. 2022. Scoping review to evaluate the effects of peer support on the mental health of young adults. *BMJ open*, 12(8):e061336.

Youngseo Son, Vasudha Varadarajan, and H. Andrew Schwartz. 2022. Discourse relation embeddings: Representing the relations between discourse segments in social media. In *Proceedings of the Workshop on Unimodal and Multimodal Induction of Linguistic Structures (UM-IoS)*, pages 45–55, Abu Dhabi, United Arab Emirates (Hybrid). Association for Computational Linguistics.

Karen Sparck Jones. 1972. A statistical interpretation of term specificity and its application in retrieval. *Journal of documentation*, 28(1):11–21.

Lee Valentine, Simon D'Alfonso, and Reeva Lederman. 2022. Recommender systems for mental health apps: advantages and ethical challenges. *AI & society*, pages 1–12.

Daheng Wang, Meng Jiang, Munira Syed, Oliver Conway, Vishal Juneja, Sriram Subramanian, and Nitesh V Chawla. 2020. Calendar graph neural networks for modeling time structures in spatiotemporal user behaviors. In *Proceedings of the 26th ACM SIGKDD international conference on knowledge discovery & data mining*, pages 2581–2589.

Lee Xiong, Chenyan Xiong, Ye Li, Kwok-Fung Tang, Jialin Liu, Paul N Bennett, Junaid Ahmed, and Arnold Overwijk. 2020. Approximate nearest neighbor negative contrastive learning for dense text retrieval. In *International Conference on Learning Representations*.

APA-RST: A Text Simplification Corpus with RST Annotations

Freya Hewett[1,2]
[1]AI & Society Lab
Humboldt Institute for Internet and Society

[2]Applied Computational Linguistics
University of Potsdam
firstname.lastname@hiig.de

Abstract

We present a corpus of parallel German-language simplified newspaper articles. The articles have been aligned at sentence level and annotated according to the Rhetorical Structure Theory (RST) framework. These RST annotated texts could shed light on structural aspects of text complexity and how simplifications work on a text level.

1 Introduction

The goal of text simplification is to reduce the complexity of a text whilst retaining the main information, in order to make a text easier to understand. In this paper, we present a corpus of German-language parallel simplified newspaper articles, at three different complexity levels. Each text has been annotated according to the Rhetorical Structure Theory (RST, Mann and Thompson, 1988) framework. RST posits that segments (or Elementary Discourse Units, EDUs) in a text are related to each other and that one component of the pair serves as a 'nucleus' and the other as a 'satellite', or in some cases both components are considered to have 'nucleus' status. An example of a relation that connects EDUs is 'evidence' where the nucleus is a claim and the satellite provides evidence for the claim. RST therefore provides information about the structure of texts; an area which has thus far not been the focus of much research on text simplification. Whilst much of previous work has focused on sentence-level simplification, text-level simplification is a promising area of research, as it represents a 'more real use-case scenario for a simplification model' (Alva-Manchego et al., 2020). For the German language, *Leichte Sprache* is a term often used in the context of simplified texts: *Leichte Sprache* texts are written according to clearly defined rules, however text-level aspects, including coherence, are often neglected in the guidelines, even though they are highly relevant when producing accessible texts (Bock, 2019; Maaß, 2020).

Aside from contributing to the general collection of RST annotated texts, this corpus could also be used to help carve out what text-level simplification actually constitutes, how simplified texts are structured and how this differs to their standard counterparts, and could also be used to answer questions surrounding the complexity of different types of text structures. Section 2 provides an overview on previous work that has considered questions at the intersection of discourse structure and text simplification, Section 3 provides details on the annotation process of the corpus, Section 4 outlines some statistical analysis on the corpus and Section 5 summarises the paper and provides inspiration for potential use-cases for the corpus. The corpus can be downloaded at `https://github.com/fhewett/apa-rst`.

2 Related work

Datasets which combine discourse structure and text simplification are relatively rare. LeiKo is a German-language corpus of newspaper articles simplified at various levels (including *Leichte Sprache*, Jablotschkin and Zinsmeister, 2022). A subset of 40 articles from the corpus has (manual) Penn Discourse Treebank (PDTB) annotations. Ko et al. (2023) expand their corpus of English-language texts annotated according to the Questions under Discussion (QUD) framework to include six Newsela articles and their counterparts at middle and elementary school level. In the context of text-level simplification, the task of sentence deletion has also been approached using various discourse structures. Zhang et al. (2022) also look at Newsela texts, and automatically annotate them with a 'news genre-specific functional discourse structure' and with sentence alignments. They train a model to predict when a sentence should be deleted and find that the discourse structure improves the accuracy. Zhong et al. (2020) also focus on the task of sentence deletion and analyse various discourse-based

Proceedings of the 4th Workshop on Computational Approaches to Discourse (CODI 2023), pages 173–179
July 13-14, 2023

features (from RST and PDTB) for this purpose and find that the position of a sentence in an RST tree as well as some specific relations play a key role. The link between discourse structure and other aspects of text-level simplification have also been considered; Siddharthan (2003) proposes a rule-based system – using cue words, for example – to help preserve coherence when restructuring texts during the simplification process. Niklaus et al. (2021, 2016) split complex sentences by using automatically parsed syntax trees. They use a pre-determined list of cue words (such as 'although') to determine the rhetorical relation within sentences to ensure that the split sentences are still coherent. Davoodi and Kosseim (2016) implement pairwise classification of texts of varying complexity using discourse features, using a subset of 30 articles from the PDTB which have been annotated with a complexity level (Pitler and Nenkova, 2009) and an automatically parsed subset of the Simple English Wikipedia corpus (Coster and Kauchak, 2011).

3 Corpus creation

The data used in the corpus is from the Austria Press Agency (APA), who publish four to six articles every weekday, (manually) simplified to two language levels: B1 and A2[1], according to the Common European Framework of Reference for Languages (CEFR). More details on the APA data can be found in Ebling et al. (2022); the version used to create the APA-RST subset contains articles up to April 2022. APA-RST covers a total of five randomly selected days from a time-frame between 2018 and 2022, with five articles each day. The corpus therefore consists of a total of 75 articles, with 25 at each level (original, B1 and A2), covering different topics such as politics, culture and sport.

3.1 RST annotations

Each article has been annotated according to the RST guidelines from Stede et al. (2017). In addition to the relations[2] present in those guidelines, we also include two additional relations from RST-DT (Carlson and Marcu, 2001): *sameunit* and *attribution*. We also remove *means* from the relation set (due to its similarity to *enablement*) as well as *unless* (due to its similarity to *condition*). The titles of the newspaper articles were excluded from the annotation, as well as glossary entries for complicated words, which were occasionally included in the A2 texts. Longer texts were (manually) split into separate parts for a total of 111 parts; information on these parts can be found in Table 1. These texts were segmented into EDUs and given to the annotators in pre-segmented form. Five annotators used rstWeb to annotate the texts (Zeldes, 2016). The annotators were undergraduate students of computational linguistics, who were trained for the annotation task and had regular feedback sessions during the annotation process.

Approximately one third of the corpus (36 texts) has three sets of annotations. The inter-annotator agreement (IAA) was calculated using RST-Tace (Wan et al., 2019), which is based on a proposal by Iruskieta et al. (2015), and considers four different aspects: nuclearity, relations, constituents and attachment points. RST-Tace is designed for comparing two sets of annotations, so to adapt it for our three sets we simply calculated the IAA for all possible combinations, i.e. between set 1 and 2, set 1 and 3, and set 2 and 3. Overall, the average Kappa score is 0.27, and the aspect with the most disagreement between annotations was the relations. Out of all non-matching relations, *elaboration* and *e-elaboration* are the main source of disagreement, i.e. one annotator chose *elaboration* whilst a second annotator chose *e-elaboration* for the same set of EDUs. Although a certain level of subjectivity is to be expected in RST annotations, due to the relatively low agreement, all annotations were manually checked by two doctoral students. Additionally, the texts with multiple annotations

Level	OR	OR parts	B1	A2
Total sent.	558	558	184	204
Total tok.	9567	9567	2009	1871
Sent./text	22.3	9.1	7.4	8.2
Tok./text	382.7	156.8	81.0	74.2
Tok./sent.	17.1	17.1	10.9	9.2
Char./tok.	6.2	6.2	5.8	5.6
EDUs/text	-	15	9	9

Table 1: General information on APA-RST. Sent. stands for sentence(s), tok. for token(s), char. for characters and OR for original level. The values which are not totals represent averages.

[1]The A2 level corresponds (approximately) to *Leichte Sprache*.

[2]For readers unfamiliar with RST, short descriptions of the relations mentioned in the following Sections can be found in the Appendix A.4.

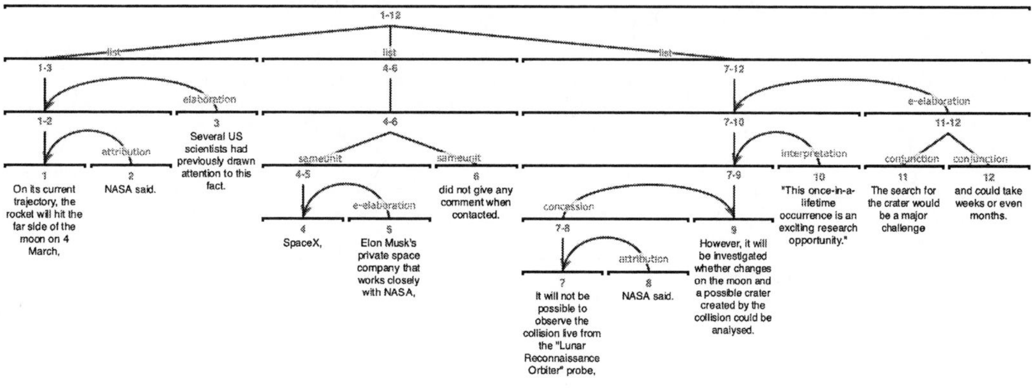

Figure 1: The tree of the second part of an original level text (4-freitag-28-1-22-or-pt2).

have been manually harmonised and checked by one annotator from the original group and two doctoral students.

3.2 Alignment annotations

The original articles and the B1 articles have also been annotated with alignments to the simplified levels. Two annotators (an undergraduate student and a doctoral student) looked at the sentences in the B1 and A2 texts and labelled the sentence(s) in the original texts which provided the content for the simplified sentences. The inter-annotator agreement (Kappa) for aligning the sentences in the original texts to their B1 counterparts was 0.77, and 0.9 for B1 to A2. Information on the types of alignments can be found in Table 3. An example of an aligned text can be seen in Table 2; the B1 sentence [1] consists of content from two sentences in the original, this is an n:1 alignment.

4 Corpus statistics

As we can see in Table 1, the simplified texts are approximately a third of the length of the original articles, showing that simplification of newspaper articles mostly results in a shorter version. The A2 texts are slightly longer than the B1 texts, owing to more descriptions and explanations of complicated concepts.

Relation distribution. Figure 2 shows the distribution of the relations at the different complexity levels. The texts at levels B1/A2 contain more *elaborations* and *e-elaborations* than the standard texts. With regards to the multi-nuclear relations – relations which consist of two nuclei segments – the simplified texts contain more *sequences* and slightly more *conjunctions*, whereas the original texts contain almost the same amount of *lists*. For the original texts, the *list* relations are found at a higher level in the tree, as they encompass an average of 8.2 EDUs, as compared to approximately 4 in the simplified texts, as can be seen in Figure 3. The example tree in Figure 1 shows a *list* relation at the highest level in the tree. When it comes to causal relations, the simplified texts contain more *causes*, slightly more *results* but less *reasons*. According to the annotation guidelines, *reason* should be used to link two subjective claims, which suggests that the original texts have more subjectivity. *Attribution* relations occur more frequently in the standard texts. Attributing information or a quote to an external source increases the number of perspectives in a text, whereas the simplified texts have less attributions and therefore less perspectives. *Sameunits* do not occur at all in the simplified versions. In the original texts they are used for nested constructions; these are not present in the simplifications.

Relations and nuclearity of aligned sentences. Figure 4 shows the relations together with the nuclearity assignments for the original sentences which align with the B1 version, i.e. the original sentences which contain the content chosen for the simplification. Only those that occurred at least 5 times were included. Any bars above the line means that the corresponding relation occurs over-proportionally in the selected sentences. *Elaboration N* and *e-elaboration N* feature heavily. As the simplified texts are more concise, they mostly consist of more salient information. *E-elaboration S* are also selected more frequently, indicating that elaborations on specific entities or examples are useful for a simplified text. The high frequency of *sequence MN* also suggests that the simplified texts may have more of a linear tone; the standard deviation for the

B1 sentences	Original sentences
[1] In 2015, a rocket from the company SpaceX was sent into space.	[1] A part of **a SpaceX rocket** could collide with the moon in early March, according to calculations by scientists at the US space agency NASA. [3] The rocket was launched from the Cape Canaveral Cosmodrome **in 2015** and had brought the "Deep Space Climate Observatory", an Earth observation satellite, into space.
[2] The rocket's fuel ran out before it could return to earth, which is why it is still in orbit.	[4] Afterwards, however, **the rocket's fuel ran out before it could return to Earth, so it's been in orbit ever since.**
[3] According to the US space agency NASA, a part of the rocket could collide with the moon in early March.	[1] **A part of a SpaceX rocket could collide with the moon in early March, according to** calculations by scientists at **the US space agency NASA.**
[4] NASA announced this on Thursday.	[2] The trajectory of the "Falcon 9" rocket is currently being monitored, a **NASA** spokeswoman **told** the Deutsche Presse-Agentur **on Thursday.**
[5] It will not be possible to observe the collision live.	[8] **It will not be possible to observe the collision live** from the "Lunar Reconnaissance Orbiter" probe, NASA said.
[6] However, it will be investigated if there are any changes on the moon afterwards.	[9] **However, it will be investigated whether changes on the moon** and a possible crater created by the collision could be analysed.
[7] The search for the crater could however take weeks or months.	[11] **The search for the crater** would be a major challenge and **could take weeks or even months.**

Table 2: Example of an aligned text. The B1 sentences (on the left) were aligned with the original sentence (on the right) that contains the content; the relevant content is highlighted in bold. The full original text can be found in Appendix A.1.

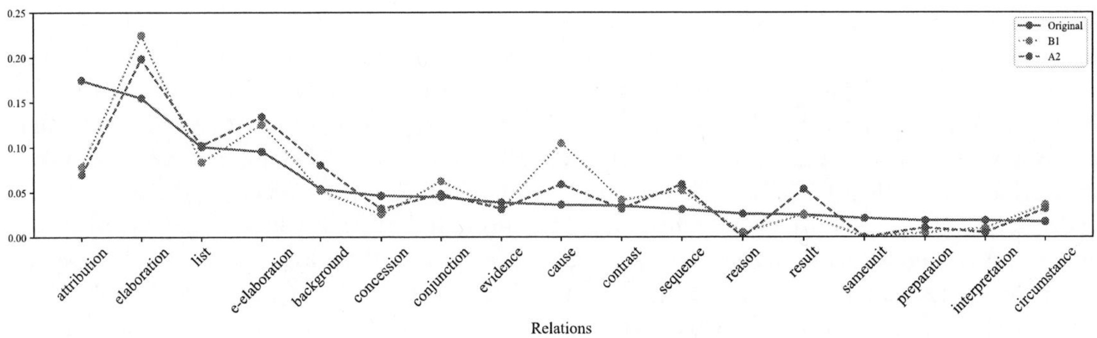

Figure 2: Relation distribution at the three different complexity levels. The counts of relations have been normalised. For readability purposes, only the top 17 relations are shown (out of a total of 30).

Level	1:1	n:1	1:n	1:0	0:1
OR:B1	85	5	33	430	30
B1:A2	123	1	33	26	10

Table 3: The types of alignments that were annotated, where n is more than one.

depth of EDUs[3] is in fact lower in the simplified texts (1.18 at A2 level and 1.33 at B1 level, compared to 1.4 in the original texts), indicating that the RST trees for the simplified texts are slightly more shallow. The mean depth of the trees of the original texts is 4.7 EDUs, compared to 4.1 and 3.9 for B1 and A2, respectively.

5 Conclusion and outlook

We have introduced a new German-language corpus of 75 parallel texts at three different complexity levels. The texts have been annotated according to the RST framework and have also been aligned at sentence level. We have shown how the relation distribution differs across the complexity levels, as well as how the relations differ in terms of what level they are used in the tree. We have also looked at the sentence alignments together with the RST annotations and shown the specific relations and nuclearity assignments of the content that is selected for a simplification. We pro-

[3]For example, the depth of the EDUs 5 and 6 in Figure 1 are 5 and 4, respectively.

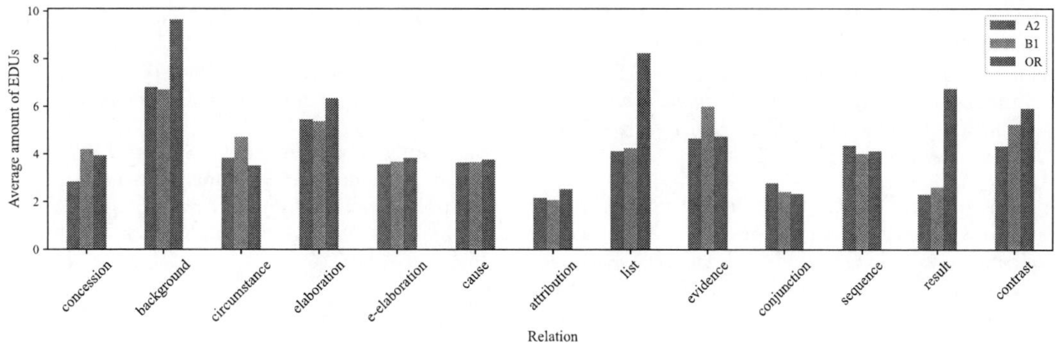

Figure 3: Average (mean) amount of EDUs that the relations encompass. Only relations that occur more than once in the A2 texts are included.

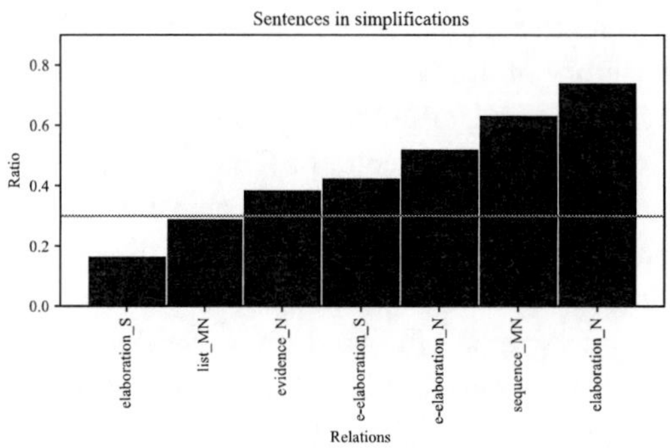

Figure 4: Relations and nuclearity of aligned sentences, out of the total amount of relations. Any relation ratio above 30% (the line on the graph) is above average. Relations and nuclearity assignments occurring less than a total of 5 times are excluded. N stands for nucleus, S for satellite, MN for nucleus in a multi-nuclear relation.

vide the corpus for download, enabling research on German-language RST in general, but also on specific questions which consider the interaction of text complexity and discourse structure.

Limitations

The corpus presented in this paper is relatively small and so the conclusions made should be considered in this context. We have also only focused on the specific text type of the newspaper article; other text types have different structures and are also simplified in different ways.

Acknowledgements

We would like to thank Dietmar Benndorf, Louis Cho, Elisa Lübbers, Hugo Meinhof, Costanza Rasi, Christopher Richter and Sara Shahmohammadi for their work on annotating the data. Furthermore, we would like to thank the reviewers for their very helpful comments. This research was funded by a grant from the German Ministry of Education and Research (BMBF).

References

Fernando Alva-Manchego, Carolina Scarton, and Lucia Specia. 2020. Data-Driven Sentence Simplification: Survey and Benchmark. *Computational Linguistics*, 46(1):135–187.

Bettina M. Bock. 2019. *'Leichte Sprache' – Kein Regelwerk. Sprachwissenschaftliche Ergebnisse und Praxisempfehlungen aus dem LeiSA-Projekt.* Frank & Timme.

L. Carlson and D. Marcu. 2001. *Discourse tagging reference manual (TR-2001-545).* USC Information Sciences Institute.

William Coster and David Kauchak. 2011. Simple English Wikipedia: A new text simplification task. In *Proceedings of the 49th Annual Meeting of the Association for Computational Linguistics: Human Language Technologies*, pages 665–669, Portland, Oregon, USA. Association for Computational Linguistics.

Elnaz Davoodi and Leila Kosseim. 2016. On the Contribution of Discourse Structure on Text Complexity Assessment. In *Proceedings of the 17th Annual Meeting of the Special Interest Group on Discourse and Dialogue*, pages 166–174, Los Angeles. Association for Computational Linguistics.

Sarah Ebling, Alessia Battisti, Marek Kostrzewa, Dominik Pfütze, Annette Rios, Andreas Säuberli, and Nicolas Spring. 2022. Automatic Text Simplification for German. *Frontiers in Communication*, 7.

Mikel Iruskieta, Iria da Cunha, and Maite Taboada. 2015. A qualitative comparison method for rhetorical structures: identifying different discourse structures in multilingual corpora. *Language Resources and Evaluation*, 49(2):263–309.

Sarah Jablotschkin and Heike Zinsmeister. 2022. LeiKo. Ein Vergleichskorpus für Leichte Sprache und Einfache Sprache. In Mark Kupietz and Thomas Schmidt, editors, *Neue Entwicklungen in der Korpuslandschaft der Germanistik. Beiträge zur IDS-Methodenmesse 2022*. Narr, Tübingen.

Wei-Jen Ko, Yating Wu, Cutter Dalton, Dananjay Srinivas, Greg Durrett, and Junyi Jessy Li. 2023. Discourse Analysis via Questions and Answers: Parsing Dependency Structures of Questions Under Discussion. *arXiv:2210.05905v2*.

Christiane Maaß. 2020. *Easy Language – Plain Language – Easy Language Plus : Balancing Comprehensibility and Acceptability*. Frank & Timme.

William C. Mann and Sandra A. Thompson. 1988. Rhetorical Structure Theory: Toward a functional theory of text organization. *Text - Interdisciplinary Journal for the Study of Discourse*, 8(3):243–281.

Christina Niklaus, Bernhard Bermeitinger, Siegfried Handschuh, and André Freitas. 2016. A Sentence Simplification System for Improving Relation Extraction. In *Proceedings of COLING 2016, the 26th International Conference on Computational Linguistics: System Demonstrations*, pages 170–174, Osaka, Japan. The COLING 2016 Organizing Committee.

Christina Niklaus, Matthias Cetto, André Freitas, and Siegfried Handschuh. 2021. Context-Preserving Text Simplification. *arXiv:2105.11178 [cs]*.

Emily Pitler and Ani Nenkova. 2009. Using syntax to disambiguate explicit discourse connectives in text. In *Proceedings of the ACL-IJCNLP 2009 Conference Short Papers*, pages 13–16, Suntec, Singapore. Association for Computational Linguistics.

Advaith Siddharthan. 2003. Preserving Discourse Structure when Simplifying Text. In *Proceedings of the 9th European Workshop on Natural Language Generation (ENLG-2003) at EACL 2003*, Budapest, Hungary. Association for Computational Linguistics.

Manfred Stede, Maite Taboada, and Debopam Das. 2017. Annotation Guidelines for Rhetorical Structure. Unpublished manuscript.

Shujun Wan, Tino Kutschbach, Anke Lüdeling, and Manfred Stede. 2019. RST-Tace A tool for automatic comparison and evaluation of RST trees. In *Proceedings of the Workshop on Discourse Relation Parsing and Treebanking 2019*, pages 88–96, Minneapolis, MN. Association for Computational Linguistics.

Amir Zeldes. 2016. rstWeb - A Browser-based Annotation Interface for Rhetorical Structure Theory and Discourse Relations. In *Proceedings of NAACL-HLT 2016 System Demonstrations*, pages 1–5, San Diego, CA.

Bohan Zhang, Prafulla Kumar Choubey, and Ruihong Huang. 2022. Predicting sentence deletions for text simplification using a functional discourse structure. In *Proceedings of the 60th Annual Meeting of the Association for Computational Linguistics (Volume 2: Short Papers)*, pages 255–261, Dublin, Ireland. Association for Computational Linguistics.

Yang Zhong, Chao Jiang, Wei Xu, and Junyi Jessy Li. 2020. Discourse Level Factors for Sentence Deletion in Text Simplification. In *Proceedings of the AAAI Conference on Artificial Intelligence*, volume 34(5), pages 9709–9716.

A Appendix

A.1 Translated example text (4-freitag-28-1-22-or)

A part of a SpaceX rocket could collide with the moon in early March, according to calculations by scientists at the US space agency NASA. The trajectory of the "Falcon 9" rocket is currently being monitored, a NASA spokeswoman told the Deutsche Presse-Agentur on Thursday. The rocket was launched from the Cape Canaveral Cosmodrome in 2015 and had brought the "Deep Space Climate Observatory", an Earth observation satellite, into space. Afterwards, however, the rocket's fuel ran out before it could return to Earth, so it's been in orbit ever since. On its current trajectory, the rocket will hit the far side of the moon on 4 March, NASA said. Several US scientists had previously drawn attention to this fact. SpaceX, Elon Musk's private space company that works closely with NASA, did not give any comment when contacted. It will not be possible to observe the collision live from the "Lunar Reconnaissance Orbiter" probe, NASA said. However, it will be investigated whether changes on the moon and a possible crater created by the collision could be analysed. "This once-in-a-lifetime occurrence is an exciting research opportunity." The search for the crater would be a major challenge and could take weeks or even months.

A.2 Original example text (4-freitag-28-1-22-or)

Ein Teil einer SpaceX-Rakete könnte nach Berechnungen von Wissenschaftern der US-Raumfahrtbehörde NASA Anfang März mit dem Mond zusammenstoßen. Die Flugbahn der "Falcon 9"-Raketenstufe werde derzeit beobachtet, sagte eine NASA-Sprecherin am Donnerstag der Deutschen Presse-Agentur. Die Rakete war 2015 vom Weltraumbahnhof Cape Canaveral gestartet und hatte das "Deep Space Climate Observatory", einen Erdbeobachtungssatelliten, ins All gebracht.

Danach reichte jedoch der Treibstoff der Raketenstufe nicht aus, um zurück zur Erde zu kommen, weswegen sie seitdem im All unterwegs ist. Auf ihrer jetzigen Flugbahn werde die Raketenstufe am 4. März auf der Rückseite des Mondes einschlagen, hieß es von der NASA. Zuvor hatten mehrere US-Wissenschaftler darauf aufmerksam gemacht. Von SpaceX, der privaten Raumfahrtfirma von Elon Musk, die viel mit der NASA zusammenarbeitet, gab es auf Anfrage zunächst keine Reaktion. Der Aufprall werde von der Sonde "Lunar Reconnaissance Orbiter" nicht live beobachtet werden können, hieß es von der NASA. Es werde aber untersucht, ob danach Veränderungen auf dem Mond und ein möglicher durch den Aufprall entstandener Krater analysiert werden könnten. "Dieses einmalige Vorkommnis stellt eine aufregende Forschungsmöglichkeit dar." Die Suche nach dem Krater werde eine große Herausforderung und könne Wochen oder sogar Monate dauern.

A.3 Original example text, B1 (4-freitag-28-1-22-b1)

2015 ist eine Rakete der Firma SpaceX ins All gestartet. Der Treibstoff der Rakete reichte aber nicht mehr aus um zur Erde zurückzukehren, weshalb sie seither im All unterwegs ist. Laut Berechnung der US-Weltraumbehörde NASA könnte nun Anfang März ein Teil der Rakete in den Mond krachen. Das gab die NASA am Donnerstag bekannt. Der Aufprall wird nicht live beobachtet werden können. Allerdings wird untersucht werden, ob danach Veränderungen auf dem Mond erkennbar sind. Die Suche nach dem Krater könnte aber Wochen bis Monate dauern.

A.4 Descriptions of RST relations

Relation	Description
elaboration	'S provides details or more information on the state of affairs described in N'
e-elaboration	'S provides details or more information on a single entity mentioned in N'
sequence	'the nuclei describe states of affairs that occur in a particular temporal order'
conjunction	'the nuclei provide information that can be recognized as related, enumerating [...] and they are linked by coordinating conjunctions'
list	'the nuclei provide information that can be recognized as related, enumerating'
cause	'the state/event in N is being caused by the state/event in S'
result	'the state/event in S is being caused by the state/event in N'
reason	S and N are 'subjective statement[s]/thes[e]s/claim[s]' and 'understanding S makes it easier for [the reader] to accept N'
attribution	the attribution predicate is the S, the attributed material the N
sameunit	used for linking two discontinuous text fragments that are really a single EDU, but which are broken up by an embedded unit

Table 4: These descriptions are taken from the Annotation Guidelines from Stede et al. (2017); more detailed information can be found there. The descriptions for *sameunit* and *attribution* are adapted from the RST-DT guidelines (Carlson and Marcu, 2001).

Author Index

Association for Computational Linguistics
209 N. Eighth Street
Stroudsburg, Pennsylvania 18360

ISBN 978-1-7138-8225-1

CURRAN ASSOCIATES INC.
proceedings.com